The Wizard's Bride

The Personal Reflections of Mrs. Thomas A. Edison

A Historical Novel

by

Gerald Seaman

May 2016

"An intimate glimpse into the family life of the most famous inventor in the world."

Novels by Gerald Seaman

Suspense

Naked Greed
Cunning Killer
Moving On

Historical

The Wizard's Bride

Edison Family Tree

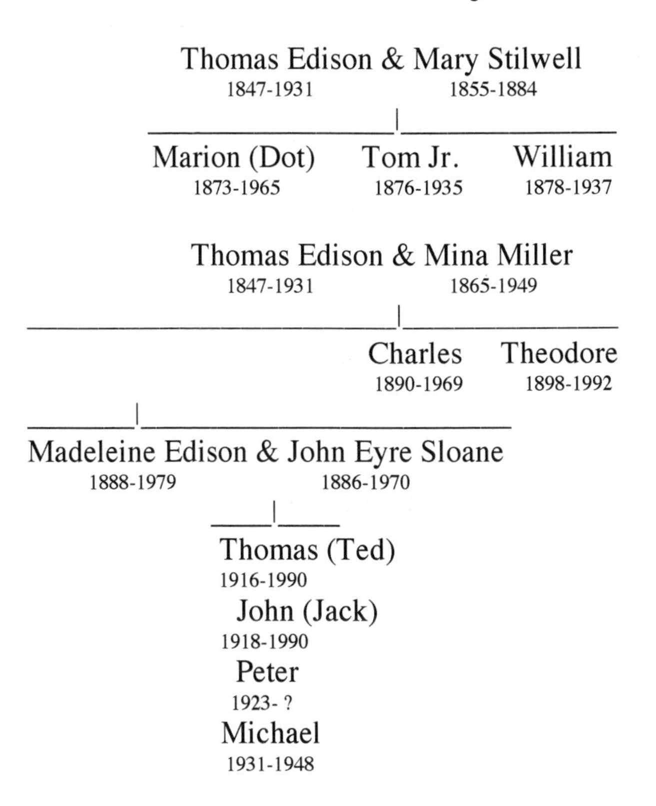

Thomas Edison's parents - Samuel & Nancy Edison
Mary Edison's parents - Nicholas & Margaret Stilwell
Mina Edison's parents - Lewis & Mary Miller
John Sloane's parents - Thomas & Alice Sloane

(Other selected characters are listed at the end of the book.)

Dedication

To the love of my life, Carol,
my bride who inspires me
through all my projects.

Published in the United States of America

Author's Notes and Sources

The Wizard's Bride: The Personal Reflections of Mrs. Thomas A. Edison is a work of historical fiction. Apart from the well-known actual people, events and locales that figure in the narrative, all names, characters, places, incidents and quotations are the product of the author's imagination or are used fictitiously. Any resemblance to current events or locales, or to living persons, is entirely coincidental.

Although this book is a work of fiction, it is firmly rooted in fact, yet I have taken liberties with the development of certain scenes and characters. Mina Edison is the narrator of this book and the ever-loving and faithful wife of Thomas Edison. I have attempted to fully understand Mina through her voluminous letters and, from those letters, create a genuine person with whom you, the reader, can identify.

I am grateful in particular for the work-in-progress online resource of letters, notes and diaries published by Rutgers University, *The Thomas Edison Papers*, edited by Paul Israel. It is truly an invaluable, exhaustive and growing resource open to the public.

For a comprehensive hands-on window into the life and inventions of Mr. Edison and his family, I recommend the following. I am particularly grateful to the historians: Neil Baldwin, *Inventing the Century* (1995), Paul Israel, *Edison: A Life of Invention* (1998), Matthew Josephson, *Edison: A Biography* (1959) and Tom Smoot, *The Edisons of Fort Myers* (2004, 2011).

The New York *Times Archives* provided specific on-the-spot news articles I found valuable and for that I am also indebted.

I have used extensive End Notes. These are identified by numerical superscripts within the text that refer to notes at the end of the book. Some readers may find these annoying and interruptive to the main story. They may be ignored, of course. Other readers will find them helpful during the reading or later since they further explain a subject, identify and credit the sources for material, including some Internet addresses for further investigation.

A Selected Bibliography precedes the End Notes.

1945

Meet Mina

My name is Mina[1] Miller Edison. I am writing this in my eightieth year, forty-five of which included my marriage to Mr. Thomas Alva Edison. My "Dearie" has been gone for fourteen years. He was my one and only love. I miss him deeply.

Much has been written in newspapers and books about my husband. In fact, Mr. Edison himself dictated and published his own life story in 1910 when he was sixty-three. This resulted in a massive, two-volume autobiography[2]. But somehow he neglected to include *anything* about how his two wives and six children contributed to his life. In fact, very little has been written by anyone about me and my family. It is almost as if we never existed or no one cared about our contributions to our revered husband and father.

I'm not asking for pity. Indeed, I have had a glorious life with my husband and among the hundreds and hundreds of people I have met throughout my life. I should have long ago written *my* autobiography.

Over the years, I have written and received volumes of correspondence and written hundreds of pages in my diaries. These are the foundation for my story here.

I was a girl of only nineteen when I was first introduced to Mr. Edison. He was deaf, twice my age, a widower, an unrefined, often crude man, yet a world-famous inventor and the father of three children, the oldest of whom, Marion, was only a bit younger than me! Who would have guessed a match like this would ever take place -- much less last well into the 20th Century?

I met Dearie. . . Oh, excuse me. "Dearie" was my pet name for him and he called me "Billie." When I asked how he ever came up with that name he laughed, put his arm around my waist and said with a chuckle, "I guess I've always liked nicknames. Now I can indulge them." We used these expressions of adoration throughout our marriage. Yes, we adored each other. I still get a tingly sensation when I recall, quite vividly, our intimacies. Yes, even in my day, sexuality was alive and well. We grew up in the Victorian era, but I think that era was misrepresented. We just didn't talk openly about sex. Yet, my Victorianism still brings color to my face when I use that three-letter word.

The entire world missed "Mr. Edison." (I'm going to use this formality throughout my story to add dignity to our sometimes undignified life.) Everyone loved the man who epitomized American inventive genius. A New York *Times* reader poll in 1922 voted him "The greatest living American."[3]

That poll may be true, but he certainly was not always the greatest living *husband* and, I must add, he was even a worse *father* to his first three children. I say that without any bitterness or regret. I state it as a fact. He spent very little time at home for most of our early marriage years. He was either in his laboratory with his men laboring over the development of a new idea or far away promoting these miraculous conceptions throughout America and Europe.

My father, Lewis Miller, had warned me that a celebrity might be difficult to live with, or without. He was correct, but I learned to live with and accept the advantages and the consequences of the Edison idiosyncrasies.

I am eager to tell you about my life with Mr. Edison, our children, the celebrities we met and the travels we so enjoyed.

Chapter One

1847-1884

Edison's early years

Mr. Edison had a unique mind. From his earliest days at school his teacher believed he was "muddle headed," a dreamer lost in another world, seemingly unaware of activities going on around him. In a word, Al, as he was called then, just wasn't like the other children.

He lost most of his hearing as a young boy in Port Huron, Ohio. Scarlet fever[4] was rampant in town and he was one of its victims. His loss of hearing affected his life in many other ways, not the least of which was communicating with me years later. It certainly affected his school classroom work and resulted in his mother, Nancy, after listening to the teacher's report on her son, indignantly removed him from his first-grade class after only three months and thereafter educated the boy at home.

Nancy Edison was a good teacher of the basics. If only one subject stood out clearly in his learning, it was reading. Under his mother's protective wing, with no siblings or classmates to romp with, and with the isolation of their home, the boy turned to reading for companionship. The child read everything he could get hold of, and this compulsion lasted the rest of his life. As an adult in the early 1880s and throughout his life, when he became interested in a particular subject he purchased every related book from bookstores in New York City -- spending hundreds of dollars in a single month. Reading was my deaf husband's only education, self-education, and he was very proud of it.

Young Al loved to experiment. He had his first laboratory in the basement of his parent's home. Here were his collections of feathers, beeswax, charcoal and acids and a miscellany of storage boxes, bags, ceramic containers and jars of every size. His prized collections were labeled "Poison" so as to keep others from touching them.

Although his father, Samuel, was available, they were never close, a trait carried along to Al's later relations with his own children. Al was forever getting into trouble and was accustomed to getting switched. But the time he was experimenting with fire inside his father's shed he would never forget. The fire got away from him and the shed burned down. His father was furious. After announcing the forthcoming punishment event to friends, acquaintences and others, Samuel marched Al to the town square and whipped him publicly.

Among the young man's first money-making endeavors included peddling newspapers and candy aboard the local train, strolling from car to car as it ran from Port Huron to Detroit and back. He has been described as a man who "inherited an intoxication for commerce. . . a homo faber in its most extreme, a self-constructor defined by pathological immersion in labor."[5]

He had been very close to his mother, Nancy, throughout his childhood, but when she died in 1871, the twenty-four-year-old inventor had not visited her for three years -- another characteristic of his relations with his future wives. Filled with guilt and grief, he attended her funeral.

The loss of his mother brought on a family emptiness that he felt compelled to fill. Five months later he began courting sixteen-year-old Mary Stillwell, a clerk who worked in the same telegraph office. She was a blond, attractive and gently innocent. They courted only three months before marrying. Mr. Edison never saw a reason for delaying any of his plans.

Their thirteen-year marriage was not a happy one for Mary. Although he provided her with a substantial and well-furnished home with a domestic staff of two and a coachman, a barn with carriages and horses, his young wife was alone most of the time. She bore one, two and then three children in the tiny farming village of Menlo Park, New Jersey, a village that had a total of eight houses, two of which were owned by Edison managers. For companionship, Mary initially had her sister living with her, but then Alice married and moved away leaving her with only the wives of the managers with whom she had little in common.

Beyond that, Mary was in poor health much of the time. Not long after their marriage Mr. Edison commented in his notebooks, "Mrs. Mary Edison My wife Dearly Beloved Cannot invent worth a Damn!" In other words, she had no imagination. Indeed, she had little education. For Mr. Edison that meant no meaningful conversation. In addition, he refused to participate in any form of domestic life -- the only life Mary had. There were no friends, no parties, no social life except family and no husband most of the time. Mr. Edison had a habit of working at least eighteen hours a day. He might even be traveling in Europe or out West for weeks at a time. When he returned, usually in filthy clothes, he was half asleep from exhaustion and immediately flopped down in the spare room on Mary's clean coverlets and pillow shams.

I have great compassion for his first wife. I suspect Mr. Edison's attraction to Mary was her beauty and, let's face it, a man in his early twenties has an abundance of testosterone. This urge to satisfy his desires undoubtedly drove him to marry this pretty elf of a young woman. Mr. Edison and I never discussed his intimacies with his first wife, but from my experience with him, I know he was no laggard. He knew how to add some thrilling moments to my life.

His daughter Marion wrote in later years that her mother, alone at night most of the time, was afraid of robbers breaking into her house. She said her mother slept with a revolver under her pillow. This almost resulted in a major problem one time when Mr. Edison returned home in the middle of the night. He had lost his house key and climbed through the bedroom window. Mary was startled, awoke in a daze, screamed and pointed her gun at the intruder. Mr. Edison answered and lived to see another day.

As the inventor grew wealthy, the family moved to New York City. Mary was thrilled beyond description. The country girl loved the excitement of the city. As the now-famous inventor's wife, she was invited to numberless parties by her new friends. Mr. Edison bought Mary costly gifts each time he returned from a lengthy absence. She became known for her eye-popping appearances at tea parties, liberally decorated with jewels and wearing gowns of the finest taste, a bodice of satin, a bustle and a lengthy train. Mr. Edison rarely had a lot of available cash for, what he called, her frivolous expenditures. He reinvested all his profits in his businesses. But when a windfall arrived, such as the payment on a patent, he felt he could be extravagant with her. And Mary made sure her young daughter, Marion, also a blonde, was appropriately dressed and decorated as well.

During these early days, Mr. Edison limited his social life to working side by side with his male employees. His men were his family, his "Muckers," as he called them. He was a hands-on guy. He micro managed. But he also dined regularly with his top managers, often at his favorite establishment -- Delmonico's.[6]

It was his "pathological immersion in labor" that occupied most of his time -- day and night. It was commonly known that he needed little sleep. Catnaps of an hour or two revitalized him. He most often slept in the laboratory or at the office because it was close at hand, even though his home was only a few blocks away.

Consider briefly what Mr. Edison accomplished with the use of his time before he was thirty-eight -- *before* he married me.

In 1868, at the age of twenty-one, he was granted his first patent. It was for an electronic vote recorder. At age twenty-two he quit his job as a telegrapher at Western Union and began inventing full time. At age twenty-three he established two telegraph manufacturing shops in Newark, New Jersey.

During his first marriage at age twenty-four and fathering three children, he began work on duplex telegraphy; at age twenty-six he tested an automatic telegraph system in England; at twenty-seven he discovered the electromagnetic principle and invented the quadruplex telegraph; at twenty-eight he conceived the electric pen and an automatic press copying system and experimented with acoustic telegraphy; at twenty-nine he constructed the Menlo Park laboratory under the supervision of his father, Samuel; at thirty be began work on carbon transmitters (the basis for telephone communication for more than 100 years); the same year, he conceived and demonstrated the phonograph, his favorite invention, and gained international recognition for it.

At age thirty-one he began electric lighting experiments and incorporated The Edison Electric Light Company; at thirty-two he constructed his first generator, developed a bipolar dynamo, toured Canada looking for supplies of platinum, and had his first successful experiment with a high-resistance carbon filament; at thirty-three he experimented with magnetic ore separation, installed the first incandescent lighting plant, built an experimental electric railway at Menlo Park and began operations at the Edison Electric Lamp Works at Menlo Park.

In 1881, at age thirty-four, he moved his business operations (and family) to New York City, and began manufacturing generators, conductors and other components for electric lighting systems. That same year he opened an electric central station in London, England and began building electric central stations throughout the United States.

At thirty-seven he was elected vice president of the American Institute of Electrical Engineers and that same year he reorganized the Edison Electric Light Company.

At age thirty-eight, seventeen months after Mary died, he married me.

Meet the Miller family

My father's grandfather, Abraham Miller, emigrated from Germany in 1776. As family lore relates it, he promptly joined the Colonial army and served under General George Washington at Valley Forge. His son John, my grandfather, was a farmer who moved west to the "unspoiled" lands of Greentown, Ohio, southeast of Akron. It was here my father, Lewis, was born into John's family in 1829 on the crossroads of a north/south stagecoach route and the east/west Conestoga wagon trail. Father told me he used to watch these "Ships of the Desert" creak and groan as they slowly passed, each hauled by three teams of horses or oxen. He said he remembers well the sound of the cracks of the whip and the Gee/Haw commands of the drivers. It was a very romantic image to him and now to me.

Father did not follow his father's farming vocation but he was not far from it. Lewis Miller's interest was the mechanical methods of harvesting crops -- reaping machines, and their use for bringing in the crops quickly and efficiently. That interest inspired him to work for Bell Aultman and Company where the first reapers in Ohio were manufactured. There he mastered the trade of a mechanic.

The company business grew rapidly. Father's inventive contributions to the company led him to become a partner. He spent many hours afield studying how the reapers worked as they harvested the fields. What he learned from observation was translated into machine improvements that became patents that were the most important and revolutionary changes since McCormack and Hussy first introduced the machines. The company name was changed to the Buckeye Mower and Reaper Co. and it was moved to Akron to be near the Erie Railroad. By the time I was born, the company was producing and shipping world-wide some twenty-five thousand of his reaping machines a year.

My father's story is where his genius for invention coincides with Mr. Edison's. Father became a very rich man. He secured some ninety-two patents for his company. His successes, and Mr. Edison's, were built primarily upon the improvement of other men's original ideas, having purchased from these men their original patents.

Both men had an affinity for their workers. Mr. Edison worked daily, hand-in-hand next to his men. He was known as "the boss," or the "old man." But my father gave himself the title of "superintendent" -- a term that implied he too was close to his workers, rather than using the more lofty title of "president."

A major turning point

The loss of Mr. Edison's wife, Mary, marked a major turning point in all aspects of Mr. Edison's life. He was not a religious man and therefore had nowhere to turn for divine comfort. Without Mary, he was in a void. For the first time he made excuses to keep away from his office and lab, extending his lunch and dinner hours at Delmonico's chatting casually with acquaintences, ignoring developing crises among his many businesses, including Edison Electric Light Company where significant personnel problems had developed.

His corporate life was immensely successful and he was already vastly rich. But now, his youthful gallop through industry ran into a wall. He slowed his frantic pace and began to take notice of life beyond his work.

His oldest child, Marion, who he had nicknamed "Dot," in reference to his early life as a telegrapher using Samuel Morse's code, was now twelve and nearly full-grown. She had blonde hair that reminded him of her mother. She suddenly became his constant companion as he tried to reconstruct his family life.[7] Marion was delighted. She now had her father all to herself. She had been attending a private day school in New York City not far from her father's office. When he invited her over to visit him, it was at the expense of her missing classes and leaving her homework unfinished.[8] But that didn't matter to her. She bloomed as she considered herself her father's favorite and never gave a thought to her younger bothers, Tom and William, pining away in the care of relatives and a governess.

A month after Mary passed away, Mr. Edison and Marion visited the International Electrical Exhibition in Philadelphia. Many of his companies had display booths that included his lighting systems for factories, hospitals and hotels, and his lamps and dynamos. It was a major show with 1,500 exhibitors that attracted some 300,000 visitors.

On his return to New York, freshly energized, he reorganized the Edison Electric Light Company on the basis of ideas he had picked up in Philadelphia and he settled the internal employee dissention.

Even today, I continue to be amazed how he managed all that was happening in his business and private life.

In mid-February, 1885, West Orange was snowy and the damp cold was penetrating Mr. Edison's limbs. His knee joints ached -- a sure sign that he was ready for his Florida cure.

He and Marion boarded a train and planned two stops along the route south. The first stop was Akron where they visited long-time friends, Ezra and Lillian Gilliland. Ezra and Mr. Edison had become close during their first-job years working as itinerant telegraphers. They had roomed together. Ezra was now a large, jovial man with a substantial handlebar mustache. His wife was a beautiful, sophisticated lady whom Edison greatly admired. She managed her home and entertained with grace and ease, talents his wife, Mary, had never learned.[9]

Significantly, Lillian had a powerful domesticating effect on Mr. Edison who never had the social polish that many of the nouveau riche of the time affected. As I can well attest, he was uncomfortable in stiff collars and fancy clothes. He was a hands-on man who proudly worked side-by-side with his employees – never afraid to dirty his calloused hands.

At age thirty-eight, Mr. Edison was worth more than $10 million -- a phenomenal sum in those days. Employees, friends and some relatives saw their association with him as a chance to ride along on his coattails with the hope that someday the great man would share with them his wealth, if not his fame.

The relationship with his buddy Ezra was different, however. He and Mr. Edison collaborated on a number of projects and Ezra was tuned in to his friend's thinking. He had a great wit and was quick with the pun. That type of friendship allowed trust and relaxation in each other's presence. In fact the two men were co-owners of a number of significant patents.[10]

As I mentioned earlier, the Gillilands were close friends also with my family in Akron. I had spent many a pleasant evening in the Gilliland home and the same when they visited our family for dinner.

The Gilliland's now joined up with Mr. Edison and Marion on their trip south and continued by train to their second stop -- New Orleans where they attended the World Industrial and Cotton Centennial Exposition. Ezra assisted Mr. Edison and his show organizers at his exhibits.

But more than that happened. My father, Lewis Miller, and I were also in New Orleans for much the same purpose. Father was exhibiting his farm machinery.

Introduction to Mr. Edison

Part of father's plan while at the New Orleans Exposition[11] was to visit Mr. Edison's exhibits and this was where I first met the man I had always heard so much about. My initial feelings about him were certainly not romantic nor do I think I was expected to be attracted to him. I was certainly well aware of the man's amazing accomplishments – as was the rest of the world. Already, at age 38, he had invented the phonograph and had improved on the light bulb,[12] among other things. All my friends thought he was the cat's meow.

Mr. Edison was on hand at the Bell Telephone exhibit where some of his inventions were displayed. We had to push our way through the huge crowd of admirers who were eager, not only to see his new gadgets, but to see the man who created them. People had begun calling him "The Wizard" because of the apparent magic that inspired the many inventions that came out of his Menlo Park laboratory.

Father and I were pleasantly surprised to run into the Gillilands when we arrived at Bell exhibit. It was our mutual friend Ezra who introduced us to the inventor.

Mr. Edison took my hand in greeting and was more than polite to me as he offered to guide us through his exhibits. He kept turning to me and smiling as he explained how his creations worked. I was flattered by his attentions. He was modest in his explanations, as if making these wonderful things were an everyday event. For him, it seems, it was.

Mr. Edison was a stinky cigar smoker, yet I was intrigued by his use of it. No one in our family used tobacco. He took a puff now and then and blew the smoke into the air between his sentences. Then, holding it between his thumb and the first two fingers of his left hand, he gestured with it. Whenever two hands were needed, he jammed the cigar between his teeth and wrapped his lips around it, dragging smoke in through the cigar and then exhaling it from the side of his mouth and his nose.

Of course there were other distractions with the hubbub, noise and confusion of the exposition crowd. I absorbed little of Mr. Edison's animated explanations of his devices. And I noticed he had difficulty hearing my questions. He repeatedly placed his hand behind his right ear and leaned toward me as I spoke. I was attempting to sound intelligent but more likely my response to his answers was as a dumb teenager and I probably blushed. Father was quick to intercede.

I have long forgotten his first words to me, but they were undoubtedly technical. All I remember is, whatever he said, he spoke with a pleasant smile and a chuckle. I felt very important. I'm sure there were some people in the crowd who wondered who that girl was to get such personal attention.

I thought he was a very interesting gentleman, not much different than my father, actually. My father, Mr. Gilliland and Mr. Edison all had a common interest in mechanics. I grew up watching my father, the inventor, working in his shop and listening to his excitement as his creations took on their own lives. I wouldn't say this to any of them, but they were like boys with their toys.

It never occurred to me that Mr. Edison might find *me* interesting. I thought he was simply being nice to the young daughter of a friend and didn't want to see me standing alone with Lillian while he talked with father. Of course I enjoyed his attention. Who wouldn't?

Incidentally, my female observation noted that my father and Ezra were far better dressers than Mr. Edison who looked like he had slept in his rumpled suit. It was cold in New Orleans on this visit and Mr. Edison was still in his summer linens!

But no matter. That was our brief meeting. I'm certain I was soon out of his memory after we departed and continued through the exposition to father's display of farm machinery.

It wasn't until after we left that father told me Mr. Edison's wife had passed away only a few months earlier.

In looking back now, I recognize that in Mr. Edison's sensitive transition in life, the widower began to notice attractive young women again. He needed a wife, someone to help reassemble his family and look after his children. He also needed someone to tell him when to wear a coat. In spite of all his money, he now lacked a home life and envied what he saw the Gillilands enjoying. He needed a new love. It appeared to me some time later that it was I who awakened feelings of passion in Edison. It might even be called "love at first sight" -- for him.

Lillian told me later that she noticed this change in Mr. Edison. She even talked with him about it and she said he responded with a rush of feelings. In fact, he recorded in his diary some months later that he daydreamed of me and even imagined our marriage and happiness together. Of course I was totally unaware of this at the time.

A few days later father went back to Akron and I returned to Miss Johnson's Ladies' Seminary, my finishing school, and the winter in Boston. I enjoyed the New Orleans get-away and I took pleasure in telling my friends about meeting the man whose name and accomplishments were familiar to all of them.

I wasn't at all surprised when the girls wanted to know more details about this world-renowned icon. How tall was he? What was his voice like? Did he smile? Was he a gentleman? Did he take my hand when we met? Why was he so interested in me? What do you know about his wife?

I basked in their shower of their questions, most of which I couldn't answer.

I graduated in the early summer of 1885 and remember it well. It was a beautiful season in Boston. The Public Gardens were bursting with tulips of every color. The Swan Boats[13] were out along with a pair of real swans. It was a wonderful time in my life and school was now behind me.

Back home in Akron, my family thought it was time for me to marry. There were two young men I had grown up with as friends. One of them was George Vincent to whom I was actually engaged since I was sixteen – thanks to pressure from mother. But now there was something about my relationship with George that troubled me.

Discovering Eden

Mr. Edison, Marion and the Gillilands continued on to St. Augustine, the southernmost Florida resort city at the time. There Mr. Edison welcomed the sun, sand and healing warmth and quickly recovered his health.

He was still searching for a light bulb filament that was more durable and longer lasting than those he had used in earlier bulbs. The ideal filament was elusive. Bamboo was one plant he was eager to acquire as a possible solution. He had sent agents as far away as Brazil and Asia to locate similar exotic plants but with little success.

While in St. Augustine someone mentioned bamboo was available further down the west coast of Florida in a place called Fort Myers. Unfortunately, there was no train service or decent road to this exotic place. But that didn't deter the man with a mission. This would be an adventure. Lillian and Marion elected to forego that "adventure" and stayed behind with the comforts of the resort.

The trip southwest was difficult, riding a dilapidated, pre-Civil War railway through Gainesville and on to Cedar Key, located on the Gulf Coast. The train went off the tracks several times and Mr. Edison and Ezra were forced to stand by idly each time as repairs were made. Mr. Edison's intrusive suggestions on how to improve the rail line and its service were not appreciated.

From Cedar Key they continued south by boat to Punta Rassa, located at the mouth of the Caloosahatchee River and within sight, across San Carlos Bay, of the recently erected iron lighthouse at Sanibel Island[14].

They stayed at a lodge called Tarpon House and were captivated by stories about the huge tarpon that were caught just offshore. The mission to find bamboo was delayed. Mr. Edison gave in to his compulsion to fish whenever a tantalizing opportunity confronted him. The anglers hired a guide who took them out into the Gulf. They then dropped their lines in vain for for several days. The tarpon remained elusive. Both men blamed the bait, then the lures, the weather and finally the guide. They would catch the "big one" another time.

The search for bamboo resumed. The men took a scheduled steamer twelve miles up the Caloosahatchee to the tiny village of Fort Myers and arrived in mid-March. They roomed in the Keystone Hotel -- the only hotel.

Mr. Edison liked the town. It was exotic, with palm trees, fresh air, a clear, clean river and abundant flora of every description. He visited the docks and walked the dusty main street. It was quiet. It was away from the clamor of the noisy, dirty, northern cities and he liked the relative anonymity. He felt free. He had discovered a personal retreat.

He stopped in at the E. L. Evans General Store and had a conversation with Evans himself. The subject of bamboo came up and Evans offered to take the explorers to see it. They rode in a horse-drawn cart to a location about a mile out of town on the banks of the river.

To be sure there was a tangle of vines, grasses and ferns but also a treasure of hardwood hammocks, Spanish moss, colorful native orchids and air plants. And, there also was Mr. Edison's long-sought bamboo, a forest of tall poles by the hundred. The spot was idyllic and immediately captured Mr. Edison's heart. He took hold of one of the plants, shook it gleefully. It rattled like so many primitive fishing poles against each other. He turned to his friend. "Finally, Ezra, an inexhaustable supply of potential light bulb filaments."

Gilliland just shook his head at his boss' burst of playfulness.

There was a small shack nearby in a clearing that extended to the edge of the river. A couple of rickety chairs sat just outside the shack. Mr. Edison looked at Ezra and pointed to the chairs. "Ezra. I think we ought to take advantage of what some kind soul has provided for us."

"I think you're correct, Tom. If people are kind enough to place them here, we have a certain obligation to make use of them."

They sat, lighted their cigars and leaned back into comfortable positions. The cigar smoke only briefly clouded their view.

"Isn't this the place, Ezra? Just look at all the colorful flowers and that magnificent river. It must be about a mile wide. How did old man Evans pronounce its name?"

"I think it was something like ca-loo-sa-ha-chee."

"Say that fast three times Ezra." Mr. Edison laughed.

"I can't. But it is beautiful, Tom."

"It's so peaceful, so quiet."

"Every place is quiet to you," Gilliland joked. "I bet you can't hear any of the squawking birds."

"I don't need to hear them. But I can see a huge variety of colorful flora. I can also see the potential of clearing out all the dead and ugly underbrush and opening this place up. I can see planting gardens where we can raise the rarest of plants from around the world. I can see building another lab here where I can study all this beauty."

"I'll admit the contrasts between here and home sure make it welcoming."

"What do you say we buy this place, Ezra?" Mr. Edison suggested.

"*Buy* this place? Whatever for?"

"Think about it, Ezra. It's a perfect retreat. When we clear away the underbrush and open it up, build a couple houses, one for me and one for you, this will be a perfect Garden of Eden. I'll bet Eden was exactly like this. Look at all the flowers. Look at all the species of trees. And the river. Have you ever seen a river so clean? All the way up here on the boat I watched the bottom of the river slide by. I could see every fish. I saw the dolphins. I even saw a manatee. Just you try to find a place like this up in Ohio, or anywhere up north."

"You're right, Tom. I've never seen any place like this. But I don't think Lillian will care for it."

"Of course not. Not in this overgrown condition. I'm not suggesting that. But we could get this place ready in a year or so. Just use your imagination on what this could be. It is definitely an Eden. It just needs a little tune up."

"Sure. I can see that now. You're right, Tom."

The pair now sat in quiet contemplation. Each with their own thoughts. Each with his cigar.

Mr. Edison broke the silence. "That sure was clever of you and Lillian to match me up with the Miller girl. She is a beauty, and she's smart. She comes from a good family. I plan to catch her. I need a woman like her."

"Are you serious? Miss Miller is rather young, don't you think? And we didn't match you up. We just introduced you."

"Ezra! She's a grown woman. She's mature. She's ripe."

"Tom. What makes you think she'd be interested in an old man like you. You have a daughter almost her age."

Mr. Edison sat up straight and looked at Gilliland. "What do you mean? I'm in the prime of my life. What difference does age make?"

"Lillian and I know her family very well, Ezra. Her father, Lewis, is a hard worker and he's an inventor like us. But he's also a very religious family man. He may have something to say about your interest in his daughter."

"I have nothing against religious family men. I'm interested in his daughter who is now of marrigeable age. I need a smart, beautiful wife. I think Miss Miller is the one for me."

Cigars and deep thought occupied the next few minutes.

"I'm not supposed to tell you this, Tom, but I think Lillian has plans to invite you and the Millers to our summer place. You'll have a chance then to test out your 'prime-of-life' theory."

Mr. Edison's look turned serious as he studied his friend's countenance. "You're not joking. Does this mean that Lillian thinks Miss Miller and I would make a good match?"

"I didn't say that, Tom. Lillian has an unquenchable knack for matchmaking. She's been successful at it in Akron. She can't bear to see an eligible man wandering alone without a woman to guide him. She has plans for you. She will invite Miss Miller, but there will be other young women for you to meet as well."

"You are a good friend, Ezra. That's very nice of Lillian to think of me. I look forward to that. I want to marry that girl. She's been in my dreams since I met her. I envision this place right here will be our Eden and our love nest."

"Aren't you a little ahead of yourself, Tom?"

"Some people might say that, my friend, but I know what I want."

Mr. Edison made a decision. He was famous for his foresight. He decided to buy the property. He expressed his vision in detail to his friend. Their entire discussion was not focused on me. He convinced Gilliland to partner with him and share the expenses of the land and the cost of building the houses.

But I've often asked myself why the dapper Gilliland would want a second home in the jungle of Florida. He was happily married to a woman of sophistication and urban grace who was certain to abhor being trapped in such a primitive location. It took some years for me to understand Mr. Edison's excitement about his Eden.

And Gilliland must have found himself in a compromising situation. They were the best of friends, but he was also Mr.

Edison's employee, a close friend, trusted and valued, but still an employee -- potentially a difficult relationship for any individual when asked to join in a financial deal. As such, with his boss' enthusiasm and acknowledged leverage over him, Ezra undoubtedly felt pressured into sharing expenses -- even though, most likely, he may not have been able to afford it.

Certainly Mr. Edison was ecstatic. The men would soon be the owners of a choice, thirteen-acre piece of paradise that Mr. Edison himself called "my jungle." Later, the formal name would become Seminole Lodge, at Mr. Edison's suggestion of course, recognizing the Native Americans who formerly occupied southern Florida and the Everglades.

Mr. Edison had instantly fallen in love with the area. He envisioned setting up another laboratory to study the rampant native flora. He was also eager to test the bamboo as a filament for his light bulb that could be carbonized and have a much longer burn life than his current materials. In addition, he was beginning a long struggle to find a plant from which he could produce rubber.

Before leaving Fort Myers, the men met and signed a real estate agreement. They also hired a local contractor, Frank Thompson, to hire a labor force to clear certain areas of the property and begin building a pier out into the depths of the otherwise shallow Caloosahatchee so that a steamer could unload building materials, utilities and machinery.

The men returned to St. Augustine in late March with abundant samples of plant life. During the long trip the men sketched plans for the two residences. Mr. Edison would hire an architect in New York and have the houses build as prefabrications in Maine using lumber sawed from local timbers. A schedule was set. He was determined to have everything completed and in place by the following January.

And then there was me. According to Mr. Edison, I was still very much on his mind after our single, brief encounter in New Orleans. Of course I was totally unaware of his Fort

Myers activities at the time, but the romantic now planned to pursue this "fair maiden," as he generously referred to me. This garden of Eden, he firmly believed, would be our honeymoon love nest.

The role of the Gillilands

In the summer of 1885, my parents and I were invited to vacation at Woodside Villa, Ezra and Lillian Gilliland's oceanside cottage in Winthrop, Massachusetts, just north of Boston. I was not fooled by the circumstances of this "vacation" invitation. As was the custom of the day, eligible bachelors of note were often treated to meeting, and being entertained by, young ladies who were in quest of a suitor.

Mr. Edison, not by coincidence, and his daughter Marion, were also guests. Lillian took every opportunity to see that he and I were in proximity. Also in the parlor were my parents, two other young ladies whom I knew, their parents and, of course, young Marion.

To put it bluntly, we three older girls were on exhibit. It was not my interest to be put on display but I felt obliged to go through with the introduction and be done with it. I didn't want to embarrass my parents or our hosts.

I put my school training to use and swept purposefully (some might call it dramatically) into the parlor. Lillian[15] announced to Mr. Edison that Miss Mina Miller would like to sing and play the piano for his enjoyment. That was not quite the truth, probably because I knew I was sorely lacking in piano proficiency. But I did what was expected of me.

Following my recital, I turned toward Mr. Edison and, using all the dignity I could dredge up, I held his gaze and my composure while accepting his compliments. I refused to be affectedly demure and shy. For the first time I appraised Mr. Edison and noticed that he was very well dressed and looked quite handsome decked out in the style of the day.

I thanked him for the tour of his exhibit in New Orleans and said how much I enjoyed seeing the fruits of his endeavors. Then I simply smiled again and moved to another chair across the room.

That wasn't the end. Mr. Edison kept looking at me -- almost as if he had been impressed with my performance. I again held his gaze and smiled, wondering if I had played well enough to satisfy my parents.

Mr. Edison broke the awkwardness by telling everyone in the room how he had been reading Hawthorne's "English Notebooks"[16] and how critical he was of it. But then he cast that thought off and admitted he undoubtedly didn't have the education to appreciate "fine" writing.

I was surprised to find myself laughing and said I had tried to read the "Notebooks" as well and also had a problem with it. We both became quite merry as we joked about the author's detailed descriptions of old churches, musty graveyards and morose coroners in London.

At dinner, Lillian made a point of seating Mr. Edison beside me, to his right, aware that his right ear was the better one. We chatted quite amiably throughout dinner, not intentionally ignoring Lillian who sat to his left. I was surprised that Mr. Edison had such a good sense of humor and he was quite pleasant. Sitting this close, I noticed he looked younger than I remembered. Although his hair was turning white, he had very few wrinkles. He was actually quite handsome for someone twice my age.

On the downside, he spoke loudly and everyone around the table could hear his side of our conversation. Also, it was obvious he was uncomfortable with table etiquette. He appeared puzzled at the quantity of silverware at his place setting. He began to eat before the hostess picked up her fork. He forgot to place his napkin in his lap and he used his dessert fork on the main course. Oh, my, I thought with a smile. The great inventor never went to finishing school.

I was at the Gilliland's for a week. Mr. Edison and I walked the beach and chatted on the porch overlooking the ocean. Marion[17] was with us often and held her father's hand in between chasing seagulls, her long blond hair streaming behind, her lilac-flowered dress bouncing up and down as she dodged the ebb and flow of the waves.

The Gillilands owned a large yacht and my parents were able to accompany us as we all went out onto the sea. Mr. Edison fished from the stern and was apparently happy simply losing his bait.

"Yes I love to fish," he said to me as I stood by. "There's something magical about it. It's a time to think and to keep the hands busy at the same time. It's not necessary to catch the poor creatures."

He surprised me by handing me the pole.

"It's a rod, Miss Miller. Not a pole."

He showed me how to manage the rod. We sat very close as I awkwardly maneuvered it. I enjoyed the experience until Marion noticed and pushed between us and asked to hold the stick.

"It's a rod, Dot, not a stick." Mr. Edison chided with a smile.

I had to laugh. I liked Marion. Even at twelve she was almost my height. Certainly I could understand how she was annoyed that I was increasingly usurping her father's attentions. Thinking of managing my younger brothers and sisters, as I had frequently been asked to do at home, I now tried to give her more of my attention. I quickly learned it was not welcomed. She wanted no part of me and was quick to express herself and her age in a variety of ways, such as sticking out her tongue or making an ugly face when her father wasn't looking.

Otherwise, it was a glorious time. I found Mr. Edison to be very attentive and interesting – and maybe attractive in the sense that we found plenty to talk about when we were near enough, and when I was on his right side and he heard what I was saying.

Our week went fast. In some ways I didn't want to leave. I enjoyed Mr. Edison's company and he told me how much he enjoyed mine. I thanked the Gillilands for their hospitality and our family departed for Chautauqua[18] for our annual summer retreat.

More on the Miller family

My father was a very rich man when he moved his company and family to Akron in 1863. By then, our family had grown to seven children. I was the youngest. Five more siblings would join me during the next twelve years, placing me, by age, plunk in the middle of my siblings.

We were a religious and prayerful family reading the Bible regularly, pillars of the Akron First Methodist Church. Father soon became a recognized leader in this community, supporting the church financially and initiating a Sunday school program that recognized the health advantages of open air teaching and the beauty of nature -- not much different than the philosophical movement of the Transcendentalists that was the vogue in New England thirty years earlier.

Father, always a vigorous proponent for education, expanded his Sunday school curriculum to include music and other arts. He built a new school building in the shape of a semicircle that faced the natural setting of the woodlands. And he became superintendent. It was this school that became the prototype for the Chautauqua Institution.

He was well ahead of his time. He became president of the Akron board of education and he served on the board of directors at Mount Union College. This college was the first in the nation to offer a four-year course of study and, most importantly, gave equal privileges and rights to both men and women -- the shocking idea of an Ohio liberal.

I had six brothers, three of whom were older. I found them far more interesting than my sisters. I'm told that I was a tomboy. My brothers and I built a treehouse. From the treetops we had a view that overlooked Akron and the villages well beyond. We went on treasure hunts. We ventured into Akron as a group on our bicycles. They taught me their version of self-defense. The boys were very protective and at times I did some pretty silly things because I knew they would save me from myself. One of those times I rolled my wagon down the steep hill from our house, but the boys were at the curve where they knew I would tip over. They caught me just in time. My oldest brother, Edward, never married until he was in his sixties. He continued to look after me and my personal finances in the years after Mr. Edison's death.

It was here the Miller family bought twenty-five acres atop the hill that overlooked Akron and built the home father named Oak Place. This was no castle-in-the-clouds, no retreat from the world. Lewis and Mary Miller opened their home to the world and made it a ritual to invite guests, rich and poor, Methodist and Atheist, to join them and their older children to their dinner table *every* evening of the week where several-course meals were served. Music and discussions, philosophical and topical, always followed, satisfying the patriarch's passion for intellectual and social education. Ezra and Lillian Gilliland were occasional guests whom we had met through our church. Christian values were always stressed.

It was within this milieu that I was raised and strongly influenced. Father's example determined my social and moral values for the rest of my life.

The Paragon of Perfection

Mr. Edison spent nearly the entire month of July 1885 at the Gilliland's beach house. There were other guests as well, including John Tomlinson, whom Edison would later hire as his private legal counsel.

As much as Mr. Edison enjoyed the summer activities in these pleasant and relaxing surroundings in Winthrop, it seems he sorely missed my presence. His diary reflected this emptiness: "Oh dear, this celestial mud ball has made another revolution and no photograph yet from the Chautauquain Paragon of Perfection. How much longer will Hope dance on my intellect."[19]

There were also a number of other attractive young ladies who were paraded before Mr. Edison. They came to the Gilliland's beach house from as far away as the mid-West knowing that the famous Thomas Edison was looking for a suitable mate.

Marion had her own ideas about who would make the best stepmother.

"I like Miss Igoe best, Papa."

"Why is that, Dot?"

"Because she has blonde hair like mother's and mine."

"That's not a good reason. Are you saying you don't like Miss Miller?"

"Yes."

"Why?"

"Because you like her too much!"

"How so, Dot?"

"I can tell. You like to hold her hand instead of mine."

"Then you are jealous of Miss Miller?"

"I want you to hold my hand."

"OK. Give me my your hand."

"Don't make fun of me, Papa. I don't mean that." Marion paused. "I guess I am jealous."

"If I held Miss Igoe's hand would you be jealous?"

"Papa," Marion snapped. "Why do you need somebody else when you have me? Don't you like me?"

"Dot, darling. I love you. You're my daughter. I need a wife. Someday you'll want a husband and then you'll want him to hold your hand instead of mine. There's no need for you to be jealous."

"I can't help it, Papa. I want to be with you always."

"Well, Dot, that's not going to happen. You'll just have to get used to it. Whoever I marry will also love you."

"It's not the same as Mama was. Miss Miller is too old to be my friend and too young to be my mother."

"Those are wise words, Dot. But it will still be best for all of us that you like whoever I choose to be my wife."

This discussion set the strained tone for my relationship with Marion for many years to come. Miss Igoe eventually married my brother, Robert Miller, eleven months after my marriage.[20]

Mr. Edison found all these ladies interesting but, as he told me later, he was already totally infatuated with me. None of the young ladies came close to measuring up to me. I know this sounds conceited of me to write this, but it was a fact. I needed to be reminded of his words in the early years of our marriage when he was away from home on extended business trips. Mr. Edison used the word "staggered" in his diary to describe his impression of me. A goddess-like image of me truly grew in his mind and he could not shake it, he wrote. He telegraphed his friend and business partner, Sam Insull,[21] and told him about the beautiful women he was viewing. He asked Insull to have two photographs of himself sent to Miss Miller.

The Chautauqua experience

The entire Miller family was fully engaged in the Chautauqua scene. I loved the social life and mixing among my interesting family friends. Noted scholars, authors, presidents and kings from around the world were invited to give lectures on a wide variety of topics. Open minds were encouraged. Chautauqua was stimulating intellectually as well as a place to relax in a variety of recreational opportunities. I spent most of my summers there throughout my life.

The summer of 1885 was my twentieth birthday.[22] I had not yet talked seriously about Mr. Edison with my parents, although they must have known we had been corresponding. My age once again inspired father and mother to ask if George Vincent and I had set a wedding date.

"No, We haven't."

"Most women are married by age twenty, Mina," mother reminded me. "Have you seen George[23] since we've returned?"

"I have. George told me his plans to teach at university level when he graduates. He asked me what I thought about that. It seemed he wanted my approval."

"Well why shouldn't he? You're engaged. Don't you think it would be nice to be the wife of a college professor?"

"Mother! I'm no longer sure I want to be engaged to him."

Mother was suddenly stricken by apoplexy. She turned red.

"Mina Miller! You are talking about the son of your parent's very best friends. We have always agreed that you two make a very good match. "

"Mother! Please. George and I were engaged because you pushed me into it. That was four years ago, before I went to school in Boston and saw that there were interesting and exciting men in this world." I sat up straight. "I want to meet other suitors. George isn't the only marriageable man in the world."

"Ah, then," mother said with a smirk. "Then it's Mr. Edison."

"*What*?" I was truly surprised. "Don't jump to conclusions, mother. Mr. Edison and I have been corresponding but that's all. Mr. Edison is interesting, but he's old."

"You had better reconsider George for the sake of our two families. I'm afraid of what the Vincents think."

"Please, mother. Don't rush me. Marriage has little to do with pleasing parents. I have to find the right man for me."

"Oh, dear. I don't know, Mina. I think you're being a little too independent."

"Are you saying I should wed George simply because the Millers and the Vincents think I should?"

Personally, I thought George was unimaginative and pompous. Handsome and dependable as he was, as good a friend as he had been all my life, I could not visualize him offering me a stimulating life. I didn't love him. I never loved him. I didn't feel the magic with him. I thought I'd rather be a maiden lady than be married to good old boring George. He told me he wanted to teach in the university because it was prestigious -- not for any particular intellectual pursuit. He admired the prestige his minister father wore as a badge on his lapel. He enjoyed the way people respected his father. I imagined George would be quite happy to have people genuflect before him. He believed the students at the university would have to show him the respect he felt he would deserve.

"Well, how about Edward Hughes?"[24] mother pursued. "He comes from an excellent and prosperous Pennsylvania family. A real gentleman."

"Mother. They are both good friends and real gentlemen and I'm certain they each will make some woman an excellent husband. But I don't see the excitement and I don't feel their passion for life. I want more, mother. I want a real man of the world who has great ideas -- a leader of men."

"Young lady," mother scolded. "You have been reading too many of those dime novels. You want a man on the proverbial white horse."

I thought a moment. "You may be right, mother," I said eagerly. "I think that describes the man *you* married. I think I do want a man very similar to father. He is a man of the world, a creator and -- a leader of men."

"Men like father don't grow on trees, Mina."

"Exactly! But I will find that man."

Mother approached and put her arms around me. She placed her head aside mine. "Darling. I'm so afraid you will never marry. Look at Jennie. Still unmarried at thirty. You two are so independent and strong willed. Not every man likes a woman like that."

"I'm not after 'every man.' I want the one man who understands me and loves me for who I am. Much like you and father. You have given me a good education. You have let me travel the world and see some of the wonderful things it has to offer. School, Chautauqua and this family, have taught me to think and to use my mind. I am well aware there are women whose only thoughts are those of their husband. I cannot limit myself to that. I have to think my own thoughts and share those thoughts with my husband. Some day, mother, women in general will arise and speak for themselves as equals with men."

"Who taught you that!"

"I do a lot of reading that you won't find in dime novels. Have you heard of Elizabeth Cady Stanton?"[25]

"Not exactly."

"Miss Stanton addressed the first Women's-Rights Convention in 1848. She sought to raise women's stature to be equal with men's. Along with this, she demanded the women's right to vote."

"She sounds like a firebrand! Does your father know about this?"

"We have discussed it."

"Oh, my. I hope you're not spreading this among your siblings."

"Perhaps I should. But don't worry, mother. I have no intention of standing on a soapbox and preaching anything. That's not me. But I do like to learn about other people's ideas -- however unconventional they may be."

"I will pray for you, Mina. I pray that you will find an honest, hard-working man who truly loves and cares for you."

I kissed mother on the cheek. "I pray for exactly the same thing." I paused and looked at her face to face. "Do you realize that this is what Chautauqua is all about -- the free expression of ideas? And don't forget. Father co-founded Chautauqua on this principle."

Father and our minister, Rev. John Vincent, were close friends, working hand-in-hand at our church in Akron to develop a diverse adult educational program that espoused their common ideas. From this, the men began to train Sunday school teachers in an outdoor-summer-school format at the facility that father donated. The concept caught on rapidly, eventually filling the area to capacity. Soon, a much larger area was needed.

Father's Christian faith took hold. The two men scouted for a proper outdoor setting that would work. They found an idyllic, secluded property on Chautauqua Lake in extreme western New York State, near Jamestown. It was easily accessible from everywhere because it was near the newly established Wheeling and Lake Erie Railroad line. They raised money among like-minded people, organized a corporation and purchased some eighty acres. The location was 150 miles east of Akron but that didn't matter because the plan was to occupy the area as a summer-long, educational tent encampment. The encampment, originally named Chautauqua Lake Sunday School Assembly, was later renamed the Chautauqua Institution. It became the spiritual vacation spot for the affluent middle class. This all began in 1874 when I was just a little tyke of ten.

It was one of those beautiful, warm, moonlit evenings in Chautauqua when George and I met at our favorite spot on the shore of the lake.

"What's wrong with you, Mina?" George said. "You're shaking. Are you cold?"

"No. I'm fine. It's just that I have something to tell you."

"Tell me?"

"This isn't easy, George," I said hesitantly. "We've known each other all our lives and I like you very much."

"What are you trying to say?"

I could see his eyes glistening in the shadows of his handsome face. He was smiling, a half grin as he looked closely at me.

"I'm going to break off our engagement." I talked fast. The words came rapidly as I had rehearsed them. "I can't marry you, George. We are not meant for each other."

"What?" George asked. "What are you saying?"

I straightened and repeated it softly. "I'm sorry, George. I just can't marry you."

"Why, Mina? What have I done? After all these years. I've tried to do everything for you. I live for you. All my life I've dreamed of marrying you and having a family together."

"It's never been right, George. It was my mother who wanted me to marry you. Our fathers are such good friends and they too expected us to marry."

"And now you are going against what your parents want?" George sounded angry.

"I am going against what both of our parents have expected us to do."

"It's another man. Isn't it?" he spit out.

"No, George. It's just that our engagement was premature. We were very young then. I've seen a different world since our engagement. I've traveled in Europe. I've lived in Boston. I want something different from what you offer."

He was totally puzzled. "The wife of a college professor? What is wrong with that? It's prestigious. It's respectable. It's honorable. It's . . ."

"I'm truly sorry. I don't love you. You don't excite me, George. The university life can be restricted and stuffy."

"That sounds very immature, Mina. Marriage isn't a joy ride on a roller coaster."

"Let me put it differently. I've never had the excitement in my heart that I am told one is supposed to feel when one is truely in love. Do *you* feel anything like that George?"

He was silent. "That stuff is the dream of adolescents, Mina. A true marriage is when two people see harmony between them. It's a match between two families with a history between them. It is a continuation of a line of tradition. We both come from educated, successful, respected families. The whole point of our marriage is to carry the richness of our genes on from generation to generation." George paused. "Marriage is not the silliness of adolescent excitement that you speak of."

"I hope you're wrong, George. But do you realize that in all our years together you have never once said you *loved* me. Don't you think it would be appropriate for a man who plans to marry a woman to say that he loves her? I truly like you as a man and I respect you and your desire to become a college professor. I know you will do well and everyone will be proud of you." Now I paused. "But I am not for you. Yes, I imagined it could work when we were children, but we are grown up now and we, or at least I, think differently now than before."

"I hope *you* are wrong, Mina. I have not changed. I am the same man with the same goals I had when we became engaged."

"It is I then who has changed, and that's enough."

"Then you really do want to end our engagement."

"I do, George. I'm sorry. I want someone who truly loves me and says it to me. I just hope we can still be friends."

"I don't know what I'm going to tell my parents."

"You could start by telling them you never loved me and Mina wanted to end our engagement."

"Should I tell them I'm not exciting enough for you?"

"That's not necessary. Tell them we were engaged before we knew what we were doing. Now that we are mature, and have experienced college and life in general, we believe we are not meant for each other. We don't love each other."

George looked at me. He was sad. I *do* love you, Mina, if that's what you want to call it." A tear ran down his cheek. He covered his face with his hands. He speech was broken. "I do love you."

"I think it's kind of late to say that. I don't detect your sincerity."

"Have you told your parents?"

"Not yet. I wanted you to be first."

"I don't know if we can still be friends. This is not easy, Mina."

"I know, but let's give it a try." I stood and brushed myself off. "I want to continue to be friends with you, George."

He stood. "May I take you home?"

"You may -- but only as a friend."

We walked back silently. We did not hold hands. We stopped at my house and took a long look at each other. Then I kissed him on the cheek, turned and went into the house.

Chapter Two

1885

Electricity comes to Chautauqua

By summer 1885, a dozen frame houses had replaced the tents lining the shore of Chautauqua Lake. Our house and Rev. Vincent's were among the handsome new structures.

At my parent's invite, Mr. Edison and Marion appeared in a carriage at our door one summer evening. "We're here to thank you for the invite and to celebrate Billie's, er, Mina's birthday. We also want to see what Chautauqua is all about," he said happily.

"We hope you can stay a few days," mother said.

"That would be our pleasure," He responded. "I've brought a little present for Mina." He stepped outside and signaled the driver who brought several boxes to the door.

I was puzzled by all the boxes. Certainly they were not all presents. My answer came in the next sentence.

"What I'd like to do," Mr. Edison began, "is set up an electric lighting system for you."

"Electric lights?" father gasped.

"Certainly," Mr. Edison said. "Mina told me in a letter that there was no electricity at Chautauqua. How would you like to be first?"

Father's inventor mind clicked into place. "I'd like nothing better."

"Very good. But I have something for Mina first."

That caught my attention.

Mr. Edison went to his boxes. Out of one he removed a frosted cake large enough to feed the whole family. He placed it on the table in front of me. I stared at it in wonder. It had an electric lamp planted in the center. In the frosting around the lamp, it said "Happy 20th Birthday, Mina." A cord ran out from under the cake to a little box.

"Can we now snuff the lamps?" Mr. Edison asked.

It was dusk outside and with the lamps out it was darker inside.

"OK, Dot. Let's make light."

Marion touched a lever on the box and the cake light came on. We all clapped. We now had a lighted room. The little light bulb burned about as bright as a single candle.

"This was my idea," Marion said proudly. "But there is one problem."

We all turned to her. "You can't blow it out like a candle."

We all laughed.

"But wait," she said in her little girl voice. "I can fix that."

That brought our attention again.

Marion placed her hand on the little box. "OK, Mina. Blow on the light."

Perplexed, I followed her directions. I blew and the light went out.

"See?" Marion said.

We all clapped again. I stood up from my chair and hugged Marion. She didn't resist.

"That was a wonderful idea -- and a good trick," I said. "Thank you."

"Better turn that lamp on again, Dot."

Father then led us singing Happy Birthday.

"This lamp is the type I want to use on Christmas trees," Mr. Edison said. "I'm developing them to come in a string so they can easily be draped on a tree. They will replace those dangerous candles."

"Papa wants to set up his electricity," Marion announced.

We all turned to Mr. Edison.

"That's true, if you don't mind, Lewis."

Father looked to mother who had been quiet all through this. "Why not?"

"Maybe we better eat Mina's cake first, if you don't mind," mother suggested.

The children set the table and took their places. The others sat and watched while I cut around the light in the cake and served it.

"Where did you ever get the idea to electrify a birthday cake, Tom?" father asked.

"Well, I'm replacing oil, gas and candles everywhere else with electricity so why not a birthday cake?" Mr. Edison answered to more laughter.

"If you don't mind, Dot and I would like to string some wires and brighten this place up," he said.

For the next hour Mr. Edison set up his system, working by the glow of our oil lamps. He strung the last one on the ceiling of our front porch.

Finally, he said with a touch of the dramatic, "You now have a light in each of your downstairs rooms and outside. It's a battery system. Let's see if it will work." He winked at me. "Mina. I'd like to have you ignite the lamps."

I saw Marion's face turned into a pout.

"Oh, no," I said. "I'm afraid. I want Marion to do it."

Marion smiled at me. It was worth a million dollars.

The family stood around in anticipation. Marion moved what he called a switch. The room immediately brightened like a flash of lightning that wouldn't go out. We were blinded momentarily and our mouths agape.

Minutes later there was a knock on the door. Father answered it.

"Is everything OK here?" a voice asked.

I went to the door. A gathering of our Chautauqua friends was in front of the house. The rays of the porch light showed on their faces as if watching a sunset. We invited them in for a closer look.

At that moment I felt in full bloom and so proud of Mr. Edison. I thought to myself that this was an exciting man. Mr. Edison's impromptu event marked the first electricity at Chautauqua.[26]

Courtship by telegraph

I don't know if George ever told his parents about our breakup. My parents never mentioned anything further about it. Certainly if it had caused tention between them I would have known about it.

That summer Mr. Edison showed up at Chautauqua several times. We went to events together. He kept appearing and reappearing and he sort of grew on me, like the presents he brought with every visit. I protested at his generosity and told him his presents would not buy my affection. He was very sweet -- a little rough around the edges, but he was a man of action, like my father, and that suited me just fine. Even mother came to like the man.

It was at our dinner with the Vincents and Mr. Edison that it became evident that the inventor had more than a passing interest in me. If our relations with the Vincents were strained as a result of my breakup with George, it didn't show. George was quiet and contributed nothing. The Vincents were here because my father thought his friend would find Mr. Edison interesting.

Stodgy Reverend Vincent admitted he was impressed with Mr. Edison's accomplishments. Now he saw another side of the man. There were a lot of laughs at Mr. Edison's more tempered story telling. He was genial and friendly and a real person, as opposed to the often wild stories that were created by the newspapers and magazines in order to drum up readership. And as the evening went on the Reverend even came out from behind his beard and told a few stories himself that made him human. It surprised father and mother who thought they knew their best friend better.

I was greatly relieved that neither I nor George had created a rift between our families.

Mr. Edison's poor hearing was of growing concern to both him and me, not to mention the rest of the family. With each visit we grew closer and I appreciated the man more and more, although it was not yet the love I sought. We began to say sweet things to each other during the few times we could get alone. But it was difficult voicing the intimate feelings in our hearts without someone overhearing. We were rarely alone, of course. Whispering didn't work. Our talk was, by Mr. Edison's necessity, loud. We were followed everywhere by the hordes who wanted to speak with Mr. Edison. We even had Marion with us as we braved Chautauqua Lake in a rowboat. Everyone wanted to be with us. We just were not able to be alone so we could talk freely.

But Mr. Edison had an idea. He always had a solution. He taught me Morse code.[27] He left me a book of the Morse code alphabet. In addition to the dots and dashes of the alphabet, he began developing code and other hand signals for our most frequently used phrases, similar to sign language, so we could communicate across a room or from a longer distance.

These teaching sessions were more intimate than any pleasant experience I ever had with a man. His simple touch of my palm as we practiced coding was a sensuous thrill.

"Your eyes are beautiful." "Your presence makes me very happy." "You have a wonderful smile." "You are so smart and are learning code so quickly." "May I kiss you on the cheek?"

I became very good at thanking him in code and eventually I stopped blushing. When mother walked into the room wondering what was going on in our silence, we were just holding hands. She looked. She smiled. She shrugged, turned and left the room. She knew we communicated -- somehow.

As accepted table manners dictated, placing one hand in the lap as we ate (or between our chairs), we held hands at the dining table much of the time. And now if Mr. Edison had difficulty understanding what was said by another person, I was able to interpret for him with code. For those who were suspicious of what was happening between us, we had to explain.

In a short while I was able to clearly send and receive messages. From that point on we were able to hold hands and tap our feelings to each other with few those of around us ever the wiser. Anywhere we could hold hands, we were able to communicate. It was courtship by telegraph.

I steadily weakened toward this man. He was young at heart. He was funny. We now used pet names and said things we probably would have had difficulty speaking to each other. The ultimate of this was when he tapped, "I love you."

It was as if he had said it aloud. I almost choked on my food. I looked around at the others. I was embarrassed. But no one was looking at me. When I finally grasped his words, I tapped, "Say again." This was my usual response when I wasn't sure what he said.

"I love you, Billie."

We looked at each other. He was smiling. I returned the smile. I was exuberant. No man, except father, had ever said he loved me. There it was in all its beauty. But what should I reply? Did I love this man? Did I know him well enough to love him? Would I be truthful if I tapped back that I loved him as well?

"Mina." I heard Jennie in the distance. I awoke. "Will you please pass the potatoes."

I reached for the serving bowl and passed it to my sister.

"Are you all right, Mina? Do you feel OK?"

I snickered. "Yes mother. I'm just fine."

Now everyone was looking at me.

The spell was broken. Our hands had separated. It seemed like minutes had passed. I turned to Mr. Edison and he replied with a look that asked for my response. I accepted his hand again.

"Thank you, Dearie," I tapped. It wasn't romantic but it was honest. I turned my head and looked him in the eye. He smiled and winked at me. I could see in his face it wasn't the answer he wanted.

The proposal

Mr. Edison was so interesting -- yes, exciting -- and involved in so much. I don't know how he found the time to visit us so frequently.[28] And once here, everyone seemed to want his attention, yet he showed little interest in them. Hardly a week went by when one story or another about Mr. Edison appeared in the newspapers. He took my breath away. Oh, yes. And I liked the way his hair fell across his forehead.

I had so many serious questions about our future relationship before I could express to him my love. His age was not a problem. I liked maturity in a man. Then there were his three children, particularly Marion. Would I ever be able to get along with her? Would she ever accept me as her stepmother? That concerned me greatly, but only time could answer that question -- perhaps a *long* time.

Late in the summer of 1885 my family was again visiting the Gillilands in Massachusetts. I knew that Mr. Edison had also been invited. And, of course, he had Marion in tow. In the course of our visit Mr. Edison somehow convinced father to let us go on a long carriage ride through the White Mountains of New Hampshire. Ezra, Lillian and Marion came with us as chaperones. Marion had accompanied her father almost continually since his wife's death. She adored her father and I suspected the twelve-year-old continued to be jealous of me, all the more so because Mr. Edison refused to let Marion sit between us in the carriage.

It was a long trip and verbal communication among the five of us lapsed into many quiet periods. Depending on the road surface the carriage could be very noisy and bumpy. But Mr. Edison kept his telegraph tapping, telling me more of his background and family. And I responded with family stories of my own. We were learning important things about our beliefs and our backgrounds. And, of course, the other passengers were unaware, although they might have seen our fingers tapping each other's hands constantly. In any case, the Gillilands didn't say anything.

It was a beautiful trip. The mountains were spectacular. At the same time a warm, cozy feeling gradually swept over me. I recognized I was very comfortable with this man. I was relaxed and felt one with him. Our conversation was personal and I was floating above the reality of the ride. Dearie's hand was warm and comfortable and I realized this must be what love is all about. I was in love!

I decided I had taken long enough to consider Dearie's statement. I coded him my response: "I love you also."

Then it happened. It seem he was still waiting for those words. His message was, "Will you marry me?"

I was thoroughly surprised. If the others noticed my sudden ear-to-ear grin, they didn't say anything. But I turned and looked at this man. I studied his face. I saw the twinkle in his eyes. I saw a man of men -- a man I would be proud to marry. My answer was delayed by perhaps thirty seconds. I tapped my answer -- dah-di-dah-dah di di-di-di!

He squeezed my hand and we looked deeply into each other's eyes. He squeezed my hand and we smiled at each other. I wanted to kiss him. I so wanted to kiss him. I coded this to him and he immediately kissed me on my cheek. A lips kiss would have been well beyond appropriate and I told him so. He respected my request.

Marion was the one who was first aware. She noticed the kiss and she noticed the both of us smiling at each other as we never had before. She knew something momentous was unfolding.

"Papa! What are you doing?" she interjected.

It took me several seconds to snap out of the world of love. The spell was broken and we turned to our companions. I was embarrassed at having been so far away -- I didn't know how long. Mr. Edison must have been away with me for he too was delayed in reaction to Marion's loud statement.

Lillian smiled. She also recognized there was some magic going on between us. She knew something significant had transpired. "Are you two OK?"

"Lillian," Mr. Edison announced. "Things between us could not be better."

"Are you two not telling us something we would like to hear?" Lillian asked with a smirk.

Ezra joined in. "Come on, Tom. No secrets here."

Mr. Edison tapped, "What should I tell them, Billie?"

"The truth, Mr. Edison. Always the truth," I coded.

"I am pleased to say," Mr. Edison began aloud, "that Miss Mina Miller has accepted my proposal of marriage." Then he quickly added. "Provided we have her father's blessing, of course."

Lillian and Ezra looked at each other, perhaps a bit smug at their success at matchmaking. "Congratulations. We are very happy for you."

Marion took the news quite differently. "Does this mean you're going to *marry*?"

Mr. Edison answered. "Of course, my sweet Dot. She will be your new mother."

Oh, oh. Wrong words, I thought. I watched Marion's face contort.

Marion shrieked a high, piercing expression of agony. Her father immediately slid close to her and put his arm around her. Marion pushed him away, slid to the floor and crouched in a corner whimpering and became uncommunicative.

We four adults looked at each other in horror. We all knew how Marion worshipped her father and clung to him since her mother's death.

Mr. Edison spoke harshly, yanking Marion out of her corner. "Dot! I will have none of this! This is the way it is going to be. I love you just as I always have, but Mina is going to be my wife. I will expect you to love her as much as I love you."

I recoiled at his harsh reaction to Marion. His words were anything but comforting. I was tempted to do something kind toward her, but then I thought better of it. I knew I should keep out if it. I had no authority. Anything I tried would be less than helpful. I found the scene very disheartening. I tried to visualize how I was going to be able to handle Mr. Edison's children once we were living together. Was I capable of genuinely loving her? Was I capable of managing her? But then, marriage and living together was a long way off. Optimist that I am, I believed that by the time we married Marion would warm up to me – or at least tolerate me. I had just accepted Mr. Edison's proposal. I may have been premature in answering. I hadn't realistically considered all the consequences of marriage to this man, much less dealing with his children.

Mr. Edison looked at me and he looked at Ezra and Lillian and he shrugged his shoulders. The tour of the mountains came to an abrupt end and the carriage turned for home. Little did I know then just how much pain and suffering Mr. Edison's relationship with the rebel Marion would affect us all.

The answer

That was only two weeks earlier. How much had changed in two weeks. Did I make too hasty a decision with Mr.

Edison? I now worried about the future and how I was going to cope with Marion's unpredictably. Before we parted I tried to talk with him about Marion but he waved it off.

"No," I said. "I can't accept your waving it off. I want to discuss it."

"What is there to discuss?" he asked. "Do you want Dot to dictate what we can and can't do?"

"Of course not. But it is my greatest wish that she accept me."

"Marion is stubborn. She can be very difficult."

"I've noticed that. And you can be stubborn also." I said without thinking, before I could check myself.

He looked surprised. That was the first time I had accused him of anything.

"That won't help. What do you suggest, Billie?"

"I don't know what to suggest, only that we treat her lovingly."

"Just how do we do that?"

"You must remember I am not her mother, first of all. But you *are* her father. It is you who have to take responsibility by convincing her we are doing the right thing."

"And how do I do that?"

"By continuing to give her a lot of attention."

"I can't do that, Billie. That has to be your job."

"I don't know that I can do that without your help, Dearie."

We were quiet for a while. I wondered if we were at an impasse.

"Do you think she'll get over it?" I finally asked.

"Honestly, I don't think so. In her mind, seven years difference is too close in age."

"Then you're saying I'm too young to be her stepmother?"

"That's what she thinks."

"What about Louise Igoe? She indicated she would have accepted her and she's a year younger than I."

"It's irrational," Mr. Edison said. "Louise had blonde hair like herself and her mother."

I dropped into thought. "This is peculiar. If I'm too young to be her stepmother, does it follow that you're too old to be my husband?"

He looked at me sharply. "I hope that's not the case."

"How then will I be able to manage Marion after we are married?" That seemed a logical argument to me.

"You'll have help. She has a governess whom she adores and has looked after her since she was born."

"So I just ignore Marion and let her governess manager her?"

"What do you want to do, beat her?"

"Not at all, but I do want to enjoy my life and live in harmony with her in the same house."

"Billie. I don't think we have a problem. She is going to be away at school in New York most of the time and away at camp for at least part of the summer. Otherwise, if she becomes a problem and you are unable to cope with her, she will have to understand I will not put up with it."

"And what would that be?"

"We'll cross that bridge later."

"I'm not fully convinced."

"In the meantime," he said, "I will speak with her to see if I can pound some common sense into her."

"This is an awful way to start out between us, Dearie. You realize that I come from a family that is accustomed to a life of harmony."

"Billie. I cannot promise you 'harmony,' nor do I think any man can. You told me you wanted excitement. You said the man you were engaged to was boring. I can't promise you excitement all the time, but I can promise you my love."

He gently took me into his arms and kissed me properly, on my lips. It was very nice. I enjoyed it. It was our first real kiss.

I looked at this man. I studied his face as he studied mine. It was a long silence. We smiled at each other. Finally I said, "I guess I can live with that, Dearie."

Mr. Edison returned to New York City and Marion was off to day school a few doors from his office. My parents and I returned to Akron. During the long train ride home I revealed the news of Mr. Edison's proposal but they had already heard from the Gillilands.

I had wanted to tell them myself. "Mr. Edison is sending you a letter, father. He's going to ask your permission to marry me. He has proposed to me and I have accepted on that condition."

Father speaks to me

"I've noticed a dramatic change in you," father began, "I would never have guessed your relationship would progress so rapidly. I knew I shouldn't have allowed you to go on that carriage ride."

"Why is that?" I exclaimed.

"I want to tell you a little bit about Mr. Edison."

Now I was nervous. Was father going to disapprove of him?

"It has been obvious that Mr. Edison is smitten by you. But honestly, I never thought it would come to this, so fast."

"Why not?" I asked.

"That is exactly what I want to talk about. First of all, I was embarrassed by Mr. Edison saying in the presence of Rev. Vincent that he 'was not of our denomination.' He has an outspoken irreverence that is not to my taste."

"But father," I protested. "He says he doesn't go to church because of his deafness. He's not against our religion. He does believe in God. You should be happy he's not a hypocrite. He speaks thoughtfully and from his heart."

"In the company of others, it is sometimes best to keep your heart and mind where they belong."

I sighed. "Yes. I agree. But . . ."

"Then there is his age and his children. He's nearly twice your age. Do you want to marry into an established family? It seems obvious to me that his daughter, Marion, is already quite jealous of you. And you're not much older than she. How about his boys?"

"I haven't met Tom and William yet. They are quite a bit younger. I will admit that Marion might be a problem. In fact she has been annoying ever since I've known Mr. Edison. She is jealous of me. And she is stubborn. But how long can this last?"

"It has been known to last a lifetime. How about the boys? Are they going to be as difficult as Marion appears to be?"

"Father, you are right. I do have to visit them before we marry," I said with exasperation. "But I grew up in the midst of your eleven children. I have dealt with the younger ones and the older ones by necessity all my life. I think I can handle Marion. I like large families. I can handle his children."

"I don't know that any of your siblings ever gave you trouble similar to Marion. If they did, it was our problem not yours."

"Again you're right. Mr. Edison's children will be my problem -- or my pride."

Father smiled. "I only pray that you are able to cope, Mina. You are mature well beyond your age and have recognized the potential problem." Father paused.

"Mr. Edison and I have discussed Marion at length. He is aware of my concerns."

"You mentioned his difficulty hearing. Apparently you have no problem communicating."

"Didn't mother tell you?" I looked at her. She hadn't said a word during our talk.

"I'm sorry, Mina," mother said. "I didn't believe you. I thought you were joking. I've been worrying a lot about this relationship, Mina -- first his children, and then his trouble hearing. These are major things, my dear."

"They are my challenges, mother."

"What did you think Mina was joking about, Mary?"

I looked back to father. "Communication is our little secret, father," I said happily and laughed. "He taught me Morse code and sign. We communicate through our hands and sign when we're not able to voice comfortably."

Father looked at me in wonder. "Are you saying you tap messages back and forth on your hands?"

"It's really marvelous, father. If Mr. Edison were sitting next me right now, we could hold hands and talk about you and the family and you would never be aware."

Father smiled again. "What a genius that man is! It's brilliant! Who would have thought? We should all learn Morse code for that very purpose. But is that really practical? Isn't it just another problem you have to cope with?"

"It's not a problem at all," I said. "Now that I'm used to it. But we always voice under normal circumstances."

"I don't know."

"You don't approve of our marriage?"

"I didn't say that. I'm simply trying to understand your relationship with this man."

"He's really wonderful, father."

"He's 'wonderful' to many many people. Another thing," father continued. "It is strange to me that a man of his age and reputation wants to marry my daughter -- and he seems to be in a great hurry to do so."

"Is there something wrong with that, father?" I asked.

"Just what is the hurry? Age difference is important. At twenty years older than you, he could become infirm early in your marriage and you would have to care for an invalid."

"I don't like that argument, father! It's not fair. I could fall down stairs and break my head early in our marriage and he would have to care for me!"

"You're right on that point, Mina. I withdraw it."

I cut in immediately. "It seems like you're looking for every fault the man could possibly have. How about his good points?"

Before father could answer, mother cut in. "Has Mina told you her ideas about women's equality with men and voting rights for women?"

Father looked at mother quizzically. "Mina and I have had some very good discussions, my dear. She has a very good intellect. We have set a good example, don't you think, Mary?"

"Do you think Mr. Edison will approve of Mina's, er, intellect and equality?" mother asked.

"Apparently he already has," father replied. "But that's between them. Mr. Edison has his ideas and Mina has hers, I presume."

Father turned to me. "Have you talked specifically with Mr. Edison about your ideas, Mina?"

"We've discussed a lot of things, father," I said. "Frankly, I don't think he puts much stock in women's equality generally, but that's his business. He says he *does* consider me his equal and he wants me to have a part in his laboratory. We have discussed our individual beliefs on things such as God and religion, politics, women's suffrage and we don't always agree. But we have agreed to respect each other's views. He mentioned his mother as a mentor who was his sole educator. She certainly taught him well, or at least pointed him in the right direction. He's a strong believer in self-education.

"The big difference between us is his dedication to science and mechanics whereas my love is the arts and social life. These differences give us plenty to learn from each other. We're not competing. We're respecting each other."

"Chautauqua has been a good influence on you, Mina," father said, turning and looking at mother and nodding. "Thank God for Chautauqua."

"Then you approve of our marriage?" I asked.

"There are some other things, Mina, you may not be aware of. He has long working hours. It's no secret that he can be in his laboratory for days at a time and not go home. And he travels a lot -- all over the world. And you know my habits. No matter how busy, I am home for dinner most every night. I separate work and family. Tom Edison cannot. Do you really think that you can live with someone whose habits are so very different than ours?"

"I do, father. It is a challenge I'm willing to make. The man is exciting. I want to be part of that excitement. When Mr. Edison is away, I will make my own challenges. You two have shown me how to fill my days with worthwhile projects. And I love to entertain. You have set me on the right path. I'm sure Marion will come around when I demonstrate how much I love her."

"I believe you are strong, Mina. I believe you will make a fine marriage and overcome, can I say, *most* adversities. In any case, you have our support."

"Then you approve of Mr. Edison?"

"Approve? Of course I do. I can tell you now that I have always admired the man, in spite of *our* differences. We all have faults and issues and I would be the hypocrite to say he is any worse than I. Mr. Edison is a good, hard-working, honest man."

I relaxed. "I love you, father -- and mother. You have always been so open-minded."

"I would rather you say I am so Christian."

I laughed again. "You are *so* Christian, father."

"One other thing, Mina dear."

"Yes, father," I said with a sigh, wondering what more he could possibly say.

"Mr. Edison is plagued by the terrible burden of fame. Fame is a two-edged sword. The terrible part of it is the demands other people lay on you. You witnessed a bit of this in New Orleans at his crowded exhibit. You have seen it here in Chautauqua. Should you marry him, you will inherit his burden. Finding privacy together will be very difficult. Coping with the attentions of the public will stretch your patience to a degree you cannot imagine now. A moment together, alone, will seem like Heaven. You cannot take this lightly."

"I am prepared to deal with that, father. You too have had your share of fame. Mr. Edison and I have discussed these things. He is the man I want. He is the man I love."

Father paused in thought. I waited eagerly for his response.

"We have just discussed Mr. Edison's long work hours and his absences."

"Yes, father."

"Men have a moral obligation to support their families, financially and otherwise, as best they can. I don't begrudge him for his long work hours. But his time away from home does seem extreme. You may have a problem with his absences, having to cope alone. I love you, Mina. I want you to be happy. You appear to understand what you're getting into. On the plus side, Mr. Edison is a known quantity. That is more than I can say in advance about partners in many marriages. I can see that he is deeply enamored with you. Both of you will have a lot of adjustments. Your mother and I will be glad to help you in any way we can."

I rose from my chair, walked around his desk, stood behind his chair and hugged him. "Thank you, father."

In Mr. Edison's letter to father, I learned later, he told him "my future happiness depends upon your answer."

Father approved and our marital happiness now seemed assured. He immediately picked up his pen and began his response to my future husband.

I walked away with his concerns about my relationship still echoing in my head -- managing his children, coping with his deafness, differences in religious outlook, the woman's place in the world, and the intrusiveness of his fame. Piled up in a single sentence, my marriage might seem overwhelming to an outsider. Indeed. It was a bit scary. But when I compared it to what my marriage to George might be like -- utter monotony and boredom -- I would still choose Mr. Edison in a flash.

Sister Jennie

My sister Jane was the oldest child in the Miller family. Ten years my senior, she had always been a strong influence. I knew I could always turn to "Jennie" for guidance and solace. But Jennie was not enthusiastic about the anticipated marriage. In fact, she and my mother were somewhat intimidated by Mr. Edison. Jennie always suspected it was Lillian Gilliland who convinced me that Mr. Edison would be a great match. But Jennie, who was now thirty, living in New York and still single, continued to have reservations about the much older Edison's motives in wanting me. She suggested I delay the wedding, arguing that February was a mere eight months after meeting this man at the Gilliland's.

"At least two things bother me, Mina," Jennie counseled. "Why is Mr. Edison in such a mad rush to get married? What is the hurry? You hardly know each other, and he's twice your age. I suspect he thinks of you as a child. After all, his first wife was only sixteen when they married. Why isn't he seeking out a more mature woman nearer his age?

"I know father and mother are worried about what the Vincents will think about your decision," Jennie continued. "Look at what happened when you broke up with George. His dream of marrying you was dashed by your sudden change of mind. His parents were shocked that father gave his approval for you to marry Mr. Edison. Rev. Vincent said it shook his faith in father's good judgment."

I tried to defend myself. "I feel sorry for George, but I can't take responsibility for his expectations. I never promised George anything. I love this man, Jennie. Mr. Edison is a busy man. He does everything in a hurry. I want a mature, established and exciting husband. I see no point in delaying our wedding."

"And then he has that little brat, Marion," Jennie retorted. "How are you going to cope with her? Are you ready to be the stepmother to a stubborn girl hardly younger than you?"

"Your arguments are compelling, Jennie. A lot of what you say may be true, but you don't know them as well as I do. We will work things out," I said with false confidence.

I thought Jennie was exaggerating. After all, what did she know about men and children?

Jennie finally did come around to support me. The two of us met in the city in mid-December and Jennie helped me pick out my trousseau. Father had given us a "tight" budget of $1,500.[29] We bought practical items like sheets, towels and washcloths, underwear and sleepwear. And, after great deliberation, we splurged on a number of elegant suits to keep me in style each day for two weeks.

Designing paradise

"Saw a lady who looked like Mina. Got thinking about Mina and came near being run over by a street car. If Mina interferes much more will have to take out an accident policy."[30]

Mr. Edison was consumed by love. He saw me as a constant image in his brain, suppressing nearly all his life that preceded our meeting. His laboratory and his business obligations had now become secondary to preparation for his life with his "Maid of Chataqua"[sic].[31]

Among his preparations for our honeymoon was the pace of his activity in what he called his "earthly paradise in the land of Flowers."[32]

"This construction project, Billie, has a must-do deadline of next February. The timeline has been established."

He was convinced that, less than a year after he purchased the land, it would be ready for our honeymoon.

He told me he had hired an architect to design a pair of identical buildings, one for him and the other for the Gillilands. There would also be another building for his laboratory -- a miniature of the lab he had in Menlo Park. He contracted with an agent to hire men to cut lumber from the forests in Maine and to oversee the pre-fabrication[33] of the buildings there. He arranged to have the completed buildings shipped in sections by boat to Fort Myers and reassembled on location.

In order to unload the lumber and the hundreds of items needed for the houses and the laboratory, he hired more men to build a very long pier out into the Caloosahatchee River where a depth could be reached that would accommodate the delivering steamer.

At the site, he hired another agent to supervise the clearing of the land for the buildings and to oversee the reassembly of all the buildings. It was a major undertaking.

Daydreams

I don't know where the summer and early fall of 1885 went. Both Mr. Edison and I spent a lot of time on the train between Akron and New York.[34] It was all dazzling parties, dances and spending much time with whoever was chaperoning me and the man I would soon wed. We talked about the forthcoming wedding, of course, but also about the Broadway shows we attended. Gilbert & Sullivan's "H.M.S. Pinafore" and the "Savoy operas" come to mind now. I loved the excitement of the city and all it had to offer, but I had no desire to live there. Although it had its beautiful moments, generally it was dirty, noisy and crowded -- narrow dirt streets, numberless horses and, of course, their smelly droppings.

And books. Henry James had just published "A Little Tour in France." I read it as it was serialized in the *Atlantic Monthly*. Another book I enjoyed was "Life on the Lagoons," by Horatio Brown. It was a fascinating account of the history and topography of Venice, one of my favorite places.

Many of our growing number of hours together led to the inevitable discussions of Mr. Edison's work. I wanted to become part of that work. I was eager to share my ideas with him, yet I recognized I had a long way to go to learn enough to contribute anything worthwhile. He gave me a lot of books to read and told me how he speed-read a book to get the most out of it quickly. Naturally, I couldn't do that with my novels. I relished every word of a good story. But I could easily speed-read his books on telegraphy, mining, electricity and chemistry although I can't say how much of the information I retained.

One of Mr. Edison's many unique characteristics was the way he talked about what I call his daydreaming. When we were out for a walk or a carriage ride, something, anything might attract his attention. It didn't matter what it was. His curiosity about anything and everything resulted in constant ruminations and he often expressed these thoughts aloud.

I particularly enjoyed his prattle on detachable atoms. "Wouldn't it be wonderful," he said, "if the atoms that make up our bodies were under our control. I'd like to be able to tell atom number 346 to go and become part of a flower or a mineral or a machine. Later I would call that atom back into my body along with all the knowledge it gained from its experience elsewhere and I would benefit from the absorption of that new knowledge."

For things mechanical, he contemplated just how it was constructed and how he might improve upon it. A perfect example was the telegraph that he used in his first real job. Samuel B. Morse demonstrated in 1835 that signals could be sent by wire making use of his Morse code. Although this was a practical and useful invention, it was limited to sending a single message, in one direction, over the single wire.

It was Mr. Edison, after much experimentation in his lab, who developed what he called quadruplex telegraphy where four messages could be transmitted, two in each direction at the same time over a single wire.

This eventually led Mr. Edison and his partner Ezra to create a voice telephone that improved on the patents held by Alexander Bell.

Another example was the phonograph. He developed this through countless phases -- improvement after improvement after improvement. He believed there was no end to improvement. Everything, other than nature itself, he said, can be improved. We all have wonderful ideas but he knew how to bring his ideas and those of others to fruition.

Mr. Edison's boys

"I want you to introduce me to Tom and William, Dearie. I think it's very important for me to begin to know them before they move in with us."

"No. I don't think that will be necessary."

"Why do you say that?" I was perplexed.

"The children will not be living with us."

"What? You never told me that!" I was shaken.

"No, Billie. I think the boys are happy where they are. Mary's mother, Margaret Stilwell, and her sister, Alice Holzer, share the care of them. They have been very kind to take charge. They get along just fine and it gives them something to do. I assist them financially and give them adequate help."

"Are you going to send Marion away also?"

"I already explained to you that she will be away at school and summer camp."

"This all seems strange. When will *you* see them?"

"Not very often."

"Once a week? Once a month?"

"Rarely."

"How old are they now?"

The strangest look came over Mr. Edison. He looked at me quizzically. "I have forgotten. By gosh. I really don't know their ages right now."

I was shocked. "You don't know the ages of your own children!"

"Well, let's see. Dot is twelve. That I know. She reminds me every year. She was the first born. Then there was Tom who I nicknamed Dash. He came a couple or three years later. That would make him eight or nine. And then there was William a couple years after Dash, so he must be five or six. I think I have that information somewhere. Oh, balderdash. That's the problem with ages, Billie. They change every year. I have trouble enough remembering my own age. You can check with Mrs. Stilwell. She'll know."

I didn't want to push this age thing as far as I would have liked. I knew he was a busy man, but so busy as to not know his children's ages? And he only had three children. My father had eleven children and he remembered all our ages.

"I want us to visit Mrs. Stilwell and the boys very soon."

"If you insist. I'll make arrangements soon, Billie. I'd prefer that you go alone."

"Then you *don't* want to see your boys," I said flatly.

"Billie. I just have no rapport with young children. It'll be different when they grow up." He seemed put out by the suggestion of taking time away from other matters to see his boys.

"How about when we have children?"

"As I say, I have difficulty with them when they're young."

This greatly troubled me. I couldn't pursue this any further. I held my tongue -- for the time being.

"Well, I want to meet Mrs. Stilwell and the boys very soon, even if I have to see them alone."

Marion

When Marion was much older, she wrote that her happiest years were between ages of nine and eleven -- before her father took an interest in me. She was the lively and vivacious one in the family. She had her mother's long blonde hair, and, I am told Mary's loveliness and personality. She was her father's favorite. These were the years the Edison family moved from Menlo Park in 1881 to New York City and into a grand four-story townhouse near Gramercy Park. There, Marion was enrolled in a succession of day schools "for young ladies" where she took an interest in dancing, music, drawing as well as courses in French and English. This was a major change from her drab and uneventlful life with her two young brothers in the tiny town of Menlo Park.

But now, in New York, her mother became progressively sick as Marion approached her teens. In the winter of 1883-1884, even Mr. Edison was stricken with neuralgia. The family escaped to St. Augustine, where Marion found life immensely enjoyable and her father and mother enjoyed relief in the predictably warm Florida climate.

Returning north, the family reluctantly moved back to the house in Menlo Park where, in July, Mary contracted typhoid fever and was regularly looked after by her sister Alice and a doctor. But her condition worsened. Mr. Edison was called home from his office in New York City. Early in the morning of August 9, 1884 Marion was awakened by her father. She saw him shaking and crying in anguish. His lovely wife Mary had passed away.

He now deserted Menlo Park, moved his laboratory and all his main businesses to New York and lived once again at the house near Gramercy Park. He said he hated Menlo Park and swore he would never return. The famous buildings in which some of his most important inventions had materialized were now abandoned.

Marion was eleven, too young to take responsibility for the household and her younger brothers, Tom and William. Mr. Edison turned his Menlo Park house over to Mary's sister Alice and mother, Margaret, who was recently widowed. They took turns caring for the boys. They knew her as "Grammach."

It was at this point that Marion became her father's constant traveling companion. She returned to the Academy on Madison Avenue.

Otherwise, Marion was often with her father in his laboratory and even made jottings in his notebooks. It was a good place to do homework in Papa's company. Often when work was set aside for the night, she accompanied him to his favorite haunt, the cigar-smoke clouded, "men-only" Delmonico's restaurant, until after midnight. The attraction for the young lady was ice cream and sweets and, of course, she enjoyed the attention of her father's men friends and other patrons.

I meet Mr. Edison's former mother-in-law

It was true. Mr. Edison had no idea how old his sons were. A week later, Jennie and I took the train from the city to the house in Menlo Park where Mr. Edison and Mary used to live. It was a comfortable two-story house which he still provided for his former mother-in-law and his boys, along with a cook, a housekeeper and a governess.

Mrs. Stilwell greeted us pleasantly and ushered us in. The two boys, Tom and William, were sitting in the middle of the room playing with wooden blocks, building a tower as high as they could reach. When I entered the room they kicked it and it crashed to the floor. They laughed, looked up and saw us.

The tallest boy, Tom, came up to us. "Grammach says you know our father."

"These ladies are friends of your father," Mrs. Stilwell said to the boys.

"Then you *do* you know father." Tom stated. His facial features surprised me. They were exactly like his father's.

"Yes, Tom. I do," I answered.

"Do you see him a lot?"

"Yes."

"Is he a nice man?"

"He's a very nice man. I like him a lot."

"Can you bring him here to see us. We want to see him."

"I'll try to do that."

"Did you know he's a famous inventor?" William asked.

"Yes. He's invented a lot of things, like that light bulb over there and this phonograph beside me here."

"When can you bring him?"

"I don't know. I'm sorry. I wish I could tell you."

"He's a very busy man," Tom said, looking at his feet.

"He is. Sometimes, even I can't see your father. But I will tell him you both want to see him."

"Tell him we want to try to fix the clock again."

I looked at Mrs. Stilwell, not understanding the reference to a clock.

She leaned toward me. "That's a test he gives his children to see how mechanical they are. They're supposed to take it apart and put it back together."

She turned to Tom and William. "OK. You boys go in the other room and be quiet. I have guests I want to talk with." The boys quickly disappeared. I was impressed with how well they behaved. I wanted to take them home with me right now.

She pointed to the chairs and we sat. I felt very awkward.

"How old are the boys?" I asked.

"Tom was nine in January and William will be seven in October."

"Do they go to school?"

"Not yet. I homeschool them here and when their Aunt Alice takes them she schools them also. We trade off now and then. Aunt Alice and her husband live on a farm so there's a lot more for them there than here. But we get along just fine. Are you looking to take the boys away after you're married, Miss Miller?"

"I would really like to. I expected I would be raising them, but Mr. Edison says he is happy with the present situation."

"So neither of you want them! Right?" Her voice was hard.

"I don't like to think of it that way. It's just that he's very busy and he . . ."

"Oh. You poor, innocent girl," Margaret began. "You have no idea what you are getting in for by marrying that selfish bastard." I was stunned by this woman's vocal outburst and fell back in my chair. Jennie was also startled.

"I have cared for and loved his children every minute since my beautiful daughter became sick and died of loneliness and a broken heart," Margaret Stilwell continued and then broke down in sobs.

She looked up at me, eyes red, tears running along the grooves in her wrinkled cheeks. But then compassion overtook me. She seemed like a warm, grandmotherly woman, deeply concerned about her daughter's children. But now. . .

"Mary was a beautiful angel," she continued. "Her marriage was hell. That man came home each time only to get her pregnant. She struggled to manage her life alone and all that did was make her sick. That poor excuse for a husband hasn't visited me since my daughter died. His sons wouldn't recognize him if they ever met. They don't know their own father."

After my last conversation with Mr. Edison, I believed she was telling the truth. I was sorry Jennie was hearing all this.

"And now you are about to marry him," Mrs. Stilwell went on. "I pity you. I truly do, Miss Miller. You wouldn't marry him if you had seen how he treated Mary. He was always off somewhere -- too busy for anyone but himself and his inventions. Sure the world adores him, but they don't see the destruction he's left in his wake.

"My Mary wasn't old enough to know what she was doing when she met Thomas Edison. She was only sixteen when he snatched her from me. On the surface, he seemed like a good catch for her. He was already an inventor and he had money. They met in the office where her job was punching perforations into telegraph tape. He courted Mary only three months. He was in a hurry.

"They married on Christmas Day -- very romantic," she continued bitterly. "But then, that very same day, their wedding day, he took off for his laboratory, leaving Mary alone and waiting for him well into the night.[35]

"Oh, Miss Miller," she sighed, falling back on her sofa. "I'm sorry to carry on like this, but I have tried so hard to make my daughter, and now her children, happy. Marion is his favored child. I'm sure you noticed. He took her away right after Mary died. I offered to care of the boys for him -- with the help of dear Miss McWilliams, their governess, and the others. I'm sure he was glad to get rid of the boys, only eight and five. He latched onto eleven-year-old Marion and I haven't seen either of them since.

"And now you are here. I'm sure you think you're going to change him. The new Mrs. Edison is going to change this man. I don't think so. It appears he always has to have a young woman companion at his beckoned call -- whether it's a wife or a daughter -- or, who knows, maybe another sweet thing. Young Marion filled in for the loss of Mary until you came along. I'm sure you've seen how he dotes on Marion.

"Oh, Miss Miller. I just can't see any changes with your marriage to this man. All I see is a trail of tears for all of us who try to be close to him. He doesn't know what love is!"

I was in tears myself at this spasm of emotion. Jennie didn't know what to do. I didn't know what to think. All was silent now. I moved next to Mrs. Stilwell and put my arm over her shoulder. I could think of nothing to say. She had apparently exhausted all her words as well.

After a few moments of silence I released her and got to my feet. I was afraid now to say goodbye to the boys. I was torn in all directions. What was I doing? I was so confused.

"Thank you for seeing me, Mrs. Stilwell. We will see what our respective futures bring us." A rather dumb thing to say, in retrospect.

Mrs. Stilwell nodded, her face still in her hands. I took Jennie's hand and we let ourselves out the door.

Jennie had a lot to say as we returned to the city. I wished I hadn't brought her. Her comments boiled down to, "I told you so."

For my part, I thought, after I'm married, I want his boys to live with us. I won't have it any other way. And when Mr. Edison and I have children, he will play a very active role in my family.

Christmas at the Millers

Christmas had always been a major event at the Miller household in Akron. But Christmas 1885 was very different. There were eleven of us mostly-adult children and then there were cousins and aunts and uncles and even grandparents. I wanted to invite Tom and William to be with us as well, but apparently the nuisance of arranging the travel between Menlo Park and Akron was too difficult for Mr. Edison to manage. I couldn't help but show my annoyance at him, but I also didn't want to spoil Christmas for the rest of the family by pressing the point.

The vestibule ceiling was three stories high. Our tree was brought in through the double doors and was erected in the center of the area. It was huge. The men needed tall stepladders in order to string the decorations. The lower branches were for the children to decorate, from near the floor to as high as they could reach.

We never used candles on our trees. Father rightly believed it was much too dangerous. Instead, we used lots of tinsel and shiny, colored balls, both of which twinkled in the light that poured in from the windows. At night they even sparkled a bit from our oil lamps.

But the tree changed when I invited Mr. Edison and Marion to our family event.

"Do you have lights for your tree, Billie?" He asked me.

"Lights? You mean candles?"

Marion joined the conversation. "No, Mina. Father means electric lights."

I immediately thought back to Mr. Edison's visit to Chautauqua this past summer when he electrified my birthday cake. I laughed. "Marion. Are you going to tell me now that your father has electric lighting for a Christmas tree."[36]

"Yes," she answered. "The lights are together like on a rope."

"Oh, my. That sounds exciting."

"Yes," Mr. Edison added turning to me. "And with your father's permission, I want to light up your tree."

"Oh! I'm sure everyone will like that."

As a result, Mr. Edison certainly contributed to making Christmas one of the best in my memory. Once again I was so proud of my fiancé. The tree, lighted with red, white and blue electric lamps, was awesome to all of us, including our help who we always invited to be with us on these special occasions. It also attracted our neighbors who saw the tree from a distance through our windows. We invited all passersby in for a cup of hot wassail and cookies on Christmas Eve.

All the young children sat near me, my youngest sibling on my lap, while I read aloud "The Night Before Christmas." And Marion, ever proud of her Papa, remained beside him.

Father took an interest in Mr. Edison's lights, well aware that the inventor was actively engaged in lighting up the world. His house in New York City was electrified as well as his businesses. Electric central stations were being set up nationwide as well as in Europe.

"I think it's time for us to install electricity in the Miller household," father said. "What do you think, Tom?"

"I can certainly arrange it for you," Mr. Edison replied. "I already have men working in downtown Akron."

Since Saint Nicholas always came after the children were asleep in their beds, it was morning before presents were opened. And, of course, it was very early morning, and those children had to wait until the rest of us *finally* appeared, most still in our night clothes.

Of course there was not room, even under the big tree for all the packages. Opening them took all morning. Our rule was, only one present could be opened at a time. This gave us all a chance to admire it and record who gave what to whom so thank-you notes could be written. Best of all, it extended the fun, although it was frustratingly slow for the kids.

As I sat watching our spoiled family opening many things we really didn't care for and certainly didn't need, I thought of Tom and William and wondered what their Christmas was like. I had sent them a dozen presents in my name and their father's name and hoped they were toys that boys their ages would enjoy. Mr. Edison suggested mechanical presents such as an Erector Set that required assembly, but I resisted that until I knew them a lot better.

I also sent Grammach a token ladies' present that I felt sure she would appreciate.

"I'm asking a lot of you by taking my hand in marriage, Billie," he began. "The most obvious challenge is my daughter. But I will expect you to love her as if she were your own. We are both well aware Dot is jealous of you, but it's up to you to show her your love and eventually she will come around," he said confidently.

I smiled and kissed him on the cheek. "I love your children, Dearie. Remember, I grew up as the seventh of eleven children. I know something about children."

"You met the boys. What do you think?"

"I met them and we talked a bit. Tom looks just like you -- a mini Dearie." I giggled. "They are cute. All their questions to me were about the father they adored. They asked when they could see you. Neither remembers ever seeing you. I think I could get on very well with them. They seemed well behaved and full of energy. I was disappointed when Mrs. Stilwell sent them to another room."

"What did you think of Margaret?"

"I think she cares deeply about the boys."

"Anything else?"

"I'm finding this awkward, Dearie. I don't want to get between you two."

"What do you mean?"

"Recently you told me that you made arrangements for Mrs. Stilwell to take care of the boys -- indefinitely."

"I did."

"She said you and Marion hadn't visited her and the boys since Mary died."

"That's true, I guess. I haven't been counting the time."

"She was, let me say, *very* upset about that."

"Dang blast it! She knows how busy I am!"

"Dearie," I began with great patience. "You are their father. I want you to *make* time, just once in a while, to visit your own flesh and blood?"

"Billie. I just don't have any patience with children."

I looked at him sternly. "Here we go again. That better not mean you won't pay any attention to *our* children." I'm afraid that angered me.

"I will do my best to make you happy, Billie."

"Let's rephrase that to 'make me *and our children* happy.'"

"I will do my best, Billie. That will be different."

He was encouraging but evasive.

This issue was a major sticking point between us. At this moment I felt I could not marry this stubborn man who had no feeling for his children.

"Oh? How will our children be different?"

"You will be their mother." He smiled at me.

There was a long pause between us.

I continued. "We're not getting anywhere. I want you to tell me what you consider your responsibility is to your children." I'm sure I sounded angry.

"Simple. You, Billie, are the mother. Your duty is to love me and manage the children, the house and all things domestic. My responsibility is to love you, provide a home for us and to run my businesses. I don't have the time or the inclination to take care of children."

Another pause.

I pulled myself together and calmed down. "Fine, I said sweetly. "I am very happy to take responsibility for our children -- as well as yours. In order to do that then, I want Tom and William to live with us after we get settled."

Another pause. I think Mr. Edison sighed.

"Billie. If that will make you happy, that is what we will do."

I leaped from my chair like a child after a surprise gift and ran to him. "Thank you, Dearie. You've made me so happy." I wrapped my arms around him and gave him my best kiss. I felt I had won a major concession.

"I know you'll be a good manager and mother, Billie. I expect you'll be very busy overseeing your household staff and my life as well," he said. "My appointments, my lectures and personal appearances. Oh, lordy how this fame is chewing into my laboratory time. I need you, Billie, to hold my hand and fight off what I call the savages that suck the creative time out of my life. I need time also to be with you and to be with myself. There is so much yet to be accomplished and time escapes me so rapidly."

"And here you are with me, Dearie. We've had such a wonderful summer together. But here I am now taking up your valuable time."

"Billie. I cherish every minute with you. I will always want you nearby."

Oh, how I pray that will be possible, I thought.

Glenmont

Mr. Edison presented me with a lot of situations in which I had to make the decisions. I liked that. Some were very big decisions. For example, we were out in the sleigh one crisp afternoon soon after Christmas. We were enjoying the countryside in and around West Orange, New Jersey when he asked me if I preferred to live in the city or in the country. He had businesses in many cities and he was planning to build a laboratory in West Orange. He said it didn't matter to him where we lived.

For me, both country and city had their virtues. Boston and Manhattan were thrilling for me. As I wrote earlier, I loved the theater, the museums, the endless opportunities just waiting for me to take advantage of them. If I chose country, the city was only a short train ride away.

"I prefer the country, Dearie. It is peaceful and clean here in West Orange, only twelve miles from the city and a good place to raise children. With your laboratory here in the country also, we will be near each other."

"I'm glad to hear that, Billie," he said with his trademark twinkle. "Now, since living here is your choice, I have something to show you. It's not too far. I want your opinion."

Our driver put the horse into a trot and we glided over the new-fallen snow. In a few minutes we approached a huge mansion located on a high ridge in the exclusive Llewellyn Park section of West Orange. It was much like a castle of wood and brick. I wondered who possibly could live here.

"This place is called Glenmont," he said. "It was owned by a tycoon who went bankrupt and left the country in a hurry. It is currently unoccupied. I can buy it from his creditors for one-quarter of what he paid to have it built and furnished."

Glenmont was huge. Its architecture was Queen Anne English style, very elaborate with numerous balconies and gables. It sat in the middle of fifteen acres and overlooked the area of West Orange where Mr. Edison was constructing his new laboratory -- near the foot of the hill. How amazingly comparable it was to Oak Place! It was surrounded by snow-covered sweeping lawns and decorative trees. I saw also areas where under the snow there must be flower beds. I tried to imagine what Glenmont must look like in the spring and summer.

We toured the ground floor drawing room, parlor and hotel-size dining hall. The rooms were tastefully furnished, although a bit too sumptuous for my taste. The house had twenty-three spacious rooms in all -- enough for an army, as Mr. Edison put it. We viewed them all. Beneath the dining hall was a huge kitchen with every imaginable convenience available. Next to it was a gathering and eating area -- a resting place for the help.

We climbed the rear stairs and looked at the help's living quarters on the third level and continued through the lower halls, peeping into the bedrooms of the second floor, stopping only at the spacious library.

"The man had very good taste in books, Billie, but I plan to fill the shelves with the titles I most love. I have a huge collection."

"I'll contribute mine as well." I looked around. "What a cozy place this is to spend the hours reading in front of the fireplace."

"And the house is only a half mile from my office," he said gleefully. "I can easily walk it."

"Oh, Dearie. I can't believe it. This is just perfect."

"Then you like it."

I took his hand. "Like it? Of course I love it. We will fill it with family and friends."

"Then I will buy it. This will be my wedding gift to you, Billie. I want you to have the best."

The best it was. I tried to recall how mother made full use of our large home at Oak Place in Akron. With my ten siblings, it didn't take much recall. In my situation we would fill Glenmont with our children and guests. Mr. Edison had countless friends, business associates and dignitaries we could invite. I just loved to entertain, just like mother. I wanted to meet, mix and laugh with the writers, actors, musicians and heads of state, many of whom Mr. Edison had already met and were clamoring for invitations. I wanted to be able to influence people's lives and reach out to help those who were not so fortunate. Philanthropy was a major part of father's life and it was ingrained in me. I wanted to play a big part in society. Mr. Edison was giving me all and more than I had ever dreamed. My youthful head was spinning with the magnificence that was happening in my life. Father and mother had prepared me well. They were no slouches themselves when it came to doing things up big.

Mr. Edison said Glenmont "made a statement." I also saw that this was more than just a house. It represented the success that he had worked so hard to reach. And for me, it gave me a lifetime of decorating and redecorating. Father saw to it that each of his daughters had sufficient incomes to insure their independence.

A new self view

Mr. Edison's self view and his view of life itself was changing dramatically. He had grown from a destitute, home-schooled boy to a versatile and productive creator of indispensable objects. He had already accomplished a great deal during his first thirty-eight years. Any one of his inventions would have given him the status of a great inventor. But he was a driven man. He went on to make his fortune, and the fortunes of others. He said the foundation had been set. He was established and he was about to be married to a woman, he told me, who was in a class above himself. He continued to flatter me by saying I will do him proud among his peers.

He was not shy to tell me how he now saw himself as an equal with the Rockefellers and the Carnegies -- the relentless captains of industry. He reminded me that the character of Glenmont was on a par with those mansions erected by the new rich of the 1870s and 1880s in cities throughout the northeast, in Newport, Rhode Island and the Gold Coast of New York's suburbia. They were homes that shouted out the status and power of the kings of railroad, iron, coal, pork, oil -- and now? Electricity! Mr. Edison stood out as the ideal man of his era, an example of the individualist and the self-made man. He stood so proudly before me as he reveled in how he saw his new image.

At the same time, the inventor was different than the others. Although always a self-promoter, Mr. Edison never sought fame or attention in itself. Fame came inevitably. Sometimes he welcomed it. Sometimes he despised it. Money in itself meant little to him, he exclaimed, except for its use in paying for his research and reinvesting it in his businesses. He scorned those who amassed money simply to increase their prestige.

From Glenmont on, Edison saw himself as of one of the country's ruling industrial tycoons and he planned to do everything on a magnificent scale. Then, perhaps contradicting himself, this meant spending vast amounts of money, as on his bride's jewels, the huge Glenmont mansion and the enormously enlarged and equipped laboratories that would replace his small, primitive laboratory in Menlo Park.

I had difficulty grasping my husband's thoughts on money and status. It was foreign to me. My education at home and away never dealt with such subjects.

Mr. Edison spoke of this sometime later. "When I entered [Glenmont] I was paralyzed. To think it was possible to buy a place like this, which a man with taste for art and a talent for decoration had put ... years of enthusiastic study and effort into -- too enthusiastic, in fact -- the idea fairly turned my head and I snapped it up. It is a great deal too nice for me, but it isn't half nice enough for my little wife here."[37]

Chapter Three

1886

Our engagement

The announcement of our engagement and forthcoming wedding was sent out just after the first of the year. As father predicted, my life took a dramatic turn into public scrutiny. Reporters, normally pursuing Mr. Edison, now showed up in Akron to interview me. My family was overwhelmed by the magnitude of the response. Fortunately father was available.

"We don't want the press banging on our door all the time," father said. "We will put together a biography and Alastair can hand it out."

That didn't satisfy the hunger of the press. They wanted details. They wanted photographs. It seemed the more details we gave them the more they wanted. The clammoring became very annoying. I appealed to my fiancé.

"They're piled up at my door too," Mr. Edison said. "You'll never satisfy them. Just send them packing. You probably gave them too much already. Now they're digging into whatever privacy you have left."

That seemed to work with Alastair, our butler, as a buffer. But I was afraid to go out. Being accompanied by one of my sisters was not enough. I had to ask my brothers to take turns accompanying me and fending off unwanted strangers.

Little old me, Mina Miller, age 20, was on the front page of every newspaper in the country and in the capitals of Europe. It was exciting, yet at the same time very frightening. What was now expected of me? I thought again of mother. How did she behave in the illumination of her husband's career as a famous inventor, philanthropist and founder of the much admired and imitated Chautauqua Institution?

"I'll tell you, Mina, the attention on me was never as intense as this one," mother said. "And some of the stories I've read about you are more fiction than fact. It's terrible. They're interviewing everyone in Akron who has ever brushed against you, including our friends and your schoolmates."

"Don't worry about the press, Mr. Edison said. They're just doin' their job. They're harmless. You'll get used to them."

I doubted that. "If you were a woman you might think differently."

"Reporters can be your best friend. They depend on you for their income."

"They are like attack dogs. They rush at me and compete for the first words I have to say."

"Give it time, Billie. Give it time. Just relax and give them simple answers."

"I'm not convinced, Dearie."

Not all the press was bad, of course. Mr. Edison had his favorite reporters and writers and his favorite papers, the ones he read every day. He was a master at manipulating the press. He often made up stories about his inventions that magnified his image as a small-town boy who made good. He exaggerated the efforts he spent developing an invention. He was a master at story telling. The public loved his stories and they sold newspapers.

He gave them limited information about me but he also used that opportunity to elaborate on his businesses.

As I look back today with a new perspective, I see mother carrying herself with dignity, strength, humility and intelligence. She rode on the crest of a wave directing those around her with a captivating elegance and charm. She wooed the mightiest to her will and, so it seemed, they fell at her feet.

Yet she was loving and warm, modest and unassuming, but she was also a fighter.

Me? Could Mina Miller Edison do this? I had to begin on the right foot and never stumble. I had to live up to Mr. Edison's expectations.

Before me now was our wedding. That was the first test of my new métier. Mr. Edison, as my husband, was far beyond what I had ever dreamed and he was now preparing me to become part of his complex life.

I protested his extravagant purchase of my diamond-and-pearl necklace. But he countered with, "Billie. Part of all this falderal is living up to what others expect of us. My reputation has taken on a larger-than-life image, for better or worse. Your intelligence, beauty and your role is that of a queen, revered by her subjects. The truth is, I worship you also. This is one way I will love you as Mrs. Edison."

Be calm, Miss Miller, I thought. Don't let it go to your head. Be true to yourself. Don't be swept up in this intoxicating notion of queen worship.

Letters, flowers and telegrams of congratulations arrived. Strangers knocked at the door offering their best wishes. I was very close to being swamped with details. Mr. Edison saw this.

"I want you to advertise for a full-time personal secretary," he said, coming to my rescue. "You will have much use for her services."

I wasn't the only nervous one. Now that the wedding was exploding into reality, my fiancé was a bundle of nerves as well. He spoke of his life-long fear was not being able to hear or understand something spoken to him, in this case, our minister during our vows.

"I'm afraid our 'binder' will not speak loud enough," he admitted to me in reference to the minister. "In fact I'm getting pretty scared, Billie. I wonder if I will pull through."

I had never heard Mr. Edison express his fear of anything, and now this seemed pretty silly to me.

"There's no need to worry, Dearie," I said in a bit of role reversal. "We will be holding hands. In a pinch I can code you."

"You're not a bit nervous. I know *you* will pull through. Women have more nerve than men."

Well he judged that wrong but I said nothing.

The bachelor party

In early February, Mr. Edison's best friends, who were really his long-time business associates, arranged what turned out to be a raucous bachelor party at Delmonico's Restaurant in the city. It gave the normally sedate, middle-aged, nose-to-the-grindstone men an excuse to let loose their inhibitions.

The leader of the revelers was Ezra Gilliland whom Mr. Edison had known the longest and to whom was probably closest. Co-leader was Charles Batchelor. He was born in England and worked for a company that did business in America where he met Mr. Edison. His arrival was part of a general knowledge-transfer from Europe to this country that was deeply involved in another revolution called "Industrial." Whereas Ezra was outgoing and loud, Batchelor was quiet, unassuming and as precise as a draftsman. Every business action he made was, like Mr. Edison, recorded in detail in notebooks. Edison considered "Batch" his most clever mechanic, able to mold his boss's unique ideas into working models. Mild-mannered Batch was for decades the inventor's most trusted collaborator and technological ambassador.

Sigmund Bergman was a German mechanic. Mr. Edison admired him for his skills at creating, but he spoke very little English. He owned Bergman & Company, some three hundred employees strong. It produced a myriad of electrical components to feed Edison's electric lighting systems. When someone commented on his lack of verbal skills, Mr. Edison responded with, "What difference does it make? His work speaks for him!" His products thrilled Mr. Edison.

Edward H. Johnson was Mr. Edison's principle business lieutenant, also a trusted manager who carried on during Mr. Edison's absences as well as when his boss was too preoccupied in developing an idea in the lab to care about anything else.

Gardiner Sims designed Mr. Edison's steam engines. He was a problem solver of mechanical devices.

Alfred Tate was Mr. Edison's adulating secretary and biographer who became a principle in Mr. Edison's Kinetoscope Company.[38]

Navy Lieutenant Frank Toppan[39] was Edison's Best Man, a mystery figure in Mr. Edison's life. He showed up at our wedding, did what Mr. Edison asked him to do and I never saw him again.

Samuel Insull was Mr. Edison's indispensable right-hand man and personal secretary. "Sammy" began his career at *Vanity Fair* magazine and was adept at shorthand. He too was captivated by romantic myths surrounding Mr. Edison and ached to work for him. A job opening sealed his success. He was always available to carry out every one of Mr. Edison's wishes and whims.

I knew the men, of course, but I was never told much about their party. The alcohol flowed freely, except for Mr. Edison who was a strict tee-totaler "for health reasons." He said he stood up to a lot of ribbing and foolishness, but it was all in fun for their "old man."

Ezra made the official toast. He took credit for introducing the young woman to the "old man" and that stirred up some jokes about foolish old men chasing after young women. But, as they say, what happens in Delmonico's stays in Delmonico's which is probably just as well.

The highlight of the party was the food. The menu included roasted oysters, foie gras, "Cape Cod" day-boat scallops, blue crab cake, lobster newberg, truffle with chicken and every possible cut of steak.

These men, and many others, helped give birth to my husband's ideas. Although he always took pains to meet and speak with every standout employee, those attending this party were the stars of his show.

They would next gather at the boss's wedding.

An urgent telegram

Between the time of his stag party and our wedding Mr. Edison received an urgent telegram from Frank Thompson, his superintendent of construction in Florida, saying the winter homes were not yet completed. Mr. Thompson asked why Mr. Edison had not been answering the queries he had been sending over the last few months.

Mr. Edison was shocked. It was true. He had been ignoring not only Thompson but the regular crises in his businesses. He now realized his intense attention to me and our plans for the future had totally distracted him from Florida and business matters. More troubling for him, it was delaying the completion of his honeymoon plans at his Garden of Eden -- his much anticipated "love nest."

Even though he had little to do with the actual wedding preparations, he was in the midst of purchasing Glenmont, hiring extra help to fully electrify our new home, and overseeing that it would be ready when we returned from Florida in the spring.

Numerous telegrams from Fort Myers had been ignored. He was now forced to face these problems.

"I want your first visit to the 'Jungle' to be as perfect as it can be," he told me.

"Everything is going to be fine, Dearie," I innocently assured him. "But if it isn't, that's okay with me."

But my casual attitude didn't solve the problems as he saw them. He told me he spent a day and a half retrieving Thompson's old telegrams, sorting out the superintendent's questions, and preparing his answers. The huge word count in the telegram Mr. Edison returned to Thompson was certain to have set a record at Western Union.

For my part, all I had to do in preparation was pack my clothes for our mysterious honeymoon trip. Despite all the travels with my family to Europe and elsewhere, we had never visited Florida. My fiancé's descriptions of the place seemed to border on hyperbole. He insisted Fort Myers was close to being a Garden of Eden, or even Eden itself. I was unable to imagine unclouded river water, vast expanses of colorful wild flowers, and day after day of balmy sunshine. Certainly he was exaggerating.

I only hoped now that I had the right clothes for this climate. I had the items Jennie and I bought in the city. I went through my closets with mother and she helped me put it all together. It was very sweet of her to spend so much time with me because she had her own pressures. She was out straight directing our help in preparing Oak Place for the wedding day.

I couldn't believe the length of the invitation list. Many of the invitees were Miller relatives. Probably an equal number were Mr. Edison's business associates and a couple of Edison relatives, including his father Samuel and brother William.

We had a discussion about inviting Mr. Edison's children. It began when I scanned his guest list. His children were not included.

"You've forgotten your children," I said as I held the list toward him.

"I haven't forgotten them, Billie. I'm not inviting them."

"Why not? They should be an integral part of the ceremony."

"Billie. Let's not get into discussions about my children again. They would only be a distraction."

"I disagree," I said firmly. "Marion would make a lovely flower girl and the boys could carry the ring and a bouquet down the aisle."

"I can't see it."

"I would feel very poorly if they are not included. If we don't invite Marion that will further increase the divide between her and me. And the boys? They have been happy and excited about the wedding. They will be greatly disappointed."

"Billie, Billie. Why do you do this to me?"

"I do it because they are part of our family. I can't imagine what the outside world will think if you exhibit such insensitivity to your children." He was weakening. "I want the children to be included. For most guests, it will bring smiles to their faces and give you a bit of humanity. The press will love it and there will be more pictures."

He gave in. "Anything for you, dear Billie. Anything."

"Thank you, Dearie." I gave him a kiss.

I invited none of my friends. I still cannot understand my motive. I wasn't even going to have bridesmaids. Now, at the last minute, I had misgivings.

My parents had really gone to extremes in their planning. They still had a lot of "special" details they wouldn't reveal to me. These would be my surprise. Oak Place was becoming more like a royal palace as my big day approached.

Our wedding day

Oh, my. Father certainly did up my wedding fit for a queen and I felt like royalty. He hired high-stepping horses and carriages to transport the guests from the railway station. And on arrival at Oak Place, he had a very long red carpet rolled out to meet them.

The aroma of vibrantly colored flowers filled the big front parlor where the orchestra resounded with strings, brass and reeds.

The wedding took place at 3 PM, February 24. Oak Place had a beautiful location in an exquisite spot at the top of a hill -- not much different than Glenmont.

In addition to our families, we reduced the invitations to one hundred guests from near and far to witness my grand occasion. A special train arrived from New York with the same friends who feted Edison at his rowdy bachelor's party at Delmonico's. Telegrams arrived from around the world, mostly from unknown admirers.

The wedding ceremony itself took place on the front lawn overlooking the Akron. It was a magnificent day. I wore a gown of white silk, trimmed with Duchesse and point lace, square neck, laced corsage, plain trim. Around my neck was Mr. Edison's groom gift, an outrageously expensive necklace of diamonds and pearls.

Mr. Edison was waiting patiently beneath a horseshoe of roses as father escorted me toward him. He looked spectacular, but somewhat uncomfortable, in his formal wear that mother had chosen for him. He had rebelled at her suggestion of white gloves that would have completed his outfit. So, when father gave me to him he bare handedly took my gloved hands.

Marion paraded just behind us with a bouquet of daylilies. She had initially responded to my invitation with mixed feelings, but the prospect of having her hair done up special and wearing a pretty pendant and a beautiful new dress clinched it.

Tom and William walked side-by-side behind Marion. Tom carried Mr. Edison's ring and William carried mine on small velvet pillows. The guests responded with smiles of approval.

We kneeled before the beautiful altar decorated with calla lilies and tea roses, our hands together, as the senior minister of our Akron Methodist Church led us through the vows.

Mr. Edison several times turned his head toward me, smiled and winked and then totally distracted me by tapping "I love you." The minister had to ask me a second time if I promised to honor and obey this man. It was embarrassing -- as if I had to think twice about this promise. I finally answered that I would. But then my groom coded another distraction about obeying him. It was very personal and it caused me to scowl. And I think I blushed. It would not be polite for me to tell you what he said. I almost dropped his hand.

At this point in our lives, messaging each other was as natural as speaking aloud. I sometimes had trouble differentiating the two forms of communication. It seems silly, but now and then when he messaged me a very personal remark, I would look around to see if anyone had heard him. Mr. Edison was not shy about "voicing" things I considered intimate, especially so early in our relationship.

He could also be irreverent. I knew he was an agnostic. My family knew he was a doubter. But, generally, my parents felt he had enough virtues to override that. At least he wasn't an atheist! Sister Jennie had her own views. She thought Mr. Edison, at 38, was after my young, virginal body. "After all," she said. "His first bride was only sixteen and you're little more than a teenager!" Need I say that Jennie often spoke her mind? But I had to forgive her comment. Jennie was already thirty and had not yet found a man to her liking. Or had men not found her to their liking?

Somehow we made it though the vows. The children performed their duties admirably and their father and I were now joined for life, "for better, for worse. . ." What bride ever considers "for worse?"

Hand in hand we circulated among our guests. The children accompanied us initially but then wandered off somewhere. Mr. Edison introduced me to guests I had not previously met. At the same time he messaged me with little tidbits about some of them that we would not have wanted them to hear.

Following the ceremony, all guests were seated at the same time and served a dinner created by a chef imported from Chicago and served by an army of fifteen waiters.

Father clinked his fork on his glass for attention and then led in a prayer of thankfulness for a loving God, the day, the guests and for people at home and abroad who were not as fortunate as us.

The gifts were not opened until we returned from our time in Florida. They were a rich and costly array, including every article known to the silver worker's art, diamond bracelets and pendants, a ruby and sapphire pin, a chalcedony encased in gold, and a host of rare articles of virtu.

Even on our special day, the press, including a New York *Times* stringer,[40] was on the sidelines taking note of everything.

I was so proud to be at my husband's side as we moved among our friends. The compliments given us seemed genuine and heart-felt. Everyone appeared pleased that he had found a suitable partner. I was relieved that not a single person mentioned how soon our marriage took place after Mary's death. Eighteen months did not leave much time for mourning. But then Mr. Edison was not known for dragging his feet.

Following all the activities at Oak Place, we and our three children took a publicly-announced open carriage ride through the streets of Akron and waved to the cheering residents that lined the roadway. I swallowed hard when saw a number of my childhood girlfriends along the route. This was when guilt overcame me. Tears blurred my sight. I had not invited one of them to my wedding. I asked the carriage to stop, baffling Mr. Edison and the children. I stepped down with help from the carriage attendant and personally greeted three close friends who stood together. Once again I regretted not having these friends as bridesmaids. I now wished I had invited them all. I blew kisses to the others, wishing at the same time I could take them into my carriage. I wondered what astonishing surprises, or lack thereof, their lives had yet to deliver them. I doubted they would be as fortunate as I.

My new husband and I and, yes, Marion took the evening train to Cincinnati, stopping briefly for Mr. Edison to say hello to friends who were not able to attend our wedding -- and, of course, to show off Marion and me. From there, our honeymoon began with an overnight train to Jacksonville. Mr. Edison had reserved a private car just for the three of us.

I know I'm being sarcastic, but I was pleased that Marion was not in bed with us that night. But she was not far away, in her own compartment. She appeared a couple times complaining that she was afraid to be alone. Mr. Edison finally escorted her away, tucked her in, and at last we were left to ourselves.

Messaging proved its value once again, assuring our pillow talk was not overheard.

Our first union was surprisingly pleasurable, contrary to my training and unmarried Jennie's words of questionable wisdom. We girls at the finishing school had had a three-minute explanation of the birds and the bees. Miss Appleton, a maiden lady, was assigned the duty of demonstrating with a pair of dolls how a man mates with his wife in order to produce children. The woman's role, she said, "must be passive and uncomplaining." Her duty is to allow her husband to be fully gratified as he takes control of his wife's body.

That was the theory. It was quite evident that my new husband had never been exposed to Miss Appleton's lessons. Mr. Edison had years of experience with his first wife. He was gentle and sweet. His touch was magic, producing sensations in my body I never knew were so well hidden. I had difficulty holding back from screaming with delight lest Dot appear on the scene again and destroy our intimacy. Time evaporated. The clickity-clack of the wheels on the rails faded away. I drifted into a new realm, a dream world of unexpected ecstasy, as Mr. Edison and I became one.

Jacksonville was pleasant. Our first activity after checking into the hotel was a romp on the beach. Dot knew her way around, having been here before and we truly had fun together. She kept whatever thoughts she had about our night on the train to herself. We walked in the surf and build sand castles together. I found that the water was indeed as clear as my husband had described.

The Gillilands arrived late in the afternoon and spent one night. They had brought a traveling companion for Marion. That was very thoughtful. Had I the foresight, that companion could have accompanied us on the train. Certainly Marion would not have objected to staying with her in a separate compartment.

We had a nice dinner together before they left the next morning for Fort Myers with Marion and her friend. The Gillilands were intent on making sure all was in order at Fort Myers for our eventually arrival.

I finally had my husband to myself for the next two weeks. It was idyllic most of the time -- beach, sand and sun. He and I had all the time in the world to be alone -- and to be intimate. I learned about a different side of my inventor husband. And I still blush as I say this but I want it to be known. He was a passionate, gentle lover. Our handholding had a double meaning. Although it was often our means of communication, it was also a sensual instrument. Actually, from the beginning when we started coding, whenever he touched my hand I was electrified -- no pun intended with this word. He certainly was the generator of my sensuality. He never let me forget that I was his queen throughout our forty-five years.

We ventured south from Jacksonville and did some touring in and around the old city of St. Augustine. We took a horse trolley part way and then boated on the St. Johns River near Palatka. Florida was such a verdant and beautiful place. I saw my first wild alligators. As our boat moved up the river, these creatures slipped into the water from the shore. I was certain they were going to pursue us, but thankfully they minded their own business.

We also enjoyed a bit of culture and dined in restaurants that offered live music and song. I enjoyed singing along with others when the situation encouraged it. My husband was more restrained. I did finally coax him out onto the dance floor but it was quickly evident his talents did not include the graceful movements I so enjoyed.

We were both very interested in the tropical plant life, each of us for very different reasons. I enjoyed the complex beauty and extraordinary variety of flowers. Mr. Edison collected leaf and stem samples whenever possible and asked me make detailed drawings while the clippings were still fresh. I was very happy to be asked to make use of a talent I rarely used. He had great plans for this flora at his "jungle" in Fort Myers. He wanted a horticultural Eden where he could experiment with every possible exotic plant. He went on and on talking about his paradise on earth while I still tried to develop my own vision of what his Eden must be like.

I would soon find out.

We were on the train again, but with much more primitive accommodations. Henry Flagler's deluxe railroad line had only reached St. Augustine at this time.[41] We were now heading for Gainesville on the pre-Civil-War Florida Southern Railway. Next came the Florida Railway to Cedar Key on the Gulf Coast. The further south we went, the more rustic things became.

The final leg of our journey was on the steamer *Manatee* that took us 200 miles south along the verdant coastline. The Gulf waters were as clear as promised. It was exciting to watch the dolphins as they raced the boat, leaping in the bow's wake. They dipped and dived playfully and occasionally leaped several feet into the air. We soon reached Punta Rassa at the mouth of the Caloosahatchee River.

"Say Caloosahatchee fast three times, Billie," and he laughed. "This is our river. Our cozy little retreat abuts this magnificent water. It's an Indian word that means 'river of the Calusa' tribe."

I *did* repeat "Caloosahatchee" three times with no effort.

"I just wanted you to remember the name. It's important."

It was an interesting fourteen miles from the mouth of the river to Fort Myers. I spotted a huge hippo-like animal just below the surface of the sparkling water. Just its nose appeared and that was only for a moment. A fellow passenger informed us it was a manatee, the namesake of our ship. Sights like these were unheard of along our dark and filthy rivers in Ohio. Maybe Mr. Edison actually did find Eden.

He was a bundle of excitement throughout this water trip, pointing out landmarks he and Ezra had seen a year earlier. Further up the broad Caloosahatchee he was intent on locating his plot of land on the south bank, just short of the village.

We were not disappointed. It was the captain of the *Manatee* who appeared where we were standing at the rail and pointed it out. Actually it was quite obvious, even to me, because of the long pier that stretched far out into the river. He had the pilot toot the loud horn and we waved to whoever on our plot might have turned in our direction. The captain handed Mr. Edison his binoculars and he was able to see his new houses quite easily. He passed them to me and I had my first fuzzy glimpse of the place I would call my winter home for many years to come.

Arrival at the love bower

We arrived on the Ides of March, tied up to the rickety Fort Myers dock and went ashore, our bags following us with a porter. There was no one here to greet us because our schedule was unannounced. Mr. Edison hired a carriage.

I had expected a lot more to the town -- perhaps, a mini St. Augustine with smaller hotels, a little less traffic and fewer people visiting the local shops. Well! Carry that thought to the extreme. The main street was dirt, and it was the *only* street. I saw a single, small hotel, a general store, a tavern and a cute little church, each with a hitching rail. Every structure was very much in need of paint. Indeed. This reminded me of the cattle towns of New Mexico and Arizona I passed through with my parents years ago. If I had blinked I would have missed it all. It was noon. I saw two people. They casually waved to us, unaware it was Mr. Edison. I returned the wave.

My husband excitedly pointed out various trees and flowers along the way and said how he wanted to transplant them on his property. I smiled and nodded, but in reality I saw nothing but an uninhabited dusty road.

About a mile later we reached our destination. To our surprise, workmen were still busy on the grounds. We spotted Ezra at the same time he saw us. His mustachioed face broke out into a broad smile and his large body trundled toward us and as he gave his greeting.

"I'm sorry to report the work here is not finished," he announced. "There's going to be a delay of about a week. They're just finishing up the final trim and a few details. Then, with a second coat of paint, it will be completed."

"Damn it, Ezra!" Mr. Edison exploded. He glared at his friend and then turned to me. "I was sure this would be ready for us, Billie. That's why I dilly-dallied so much in St. Augustine."

I was shocked. I had never seen my husband so angry or heard him utter a profanity.

"Where's Thompson?"[42] he continued. "Do we have a full crew? I want to know what the hell is going on."

"Thompson's here. I'll get him if you want. We have every tradesman in Fort Myers on the site as well as those we've imported."

Mr. Edison turned back to me. "I don't want you to see this place until it's finished, Billie. We'll stay at the hotel."

"I already have rooms for you," Ezra said. "Lillian and the girls are there."

"Good," he answered, still angry. "We'll go back to the hotel and get settled. I'll return and talk with Thompson."

"Thompson's had questions," Ezra continued, attempting to explain. "He says you've been incommunicardo until recently when he received your lengthy telegram and that's what caused the delay. When I arrived he fell all over me with questions. I gave him some answers and they have since been going as fast as they can. I wouldn't be too harsh on Thompson if I were you. He's pretty stressed himself. He's ornery enough that he might walk off the job with his men."

"OK, OK!" Mr. Edison brushed his friend off. "I'll be back later. I don't want to get into that now."

I hadn't yet stepped down from the carriage so I heard it all. Mr. Edison now returned to his seat with me and we turned back to town with him in a snit. He was sullen. I tried to cheer him up by showing my excitement about being in Fort Myers and how I loved the tropical trees and flowers. But he changed little, just repeating how disappointed he was in the delay.

We entered the Keystone Hotel where we immediately saw Lillian, Marion and her friend.

Mr. Edison stepped out and Marion ran to her father. "Where have you been?" she asked with a frown. "It's been forever."

He finally smiled and hugged her. "I've been showing your new mother the Florida jungle. Now go and greet her." He pushed Marion toward me.

Marion looked toward me and reluctantly, with a pout, we hugged. I held on for longer than she wished, it seemed, for she struggled and pulled away. Apparently the memory of the fun we had in Jacksonville had been forgotten. But then her friend came to me, gave me a polite greeting, a big smile and a far more genuine hug. Marion observed. I wondered what words they might later say to each other.

The week went very slow. Lillian, the girls and I wandered the dusty streets. I couldn't blame Marion for her unrest waiting for our arrival.

"I don't know why I left St. Augustine," Lillian said. "If I had only known how primitive this place was . . . There's nothing to do. I'm so damned tired of playing cards and brushing the dust off me and the furniture. We've been here three weeks already. Ezra took us to see our new houses but, you saw, they are in the middle of the jungle -- all by themselves. I can't believe Ezra thought I'd like it here."

I felt much the same, but I was here because Mr. Edison had a dream that his property was going to be Eden itself. I forced myself to think positive and keep an open mind.

Fashion shopping and entertainment just did not exist in Fort Myers. The town was a backwash, a primitive outpost. I missed my music, the theater and cultural stimulation in general. Fort Myers had nothing, not even a public library. There were certainly no automobiles, not even bicycles.

It was the general store that was the center of activity. It held the post office, a tiny eating nook, and a few books on a circulating bookshelf. Other than that, it was devoted to hardware, fishing gear and all the practical stuff that Mr. Edison liked.

"We've been taking boating excursions," Lillian continued. "The steamer has more to offer than the town. It has better food and drink, a nicer area to lounge and a changing view. I'm tempted to get on that boat again and return to St. Augustine. If you and the girls want to go with me, all the better."

I had known Lillian for the five years they wintered in Akron and during the summer weeks when we were guests at their beach house near Boston. During this time I had never seen her so out of sorts. Her negativity raised my defenses. Mr.

Edison had a dream and, knowing him, I fully expected that all he dreamed about would come true. My attitude was to give it a chance. Wait and see. My husband knew what he wanted and I wasn't going to spoil it by complaining.

"Give it a chance," I told Lillian. "I'm sure it will all turn out well."

"I'll believe that, Mina, when he delivers St. Augustine itself up the Caloosahatchee."

Noticing our frustration later, Ezra understood. He telegraphed Sammy Insull and told him to ship down a piano, but that wouldn't be here in time for this visit.

Mr. Edison and Ezra were at the site much of the time, except when we all went on a several-day boat excursion to Fort Ogden to pick up my parents who, of course, were curious about their daughter's life as a wife and what kind of shelter her new husband had provided. With them were our cook, Gracie with her kitchen help and two maids the Gillilands provided.

Finally, all of us were able to move into the new cottages. I was delighted and I had a wonderful time decorating walls and rearranging furniture in the house designated as ours. Of course there were still a great deal of items we still needed and Sammy was again wired with a list of necessities, but we wouldn't receive them either for this visit.

This was our honeymoon, but my husband and I were never alone except for a few hours at night. Marion and her friend shared both houses -- unable to decide who of the family and guests were the least boring.

The houses were identical but arranged as a mirror image. Each had two stories with dining and living rooms, a master bedroom and a single bathroom with modern facilities. The kitchen was in an ell off the dining room. A wide, airy porch wrapped two adjacent sides of each house. The upstairs of each had four small bedrooms for guests and the help and a modern bath above the kitchen. The kitchen too was well-furnished with the best and it had its own porch.

The house required quite an adjustment from Glenmont. Often, our guests chose to stay at the small hotel, provided it had rooms available.

Gracie expressed her frustration at the limited varieties of food at the local grocery and the shortage of vital cooking pots and utensils. But she was imaginative and her output was tasty. This was not the time for complaints. Mr. Edison's Eden, like the one in Genesis, was being created from nothing.

The anticipated joy of my honeymoon was rapidly falling apart. Mr. Edison's billing of this "jungle" as our "love bower" was a gross exaggeration as the numbers of our relatives and friends and additional help increased. Fortunately our guests' visits were short, but on the plus side, they brought with them necessities we had requested in telegrams. Mother fully understood the new bride's deprivation and offered her sympathy along with some pots and pans. My parent's visit lasted only three days. In retrospect, I'm afraid I was young and I was very spoiled. I had a lot to learn and it was often very painful.

During the final two weeks of April we were alone at last except for Gracie, her assistant and a maid. The Gillilands Marion and her friend made their "escape," as Lillian put it, after only one week in their completed home next to ours. She had done nothing to make it more comfortable. They gracefully offered their house for our use should we have any more guests.

With the new laboratory behind the houses completed and fully stocked, Mr. Edison immediately began work and, by necessity of keeping my man part of my life, I joined him. He began a series of Florida notebooks in which he continued his development of telegraphy and the telephone. He also moved deeply into the relationships between the forces of gravity, electricity, heat and magnetism. My contribution was recording the phases of his experiments in the notebooks making detailed drawings[43] of each.

These days were most interesting -- and exhausting. As Mr. Edison developed his ideas, each minute stage had to be recorded. I tried valiantly to follow his thought process. I learned his frustrations. I saw just how hard he worked at each detail as I toiled just to keep up with him.

We continued to learn a lot about each other, good and bad. I began to question the wisdom of my working so closely with my husband. He growled and he grumbled and he complained. Would I ever be able to anticipate his thoughts, his goals or his next action? Would my talents ever meet his expectations?

Then there was the garden. The requested open areas of our land had been cleared in anticipation of lawn and gardens. We both worked on sketching the details. One of the notebooks grew to twenty-five pages. This was no ordinary plot plan. He wanted a twenty-square-foot banana bed and a thousand pineapple plants!

Mr. Edison was also concerned about privacy. It seems the local press and residents had a growing curiosity for us. They visited without invitation and wandered around as if it was a public park. I politely informed them that this was private property and they were welcome at our invitation. They were surprised at this. They informed us that in this tiny village everyone knew each other and shared the little that each had. Everyone tried to be friendly with each other. That all sounded reasonable and nice, but Mr. Edison was not about to become host to every nosy curiosity seeker. I expressed our feelings to the reporter from the Fort Myers *Press* and gave him a full tour. The result was a story I was pleased to see did carry the gist of what I told him. But it also listed some of our valuable household items, like the modern household appliances, the electricity and its related fixtures and the inventor's chemical inventory in his lab. The article generated additional curiosity. To protect my husband's privacy and our assets, we planted thick walls of shrubs along our boundaries to discourage prying eyes.

Finally, on April 26, our time in Fort Myers came to an end. We said goodbye to our newly named Seminole Lodge and rode by horse-drawn buggy fifty miles north to Arcadia, now the nearest railroad terminal.

Arriving in New York City, the Gillilands had returned Marion to her school in the city and then continued north to Boston. Mr. Edison and I returned to his previous city home where he and Mary lived near Gramercy Park.

I enjoyed being back in the city. I liked the house and its address, on 5th Avenue and East 14th Street. It was spacious with plenty of room for guests. It was very near the theatre district, close to my husband's office and a brief ride to everywhere else in the city. This address became our city home.

Settling into Glenmont

During our long return trip from Fort Myers, Mr. Edison and I discussed my responsibilities at our new country home at Glenmont.

"We each now have our respective duties, Billie. I have my work, of course, and," Mr. Edison emphasized, "that does not include domesticity."

In short he repeated the expectations he iterated before our marriage. I nodded.

He smiled. "You can handle it, Billie. You were raised in a similar household. I have given you a generous budget. Make Glenmont a home where we can build a life together."

"You can count on me, Dearie."

"Glenmont must reflect my new status in America. You are my queen, my love. Elevate Glenmont to the status of the Carnegies and the Rockefellers. I want you to reign over our castle in a way that the world now expects of successful entrepreneurs. Listen carefully and you can hear everyone taking notice of my new wife and my inventions."

Mr. Edison expected a great deal of me very soon. I girded myself. I took charge. I was only twenty, just short of twenty-one but youth has a way of overcoming. Somehow I managed to win his approval.

We moved directly into Glenmont after a week at our city home which I now simply called Gramercy. In our absence a lot of work had taken place, under Mr. Edison's instructions, making the huge house more suitable to his style. Quite naturally, he had electricity installed in every room. Chandeliers and wall sconces were electrified. Electric outlets by the hundred were everywhere. Mr. Edison said at the time there were more electric fixtures in Glenmont than in all of Boston.

He also had his massive book collection moved into the library and the previous owner's books set aside for his scrutiny. The unwanted balance would be sent off to the local public library. I would have liked to send them to Fort Myers but, without an existing public library, it was not feasible.

Mr. Edison also had his favorite chair, smoking stand and personal effects set up in his study. After a quick walk through the house checking that all his instructions had been followed, Mr. Edison gave me a kiss and disappeared to his New York office.[44] In short, the "queen" found herself very much alone in her castle.

Hiring the help

The honeymoon was over. I was not quite overwhelmed by the multitude of tasks that faced me, but there was no way I would admit it to my husband. I took charge with a vengeance. My generous budget was indeed generous. It, and my own finances, allowed me to do whatever I wanted at Glenmont.

Over the next few weeks I hired a butler, Henry Horsey. He came with a high recommendation from Alastair, our Miller butler. He was without work because the master of his former house had died. He was also British and spoke with an accent I like so much. Henry would see to it that the help accomplished their chores smoothly and efficiently. He was an extension of me. He maintained a lot of on-call help when we entertained. He supervised all of the help except for Gracie and her scullery maid.

Gracie had been hired before we were married and she now went with us to our various homes. Her recommendations were impeccable. She showed me her menu specialties that appeared very elaborate. But after a few days of dining on Gracie's elaborate, I suggested more simplicity. I wanted more fruits and vegetables and fewer spices and herbs. Mr. Edison could continue his habits as he wished. I asked, in fun, if she could also satisfy the appetite of a meat-and-potatoes man. That was Mr. Edison's favorite meal.

There were just the two of us in Glenmont so far, and Marion on occasion. I saw that Gracie was disappointed with preparing such plain food. I told her she could give us a surprise now and then but generally she was to save her elaborate creations for when we had guests. We hired a footman, Michael, who served Gracie's meals and kept the first-floor rooms in order.

I had Henry advertise and interview other help I felt was needed. Laura was hired as upstairs maid. Her responsibility was maintaining order in all the upstairs rooms. I planned to have a lot of guests and this required a good deal of bed changing and linen washing.

Mallory became the houseman. He performed general maintenance around the house and out buildings. He also did the heavy housework such as rearranging furniture and hanging pictures and drapes. He would do painting and small repairs of all kinds.

Scarth was our chauffeur. He was available whenever transportation was needed. He ran errands and he drove us on pleasurable Sunday carriage drives and later drove our motor cars. Mr. Edison never drove. He admitted his mind wandered so much it would endanger the lives of everyone on the road. Scarth also had the special duty to see that Mr. Edison was delivered his meals at the West Orange laboratory. This turned out to be far more often than his meals eaten at home.

Scarth had an assistant who managed the stable and horses.

Tom was the head gardener. Fabius was his assistant during the growing season and the spring and fall cleanups. During winter, they removed snow from the walks and porches and cleared the deep snow from the sleighways. The indoor help lived in and the outdoor help lived elsewhere in town.

And then there was Angela, my delightful personal maid and secretary whom I had interviewed in the days before our wedding. She was for me my most difficult hiring choice. I had to like, trust and depend on her because of our intimate relationship. She managed my wardrobe and all my personal needs. She was the one person who accompanied me wherever I traveled. In the wake of the wedding I had countless notes of thank you and appreciation to send. She opened and inventoried all our wedding presents and sent the thank-you notes. Angela would also set up my office and keep me organized and informed. She would maintain my daily schedule, filter my mail and simplify my domestic and public life. Angela was hired from Miss Johnson's school. She was two years behind me and she excelled in organization and letter composition. She said she was still single, was available and was eager to work for me. She was a blessing for years.

Loneliness

I had to admit I was pretty proud of myself. The household was purring by summer. With Henry's mature and serious demeanor, the help fell into place smoothly. Angela was marvelous. She had answered all correspondence and put together an office for Mr. Edison and me. My husband's desk faced mine. Theoretically, that was to allow us to chat and work at the same time. Unfortunately, Mr. Edison's desk was rarely occupied.

Not yet six months into our marriage and I was lonely for my husband. Yes. I knew he was very busy with very important things that he only sometimes shared with me. Yet, this did not solve my problems for which he expressed very little interest. We had spent a great deal of time together in the months before our wedding and our honeymoon. I was spoiled. I admit it. Much like Marion, I missed him.

My sister Mary Emily and I corresponded frequently. I admitted to her I was lonely and found it difficult to share my husband with the rest of the world. Father had been right, so, so right. Mary Emily reminded me that things would be different after Mr. Edison finished moving his new laboratory to West Orange. It would be within walking distance. She said she was certain Mr. Edison loved me deeply "and would love you more if you would let him."[45] Sister was not the most tactful. I didn't know just what she meant by that last phrase, because I did give my husband everything I had -- when he was available.

Sister Jennie reminded me I should continue to invite friends and neighbors to the house and return the visits as soon as possible. Do some studying and practice the piano. Start a book club. Arrange baskets for needy families. "You should be the happiest young lady in West Orange," she wrote.

The boys visit Glenmont

My caustic visit to Mrs. Stilwell's home last fall before our marriage still haunted me. I thought of the two young boys who didn't know their father -- who didn't know me. I couldn't bear having them abandoned by their father. They were now my stepsons. As a stepmother, I wanted a relationship with them -- despite how their father felt. At the very least, I wanted them to visit Glenmont periodically and to see their father. I took action.

Mr. Edison had last seen his sons at our wedding. They performed well during the vows delivering the rings. He spent a few minutes with them and with Marion during the reception, but that was fleeting because of the need to circulate among the guests. Then the three children returned to their respective environments.

Confident in my decision, I made arrangements with Mrs. Stilwell for me to pick up the boys and take them home for a few days. Scarth, my chauffeur, accompanied me to Menlo Park on the train.

"So. Your conscience got the better of you," was Mrs. Stilwell's greeting.

"I am anxious to know my stepchildren," was all I replied.

Tom and William were dressed in their best and looked handsome. Tom, now eleven, stood at my shoulder height. William was two years younger and hadn't yet had his flash of growth. They were excited about their anticipated adventure. Their governess, Miss McWilliams, accompanied us.

The trip home went quickly. Scarth and Miss McWilliams were a help with boy talk. The boys had grown up with her.

"What games do you play?" I asked.

"We do lots of stuff like hoop and stick, marbles, ring toss, blind man's bluff, pickup sticks, ride our bicycles. . ." said Tom.

William chimed in. "And checkers and blocks and hide and seek. . ."

"Do you ever go fishing?" Scarth asked.

"Yes. When we go to Aunt Alice's farm. There's a lot of stuff to do there."

"How about books?" I asked. "What books do you read?"

"I like Huckleberry Finn," Tom said.

"And I like *Treasure Island*," William added.

"Grammach says you married my father," Tom said.

"Don't you remember? You were in that wedding. You two carried the rings to Papa and me."

"Oh, yes. I forgot."

"And now you are our Mama," William quickly added.

"You're both right," I said. "And I am very happy to have you as my sons."

"Will we see our Papa now, Mama?"

"I hope so. I want you to see him a lot."

"Oh, good," they said in unison.

"When can we see him?"

"We're going to get you two and Miss McWilliams to my house first and then we'll see what happens."

"Is Papa nice?"

"Of course he's nice," Miss McWilliams cut in.

"You talked with him at the wedding," I reminded them.

"I don't remember."

This was not surprising with all that was happening that day. Their exchange of conversation with their Papa was limited or non existent because of Mr. Edison's great difficulty understanding children's voices.

They seemed like normal boys, not much different from my younger brothers. They enjoyed the trip, looking out the windows, watching the people at the stations and commenting on the sights they saw.

Arriving at Glenmont, I gave Miss McWilliams and the boys a tour and showed them their rooms. Miss McWilliam's room was adjacent to theirs. In anticipation of their arrival I had bought a miscellany of boy toys and games. They immediately asked if they could open the boxes and play with them.

I was pleased. Our visit was going well -- until dinner.

"When do we see Papa?" William asked. "You said we would see him."

The question startled me, but I should have expected it. "It's difficult to tell when he will arrive."

"When will we see him?" Tom asked, repeating William's question.

I hesitated. "I don't know. He could show up at any time."

"We want to see him. Are you sure he lives here?"

"Yes. He lives here but he is away a lot."

"Is he famous? Grammach says everybody knows him."

"Your Papa is famous. He has done a lot of wonderful things."

"Like what?"

"He's an inventor. He makes things like light bulbs and phonographs. You have those at Grammach's house."

"Do you have them here?" William asked.

"Sure. Let me show you."

It was getting dark. I turned on a light. The children had never seen multiple electric lights inside a house. "Grammach only has one of these." They were awed and both of them examined each closely. They each turned them off and on a few times.

"How does it do that?"

"I don't know," I said. "You'll have to ask your Papa."

Both of them looked at me and asked at the same time, "Yes. I want to ask him."

We then played the phonograph.

"Grammach has one of these too but she never uses it."

"Where does the music come from?"

I showed them the cylindrical records.

"The music is inside that?"

"Yes," I said cautiously. "It's recorded on the outside of the cylinder."

Obviously they didn't understand and neither did I!

"I really don't know how it works," I admitted to them.

"It must be magic," Tom pronounced.

"Does Papa do magic?" Will asked.

I thought about that. "Some people think he does."

And so the visit went. Miss McWilliams unpacked the boy's suitcases and she laid out their night clothes. The boys went to bed without any cajoling. I was pleased. They were well behaved and polite.

"Will you read us a story?" They asked after I had tucked them into bed.

I looked at Miss McWilliams. "I hope you don't mind my usurping your job. It's just that I'm really enjoying them."

"Oh, surely that's fine, Miss Mina. I'll just go to my room. Call me when you're finished."

I browsed my book collection on the shelf. Did I have something they'd be interested in? I had a lot of girl's books, *Alice's Adventures in Wonderland, Little Women, The Blue Fairy Book*. But then I saw *The Merry Adventures of Robin Hood*.

"Oh, good. Do you know about Robin Hood?"

"Robin Hood?"

So I read to them. I sat on one of their beds and they cuddled close to me. It had been a long day. They were soon asleep. I gave them a lingering look as I stood at the door. I really enjoyed them. I then slipped out, tapped on Miss McWilliam's door, and went downstairs.

Mr. Edison didn't get home until after I had gone to bed. I told him about my day and how much I had enjoyed the boys and how they looked forward to meeting him.

"I want you to see your boys. They are going to be here for as long as it takes."

Before I finished talking he had fallen asleep.

He was gone in the morning before any of us were awake.

I was irritated. I wasn't asking much. He knew how much I want them to see him.

For the next several days the boys and I went on rides through the countryside in the big open carriage with Scarth driving. We all enjoyed it including Miss McWilliams. We had picnics in open fields beside trickling streams. We chased butterflies.

As the days went by, there was no sign of my husband. The last word I had, he was "traveling."

My mission was *not* accomplished. After a week, I took the boys back to Grammach. Naturally they were disappointed at not seeing their Papa, but I promised them another visit.

After listening to what amounted to "I told you so," from Mrs. Stilwell, we settled down to some meaningful conversation. I told her my plan was to have the boys live with us at Glenmont full time. When that would be I did not know.

She agreed the plan might work best for her as well. She was in her late seventies and was ready to rest a bit and maybe move in with her daughter Alice Holzer on the farm.

Factory consolidation

Mr. Edison had begun hearing stories of employee dissention while we were in Florida. But he ignored the warnings as he was so wrapped up in his activities at Seminole Lodge. But when he returned he had to face these unpleasant tasks. He was fed up with the threats of unionization and touchy employees as he attempted to deal with them. He decided it was time to move his businesses out of the New York City area. He began the difficult task of consolidating his factories and moving them to Schenectady, New York, and taking with him some two hundred employees willing to make the move.

At the same time, he moved his personal laboratory out of the city to East Newark, N.J., not far from Glenmont. But this was only a temporary move. He had grand plans for building his new laboratory -- ten times the size of his previous lab. It would be located in West Orange, within sight of Glenmont -- a half-mile walk. This would become known as the first centralized site in the world for organized industrial research.[46]

Mr. Edison described this project in his 1886 Notebooks:

I will have the best equipped & largest Laboratory extant, and the facilities incomparably superior to any other for rapid & cheap development of an invention & working it up into Commercial shape with models patterns & special machinery. In fact there is no similar institution in Existence. We do our own castings forgings Can build anything from a lady's watch to a Locomotive . . . Inventions that formerly took months & cost large sums can now be done 2 or 3 days with very small expense, as I shall carry a stock of almost every conceivable material.[47]

Christmas at Glenmont

I fulfilled my promise to myself in several ways. I held my first family Christmas at Glenmont and, in addition to the Miller families, I invited Grammach, Tom and William and Miss McWilliams, to be with us. It was thrilling to have my own tree set up in our foyer, draped with Mr. Edison's red, white and blue Christmas lights. I thought the tree was as spectacular as it had been the previous year at my childhood home.

Despite all the other "firsts" taking place in my new home, my focus was Mr. Edison's children. It was most important to me develop a relationship with them now that I was their step-mother and to get their father involved.

Marion and her brothers were together for the first time since our wedding the previous February and only the second time since their mother had died. I was curious to see how they interacted. I had not yet told Marion that I planned to have the boys move in with us. I had decided to watch what happened between them during the holidays.

Decorating the tree together was the first test. Marion, three years older than Tom, and already a teenager with far more worldly experience and time with their father, took a superior view of herself. She was taller than her brothers and she let them know through her actions that she was the favored one.

Tom and William were intimidated by Marion and were in awe of their father whose reputation hung over them like an unknowable god.

Marion felt she had to tell both boys how and where to hang each tree ornament. This became so overbearing the boys wanted to quit until I moved them to the opposite side of the tree. And even then Marion wanted to go with us and "help."

It was tricky for me. I wanted them to get along. Yet I didn't want Marion to fall into a snit and stomp out of the room.

"Marion," I finally said. "Each of you hang your own ornaments. The boys are doing a good job by themselves."

This worked especially well when Miss McWilliams and I hung ornaments between the children.

And then there was Mr. Edison. It took some effort to coax him into the Christmas spirit. It was obvious he was uncomfortable amid the children and women. I knew he wished he was in the laboratory with his men, but he knew most of his men were at home with their families on this special day.

He grumbled at the presence of Mrs. Stilwell, but I reminded him that it was my place to manage our domestic life and Christmas was a major part of that.

"None of this grouchiness, Dearie," I said, pressing close to him. "I want a happy family."

He weakened. "What? Me grouchy? Since when?" And then he laughed.

He relented and Christmas was saved. I asked him to give Tom and William a chance at family happiness that had been missing in their lives since before their mother became sick. I said I loved them and I hoped he did also. It took some subtle maneuvers, but Mr. Edison did discovered the boys were now be of an age where he could enjoy them -- at least through Christmas.

He spent some time with them at a mechanical project his men had created in their spare time. It was a box of left-over parts from his laboratory -- a well-planned miscellany of strips of light-weight metal along with nuts and bolts. He explained to his sons that the box contained the makings of a simple tower. He showed them a detailed drawing of what it should look like when completed. The goal was to follow directions and at the same time learn how to use nuts and bolts.

The boys were very shy in their father's presence. Marion sat next to her father and observed. This may have been the first time in their lives he had actually sat down with them and tried to communicate.

Tom asked a question, but it was obvious his father didn't hear him. Marion intervened by repeating the question, but Papa showed little interest.

"Here are the parts," Mr. Edison said. "And here is the drawing of what it looks like. See if you can put it together."

"I'll help them," Marion said.

"No you won't. You come with me."

He left the room with Marion happily tagging after him.

Anxious to please their Papa, they set to work as I watched over them. They had some problems, but I could see where they had gone wrong and pointed it out. After a few tries, and a mild temper tantrum, they completed the tower.

Mr. Edison returned, looked at the tower and beamed. "Good work, boys."

But then William, in all innocence, looked up at Papa and said loudly, "Mama helped us."

My husband looked at me, said nothing, shook his head, and walked out of the room again. I had not been helpful. Mr. Edison gave the boys no credit.

I watched the children from a distance as they mixed with each other. Tom and William chose to play with the young Miller boys rather than their sister. Marion was with my younger sisters showing each other the clothing each had received as presents.

For the very first time I felt like a mother. I now had three children I had to raise properly. I was very happy.

My father and mother were quiet, content to sit and watch the activity. Sister Jennie I think was envious of my new station in life. She found several things she could criticize as I gave my family their first house tour.

Mr. Edison put up a good front through dinner. I sat beside him and coded what was necessary, but then the commotion became too much. He disappeared to his study. He understood little in the chaos of family chatter.

Then it hit me. It suddenly occurred to me why he often said he never got along well with young children. He simply could not understand what they were saying. Their voices were high pitched and they talked rapidly. Now, with that realization, it all began to make sense.

When all was quiet that evening, I went to him in his study and brought up the subject of children and their voices.

He looked at me sadly. "You are right on Billie. I just cannot understand the younger ones. Marion I can understand. She speaks slowly and her tonal quality is similar to yours. If those boys are going to be around here permanently, you're going to have to train them how to talk so I can understand."

"I'll do my best," I said. "It's time they went to school. That will help them greatly, mixing with other children and interacting with the teachers. We have a very good private school right here in West Orange."

Christmas was over. A new year had started. I enrolled the boys in the Dearborn-Morgan School.

Chapter Four

1887

Devotion to work

Mr. Edison had been working very hard, traveling frequently between New York, Schenectady and the Newark laboratory ever since we returned from our honeymoon, nearly a year ago. He was away for days and weeks at a time. Those times he did come home, he was totally exhausted and went to bed. Otherwise, I saw him in the laboratory when he asked me to precisely record experiments of how long various coated lamp filaments burned. Being needed and being by his side pleased me despite it being tedious. But it also took me away from my children and my domestic responsibilities.

In any case my work with him didn't last long. Mr. Edison was knocked down in the first days of January by what the doctors described as pleurisy or pneumonia. His sickness was very frightening and took its toll on me as well. He had been working far took hard. At times we thought he was near death. It dragged on until he was finally able to sit up in bed at the end of January and then he insisted on managing some of his affairs with visits from Ezra and other managers.

This was the time that I came to the full realization of my husband's complete devotion to work. I felt very much alone, even in the midst of all the activity. I sought comfort from mother who wrote, "The first year after being married everything is so different, with so many things to learn and to do. But after a little you will learn that things will become easier and not to worry. You will be better all around, both for yourself and family and friends. In every way you will be happy and contented."

Thank you, Mother.

Troubles with Marion

During Mr. Edison's sickness I was having trouble with Marion again. She was now fourteen. Thankfully, Tom and William, who began their permanent life with us directly after Christmas, were no trouble at all. But Marion's resentment of me, and now her brothers, seemed to be growing. Mother suggested small talk with her, to ask how she liked her tutor and if there was there anything she wanted from me.

I found Marion in our study, reading a book at her father's desk. I went over to her and pulled up a chair beside her. "Can we talk?" I asked.

She slammed her book shut and looked at me. "About what?" she spit out.

"About us. About why I can't make you happy."

There was a pause. "Because I don't like you."

I leaned forward and tried to touch her arm, but she yanked it away. "Can you tell me why you don't like me?" I said calmly.

"You don't belong in my family. You think you're my mother and you aren't. My mother is *dead*," she emphasized.

I spoke softly. "I will never replace your mother, Marion. I'm not trying to replace your mother. I am your father's new wife. I love your father and I'm trying to love you. I'm sorry I never knew your mother. She must have been a wonderful woman. I'm sure you were very close to her and loved her very much."

"I did and I still do. I will always love my mother."

"That's wonderful!" I said cheerfully. "You should. But can't you just *like* me? Sometimes I think you don't like me at all."

"I don't want you here. If you weren't here, I would see Papa more."

"What do you mean?" I acted surprised, but I knew she believed I was the reason she rarely saw her father. "I don't see your father very often either. He is very busy."

"Before you came I saw father all the time."

I countered with, "Before *I came* I saw your father all the time also."

Her face turned to a pout.

"How about your brothers? I brought them to Glenmont so they could see their Papa more often, but that's not happening. They want to see their father as much as you do."

"They're too young. They don't know Papa like I do."

"Why do you think that?"

"Because I'm Papa's favorite."

I continued. "I wish I could see your father much more too, Marion. But I have accepted the fact that he has an important job to do and that job keeps him away from us a lot of the time."

Marion turned away from me. "If you weren't here, I would see my father a lot. He loves me and misses me, but he won't come home because you're here."

I was deeply saddened. "I'm sorry you think that way, Marion. Don't you think I miss him as much as you?"

She jumped up from her chair. "No. You can't miss him as much as I do." She left the room.

In desperation, I spoke with Mr. Edison about how Marion resented me and said she didn't like me.

"Dot will be very much influenced by you," he said. "No doubt she sees your feelings about her. You must win her or else it will not be what I hope and desire."

That counsel simply put more pressure on me. He was not going to speak to Marion about it. In essence he was saying it was up to me to work it out with her. He reminded me often that he wanted nothing to do with domestic problems. Apparently Marion was a domestic problem.

On top of all this, because of Mr. Edison's sickness I had to decline the invitation to my brother Robert's wedding to Louise Igoe. I had met her at the Gilliland's two years earlier. Miss Igoe was the one Marion wanted as her stepmother because she was blonde like her mother, whereas I was a brunette.

Disagreement on phonograph use

A certain relief came by mid-February, near our first anniversary. Mr. Edison was finally on his feet although not fully recovered. Amazingly, he had followed doctor's orders. We left for sunny, warm Fort Myers.

There was an army of us, Mr. Edison and me, Marion and the boys, Miss McWilliams, the Gillilands plus our respective help. We arrived at Seminole Lodge on February 19 aboard the steamer *Alice Howard*. This was front-page headline news for the Fort Myers *Press*. The paper followed every detail of the coming and going of my inventor husband.

Indeed the hamlet of Fort Myers was benefitting in many ways from its new residents, not the least of which was the Long-Legged Mary Anne dynamo,[48] a generator that promised to electrify the town.

Mr. Edison was still not feeling his best. Recovery was slow. Our friend Ezra took charge of supervising the completion of the small laboratory building. He also held back the wave of reporters anxious to see Mr. Edison, having heard that he was a physical wreck or worse.

Our first wedding anniversary slipped by with hardly a mention.

I recall now that it was during this trip in that Ezra expressed his wish to resume work at improving Mr. Edison's primitive tin-foil[49] phonograph, also known as "The Talking Machine."

"I think we have to get moving at improving your phonograph, Tom. I see that the Victor machine and Bell's gramophone are catching up with us. Both men are pursuing the entertainment market which I think could result in big sales for us."

"I'm not yet convinced about the entertainment market, Ezra. I think my original idea of businesses using it as a serious recording device -- for dictation and court cases -- is a big market. Just think how many businesses there are out there. They could all use it."

"I agree that could be a big market, but not as big as the entertainment market. If you think there are a lot of businesses, think again how many more *families* there are that could buy it. There are millions of families that would love to listen to the music we've been experimenting with."

"Maybe, Ezra. Maybe. But I'm not yet ready to make the improvements you want."

"Couldn't we pursue the entertainment line in addition to the business line?"

"That would involve many more engineers than I can afford to move from other activities. I can't see it."

"What if Victor surpasses us in the meantime?"

"Damn it, Ezra! Not now. Drop it."

Ezra was totally frustrated. He could see clearly that the future of the phonograph was for family entertainment. He foresaw the promise of vast profits -- if they could keep ahead of Victor, Bell and other companies. I secretly agreed with Ezra. To be able to listen to opera, piano or jazz music in my own parlor would be wonderful entertainment. But I now had my own piano here in Florida and I could entertain myself and anyone within earshot. We now were able to continue the children's piano lessons under the talented Miss McWilliams. But recorded professional music would be a welcome relief from us novices. I didn't understand Mr. Edison's reluctance.

My parents arrived just after Mr. Edison was finally up and at it again – the master of his ship. We all went out on his new yacht, the *Lillian,* a tribute, of course, to Lillian Gilliland whom he so admired. Lillian was flattered, of course. With its captain and crew motoring up the Caloosahatchie with flags flying, Mr. Edison was on the bow dressed in his usual dark suit, white shirt, red neckerchief and sporty straw hat. He even had a tan from his hours in the sun recuperating. He looked wonderful. He waved his hat and the crowds along the riverbanks gave him rousing cheers. I was so proud of him. Tom and William, proudly dressed in sailor outfits, stood close by and imitated their hero father, sailor hats in hand, waving to the people.

I told mother that I was happier this February than I was a year ago, although I still felt I did not have Mr. Edison's full affections. But father told me Mr. Edison seemed just as he did a year ago. He said Mr. Edison "seemed kind and affectionate in all his ways and true to me and true to what he appears to be."

It appeared Mr. Edison didn't need the affection I needed. Was I asking too much of my husband? Mother didn't have this problem with father. Father made it a point to be home most nights, and every weekend. I admitted I was spoiled and I knew I had to correct that.

In early May, just before we left for home, I thought I was pregnant. I was ecstatic. We announced my "expectation" to our friends and, unfortunately, the press heard about it as well. The coverage was wide and the creative non-facts would have been funny if it hadn't been such a stupid mistake. Alas, a month later I was downcast and embarrassed. The news was as false as the pregnancy. Discussing this later, we decided, that in the excitement of *wanting* to be pregnant, I somehow misjudged. I began to worry that I might not be able to become pregnant. Mr. Edison wanted children by me. What if I couldn't deliver? I was comforted when I was told premature announcements are not unusual among newly weds.

But I had already written Jennie and she counseled me to be sure to tell Marion the news and keep her in on what was happening so as to gain her friendship.

At the end of our first month in Fort Myers, Charles Batchelor arrived to help set up the new Florida laboratory and to begin drawing up plans for the big new laboratory at home. During this time, Mr. Edison developed an abscess below his right ear that required an operation. The poor dear. He was in agony, as was I. And then in early April he developed another abscess that led to infection, a fever and the inflammation of his skin. It was another horrid event that greatly troubled all of us. Then, miraculously, it all went away.

Lillian, Marion, the boys, my mother and I left for home together in May. In the company of my matchmaker, I am pleased to say, this put Marion in a frame of mind in which we got along very well for the entire trip. I saw another side of Marion of which I had been unaware. She was a very bright girl, quick of mind and full of ideas and dreams. She looked forward to returning to her school in the city and seeing her friends.

My father and Ezra stayed at the lodge with Mr. Edison and the other men. Father told me this would give him time to get to know my husband better. As it turned out, they all went hunting as well as fishing and boating on the *Lillian*. When not out and about, he said they talked and read their books.

Father later told me his visit increased his estimation of my husband and he assured me of Mr. Edison's generous feelings toward me. He said Mr. Edison was very pleased with my sense of economy at Glenmont and of my great desire to make the home a place for entertainment instead of my "running about," whatever that meant.

This heartened me. But at home, I was concerned that Mr. Edison, in Florida, was not answering my letters. Marion was concerned as well about the silence from the South. I was pleased when she showed me the letter she had written to him which said, in essence, "If you don't write soon you will surely have a cyclone at home."

Finally, my husband returned to Glenmont. Little did I know it was to be our last visit to Fort Myers for fourteen years.

Educating the children

Over the next several months Tom and William were growing rapidly and enjoying their life at Glenmont. We liked each other. We got along just fine. Mr. Edison attempted to converse with them at the dinner table. Becoming more accustomed to being in Papa's presence, they were gradually easing out of their bashfulness and this brought out their ability to speak louder and more clearly. They were still adjusting to school but not performing as well as we thought they should. He quizzed them at meals and gave them pages of reading assignments in the encyclopedia. Miss McWilliams also spent time tutoring the boys on the subjects that troubled them at school. I read with them before bedtime and they both cuddled next to me which I enjoyed immensely.

Mr. Edison's greatest desire for his sons was have them follow in his footsteps, to have them be like him, to be mechanical and to understand how things worked. The boys were now eleven and nine. They had finally satisfied their father at building, on their own, the metal tower he had given them at Christmas. Now he went on to the next stage. He gave them mechanical things to experiment with, such as wind-up alarm clocks. He would sit cross-legged on the floor with them and slowly disassemble one, explaining what he was doing and why the clock worked the way it did. He then reassembled the clock and handed it to one of them to repeat what he had just done. But William had lost his attention and turned to a wooden train he enjoyed pushing around the room. This angered his father who told him the train was a child's toy and yanked it away. William objected, of course, and cried.

In time, and many tries and failures at reassembling clocks, and with less and less of Papa's patience, he gave up in disgust on both his "mechanical education" for the boys and, finally, the boys themselves.

On the other hand, Mr. Edison loved jokes and was often full of innocent mischief. But on the rare occasions when he played with the children the mischief bordered on cruelty. In one example he had a glass duck that was filled with water. He asked young Tom to blow through a hole at the end of it. He did and water spurted out into his face and eyes. Mr. Edison rolled on the floor in laughter telling Tom that, if he had examined it first, he would have seen what was going to happen.

Another of Mr. Edison's jokes took place was when I gave Marion a birthday party at Glenmont with a lot of her friends. Outside it was already a dark, a late afternoon in February. All the lights in the house were on for the event. Mr. Edison found time to drop in for an appearance but then exited and went down cellar where he turned a switch and all the lights went out. We were suddenly in the pitch dark. Some of the girls screamed in fright. But then the lights returned and Mr. Edison reappeared with a big grin. No one appreciated his "humor."

Since Tom's countenance was nearly identical to his father's, Mr. Edison believed his son should be like him in abilities also. But the poor boy was delicate and sickly and a major disappointment to him.

Poor Tom. His greatest talent was for getting into trouble, which was also one of his father's talents at the same age. Family lore has it that, one time when Tom was six and living in Menlo Park, he wanted to visit his father's machine shop.

He was fascinated by the roaring engines and the myriad of endless belts. Afraid Tom would hurt himself or get caught up in the dangerous belts, Mr. Edison ordered him to leave. But sometime later he saw Tom was still in the room. Furious for disobeying him, Mr. Edison went to his newly installed telephone and called his wife, Mary, saying that she should give him a good spanking. As soon as Tom came through the front gate Mary caught him and gave him a switching. Tom was more puzzled than hurt and asked her how she knew he had disobeyed.

His children just didn't understand their father, and I might say, vice versa. He was baffling. He was never a warm and loving parent. The only time he had held them was when they were infants. Mr. Edison believed it wasn't manly for him to hug his sons, no matter how they craved it from him. That was the woman's job.

During his marriage to Mary, as Mr. Edison's affluence increased and circumstances changed, he moved his family to the Gramercy Park neighborhood in Manhattan. He placed Marion in fine private day school that put her in contact with other upper-middle-class children. After her mother died, the maternal-starved Marion was suddenly spending a lot of time with her father.

The boys had no such educational exposure. They languished at home with their mother and under the care of a part-time governess or with their grandmother Stilwell. Rarely did they see their father.

The loss of her mother coupled with our marriage, brought great change for Marion. She wanted most to continue to be near her father who she now believed was more interested in his new wife. This turned her against me. She no longer wanted to go to school. She wanted to stay home where she was most likely to be near her father. But her father was rarely at home.

After we returned from Florida, we tried tutoring Marion at Glenmont with Miss McWilliams, but Marion was not cooperative. It was a tough time for her and for me. I had a full plate. I was adapting as a wife as I also tried to create our new household at Glenmont. As much as I tried, Marion attempted to undermine me in the absence of Mr. Edison.

We finally sent her away to Bradford Academy, a private residential school for girls in Bradford, Massachusetts. It had a superior reputation for preparing students for college. Here she initially enjoyed the school and did well in the arts, history, arithmetic and Bible study. But she also took science classes, a study for which the academy was best known and which Mr. Edison advocated. To her father's dismay, she did poorly in the sciences.

At the same time, Tom and Will, now thirteen and eleven, began their third year at the local Dearborn-Morgan School. This was co-educational with the goal of preparing the students for business or college. The boys had not been doing well in their academics. With Mr. Edison's encouragement and his wish to have them be exposed to sophistication they sorely lacked, we sent them to St. Paul's School in Concord, New Hampshire, known as one of the best preparatory schools in the country.

Formal education had always been contrary to Mr. Edison's preaching. But now he admitted his homeschooling methods were a total failure. His status in the world had greatly changed. He was a rich man. He now wanted to be an equal to the great, educated men of his day. These men were sending their children to the best schools to prepare them for the lives their fathers has created for themselves. But like many of his contemporaries, he left his children's education and domestic duties to his wife. That left it to me to make the education decisions. I truly felt my stepchildren would eventually go on to Yale or another Ivy-League school or, as Mr. Edison said, he preferred MIT or Cornell for an engineering education.

But, in the meantime, things were not working out for me. Marion returned home from Bradford Academy and continued to be a pest.

The phonograph deal with Ezra

For most of 1887 I was able to watch from my Glenmont veranda the progress of Mr. Edison's impressive new laboratory as it rose from his industrial acres at the foot of the hill. He described his plan with considerable pride saying it would be ten times larger than the Menlo Park laboratory with an equally larger staff. His goal, he said, was to produce ten times the inventions with ten times the genius. His expection was that the result would be ten times the number of brilliant inventions.

Mr. Edison finally stirred himself to excitement at having his men return to making further improvements to his favorite creation -- the phonograph, first conceived ten years earlier as "The Talking Machine." Seeing struggles of competition arising, he said he wanted to make his phonograph "a better and cheaper machine" than both Alexander Graham Bell's gramophone and Victor's machine.

"I have reluctantly named Ezra Gilliland my exclusive agent to sell the phonograph," Mr. Edison told me.

"'Reluctantly?'" I asked.

"Ezra is already a very rich man, thanks to our cooperative pursuits. But he always wants more. Sometimes I suspect him of opportunism."

"Why shouldn't he always want more? Don't you?"

"Billie. I'm different. I only want to make a better phonograph. Making money for its own sake doesn't interest me. But the more money I do make, the more capital I will have to invest in research. That has always been my sole interest. Research is what it's all about."

"Then it's endless, isn't it, Dearie? There's no end to your pursuits. There are always more things to chase after."

"Of course. That's the answer to building civilization. Chasing dreams. Competition. Improvements. Building something better than the next person. Once perfected, my phonograph will be far better than Bell's. Ezra knows my machine better than anyone. Thus, my rationale for giving him this opportunity."

Chapter Five

1888

Pregnancy

By early 1888 I *knew* I was pregnant. It was obvious. I felt wonderful. I was finally going to be a mother. The doctor set the date for May. I could now announce it to the family.

Creating my legacy

Father counseled me on my husband's work habits in a letter dated March 22. He "must not work nights any longer," he wrote in response to my complaint about the days, nights, and weeks that Mr. Edison was away from home. This counseling came at the peak of Mr. Edison's battles with Alexander Bell over the phonograph. But it also happened during the final three months of my genuine pregnancy.

Father continued. "Working nights will most surely break him down. It's very easy for me to prescribe to others when I speak from experience, but it is much harder for others to accept and act upon another's advice."

My sister Mary Emily's advice was more to the point. "I hope you make it interesting for him by using your charms to make him want to stay home."

So much for this advice, I thought. It's easier said than done. I now thought of his first wife, Mary, and why grandmother Stilwell was so upset at our first meeting. It appeared to me, the great man simply lost interest in Mary who was so wanting, so insecure, so lacking in education. And his same attitude toward his two young boys who were unable to perform to his standards. It was disgraceful. They were forever asking about their father who was never here for them, never did anything for them, and who it seems did not love them.

I wondered if my husband perceived me as he did Mary?

But I'm not like Mary and I don't think Mr. Edison will ever change his work habits. It is I who have to stop complaining and and build my own life. I must be able to stand on my own and accept the hours it takes my husband to be the great inventor -- the way the rest of the world sees him.

I must create my own legacy.

Competition with Alexander Bell

Mr. Edison admitted he was jolted into action to improve his phonograph after two stunning events occurred. He learned that Alexander Bell had, not only been working at perfecting *my husband's* primitive tin-foil phonograph, but he had also applied for a *patent* on it, naming the improved machine a "gramophone." Bell's patent was actually awarded. Bell then had the gall to approach Mr. Edison privately and suggest they work *together* to improve the machine further and promote it. Bell acknowledged that my husband was the true inventor of the "talking machine" but he said that together they could both gain by sharing costs of all experimental work and raise capital together to exploit it.

"Our two big names together," Bell said, "will have more impact than either one of us."

As reasonable as the proposal might seem to outsiders, Edison was irate over Bell's confiscation of his ideas.

"No way will I work with him. This is *my* baby. That Bell and his men are a bunch of pirates!"

The second event was a letter from a businessman in Boston who wanted to miniaturize Edison's phonograph and use it to manufacture talking dolls.

Finally, something clicked in Mr. Edison's head.

"I deplore having to admit it, Billie, But perhaps Ezra's idea of selling the phonograph as an entertainment device is worth considering afterall."

Within weeks he set up a new corporation called Edison Phonograph Company and formally announced he was abandoning the old phonograph company of ten years earlier.

He then set his laboratory men to work full speed to improve his phonograph, telling them to use their greatest efforts to succeed and the money will soon flow -- presumably the profits would "flow" to the workers themselves.

Throughout this stressful period in Mr. Edison's life I asked myself, how does a deaf man create a talking machine? How can he determine if his machine replicates the subtle sounds of a soprano's aria or the violin's extreme ranges?

Mr. Edison was well aware of his hearing problem but he was also well aware that he never let any problem interfere with his goal. He could hear nothing with his left ear, so to hear correctly, he placed his right ear in contact with either the phonograph horn or the phonograph itself. His other method was to actually bite on the instrument so as to allow the sound vibrations to enter into the hearing nerves of his head. But he also had backup listening options -- Ezra, Batchelor and I were often recruited as Mr. Edison's ears.

Ezra now worked closely with Mr. Edison on phonograph experiments to improve it. He reassured my husband the new phonograph would be a splendid popular success someday.

As a result, Mr. Edison appointed his long-time and trusted friend as the reorganized phonograph company's general sales agent. He and Ezra signed a contract to this effect and it was executed by John Tomlinson, a smart young patent attorney and friend of Ezra's.

By early 1888, Mr. Edison believed the phonograph had been improved enough to raise capital and announce the new and improved machine to the world. He invited prospective financiers to his Glenmont library for a demonstration. He began by talking into the machine, recording his grand plans for its business prospects. But, when he tried to play back his speech, the eager men heard nothing but a scratching hiss. Mr. Edison was totally puzzled. He examined the machine to find the problem. Time went by as he tried to fix it. The money men slowly departed leaving behind a bewildered Mr. Edison. It was a disaster. It was very embarrassing.

He called together his veteran workers and told them that they were to stay on the job at the laboratory and work with him day and night until the phonograph was perfected to his standards. Somehow the news of this reached the press. This was an unheard of effort in West Orange. The doors were locked, keeping out the reporters as well as me. The frenzy began. They worked continuously for five days and nights before the goal was reached. A photograph of Mr. Edison at five in the morning of June 16, 1888 showed him stretched across a table listening through earphones to his completed phonograph. He looked exhausted as his arm held up his head. His hair and clothing were in total disarray. He looked like a soldier who had just been through a mighty battle. The photo was made into a painting that was reproduced and sent out as an advertisement for the Edison Phonograph Company. This episode precisely illustrated my inventor's brilliance at self-promotion and creating myths about himself all of which eventually generated sales and admiration.

In the weeks following, Mr. Edison began making recordings of famous artists. Beethoven's and Caruso's works were his favorites.

This was also the time that the famous African explorer Henry M. Stanley visited Glenmont and the new lab. Mr. Stanley was invited to speak into the machine. When he heard his voice played back, like everyone else, he was amazed. At dinner with us that evening it was obvious that the importance of the phonograph was still on Stanley's mind.

He asked, "If there were any person throughout history that you would like to have recorded, just whom would you choose?"

Mr. Edison immediately answered. "Napoleon."

Stanley replied that he would choose the voice of the Saviour.

In response, Mr. Edison laughed and said, "You know, I do like a hustler! That would really sell records."

All appeared well to Edison as plans for his favorite invention came together. What he *didn't know* was his best friend Ezra was going to take advantage of Mr. Edison's trust.

Ezra's disastrous alliance

Perhaps the most thunderous and emotionally draining event of our early marriage, was Ezra's disastrous alliance with Lippincott.

Jesse H. Lippincott,[50] was a venture capitalist who made his fortune in Pittsburgh producing glass tumblers at an output of some seventy-five thousand a week. In the spring of 1888, Lippincott foresaw an opportunity to make another fortune in the new technology by pitting Mr. Edison's phonograph against against Bell's gramophone. He offered each inventor $500,000 for the rights to produce their machines. He then sat down with Ezra and Tomlinson and discussed *secretly* the terms of the deal that included buying out the Edison Phonograph Company as well as Ezra's separate interests that Mr. Edison had signed over to him. In addition to $500,000, Mr. Edison would be given a five percent royalty on every machine sold and he would be expected to continue to improve the phonograph but would no longer have to worry about sales and distribution. The men believed Mr. Edison would like the deal because his dream machine would surely outsell Bell's.

Tomlinson took the proposal to Mr. Edison and urged him to accept the deal. But Mr. Edison was not told that an identical proposal had been presented to Bell. Meanwhile the Bell negotiators wanted to modify the deal that would take away Mr. Edison's exclusive manufacturing rights and royalties.

Lippincott took the revised terms to Mr. Edison who was unaware of Ezra's and Tomlison's separate and secret involvement with Lippincott that included cash to the pair of $250,000 plus stock options. But when Lippincott immediately ran into a cash-flow problem and was unable to make the promised payments, Mr. Edison challenged Lippincott who was forced to reveal the secret benefits promised to Ezra and Tomlinson.

The unusual scheme crashed and Mr. Edison was enraged. *His trusted friend of many years had tried to sell him out behind his back.* For the next twenty years he actively went after Ezra and Tomlinson with expensive fraud litigation. It was a long, emotional disillusionment for my husband.

As for Ezra, he had fallen for the lure of immediate financial gratification and had not considered my husband's shrewdness and deep attachment to his invention.

For me and for his daughter Marion, we saw that Mr. Edison was deeply bruised. His hurt filled Glenmont with a dark, impenetrable cloud for months.

"I loved Ezra as the best and most trusted friend I ever had," my Dearie mourned. "I can't believe he fell for this scheme -- a scheme for money he didn't need, but more importantly, against my friendship -- the likes of which he will never find again."

He paced the floor, shaking his head in dejection.

"I will never trust anyone again," he vowed.

Mr. Edison never recovered from this distrust, with one exception -- Henry Ford.

Madeleine enters my world

Anticipating my first child, Miss McWilliams decided it was time to retire. She said she was too old to work full time and to cope with another infant.

I hired a new governess. Her name was Lucy Bogue. She was middle-aged and an experienced midwife. Although she had never married, she had delivered countless babies and had cared for and educated young children. She would be our full-time, live-in governess.

All of my hires had been thoroughly screened. They knew the advantages and disadvantages of working in an Edison household. They knew that privacy was of utmost importance and they would never, ever communicate with the diligent, persistent press.

In the midst of all the phonograph upheaval, on May 31, my lovely first child and daughter, Madeleine Edison, came into this world. Mr. Edison interrupted his hectic schedule and came to my side during the birth in our bedroom. He then spent about an hour with me after the initial excitement subsided.

I insisted he take and hold the baby which he did after minimal resistance. Something wonderful happened after a few moments. He rocked Madeleine gently for about fifteen minutes and even smiled at her before handing her back. I believed I saw an attachment, a bond taking place between them. Then again it may have been my wishful thinking. A new mother so much wants her husband to connect with their child.

Then he excused himself and rushed back to the laboratory. It was only a few days later that he and his men went into their five-day-night session on the phonograph.

The poor man was terribly burdened with problems of every sort. He was working far too many hours and he wasn't eating properly. Food sent to him was often left on the tray. For the phonograph lockdown, I arranged for a caterer to provide a continuous day and night, food and drink, convoy. They might be able to survive without much sleep, but without good food their brains would be unable to function and solve their impossible task.

I was now a mother. I was excited. I held Madeleine for several hours and memorized her features. I held her to my breast where she satisfied her hunger and then fell asleep. I passed her into Lucy's capable hands for the first time and I took a much-needed nap of my own.

Tesla vs. Edison

This was another emotionally draining event for both Mr. Edison and me. Want it or not, he more and more often brought his business problems to me, not for me to supply him with a solution, but for him to bounce off me as he looked for answers. I lent him my ears, glad to have him near me and tried valiantly to understand him, given my lack of education in his technical subjects. But some understanding did come my way.

Nikola Tesla's thinking process was the exact opposite of my husband's -- yet both were brilliant. Mr. Tesla was an Eastern European immigrant who just by chance worked for Mr. Edison as an electrical inventor and scientist for about a year before quitting in 1883. He walked out when he became frustrated with his boss' methods of operation.[51] One of the disagreements between the two men was the best method of generating electricity. Each man rigidly opposed the other and their "A/C-D/C wars" were thoroughly documented in the press at the time.

Mr. Edison had always used direct current, D/C, in his light bulbs, his dynamos and for all of his electrical uses. His generators could only function at direct current low voltages or else potentially a dangerous sparking would occur between the dynamo brushes and the commutator. Most significant and unfortunate, direct current could not be economically transmitted more than a mile or two because excess heat was generated when the voltage was increased to drive it further distances. The excess heat required larger copper wires and heavier insulation and therefore, greater expense and danger. Direct current worked just fine within the area of a city block, in homes and factory buildings large and small, and in other closed systems such as electric railways and freight elevators.

Mr. Tesla developed his theory called "alternating current," A/C. His generators created current that alternated in direction as the dynamo armature turned. There was no sparking. The system was safer than direct current. And, most importantly, A/C could be safely transmitted over high-tension wires for long distances -- hundreds of miles. Mr. Tesla further developed "polyphase" A/C that permitted voltages ten times that of Mr. Edison's.

Tesla gained a major advantage over Mr. Edison in 1888 when he delivered a speech to the American Institute of Electrical Engineers[52] describing his research on his polyphase generator. His speech attracted George Westinghouse, a Pittsburgh railroad entrepreneur, who jumped into the act and supported alternating current. Westinghouse began buying up electrical patents. He hired Tesla as a consultant at $2,000 a month to help him develop a plan to beat Mr. Edison at his own electrical game. Westinghouse saw alternating current as a way to get into the electric business with his own patented system and this resulted in establishing the Westinghouse Electric Company.

The competition between Tesla/Westinghouse and Edison became ugly fodder for the press around the world as each man fought for the hearts and minds of industry. A great deal of money was at stake. The battle of the currents involved heavy investments by American and European countries in one type of current or the other. Those who adopted A/C hoped to see the demise of D/C, and vice versa.

I have to admit my husband was rigid and stubborn in his defense of D/C and refused to submit to the many advantages of A/C.

Mr. Edison would eventually lose the battle.[53]

Chapter Six

1889

Marion and I fight it out

Marion at sixteen was more than a pest. She was rebellious and angry. She decided during Christmas vacation that she was not returning to Bradford Academy. Determined to tell the same directly to her father, she marched down to his laboratory and amongst all the workers she ran to him and put her arms around him.

"Papa! I'm not going back to the Academy. I don't like it there. I want to be here with you."

Mr. Edison was startled. He was deep in discussion with his men over a problem they were having difficulty solving. He spun around and faced Marion, nearly knocking her to the floor as she clung to him. He looked at her blank faced.

"Dot! I don't want to hear it. You get back to the house. I don't want to hear your foolishness. We'll talk about it later. Now go home."

He was harsh. There was no hint of affection. He rejected his daughter who so craved his attention. She returned to the house sobbing. I followed her through the house, pleading with her to talk with me. She ran past me, went to her room and slammed the door.

In the days following, Lucy told me Marion was taking her frustration out on the maids.

"I don't know what to do, Miss Mina. Miss Marion's room is a mess and when Laura tries to pick things up, Miss Marion just messes it up again right in front of her. She even threw things at Laura who said she was going to quit her position. I try to intervene and she screams at me."

It was true. Marion just lounged on her bed and made Laura wait on her hand and foot, literally, making the maid put her stockings and shoes on her feet while she reclined and read her book. I truly believed she was trying to be so horrible that her father would be forced to discipline her. It was obvious she was trying everything to get her father's attention.

I met with Laura, commiserated with her, wiped away her tears, and asked her to keep out of Marion's room for the time being.

Shaking with anger as I heard Marion banging around in her room. I took up my courage, entered her room and faced her, slamming the door behind me. She saw me and froze in place, totally surprised. I grabbed her arm, flung her face down onto her bed, held her down with one hand and spanked her rear end with several good whacks and then jerked her to her feet again. It was automatic. I lost my control. I had never hit any child.

She didn't cry. She looked at me with a hatred I could feel.

Still seething, I yelled, "You act like a child, you will be treated like a child from now on. And, if that doesn't work, there are places that naughty girls can be sent -- and I mean it!"

She turned, went to her bed and buried her face in the pillow.

I sat on the edge of her bed and waited for what might happen next. Time passed. I cooled down. I continued.

"I love you, Marion. Your Papa loves you, but your foolishness will no longer be tolorated in this house. I want to see you grow up. Your Papa wants to see you grow up."

I then took a chance and went a step further. "Now, to show us that you are grown up, I want you to pick up this room the way it should be. I will not allow Laura to do it for you."

There was no response.

I left her room and shut the door wondering what I would do next if she did not follow my instructions.

Two hours later, Marion found me in the library. She stopped short of me and we looked at each other. Her look of hatred had disappeared. She looked at me blank faced and wordlessly.

I held out my arms toward her. She came to me and we hugged silently for a few moments.

"Why doesn't Papa love me?"

"Papa *does* love you, but you have to understand his love. He is not the hugging type. I'm still trying to understand your father's love. He's a man whose mind is always somewhere else. Even when he's with us he's not always with us, if you know what I mean. I find it very difficult."

Marion gently pulled away and looked at me again. Sheepishly she said, "I cleaned my room."

"That calls for a celebration," I said showing my pleasure. "I'd like a dish of ice cream. Let's go downtown and get one. Are you interested?"

She smiled. "Yes. I'd like that."

I called Scarth and he drove us to the pharmacy. We invited Scarth to join us. The three of us sat on stools at the lunch counter.

"How can I help you?" the young man behind the counter said.

"We would like ice cream," Marion said, taking charge.

"You have the choice of ice cream in a dish on on a cone," he said. "We have something new we're are experimenting with." He showed us a cone-shaped waffle.[54] "It's an edible dish you can carry in your hand. It holds a scoop of ice cream on top and you can eat the whole thing. Want to try it?"

"Yes," Marion said immediately.

"Vanilla, chocolate or strawberry?" young lady.

"Strawberry, please."

The man held a cone in his hand and placed the scoop of strawberry into the cone.

I hesitated. "How do you eat it? You don't use a spoon?"

"Nope. You lick it or bite it."

"*Lick* it? That's not very lady-like," I said.

My companions laughed.

"That's what some people say," the man responded. "But it's a fun thing to do on a hot day and a lot of daring people have been trying it." He smiled at his word of challenge.

"Are you going to have one, Scarth?"

"If you do, Madam."

"Come on, Mama," Marion urged, grinning. "Try it. It won't bite. Don't be a fuddy-duddy."

I looked at Marion and smiled.

"OK. Let's have three of them. I don't want to be a fuddy-duddy," I said, with a smirk, looking at Scarth. "I'll have strawberry ice cream also."

"And you, Sir?"

"Strawberry, please."

Marion giggled as the man passed her the first cone. She was happy! I was thrilled.

The man passed the rest of the cones and we took them in our hands, awkwardly. We licked. I felt very conspicuous with my tongue out. Hmm. Interesting.

"You don't have to sit at the counter," the man said. "You can walk around with it. You can go outside and sit on the bench and eat it. Here. Take these napkins."

I hesitated. I was making a spectacle of myself in public sticking my tongue out and licking at the cone like a cow at a salt lick. I hoped I wouldn't see anyone I knew.

"Come on, Mama. Let's go sit on the bench."

Marion saw my embarrassment and I imagined she was taking advantage of it. She had the upper hand now. I couldn't give in. I had to join her fun.

We sat on the bench at the front of the building in public view. I thought, if Mr. Edison could see us now. Pedestrians passed, some looking at us curiously. One well-dressed lady with a companion actually stopped and asked us what we were eating. Marion was quick to answer.

"These are ice cream cones. They sell them right in here," gesturing with her free hand.

"That looks good," she said to her companion. They entered the pharmacy and came out with chocolate cones. They didn't sit, but continued on their way, cone in hand, tongue flashing out and back again.

Another passerby showed his curiosity. "What will they think of next?"

In spite of my self-consciousness, my joy overruled as we sat together. It was one of the most memorable times in my life. Frankly, I was still in disbelief. How long would Marion's pleasantness continue? But now we were having fun and chit-chatting as passersby looked at us and we spoke with strangers. It was a very new experience for me.

Mr. Edison never faced Marion, never asked her what her problem was, never changed in his attitude toward her -- an attitude that might be described as apathetic.

Not long after this, my sister Jennie invited Marion to accompany her on an extended trip to Europe to celebrate her sixteenth birthday on February 18. With Jennie as chaperone they planned to join my other two sisters, Mary and Grace, who were studying in Paris.

"The trip will be character building," Mr. Edison said, confidently.

Edison General Electric is organized

In the middle of Mr. Edison's conflicts with Tesla and Westinghouse over electrical currents, Henry Villard returned to America after three years in his native Germany. Villard was Mr. Edison's most dependable moneyman who excelled at raising millions of investment dollars for my husband's business adventures. Spurring Villard's visit was the fact that George Westinghouse already had more than one thousand working electric power plants across America, each using alternating current!

Villard brought news of an international syndicate that promised to underwrite the consolidation of a number of Edison businesses under the name of Edison General Electric.

In the process, a dozen Edison businesses were merged into a single company that was eventually named General Electric. The new company had a par value in new stock of $3,500,000 when the deal was settled.

When General Electric's value was added to The Edison Illuminating Company (later named Consolidated Edison) and his other smaller companies, their total gross annual sales revenues were more than $7,000,000 with profits of more than $700,000 in 1889!

Mr. Edison came away with 10 percent of the stock of General Electric and sat on the board of directors.

The gallows vs. electricity

The AC/DC battle took an ugly turn when Mr. Edison, in the fall of 1887, became involved in dramatizing the dangers of alternating current for his own benefit. Dr. Alfred Southwick had been appointed to a New York commission to find a more humane method of executing criminals than using the gallows. Dr. Southwick had been a witness to the accidental electrocution of a factory worker. The result, he noticed, was instant death. He contacted Mr. Edison and asked if he would be interested in conducting experiments with animals using electrocution as a quick, painless death. He told my husband, that with his impeccable reputation as an electrician, it would help influence the lawmakers to change the state code.

Mr. Edison responded. "I would prefer an effort to totally abolish capital punishment." But since capital punishment was already recognized by New York State, Edison said, "I agree that it is the duty of the state to adopt the most humane method of disposing of criminals."

Agreeing that electricity would be the most humane method, he suggested alternating current be used because it was "manufactured principally in this country by George Westinghouse." Mr. Edison went on to say there is "practical evidence" that alternating current can cause "instant death," and he gave an example of two men recently killed in New Orleans by this current.

Thus, Mr. Edison became involved in a public debate that was relished by a press that thrived on macabre stories. With the support of Dr. Frederick Peterson, a New York Medico-Legal Society member, a medical team conducted experiments in Mr. Edison's laboratory. Using, in turn, high voltages of alternating and direct current to electrocute dogs, it was determined that alternating current was "beyond all doubt more fatal" than the direct current. Mr. Edison's desired results, of course, was to turn the pubic against the use of alternating current.

But in the end, it was Mr. Westinghouse who won out. He hired a team of inventors who overcame the dangers of alternating current by increasing safety measures and developing motors and meters that better controlled its use.

Mr. Edison eventually gave up the battle of the currents in America while thriving in Europe with direct current. Edison General Electric went on to develop its own method of alternating current that was closely related to the Westinghouse model, and more practical competition began between the two companies.

All winter my forty-two-year-old husband suffered exhaustion again, claiming to be more tired than ever. I tried to get him to rest as I looked after his health. Finally he agreed to a vacation. We were going to Europe *alone* for two months.

Joy of joys, we were traveling together but, alas, he insisted I leave our fourteen-month-old Madeleine at home with Lucy. Mr. Edison would not listen to my pleas to take the baby and Lucy along with us.

"Billie. I sympathize with your maternal propensities, but extensive travel with the young one would not be good for her health."

"Hogwash, Dearie. Babies travel all the time. It's your health I'm worried about, not hers."

"We will be spending a lot of time among the hoity-toity and I don't want you fretting and fidgeting with the babe in your arms."

"Lucy will have her on such occasions. She . . ."

"Billie! *Not* on this trip."

"I disagree with you, Dearie. I must take Madeleine. She is part of our life now. I want us to be close to our children. Lucy will manage the baby just fine and keep her out of your sight, if that's what you want. You won't even notice she is with us.

Mr. Edison grumbled. "Sometimes you try my soul, Billie."

I laughed. "Madeleine will keep me busy while you are talking with your European buddies. You may even find that some of your men friends and their wives enjoy little children. Who could possibly resist our beautiful Madeleine?"

"You have such a way with words, Billie."

I would always want my first born close by me. Yet at the same time I knew I had to devote myself to my husband and take advantage of our rare times together. He needed a rest now after the intense negotiations of the General Electric deal.

We left America in early August and sailed incognito on the French vessel *La Bourgogne* under the name of Mr. & Mrs. Sam Insull, his private secretary's name. His goal was to attend the huge Paris Universal Exposition.

At sea his boyhood returned. He felt carefree after leaving behind the pains of the Gilliland affair and the AC-DC maneuvers with Westinghouse. And he did rest. He walked the deck alone and then sat for hours in a deck chair, wrapped in a blanket against the cold North Atlantic wind and spray. Yet his usual creative instincts never rested. His thoughts meandered as he wondered how long it would take before the wave and tidal power of the sea would be harnessed for electricity.

His travel plans included visiting the recently erected Eiffel Tower and studying the inventive exposition displays of all the 19th Century inventors, including his own, of course.

I couldn't be happier traveling with Lucy and Madeleine. In our two years of marriage I had spent nearly all my time at home as the rest of the exciting world passed me by. I loved Paris.

On our arrival in Le Havre we were met by a local delegation as well as a barrage reporters from all over Europe. So much for incognito! And behind them was a cheering crowd that trailed us to the train station hoping to get a glimpse of my famous man. So much for being alone! In Paris there was an even larger crowd. They even recognized little old me. The press was captivated by the "Wizard's baby." I felt beautiful and happy and so proud to be at the side of my inventor husband.

It was no secret that Mr. Edison was a master at generating public curiosity. Throughout this trip, his men conducted an endless publicity campaign to promote him and the products of his companies. After all, this was the purpose of an exhibition. But there were also news articles about me -- "the lovely young wife, twenty-two years old and in her full beauty." I found myself sharing the acclaim the Parisians showered over us.

Mr. Edison's displays had always taken up the bulk of the available area at past exhibitions. Months earlier, his advance party, led by William Hammer, had set up displays of all his inventions and this covered more than an acre in the Galerie des Machines. They were manned by representatives from each of his European companies and overseen by Mr. Edison's tireless secretary, Alfred Tate.

This was my second major exposition. My first, of course, was in New Orleans where I met Mr. Edison but I am at a loss to recollect any specific displays there. This time everything was different. The massive Galerie was brightly lighted by Mr. Edison's central (D/C) electric station. At its center was an electric sign such as the world had never seen. Its colored lights were arranged to display massive flags of the United States and France. Another display was called "The Fountain of Light." It provided a glimpse into the future uses of Edison electric lighting. Just imagine the wonderment of the visitor who had never seen an electric light array -- never seen anything brighter than a candle or gas lamp? The display was like the rays of the sun broken into a million colorful particles.

Mr. Edison and I were at the leading edge of an ever-growing group on this tour led by Mr. Tate. The details were a blur to me but they came into sharp focus when we arrived at the phonograph displays where visitors were able to listen to twenty-five phonographs speaking in a dozen languages. This was the first time Mr. Edison's "perfected" phonograph was exhibited on the Continent. We were told some 30,000 visitors viewed his display every day, second only in number to visitors at the iconic Eiffel Tower.[55]

I never mentioned it to him, but as Mr. Edison recognized the huge public interest in the phonograph, he certainly must have had twinges of the past when his former best friend Ezra

Gilliland tried, over his bosses blind objections, to get him to promote the machine as an entertainment device.

We attended party after banquet after fete that tended to weary Mr. Edison but which I felt I could endure forever. I often had to cajole and drag him out to these events. He remarked one time as we were returning from a dinner after meeting a barrage of other guests eager to meet him, "Oh they make me sick to my stomach."

I looked at him sharply. "Just *what* do you mean by that remark?"

"I hate the fawning public."

"Are you refering to the men and women who spend their hard-earned money to buy the things you spend most of your life creating? Are you sneering at the people who hold you in very high regard and honor you for your talents and accomplishments. If so, I think you are a pathetic and totally ungrateful human being. It is only because of these wonderful people that you are what you are. What do you think would happen if the press got hold of your remark?"

"Billie, Billie. You have horsewhipped me. I pain all over from your justifiable thrashing. My words were too harsh. Allow me to clarify. It tires me greatly to have the masses constantly at our heels."

"Oh, you poor man. It seems that you have a propensity to reject those who love you. I just hope you never find yourself alone in this world. Is that what you want -- to be alone?"

"Drop it, Billie. Drop it. You are right once again."

These honorifics, of course, were sponsored by other celebrated people who chose to place us in prominence at their expense. The City of Paris honored us; French President Sadi Carnot named Mr. Edison Commander of the French Legion of Honor and decorated him with a red sash; King Humbert of Italy named him a Grand Officer of the Crown of Italy which automatically made my husband a Count and me a Countess;

and among all the newspaper coverage, *Figaro* called Mr. Edison "the man who tamed the lightning."

Honor after honor was spoken, preached and orated but often Mr. Edison depended on me to code him the specifics he could not hear. It was the same at dinners. I always sat beside him, to his right, and either answered for him or coded something for him so he could respond.

Although invited to speak many times, my husband always refused. On one occasion when he felt he should speak, he asked the American Ambassador, Whitelaw Reid, to stand in for him.

Following all the formal speeches, we moved to the next room or hall where each wall was covered with floor-to-ceiling mirrors. The effect was astonishing and at the same time mind boggling. The dimensions of the room were thrown out of whack. I saw myself in the distance at every turn. The orchestra was playing. Some guests were already dancing.

"Come on, Dearie. Make me happy I haven't danced since our wedding. They're playing a simple waltz.

"No, Billie. You know I don't dance. I'd make fools of both of us."

I then saw the handsome King Humbert walking in my direction. He stopped beside us, looked at my husband and then at me. "May I have the honor of this dance, countess?"

I had to think twice to remember that I was the countess he was speaking to. I turned to him. "I accept your request with pleasure, Sire."

The king swept me out onto the floor. It was the most exciting, and frightening, dance of my life. The toes of my shoes just barely touched the floor. It was almost like flying. Spin and swing and lift me off the floor. I managed to look back at Mr. Edison and he was chatting with another man -- paying no attention to me. We didn't talk. My whole experience was concentrating on remaining vertical.

Before I knew what was happening, I was in someone elses's arms and in the middle of the floor. He too was a handsome gentleman with gold sash across his chest and gold epaulets on his shoulders. Thankfully our movements were more refined. He introduced himself as Pierre, one of the curators of the Musée du Louvre. He spoke perfect English and invited my husband and me to the museum and he would be our personal guide. Finally, I was led back to my seat. Two more young men approached me but I declined their offers. I claimed exhaustion. Mr. Edison finally took notice.

I had an occasional opportunity to make use of my spoken French. When President Sadi Carnot approached us later in the evening, I startled my husband by thanking M. Carnot en Français. At this the president smiled broadly and the two of us had a brief discourse about how wonderful it was to have Mr. Edison and me in Paris where all the citizens shared his enthusiasm. Then President then kissed me on both cheeks.

Mr. Edison looked at me quizzically and said. "I didn't know you spoke French."

"It's just one of my many talents, but I only use it when there is someone French to use it on," I said jokingly and both men chuckled.

"Your wife is very charming," Carnot said in an aside to my husband.

"Merci," my husband responded. "That's the only French word I know." Another chuckle.

When were were alone, he said, "You expected me to dance like that? You looked like a pair of cats with a balloons tied to their tails!"

"That bad?"

"I'm kidding, Billie. I was impressed. I didn't know such speed was possible." Then he added, "You certainly attract the young men."

"Maybe you'll take dance lessons now."

"Sorry, Billie. I don't want to get too close to this hoity-toity society."

"Oh, Dearie. I love it."

We had a box seat at the Opera House and as we entered it, the orchestra greeted us with "The Star-Spangled Banner." The audience stood looked up at us and applauded. This was not the only time that my gentle husband was filled with emotion.

Meeting M. Gustave Eiffel, a fellow creator and mechanic, was his long-anticipated highlight. Mr. Edison commented to me that he was the nicest fellow he had met in Paris -- a simple and modest man. My husband inscribed in M. Eiffel's guest book, calling him a brave builder of such a gigantic and original specimen of modern engineering. We declined the invite to climb the 1,710 steps -- a bit of M. Eiffel's humor. He said he had climbed the steps once, on inauguration day the previous March,[56] but this time he escorted us on the elevators to the summit -- the highest structure in the world! He took us to his private apartment where we enjoyed a 360-degree view of the city. I must add that looking down at the street made me instantly dizzy. I had to step away from the window. Neither of us had ever been at so great an elevation.

Another highlight for Mr. Edison was meeting Colonel William Cody, alias Buffalo Bill. Mr. Cody was in Paris with his Wild West Show, set up in the Paris suburbs. Hoity-toity people Mr. Edison merely tolerated, if that. But eating an American breakfast of pork and beans next to that famous Indian scout, and being chased by a "savage hoard of howling redskins" while riding at hell-bent speed in a coach around the show's oval track was the peak of enjoyment for for my husband.

We circulated in Paris for a week and a half and Parisians became used to our presence. We roomed at the Place Vendome and were often recognized by individuals who had an invention in mind and were anxious to hear what Mr.

Edison thought about it. He waved them off like flies around his head, towing me after him.

My interests was more serious than my husband's. We toured the Louvre, without taking advantage of the curator's offer, and browsed scattered collections of its extensive treasures. Mr. Edison was not quiet about his feelings.

"To my mind the old masters are not art. Their value is in their scarcity and in the vanity of men with lots of money."

Surprisingly to me he found the Impressionists particularly interesting.

On *his* more serious side, we were invited to visit M. Louis Pasteur and toured his Institute. He greatly respected this scientist and thought that his "germ" theory was one of the greatest discoveries in history. We were invited to watch as M. Pasteur inoculated dozens of people with his vaccine.

When he finished with the crowd, he asked us if we wanted to be vaccinated. My husband didn't hesitate to commit us both. It would have been an insult for me to refuse.

I found it interesting how different these two men were in their careers. Napolean III, in 1865, had expressed his surprise that M. Pasteur never used his inventions for personal gain or profit. It was true. M. Pasteur's joy about his discoveries was watching the immediate and beneficial effect they had on his patients' health. But, exactly like my husband, I learned that M. Pasteur was the one other man in this world who was rarely drawn away from his laboratory experimentation.

The death of three of M. Pasteur's five children from typhoid was his motivation to search for cures to infectious diseases.

We meet with Marion

Traveling in Europe with my sisters was not as "character-building" as Mr. Edison had hoped for Marion. Jennie had written from Europe that Marion told my sisters she had never liked them from the beginning. She said she didn't like living in rooming houses and preferred five-star hotels. She refused to do her French lessons and took off on excursions on her own without notice. She also warned Jennie that she was going to London to see her father alone and she didn't care a fig for the touristy things Jennie and her sisters thought the sixteen-year-old might enjoy. After only two months in Europe, Jennie continued, Marion had already spent more than half her annual allowance.

Finally, Jennie wrote, she "doesn't seem to want us around. She wants to travel Europe by herself and for a girl of sixteen with her disposition, we do not think that is the right thing."

So much for the bit of ground I thought I had gained at home with the ice-cream outing.

We finally met with Marion in Paris and she hugged both of us. Jennie returned to America and Mary and Grace happily went back to their studies.

We toured the Exposition with Marion and visited the Eiffel Tower again. She was most pleased to be with her father. She tried again and again to hold his hand but he would have none of it for more than a minute or two. Her father showed no joy of reuniting with his daughter after her absence.

As a result of that disappointment she appeared friendly toward me again but she always had one eye on her father. It was very sad.

It struck me how much Mr. Edison was missing by rebuffing his children. Their love for him was tangible. How much fun, how much joy my husband was missing.

She was coming to realize she was no longer her father's favorite but neither were Tom and William. And it was I who took the brunt of the blame for that estrangement. Certainly I could feel the tension between them.

"I can't deal with her childish behavior, Billie. I find her tendency toward extravagance intolerable. I'm also embarrassed at the brassy way she's treated your sisters."

"She is only sixteen, Dearie, still an adolescent. I'm certain she's still very jealous of me. I've taken away the attention you gave her after her mother died. I think it's quite natural for her to act this way." I paused waiting for his reply. There was none.

"I think you could do a world of good," I boldly suggested, "if you'd spend an hour or two alone with her. Take her for a stroll along the Champs Elysées. She'd probably like a boat ride on the Seine. She desperately loves you. You're her hero. She deserves your love and attention."

"Billie, that may be true, but I just can't do as you suggest. In fact, until Dot shows some fiscal responsibility, I will to cut her allowance in half -- from eighty dollars a month to forty."

"You should be teaching her about economics. She needs your guidance."

"There you go again, Billie. That is your job. Why do you keep passing all this back to me? How many times do I have to repeat, I have no interest in domesticity. No more, woman!"

I felt anger rise inside me. I wanted to shout at him, pound some sense into his head. But that is where I failed. That was something I wasn't capable of doing. As usual, I was in charge of the children. I was in charge of Marion. I didn't know what to do next.

When I cheerfully asked Marion to join me on a boat ride, I was rejected.

I wondered if there was something other than her father's rejection that might have caused her attitude. It could have been rebellion against the Victorian climate of the time when girls were far more restricted than boys. Girls were always being reigned in, even more so in Europe. Girls who wandered the streets of Europe alone had questionable reputations -- even if they were American.

And then there were Mr. Edison's actions at home where he had given her unlimited freedom to come and go after her mother died. He introduced her to the freedoms he enjoyed when he traveled with her to Florida and elsewhere. She was his pal, like a son and she mixed often with the rabblerousing guys at Delmonico's who treated her like a queen. Indeed, her father gave her everything she wanted, including his attention, during those months -- before me.

Certainly it must be difficult for any child to be granted unlimited freedoms and *apparent* fatherly love during that period and then to perceive that it has all been taken away -- by another woman not much older than herself.

Surprisingly, Marion accepted the cuts in her allowance without complaint. She even admitted she had been very careless and extravagant.

Although her words may have surprised and pleased Mr. Edison, he didn't show it.

Some time after her short visit with us, Marion wrote to me. "I miss you very much and wish you were here. I like you more and more every day and hope you like me better."

In another letter she remarked about her father, "Ever since we were in Paris together I could not help but feel that he was very much changed toward me."

Contradiction followed contradiction with Marion. I had to blame her callous father. Neither of us understood that man.

Germany, Belgium and England

Mr. Edison and I left Paris and spent the next two weeks in Berlin as a guest of Herr Werner Siemens, the German electrical engineer and inventor. Mr. Edison received as much adulation in Berlin as he had in Paris. He toured the Siemens-Halske works while I spent time with Madeleine in the park feeding the pigeons and looking at the flower gardens. I later joined him at a wonderful banquet put on by Herr Siemens.

In spite of their mutual admiration, the men were fierce competitors.[57] They had a great deal in common although they approached it from very different directions. Siemens was a scientist and was surprised that my husband, for all his accomplishments was "only" a businessman and not one of their own. German culture admired and promoted the learned scientist whereas American culture honored the practical, often uneducated, man. Mr. Edison's friends were all businessmen. The scientists at Siemens studied Mr. Edison's amazing phonograph and did their own experiments with it.

We also met Herr Hermann von Helmholtz in Berlin. Mr. Edison said he was one of the most imaginative physicists of his time, having delved into the Euclidean geometry, energy conservation, fluid and thermodynamics and the invention of the ophthalmoscope. Exchange of information between these two men was difficult. Herr Helmholtz spoke no English and Mr. Edison spoke no German *and* couldn't hear. It's amazing how their gestures and drawings were able to overcome the language handicaps.

When we left Germany, Marion had gone on to Rome with my younger sister Mary and their chaperone and tutor, Mrs. Elizabeth Earl. To Marion, her Papa seemed very far away in all respects.

"Please travel with us, Marion," I begged before we left. "Nothing good will come of remaining in Europe. Return to Glenmont and be with your friends."

"I have no friends at home," she retorted. "I have no *family* at home. I don't even have a home in America."

She then broke down in front of me. "I want a *father*! That is all I want! Why can't I have a father?"

She paused and looked at me. "It's all your fault, Mina. You came between me and Papa. You wrecked my life. I was so happy before you showed up. I . . . I *hate* you."

I felt that stab in my heart. It was physical. My pulse halted momentarily until I sat down to recover. I looked up at the girl through my tears. I held my arms out to her.

Raked with tears herself, the girl spun around and walked out of our lives. We were not to see her for another three years.

Her father rarely wrote to her and then the letter was brief. She ceased writing to him except to ask for money. Mrs. Earl became a mere caretaker while Marion recklessly wove through her undirected adolescence. My sister Mary returned home, disillusioned by Marion's up-and-down behavior.

The girl was constantly on my mind. I worried for her. Mr. Edison ignored my pleas to write her and encourage her to return. I could not convince Marion in my letters to return to West Orange and the safety of Glenmont.

Our entourage continued on to Belgium where we spent a very long day with engineers in Brussels.

We arrived in London in late September. We lodged and rested at the country home of Sir John Pender, an early telegrapher who had ties with Mr. Edison when he was promoting his automatic telegraph in Europe twenty years earlier. The men visited London for a day to inspect Mr. Edison's power stations.

Lady Pender and I had a delightful day touring their extensive estate on their red roan mares. I hadn't been on a horse since my mid-teens and I had more than a few adjustments to make. As an American teen I had always ridden astride the saddle. But here, because of tradition and because we were in long skirts, Lady Pender offered me a sidesaddle. I hesitated.

"I've never ridden sidesaddle," I confessed.

"But you do feel comfortable riding."

"I do."

"Then this will be no problem," I was assured.

Lady Pender explained. "You see there are two curved pommels. Your right leg goes around the top pommel and across the middle of the saddle and down the left side of the horse. Your left leg goes under the lower pommel and your left foot goes into the single stirrup. Both pommels curve to your thighs, one above and one below.

"Try it. You'll see that it locks your legs into the saddle. It is quite comfortable and, very lady-like."

With the help of the stableman, I moved myself, and my skirts, into place. It *did* feel comfortable -- and safe.

And we were off, with her two Labrador Retrievers along side. We began slowly, a medium walk at first, then into a trot, and then a canter. Feeling quite comfortable we even went into a gallop briefly and I felt just fine. Lady Pender was pleasant company and the horse was magnificent and responsive. I had a passing thought of how nice it would be to have one of these handsome creatures at Glenmont. I giggled to myself at the impossible thought of my husband astride this beast.

I've always loved the beauty of the English countryside, its rolling hills, the grand vistas and friendly people. Unfortunately, our visit was very short. We had to leave for home the next day.

Secret experiments

On the voyage home, beginning with the rough crossing of the English Channel, I became sick and was forced to go below. But Mr. Edison remained himself, sitting on the deck smoking his foul cigars, sending up clouds of smoke which annoyed other passengers who had come on deck for a breath of fresh air.

We both were thoroughly relaxed when we returned to America. Mr. Edison was pleased at meeting the men he had always admired. But as soon as we landed in New York on October 6, he hired a launch and rushed us across the harbor to the Jersey shore and took a carriage to his West Orange laboratory. He was very eager to check the status of the secret experiments.

A new building, a studio, had been constructed by Charles Batchelor and William Dickson for moving-picture activity. They had tried to use a room in the laboratory itself for this but the vibrations of the dynamos blurred the effort. They named the studio the "Black Maria" because the entire building was draped in heavy black material and had no windows.

Mr. Dickson seated his boss and me in chairs that faced a projection screen. He went to the rear of the room to what looked like a large optical lantern that had an Edison phonograph connected to it. He shut off the lights and turned a crank. In front of Mr. Edison, a flickering image showed Dickson stepping out into the screen. He raised his hat, smiled and spoke the words "Good morning, Mr. Edison. Glad to see you back. I hope you're satisfied with the Kineto-phonograph."

This was the first demonstration of an operable motion-picture camera. Not only that, it was the first *talking* motion picture. It was a secret project because it had not yet been patented.

Mr. Edison was beside himself with excitement as he explained it to me. It was revolutionary. It was mind-boggling.

Yes. That was all wonderful, but I was eager to get back to Glenmont with little Madeleine. It was a long absence from my home and family.

Lucy, Madeleine and I received an open-arms welcome from the help. Madeleine didn't recognize any of the help and put up a fuss when one of them wanted to take her from me. But then, a warm bottle of milk immediately brought her around. I took her back and she fell asleep in my arms. She was beautiful.

I returned her to Lucy for her nap and I circulated through the house loving every inch of it. Angela left my desk neatly stacked with letters that she had answered and with other correspondence she had acknowledged but needed my follow-through attention.

Chapter Seven

1890

Marion contracts smallpox

By January 1890, almost seventeen now, Marion had toured Rome and had gone on to Dresden, Germany. Her adolescent hostility toward her father and me had grown to such an extent that she decided to exercise her independence further and remain in Germany indefinitely.

My sister Mary, in Paris, still attempting to take responsibility for the girl, by now had been adversely affected by Marion's irrationality.

"I can no longer put up with Marion's attitude," Mary wrote to our parents. "It would be best for me to leave Marion here. It bothers me because she does not know the best thing to do for herself and she does not always do the right thing."

My father readily agreed. Marion also sent her tutor chaperone packing as well. Her only correspondence home was to ask for living expenses. Mr. Edison continued to send enough for her bare essentials as he saw them, along with a new tutor chaperone, Mrs. Sadie Bingham.

As if in punishment for her sins and her rift with her father, Marion contracted the dreaded smallpox.[58] The disease put her in the Dresden hospital for several weeks. It scarred her face and further complicated the already traumatic life of a teenager who was about to turn seventeen.

She began to correspond with me. First of all I was shocked to hear her news and my compassion went out to her in my letter the next day along with a gift. Secondly, I detected she was looking more favorably toward me, again.

"I miss you very much," Marion wrote. "I wish you and I could go out for a strawberry ice cream cone together."

Unfortunately, Mr. Edison showed no such compassion.

Another letter from Marion was more extensive and she thanked me for the gift.

"You surely do not blame me," she wrote, "for feeling hurt that I only heard from home twice during those long dreary weeks I spent in the hospital. It was quite the talk of the hospital and you can imagine my mortification. I do not blame you so much but Papa is my own father & I never thought that he would treat me with anything other than kindness. I know that he did not mean to add a pang to my sufferings but it was at a time when I needed every proof of affection and two short letters in seven weeks did not prove that there was much. I wonder if I had died if you or Papa would ever have regretted not sending a few words of sympathy for those awful hours."

Mrs. Bingham expressed her thoughts also in a letter.

"It was a great grief to her & a surprise to every one that you have not written to her during this the most awful trial that came into her life." She added that Marion blamed herself for the problems with her father, but "a loving letter from her father would have been comfort unspeakable to your poor afflicted child."

Mr. Edison and I had the most stressful words between us over this issue, words that still hurt so much I do not care to repeat them here after all these years. He was obstinate and cruel, but he was firm with her. He would not let me go to Europe to see his daughter. "I don't want you contracting smallpox. Instead, he sent his personal secretary, Sam Insull, to visit her. His only other attempt to placate Marion was an offer to send her former tutor and chaperone to see her. But Mrs. Earl was busy with another family.

The continuing conflict between father and daughter disturbed me greatly. I felt deep down that I was the wedge, although I knew also I had every right to marry her father. But Mr. Edison did very little to reassure Marion that his feelings toward her were unchanged after we were married. Instead, through his actions, he demonstrated that as long as her stepmother was around, their relationship would never again be as close as it was after Mary's death.

Marion was to remain in Dresden until 1892.

Troubles at prep school

Young Tom, fourteen, was very unhappy at St. Paul's prep school. Since writing to his father rarely resulted in a reply, he wrote to one of Mr. Edison's assistants in the lab. He asked for a package of parts for developing inventions that he could play with and emulate his inventive father. He wanted to be an inventor.

Tom also wrote asking for me to intercede and let him return home where he promised he could study for hours.

"I worry," he wrote, "and therefore I cannot study here which knocks me all out of sorts. I have failed at every attempt to succeed here at school."

The letters revealed the boy's pathos. It hurt me a great deal to read the letters his father ignored.

"If I could study at home I could look forward to unlimited time. I mean I will study as hard as I possibly could because it is for my own benefit that I should do so, because then I could get through a great deal quicker, which I know is exactly what you want me to do, is it not? Write as soon as you possibly can, Papa, will you please. I feel badly."

And then to me. "Dear Mama. My juicy cough is worse than ever, my nose is swollen and my eyes keep me from reading. I've been in the infirmary ever since Saturday night.

All the other boys are so strong and well as anybody can be. What shall I do Mama? Will I have this catarrh all my life?"

Tom's complaints, maladies, and yearning for fatherly attention were to mark his character for the rest of his life.

William, twelve, had a tendency to ape his brother's problems and anxieties. He too sent letters to no avail.

"I can't stand it up here. I don't like the masters and they don't like me. I can't study because I am so unhappy. May I come home and go to public school or any school near home. If you want to put me out of my misery you will say yes. If you don't you will say no. Some of the boys are really cruel. They made me run the gauntlet and they used straps and sticks."

Mr. Edison was firm, but he failed to offer instruction and counsel. His letters were not fatherly. They showed impatience and he didn't hesitate to criticize his son's failings, their disregard for money and their failure to write more often to me.

"I'm disgusted with them," Mr. Edison said to me. "They will stay at school and learn to cope with it. They have to grow up and stand on their own -- just as I did even *before* I was their age. They have all the advantages I never had and yet they continue to whine. If you bring them home now I know they will be mollycoddled by you, their tutors and governess."

I was believing more and more that Mr. Edison simply wanted his children out of Glenmont, out of sight, and off at some distant place while we raised our own family. I never dared approach him with that thought.

Too busy for Seminole Lodge

The Florida retreat was abandoned but not neglected by our family from 1890 to 1901. Part of the reason was the raw memories Mr. Edison harbored from the breakup with his long-time friend Ezra Gilliland who still owned the twin house just a few yards from ours.

I didn't venture to Seminole Lodge because of the growth of our second family with the births of Madeleine, Charles and Theodore. I wanted to be near the comforts of home, family and local doctors to ensure their proper care during their early years.

A third reason was Mr. Edison's total obsession during the 1890s decade with mining iron ore at his Ogdensburg facility in New Jersey as he competed for quality ore with the mines in the Lake Superior region.

During our absence from Florida, Mr. Edison's secretary, Alfred Tate, corresponded with caretaker William Hibble regarding maintenance and upkeep of the house and yard. I also kept in touch with Mr. Hibble regarding the decoration of the lodge. When Mr. Edison and I were last in Fort Myers, the decorative aspect of the house had not been completed to my satisfaction. I asked them to finish off the exterior with the pretty yellows and whites to contrast with the reddish brown of the roof. I included sketches indicating where on the building to paint each color.

Mr. Hibble sent letters on expenses and frost damage and he asked if he could remove a fence to give a cleaner look to the beach along the Caloosahatchee. He said he had to eradicate a lot of fast-growing brush to open the grounds up because it was becoming a "malaria factory."

Sometimes I questioned the appropriateness of Mr. Hibble himself. He was not a Florida native and his letters often included derogatory remarks about the locals. He was from New York and spoke of his state as "God's country." Maybe we should have hired a local overseer, but it was not for me to interfere with Mr. Tate's hiring abilities.

Phonograph spin-offs

There were two spin-off products from Mr. Edison's phonograph that had longer lives than his phonograph itself.

The first "Edison Automatic Phonograph" arrived about 1890. We had one on display at Glenmont. It was the precursor of the "Slot Machine" and "Jutebox" that became popular in bars, billiard halls and other public locations. The Edison phonograph played a selected cylindrical record for a nickel. The user listened through ear tubes since speakers had not yet been invented.

The "Edison Talking Doll" was also popular in the 1890s. A miniature phonograph, called a "voice box," was installed in dolls with imported porcelain heads, metal trunks and wooden hands and feet. Often, though, the voice boxes were removed and sold as separate toys. Frankly, I didn't give the doll to Madeleine because the early ones had a tendency to fall apart with my children's natural roughness.

Mining iron in New Jersey

Mr. Edison ventured into the mining business because he saw a need by the east coast iron and steel mills for a low-grade iron ore. Ten years of his intense personal pursuit in this venture resulted in the loss of much of his personal fortune and it became his greatest commercial failure.

His absence left my family without an adult male for most of these ten years. I was alone in coping with his children while he dug holes in the ground like a giant gopher.

The mines were located in the town of Ogdensburg, later renamed Edison, New Jersey, just north of New Brunswick. The mine was familiarly known as the Ogden mines.

Mr. Edison always relished a technical challenge and the mines offered that opportunity in quantity. This was the era of Teddy Roosevelt preaching the "doctrine of the strenuous life" as a way to save American manhood from the corruption of bourgeois domesticity.[59]

My husband's "roughing it" did not contribute to my desire for marital harmony at Glenmont. Our children saw even less of their father during much of that decade.

The Edison Iron Concentrating Company was a family venture involving my father Lewis Miller, father's brother-in-law Ira Miller, Walter Mallory and his father. Their first discussions on the project took place at Chautauqua in 1885.

The centerpiece of the mining operation was an Edison invention -- a *magnetic* ore separator. After the ore was mined and crushed, the iron was separated from the rock and sand electromagnetically.

By 1893, the Ogden mill was the largest crushing plant in the world, double in size to those in California and the Lake Superior area.

Blasting and crushing 6,000 tons of ore per day was not a fun job, but for Mr. Edison it was "manly." The size of the machinery was enormous. He had a giant traveling crane that had a span of 210 feet. There were miles of conveyors transporting the production of the huge crushers. There were many worker injuries of broken arms and legs. Mr. Edison worked among the laborers, five of whom were killed during the decade. The "old man" was known for never asking any man to do a job he wouldn't do himself.

One day a tall dryer tower became blocked with ore. Even though Mr. Edison was warned not to enter the tower, he and superintendent Mallory crawled in through a manhole to locate the problem. Suddenly 16 tons of ore emptied from the 80-foot tower. Moments later the men reappeared.

"Well," Mr. Edison said shaking his head and giving a gritty smile at the anxious bystanders, "I guess that takes care of that."

Getting into the filthy mix of things was my husband's forte. I remember meeting him with the children at the railroad station on his return from the mines one afternoon. He struggled off the train and wobbled toward us, his clothing stiff with mining dust, his face smeared with grit. He was exhausted and unwashed. He had few words. We took him home and he instantly flopped onto our bed and slept for hours.

The last major sale in this losing venture came in the fall of 1898 when an order arrived from Bethlehem Steel for 10,000 tons of separated iron ore. Still hopeful of making a profit in the near future, he fulfilled that order, working at full capacity and was totally absorbed by the problems associated with it.

It was soon after this that his faithful friend and former employee, Charles Batchelor, delivered a newspaper clipping about mining in the Mesabi Range in Minnesota. It was in this range that a mountain of high-grade iron ore had been discovered after John D. Rockefeller and W.H. Oliver of Pittsburgh had purchased the expanse. They planned for large-scale extraction and the use of special ore trains and huge Great Lakes ships to transport the production.

Mr. Edison's instant depression at his inability to compete was masked with a burst of laughing. "Well," he said to Mr. Batchelor, "we might as well blow the whistle and close up shop."[60]

Later, when he discussed with Mallory how the General Electric stock he had sold to pay for his share of the Ogden mine venture had risen to $330 per share, he remarked, "Well, it's all gone, but we had a hell of a good time spending it."

Lewis Miller's activities

Father survived well. His losses in my husband's mining venture were relatively minor. His main interest remained with the Buckeye Reaper business which continued to thrive. He was on the road most weekdays during the summer visiting his sales offices across the middle American farmland and observing his machinery in operation. He went to Texas and watched the wheat harvest while, because of the contrast in climate, the crop in Akron had not yet begun to grow. He once explained to me that a wheat harvest was always taking place somewhere in this world. It was up to him to see that his Reaper was doing the job it was designed to do wherever it was in operation.

Father's other interest was Chautauqua. The main amphitheater was under construction as was a web of sewer pipes to replace the outhouses. Broad brick streets were now replacing the often-muddy dirt avenues. And the Chautauqua Literary and Scientific Circle was expanding into a correspondence-course effort making home-learning available for everyone around the country.

At the same time my parents expressed their worries about my husband's lifestyle. Although they always looked favorably at his many accomplishments, they knew first-hand how the Ogden mine was wreaking havoc with the man himself and our family.

"How are his boys doing?" my father asked. "The last I heard they were having trouble in school."

"They're still having school troubles," I said. "Tom is ready to quit and William is probably not far behind him. They write to me regularly and I try to encourage them, but its not working."

"What's their father doing about it?"

"Frankly, he's being stubborn. He won't write to them. He tells me domestic issues are my problem."

"They're *his* boys, Mina," father said, getting alarmed. "He has to take some responsibility."

"I don't know the answer, father. It is very troubling and we have to work it out. I really think it's a larger problem than school. It's almost like he has given up on them. He said he had always dreamed of his boys working for him eventually. But in his eyes, Tom and William don't have a talent for mechanical things. That leaves my husband confounded. They have no engineering abilities. He doesn't know what to do with them."

"Has he sat down with them and tried to work out what their talents are and then adjust their educational curriculum?"

"That's not his style. He truly believes they should be like he was and cut out their own paths. He doesn't know how to direct them to find other creative talents."

"That is sad."

"It is. And I don't feel right second-guessing him and taking charge of their education. I don't want to tell him that he is wrong. Besides, I don't think he'd listen to me on that subject."

"That's even more sad."

"It will be different with my own children. I'll have full authority over their education."

Mother now visited her grandchild Madeleine at Glenmont so often we decorated a special room for her. With my second child expected shortly, I sincerely welcomed her visits. She helped me cope with Mr. Edison's absences.

Another worry mother expressed was the weakness of the 1890s economy. "Money, money, money," she began. "That's what you hear all around the country. We have to be content with what we have and how sparingly we use it."

"Frankly, I don't believe I have any money worries, mother. Mr. Edison said Glenmont was mortgage-free and my income was assured from a variety of sources."

"Don't be so sure of those "sources," Mina. "Nothing is guaranteed. It's amazing how money erodes in a bad economy. Be sure to keep an eye on your finances and economize when you can. Your father takes nothing for granted with his income."

"You worry me, mother. We have a lot of very large expenses here at Glenmont with all the help and the estate upkeep. I don't see how I can economize. I have to rely on my husband's confidence on financial status. It's he who wants to keep up with the Carnegies and Rockefellers."

"I certainly hope he's right."

Mother always kept my home decorated with colorful fresh flowers. She delighted in growing a wide range of botanical species and potting them in our greenhouse. She happily dug and planted in the rich soil of our many gardens, often in her bare feet. When she needed help, she could call on head gardener Tom and his assistant Fabius who were not far away.

Charles enters our world

Charles was born on August 3. His father took a break from the Ogden mines and spent the evening and part of the next day with our first son, two-year-old Madeleine and me. I had just handed the little fellow to his father when, staring intently at the little face, he said, "My God, Billie! He looks just like me!"

He held him toward me and I looked. "You're right, Dearie. We have a clone."

"Let's hope he is a clone," he said excitedly, doing a little dance around the room. "Do you think the rest of my faculties will come with this little package?"

"I guess we'll have to wait on that."

He pondered. "You're right. It is a bit early to give him a clock to take apart."

I just laughed, very pleased to see his excitement. I could only pray that we would have a son with my husband's mechanical abilities who could one day take over my husband's business obligations. Tom, his first clone, had not yet shown that ability.

The inventor then rushed off to see how Dickson was doing with the kinetograph and the kinetoscope. He also had an appointment to deal with his moneyman Henry Villard. He was very much strapped for cash to cover his huge payroll.

Thankfully, I had my doctor and Lucy and my parents at my side in my husband's absence. It tickled me that I now had a girl and a boy of my own. They were both healthy and beautiful and I could ask for nothing more.

My father just shook his head, puzzled at my husband's brief stay at such an important time.

"Why can't he be more organized?" father asked me. "Why can't he delegate more? I just don't understand him."

I defended my man. "I learn more about his ways every day. He is special, Father. He is a great man. There is no one like him. He is his own world. And best of all, he loves me and I know he would do anything for me -- if I insisted. I understand what he is doing. But I do get lonely."

"How can you possibly have a happy marriage," mother asked, wringing her hands, "when your husband is never at home to act like a husband?"

"I have a job to do as well, mother. I have to raise his children and I have to manage this estate. I also have responsibilities to other people. I have the money and time to donate to worthy causes. I belong to several organizations in West Orange that provide food to hungry families. I belong to and attend the West Orange Methodist Church and I head the Women's Club there. We have a lot of worthwhile programs that I find satisfying. I am thankful I have help at Glenmont. I am not tied to home by young children, thanks to Lucy. I am able to circulate. I have a great deal of freedom. And my husband respects and supports all that I do."

Mother nodded appreciatively. "You are a busy person."

"My life is not really that much different from yours," I added. "No. We don't sit around the dinner table with guests every night as I used to do with you at home. I do miss that. But my life doesn't have to be like yours. I wanted an exciting man and I now have my exciting man. We have been together on several wonderful extended trips and we're at each other's side during those times. It's fun to mix with the hoity-toity here and there. That's one of the times I find my excitement. I usually have to manage *his* time when we are away. He dreads the adulating crowds and I have to push and pull him places where he's expected, but reluctant, to show. It's a full-time job and I love it."

Mr. Edison's brother William dies

Mr. Edison's older brother, William, had lived his entire life in the small town of Port Huron, Ohio where he was born. This was also the town where my husband, as a first grader, was ridiculed by his teacher and where he was publicly beaten with a stick in the town square by his father Samuel. Mr. Edison had no fond memories of Port Huron. At one point he wrote to his father saying, "I don't think that any living human being will ever see me in Port Huron again."

William was always slow and could never really get his life going. With the encouragement, passive interest and funding by my husband, William attempted to found a street railway in the town. But he couldn't manage it alone and Mr. Edison didn't have the time. The project fell apart and the $10,000 invested disappeared.

His brother had been living in a rooming house alone when he died a slow death of pulmonary tuberculosis in the last months of 1890. Mr. Edison attended and paid for his funeral expenses as well as his outstanding debts. He was buried in the family plot near his mother Nancy. He was only 59.

Chapter Eight

1891

Glenmont ownership transferred to Mina

Glenmont was officially transferred to my name in the first months of the year.

"I want to be certain, Billie, that my wedding gift to you is safe and secure from all of my follies."

It never entered my head that our home might be subject to someone else's demonic desire to seek reparation from one of my husband's business relationships. Yes. Mother had warned me that there was no such thing as a guarantee on financial stability.

"Are you in financial trouble, Dearie?" I asked.

"Not at all. It simply gives me peace of mind to know that my family has a secure haven. I'm involved in so many financial situations that have the potential of becoming tangled or mismanaged, a lawsuit is always possible. Glenmont is a delicious plum that is the envy of any number of sharks in this economy."

"Well. I'm flattered and I love you for it." This was a perfect excuse to give my husband a hug and a kiss.

"Billie. You mean everything to me." He pulled me to him again for another hug and kiss.

This was a rare moment in our marriage. To have him near me, to have him express his intimate feelings in the light of day. This confirmed to me our love and my family's security.

I began a re-decorating binge, erasing all vestiges of the original owner's efforts.[61] The drawing room came first. I covered the walls with embossed paper featuring green-gray figures on a dullish gold-lined background. Over the fireplace I hung a huge, beveled mirror set in a mahogany frame. For our den, I bought a sixteen-foot tall painting of a nude woman dressing for nighttime, by the Italian artist, Virgilio Tojetti. The theme and style was classic and I hoped my husband would adapt to its sensibility. Personally, I couldn't take my eyes off the lovely woman.

I remodeled the living room next to my mother's oft-used bedroom on the second floor above the porte cochere. From here the view over our front lawns and gardens, down to Mr. Edison's buildings and West Orange itself was spectacular. Now that I had children, mother spent a lot of time in that room looking after her grandchildren.

On the third floor over our library was the sewing and dress-making room where I could spent time doing alterations to my wardrobe. It was fun. Although I had access to an expert dressmaker, I kept a wide selection of fabrics on hand for when the urge struck me.

Then there were the fourteen acres of trees, shrubs and open lawn that surrounded Glenmont. I had groups of lawn chairs here and there amongst the gardens where guests might seek the view, the shade or the sun. I had my own spot where I could sit with my binoculars and watch and listen to the birds that frequented my feeders.

I had numerous flower gardens and a large vegetable garden. Often, along with mother, I developed a horticultural knack over the years, learning and working also with my talented gardeners. I was able to have fresh flowers throughout Glenmont whenever we were in residence. And Gracie, my cook, always welcomed our harvests of fresh vegetables for summer meals and for canning.

Young as they were, Madeleine and Charles enjoyed sitting by the little frog pond located at the back of the house. We stocked it with colorful Japanese Koi and goldfish and they watched them for hours. There was one drawback. They wanted to join them in the pool. It took constant watch by one of us.

Our friends were encouraged to stop by at any time. No reservations were necessary. Friends didn't need an appointment. They might even stay for a meal. We had plenty of room for those close to us.

Edison's father at Seminole Lodge

Mr. Edison's father, Samuel, was old school, dependable, loyal and hard working. He had supervised the construction of his son's original Menlo Park buildings. He was now eighty-seven, white bearded, over six feet tall, still athletic, the patriarch of the family. He still enjoyed traveling, thanks to his son who sent him regular checks.

This winter he decided to spend time at Seminole Lodge with his buddy Jim Symington. Their route to Florida was meandering but not without purpose. We had regular letters telling about the sights along the way through St. Louis, Richmond, Washington, D.C., Charleston, New Orleans and elsewhere. The men were carefree and happy, and because he bore the name Edison, the press followed the duo's gentle adventures along most of the trip. In Richmond the local press escorted the men to the statehouse where they met newly elected Governor Philip W. McKinney.

The pair most enjoyed their visit to the nation's capital, touring the public buildings. They watched money pass through the presses in the Treasury building. They gazed in amazement at the Lincoln Memorial and the Washington Monument and had a guided tour through the Capitol. The highlight, they wrote, was the White House where they were invited to sit and chat with President Benjamin Harrison in his Oval Office.

The men finally arrived at Fort Myers. Mr. Hibble, superintendent of the Edison property, greeted them. He reported to Mr. Edison that his father and friend arrived tired, but after settling in they sprang to life. They took wagon trips around the area and Samuel, like his son, was captivated by the brilliance and variety of the native flora. The Fort Myers press discovered the visitors and learned that one of them was an Edison. This resulted in an interview and a feature story describing the old men's travels.

They spent two months at the estate and wrote that they were helping Mr. Hibble with maintenance and upkeep. What they were actually doing was performing hard labor. As a result of Mr. Hibble's negligence, and Mr. Edison's four-year absence, the grounds had become overgrown. The jungle had returned. The eighty-year-olds spent most of their visit attempting to rejuvenate the acreage in the hot Florida sun. Senior Edison found the work itself rejuvenating. He wrote that he had given up drinking his "rot gut" alcohol and the rheumatism in his knees had disappeared. He proudly exclaimed that his youthfulness had at least partially returned.

At the end of their workday, they relaxed by fishing from his son's favorite spot on the long pier that extended far out into the Caloosahatchee.

This was Samuel's first and last visit to his son's winter retreat. He told the press he couldn't understand why the family was not making more frequent use of the place.

Mr. Edison and I were shocked that our hideaway had deteriorated so badly. He considered selling the place and even sought out his broker, Major James Evans, in Fort Myers. He asked Mr. Evans what he thought the estate, with only one of the houses, was worth. But in the end, he scrapped the idea, fired Mr. Hibble and, at the Major's recommendation, hired Ewald Stupler, a local, as caretaker.

Marion arrived at Glenmont on April 7 after three years studying and traveling abroad. She was now eighteen. It shocked us to see her face so badly pockmarked.

"Of course you're shocked," she said. "How do you think I felt when Papa never showed any concern for me?" She looked at me. "At least you, Mama, sent me a gift, showed some concern and wanted to visit me."

She said she used a scarf to hide most of her face when speaking with a stranger. Otherwise people stared at her, making her feel very uncomfortable. But otherwise she was a very attractive young woman, dressing well and maintaining her hair nicely.

For the first few months we got along famously. I smile when I recall our reminising the pluses and minuses of our relationship before she left home. We even went out again for for another strawberry ice cream cone. I was delighted. We took pleasant drives and shopped together. She loved my dear little Madeleine and baby Charles and enjoyed holding and playing with them and pushing the baby up and down our carriageways in the stroller.

But then there was a change between her and her Papa while the rest of were in Chautauqua. It seemed Marion was, once again, trying desperately to return to the days before my arrival when she and her father had, what she remembered, as gay times together. This was doomed to failure.

It seems they fell into an argument over father's lack of empathy and show of love and the absence of a single caring letter during her hospitalization with smallpox.

Once again she reverted to calling me Mina and began visiting, and then living with, her former European chaperone, Mrs. Earl.

Finally, she asked to be invited to stay with her mother's sister, Aunt Alice, at the farm in Newark. She had visited the farm occasionally as a child when her mother was ill. That was where she remained, out of communication, for the rest of her visit.

The first showing of motion pictures

The World's Columbian Exposition, also known as The Chicago World's Fair, celebrated the 400th anniversary of Christopher Columbus' arrival in the New World in 1492. It was to open on May 1, 1893.

Only two years away, Mr. Edison planned a major splash as he had at all previous expositions. This would be the first international presentation of his Kinetoscope. However, his first presentation of the prototype *anywhere* would be at the National Federation of Women's Clubs that was meeting at Glenmont.

I was ecstatic. This was my milieu and it would be on my turf, the result of my efforts during the previous six months. On a lovely summer day, 147 women converged at Glenmont on May 20 -- likely the largest luncheon I had ever hosted. Necessitated by the number of people, the food was served buffet style and the guests were encouraged to take their plates anywhere in the house or around the grounds. Islands of lemonade, tea and coffee were distributed throughout.

I had many compliments about Glenmont itself since I had offered everyone the opportunity to circulate and examine its every niche and cranny.

The meal behind us, the women were transported by carriages to the new photographic auditorium in the laboratory at the bottom of the hill. The suspense of Mr. Edison's forthcoming show had been building since the invitations were sent out, hinting "pictures that move" will be shown.

Mr. Edison arrived and explained the technology of what was about to take place. In brief, he said the prototype kinetoscope device was a peephole viewer of a scene that had been taken with a motion-picture camera. The camera took hundreds of individual action portraits on celluloid film. This film fed horizontally between two spools at a continuous speed while a rapidly-moving shutter gave the impression of motion from one portrait to the next. The women were invited, one at a time, to watch the action through a peep hole in the side of a cabinet. What the ladies saw was a man in a straw hat, dark vest, and white shirt. The man waved to the viewer, bowed and smiled with perfect, graceful human naturalness.

The character in the film was William Dickson who was credited for most of the device's inspiration and development. He also held the patent under his name.

Although the peep-hole show took less than a minute, the wait was long, but most of the ladies were impressed. They would remember that they had witnessed the very first (silent) motion picture.

Battle won, war lost

On July 14, Mr. Edison won the patent for his carbon filament electric lamps.[62] The judge ruled that his filament lamp, over all others, was complete. But the cost to Mr. Edison was enormous. He had won the battle but had lost the proverbial war. The cost to him was about $2 million; the balance of the patent life was only two years; and it also cost him ownership of Edison General Electric. He commented, "My electric light inventions have brought me no profits, only forty years of litigation."

This problematic victory had further ramifications. Other lamp factories had to close up shop as a result of the court injunction. Some of the companies, such as Westinghouse, made great efforts to create a non-infringing light bulb with a different filament but it was at great research expenditure. Westinghouse succeeded at this in time to win the contract to light up the Chicago World's Fair. This was a terrible embarrassment for Mr. Edison after having recently lighted up the Paris Exposition.

Menlo Park deserted

Soon after the death of his wife Mary, Mr. Edison lost all interest in the Menlo Park facility where all of his early inventions originated and where he became known as "The Wizard." He phased out work on his electric railway and all experiments in this laboratory and moved operations to New York City and, eventually, to West Orange. There were too many memories for him. He never returned. He told me he hated Menlo Park.

Before long it was waist high in weeds, windows broken, doors swinging in the breezes and rusted parts of machines scattered all over. His attorney begged him to retrieve and save such things as railway motors and dynamos that could be used as evidence to protect challenged patents. He ignored that advice. He refused also to maintain the property, yet for his own unexplained reasons, he made no attempt to sell it. The place became an eyesore in the little town.[63]

Eventually, we learned one of the buildings was being used for a dance hall and another as a chicken coop for experiments using an electric incubator for hatching chicks.

Mr. Edison chuckled at that thought. "Just think," he said. "Electricity is being employed to cheat a poor hen out of the pleasures of maternity. Machine-born chickens! What is a home without a mother?"

Chapter Nine

1892

A week in Mina's life

I did find plenty to keep myself busy in my husband's absence. I had cast aside the self pity I wallowed in during the first years of our marriage. I wrote to my family every day since my marriage.[64] My Mondays were devoted to what I felt were duty calls, in which I visited, as well as received, the ladies in my neighborhood of Llewellyn Park. This involved tea and bite-size sandwiches, slices of fruit and candies -- nothing too filling but very tasty and delicate. When Madeleine became old enough, she and her girlfriends were given dance lessons at our home on Tuesday afternoons. We ladies of the West Orange Women's Club met on Wednesdays for lectures on art. On Thursdays we met at the Country Club for chamber music concerts. And at late afternoon on Friday we women in the Odd Numbers Club assembled in my grand dining room at Glenmont for strawberries and cream.

Saturdays were set aside for rides in the country if the weather permitted. Scarth always handled the reins. Mr. Edison never drove. The one time he did, he frightened the horses and put us in a ditch and one of the boys had to take over. It was always hoped that Mr. Edison would be home for at least part of the weekend to spend some time with his family. If not, Scarth transported me and whatever children were available.

Sundays were church days. Mr. Edison and I were members of West Orange Methodist Church. The service began at eleven and usually lasted an hour. A gathering time followed with Sunday School for the little ones and a light luncheon for the adults. There usually followed a selection of inspirational classes, including Bible Study, Refugee Awareness, donations for the Community Food Pantry and, perhaps a deacon's meeting, a budget assessment overview and then planning visitations for the homebound.

Church activities could very well have overflowed into my entire week so I had to severely discipline myself to keep my activities in their proper cubbyholes.

In addition to this were my Glenmont administrative responsibilities. The use of Glenmont for any activity had to be coordinated with all of the help. If guests were expected overnight, Henry had to know how many and which bedrooms to use; would drinks be served in the library; would any guests need to be picked up at the railroad station; was there anything out of the ordinary that one or more of the guests might need. Knowing these basics, led to the multitude of details that followed. Often guests brought their maid with them to attend to their personal needs. Maids were doubled up in rooms if space was short. Depending on the length of stay, we serviced their laundry and pressed their clothing and ran personal errands when necessary. Flowers were distributed throughout the house, including each bedroom. Ask which guests preferred tea, coffee, water or another beverage. Although alcoholic drinks were not readily available in the house, certain guests expressed a "need" for specific cocktails. I made sure their preferences were available on request.

Gracie had to know how many guests would be seated for each meal and who in our family was expected to be seated, next to whom, as well. The two of us went through the menus early enough so the food items could be purchased. Special diets had to be considered. Special foods, such as fresh lobster and oysters on the half shell sometimes required leaping through hoops to obtain. Anticipation was the name of the game for delicacies.

The level of service I insisted we offer our guests had to match that of a five-star hotel. All our help was aware of what was expected of them during these bursts of energetic, and often lavish, affairs. Mother was a big help in my first months of marriage. I still marvel at the details she considered for my sumptuous wedding.

How did the Wizard do it all?

It was the widely believed folklore that the Wizard single-handedly churned out his brilliant inventions. This was close to being true in the early years at his little laboratory in Menlo Park. But as his creations took on a life of their own, such as the vast number of uses for electricity, more people were required to manage this growth.

But it was the Menlo Park lore of single-handed inventiveness that persisted over the years and my wizard found it to his advantage to encourage that notion. The press was always looking for another human-interest story. My husband was a master at providing those stories that the readers relished. To the public, his inventiveness was magic as one amazing device after another sprang from his laboratory. Without question he was the idea man, but behind him was an elite cadre of dedicated, creative engineers and behind them a vast army of dedicated workers.

From the beginnings in Menlo Park, Mr. Edison had total confidence in his key men, his superior equipment and his unique laboratory. He hired men with knowledge in areas in which he knew he was weak. To achieve the results he wanted, he played his own practical, seat-of-the-pants intuition against his university-trained engineers and scientists on a particular problem. Among these men were inventors in their own right who were recognized as experts in their particular fields.

First comes the intuition, he told me. It comes with a burst of energy. Then come the problems as the ideas develop, then the resolution, then a failure and the question of whether to continue or not. Back and forth. Finally a successful result -- after a good deal of luck.

When we married, Mr. Edison already had dozens of manufacturing operations and laboratory experiments working simultaneously. It baffles me how he kept track of everything. How well each was succeeding. It took hundreds, and eventually, thousands of dependable managers and loyal workers to keep this huge enterprise moving and on track.

With all this activity churning in his fertile brain I can easily understand why, when his being was with us at home, his mind was often somewhere else. It took an army of men to follow through and actually produce the results of the boss' wizardry.

Gilliland sells his Fort Myers property

We learned early in the year from our caretaker, Ewald Stupler, that Ezra Gilliland had sold his half of the Fort Myers property. The buyer was Ambrose McGregor, a multi-millionaire oil baron and a large Southwest Florida landowner. Mr. Edison was delighted to finally be rid of his former friend and was not surprised, yet was certainly disappointed, that he was left out of the opportunity to purchase the property himself.

I was pleased to find common interests with Mr. McGregor's wife, Tootie. Over the next decade, and after her husband died, Tootie and I cooperated in helping Fort Myers develop into a desirable, beautiful and relatively sophisticated community. In appreciation of her efforts, and in memory of her husband, Riverside Avenue, that bisected our property, was renamed McGregor Boulevard in 1912.

The Gilliland house passed through two more owners before we finally reacquired it in 1906 and placed the property in my name. That twin building became our guest house and the grounds that accompanied it allowed us to fully develop my interest in flower gardens and Mr. Edison's experiments with exotic flora.

I'm not going back!

I blamed Mr. Edison for his sons' inability to adapt to their life at St. Paul's. By the 1890s college education was becoming a necessity for obtaining a job in the technical fields. Even Mr. Edison realized this in his hiring practices. He failed to send his boys to schools that could have prepared them for the technical life, yet he still believed they would eventually be working for him at technical jobs. It was inexplicable to me and it became another set-up for Tom's and William's lifetime of failures.

Of course I have to take some blame as well. Their letters home to me expressed their homesickness, their general unhappiness and the frequent sickness both of them imagined they suffered. I replied to them that they needed a positive attitude. They needed to participate in some of the many activities at the school. They had to overcome their low spirits.

It was not enough. My encouragement had little effect. They needed close, fatherly guidance.

Tom looked after his younger brother during their early years away at school. He was William's protector and helped him with his studies as a big brother should. However, Tom was the first to quit St. Paul's. He told us his reasons were too numerous to count. He said he had tried to be popular with the boys and the masters but said he had failed at every attempt.

"I've never been interested in school," Tom said. "My grades are terrible and I have no interest in going to college. I hate studying." It was Christmas vacation when he told me, "I'm not going back!" It was echos of Marion.

"Just what do you plan to do at age seventeen without a secondary school education and diploma?" I asked.

"I want to work for Papa. I'll do anything."

"What skills do you think you have?"

"I don't have any real skills," he mumbled. "I'll do anything. I can probably mop floors or hammer nails. I just want to try something."

"Do you really want to work at mundane jobs all your life? You know you're better than that. I know you can do much better in school. Do you really dislike St. Paul's that much?"

"Yes Mama, I do. But I need time to think. I have to try some different jobs. Papa never went to school. Why should I? I really want to invent. Papa didn't have to go to school to become an inventor. I might find something I can invent as I try new jobs."

"How much reading have you done? Papa's education was the result of reading hundreds, thousands of books."

"I don't read much. I just can't concentrate. I need to be active and doing something with my hands."

"Oh, Tom. I fear for you. Have you looked for jobs at other places?"

"No. I want to work for Papa, whatever it is."

I reported Tom's request to Mr. Edison. His reply was, "Oh, yes. I have a job for him." He made it sound ominous.

I was relieved, but he didn't tell me what he had in mind for Tom.

Jennie Miller marries

My oldest sister and perennial confidant, Jennie, was finally married at age thirty-seven to Richard Marvin in Akron,

Ohio on April 20. The entire family had thought she was destined for elderly maidenhood. But then the right gentleman came along. Father, again, joyfully sponsored the event, although it was toned down considerably compared to my marriage. The couple insisted on simplicity. Jennie invited several of her friends and all of the Miller family.

Chapter Ten

1893

Tom goes to work at the mine

Tom, now seventeen, revered his father but at the same time was intimidated by him and therefore had difficulty expressing to him his true feeling about himself and his dreams.

His dream was becoming an inventor like his father. But Tom's reverence was met with a mystifying hostility. Mr. Edison saw a young man who knew nothing about business and was not at all mechanical. He was not an avid reader. He couldn't even reconstruct a mechanical alarm clock, much less improve on the clock by reinventing it. He was also a complainer and a quitter.

Without any discussion, they took the train out to the mine. Mr. Edison studied papers and made notes. Tom didn't dare interrupt, so he sat in uncomfortable silence staring out the window. If only he had been reading a book on mechanics, I thought. That would have peaked his father's curiosity and a conversation might have been started.

His father set him to work as a common laborer shoveling iron ore. He lived and ate in rough temporary barracks with the other laborers while his father lived in neighboring farmhouses paying for room and board.

The work was hard. He developed blisters on his soft hands the first day. The other men ignored him because he was not one of them. They wondered why the boss's son was doing drudge work. He received no privileges from his supervisor. There was no one his age with whom he could relate.

Tom regularly wrote to me and I responded with encouragement. Over time an attachment grew between us. I thought I understood him. The hard work, as he explained it, seemed criminal. His appeals to his father, he said, were ignored, but he kept working at whatever was thrown at him. The worst thing of all was, Tom said, there was never a comment or an appreciative word about his diligence and hard work from his father.

"What did I do to deserve this?" he asked me.

I had my answer. Someone had to tell him this.

"Papa is showing you what it is like to work in the real world for someone who has not found his talent. You have had every opportunity to get an education and you rejected it. You had, and still have, the opportunity to read educational books as your father did, and you have not.

"I'm not saying the same will happen to you if you knuckle down to reading, but it will be a good start. One subject to start on might just be iron mining. You'll then have something to talk with Papa about.

"Tom. I love you. I care a great deal about you. But you must get hold of yourself and take charge of your learning. And, of course, it's not too late to go back to school."

The Great Bank Panic

Much like the Panic of 1837, the bank panic that began in January of 1893 was the result of businessmen who became too confident, invulnerable, in fact intoxicated by the natural law of free competition. But the structure, built upon the banks' madness of endless credit, and the blind confidence in unrestrained capitalism, finally collapsed and the domino effect spread through American industry and the marketplace in general. The overbuilding and shaky financing of railroads was another cause. The run on gold was another. It was the worst economic depression the country had ever experienced.

Mr. Edison felt the tremors in February even as he hoped to get the Ogden mine up to full operation by summer. But by April, requests for ore were falling off and a few months later the plant was silent. Mr. Edison was forced to lay off hundreds of long-time, loyal workers and sharply cut the activities in his laboratory. He had no cash to pay his workers.

There was a run on currency. Banks were closing. The stock market dropped precipitously. Wall Street brokerages were failing. The panic began in New York and spread through the country.

My husband found himself forced into unprecedented idleness and spent several weeks that summer with his family in our Chautauqua haven.

The depression affected my father's business as well. He was now almost sixty-five and the anxiety of creditors amassing at his factory gates took its toll on him physically. Lewis Miller became plagued with upper respiratory ailments and frequent and debilitating colds from the stress of the hard times for himself and his son-in-law. Father could only take comfort in his recently developed mower, binder, corn harvester and thresher, but nothing financial would come of it until the economy recovered in the unpredictable future.

William Dickson's Kinetographic Theatre was now completed, ready to startle the public with its revolutionary moving pictures. It was ready, but Dickson himself, the theater's creator, was on indefinite rehabilitative leave in Florida, alone, exhausted, trying to reclaim his energy. All this to the frustration of Mr. Edison who finally foresaw how entertainment and the theater could bring some much-needed escape from reality for the public. But there could be no movies without the man behind the camera.

For the first time Mr. Edison approached my father for a cash-flow loan and, with difficulty, father was able to help substantially. It was a humbling experience for the wizard to ask this of my father who, thus far, had been able to corral his own business interests into a financial safety net.

William transfers to Trinity

William was a tall and handsome youth. He remained at St. Paul's until the end of the school year. Without Tom to rely on, he told his parents St. Paul's was too far away from home. He wanted to go to another school, even a public school, nearer to home, ideally one where he could live and study at Glenmont. At age fifteen, he still wanted to be near me who, presumeably, would be sympathetic to his perceived problems.

"I hate this place," William wrote me. "It's like a prison. I would give everything I have to be released from here. I can't get anywhere with Latin and Greek. What good are these languages anyway? Where will they get me?"

Mr. Edison agreed with William on that point. And hearing similar complaints to Tom's and not wanting him to leave school altogether, he enrolled William as a junior at Trinity Preparatory School, a residential institution on Staten Island.

With my coaxing, my husband took a different tack at Trinity. He conferred with the headmaster and asked him to give William a course of study that would prepare him for Cornell University, period, having heard that Cornell had an excellent reputation in science and technology. But Mr. Edison was unaware that a university was made up of several schools of education.

As a result, based on the results of an achievement test, William, unaware of his father's intentions, was prepared for Cornell's College of Philosophy rather than the College of Engineering. William was happy. The courses were easy and he slipped through the next two years with a different attitude.

During his senior year at Trinity he became aware that some of his friends were applying to the Sheffield Scientific

School at Yale and this was also the school where my younger brothers were attending. He made Yale his choice.

Peep shows

It was May 9 when I accompanied my husband to the Brooklyn Institute of Arts & Sciences. It was here he made his first public demonstration of nickel-in-the-slot motion pictures. The uppity experimental projector did well and the demonstration of moving pictures was a big hit.

He explained that nickel-in-the-slot machines were designed to be placed in restaurants, bars, grocery stores and other public places where a passerby could place a nickel in the slot of the machine and then peer through a glass and select a short movie to watch.

At this occasion, my job was to supply the nickels to Institute patrons as each took turns watching one or more movies that could be selected for a five cents each.

Mr. Edison had planned to have this nickel-in-the-slot projector at the Chicago World's Fair that had just opened, but his slot projector was not yet functioning well enough to trust it during the entire course of the Fair.

As a result of this failure on his part, he had to swallow a good deal of pride by having to ask Nikola Tesla to borrow his moving picture projector for use at the fair to show his motion pictures. Mr. Tesla was gracious enough to lend his machines to Mr. Edison without a single negative comment because he was quite self-satisfied that his alternating current had won the electrical contract for the entire fair. In an additional swallow of pride, it was Tesla's alternating current, not my husband's direct current, that was powering all of Mr. Edison's exhibits.

Preparation for the Chicago World's Fair,[65] celebrating Christopher Columbus' discovery of America, had begun years earlier with Mr. Edison's team. The goal was to make the Edison presence even more extraordinary than the 1889 Paris Exposition.

Two years before the opening, Mr. Edison had visited the site and met with its architect, Daniel Burnham, forty-three, who showed him around the site. Mr. Edison suggested the use of incandescent bulbs rather than arc lights and the use of direct current.

A serious battle ensued over electricity between J.P. Morgan, who now owned General Electric (backed also by Mr. Edison), and George Westinghouse (backed by Mr. Tesla). It was direct current versus alternating current once again. Westinghouse won the competition with the lowest bid because his alternating current was far less expensive to operate than direct current. It was a blow to Mr. Edison but, as with other losses, he was able to laugh it off and go on to other challenges.

We traveled with my parents to Chicago in mid-August, three months after the Exposition officially opened. I could not believe the size of the grounds -- more than six hundred acres with about two hundred new buildings, Mr. Ferris' huge wheel, canals, lagoons and even streetlights. I immediately saw that its immensity and grandeur far exceeded the other expositions at which I had accompanied my husband.

The largest building, covering some thirty acres, had as its spectacle Mr. Edison's forty-foot high Tower of Light, capped with an eight-foot replica of the Edison bulb. It was created from a mosaic of thirty thousand miniscule prisms within two huge frames that gave the appearance of gigantic pillars of fire, lighted from bottom to top with five thousand incandescent bulbs that blinked on and off. All this was set into a background of mirrors that multiplied the effect.

Imagine the blaze of glory this was for my husband! He saw it. His men had created the spectacle. I was at his side.

Electric lighting was the theme of the Exposition, hence the name "White City." Garish as it was, it achieved the desired, overwhelming effect on the public.

Beyond the flash in the Hall of Electricity were Mr. Edison's extensive collections of his years of labor. Here were his rows of dynamos, sewing machines, speaking dolls, phonographs, flat irons, ceiling fans, elevators, model electric railroads and locomotives -- all electrified and illuminated by George Westinghouse's alternating current. But who among the hoards of visitors really cared about alternating current?

In the center of the room was a particularly large group of spectators. They were watching, spellbound, Mr. Edison's first motion pictures on the Kinetoscope. But let me say again, who of the viewers cared that it was Mr. Nikola's projector?

Far more interesting than the equipment was what the public was watching. All the camera work had been produced back home, live, by Mr. Dickson in the Black Maria.

Dickson drew performing artists from every walk of life. He paid regular actors about ten dollars and celebrities fifty dollars for their performance. Of course the real incentive for the actors was to be part of an historic event -- to have their act preserved forever on film.

One show was a boxing match between professional, well-known pugilists in a ring that had been set up in the Black Maria. The two men, who actually despised each other, fought to the bloody knockout. Now, watching the movie, the observers were cheering and booing as if it were a live show.

Other motion pictures included well-known muscleman Sandow lifting weights and flexing his muscles; dancers in full costume from Japan; ballet girls from France; cockfights by roosters donated by neighbors; Edison's friend Buffalo Bill with Indians chasing him down. (This was the first "Western"); and acrobats swinging from the rafters without the benefit of a net. Dickson even had sharpshooter Annie Oakley knocking coins out of the sky. Without sound, fast-moving action was the draw.

The duration of each moving picture show only averaged one minute. The camera could only handle a show length of a minute and a half. The screen image was only six inches high so the audience was provided with binoculars to watch them. But the action details were in sharp focus. This was the beginning of a whole new industry. We could readily see that this would be popular mass entertainment.

William's rebellion

Before William could follow the lead of others to Yale, he had to graduate from Trinity and this preliminary step was not going to be easy -- not for William the rebel. He put off preparing for exams because he knew they were going to be difficult. He spent his time instead in sports activities and with the co-eds. He spent money rashly which was a characteristic of Tom and Marion as well. He rebelled against the headmaster who urged him to pay attention to his studies. But he was too busy free wheeling as a senior and as a big man on campus, yet only seventeen years old.

Nearly two years had passed and his father had paid no attention to the details of William's education. By default, that responsibility was back in my hands under the category of domesticity. When he did write to his son, it was to criticize his bad habits, particularly the way he threw money around. William freely admitted he had bad habits but it seemed he was in no hurry to correct them.

In a last-ditch effort to influence William, I visited Trinity Prep and we had a heart-to-heart. I had at least two reasons to see him personally. First of all I didn't want to expose my thoughts on paper. Secondly I knew a personal visit would carry more weight and love than a letter.

"Have you had any correspondence with Tom?" I began.

"Yes. Once in a while we write. Why do you ask?"

"Are you aware of his job at the mines?"

"I know he's working for Papa in the mines."

"He didn't tell you about his work, how difficult it is and how he hates it?"

"No." He looked at me curiously. "As a matter of fact he wrote about his new freedom. He said how glad he was to be away from St. Paul's prison – just like I was."

"Tom," I said, "is doing a laborer's work of shoveling iron ore at the mine. He sees no future for himself. His father is teaching him what work is like in the real world when you have no secondary school diploma and no skills."

"I didn't know that."

"I'm telling you that because you are on the very edge of a choice. Graduate from Trinity or work at menial jobs. Your father will never give you a decent job if you have no education and no skills. Believe me.

"Tom is telling only part of the story," I said. "He complains to me that he never gets to talk to Papa and Papa shows no appreciation for all the work he's doing."

"I don't hear anything from Papa. Is he still alive, Mama?"

"That's not funny, William. He's. . ."

"I know. I know. He's very busy. He's always very busy. But he does send me a nice allowance."

"Headmaster Hawkins says he may have trouble graduating you. Are your courses too difficult?"

"No. The courses are a snap. Any course is a snap when you don't have to study Latin and Greek."

"If your courses are a snap, why aren't your grades better?"

"Oh, Mama. I don't know. I want to be an inventor too. I hate school just as much as Tom."

"Do you want to shovel mining ore all day?"

"I wouldn't take a job like that. I think Tom's stupid to put up with that."

"I understand you want to go to Yale."

"Yes. My friends want to go there also. I want to get into their School of Engineering. That will help me with my goal to be an inventor and then maybe Papa should want to give me a good job in his laboratory."

"That sounds like a very good goal, but first you have to graduate from Trinity."

"Oh, Mama. You worry too much. Of course I'm going to graduate. I have a whole semester to put it all together."

"I hope you're right, William. I pray for you. I want you to be able to do exactly what you want. I'd love to see you as an inventor in Papa's lab."

"I will, Mama. I really will."

William's graduation continued to be tenuous.

Chapter Eleven

1894

Marion returns to Europe

It was a Friday in early March that Marion showed up at Glenmont and announced she was returning to Europe. Three years had passed since she returned from her previous tour. But now she was twenty-one, independent and ready to go back.

"I miss my friends over there," she said. "I find Germany more to my liking now."

"We're going to miss you, Marion."

"Perhaps you will miss me, but I wonder about Papa. Is he here now? I want to say goodbye."

"He's upstairs. I'll get him."

"No. I won't see her," her father said. "If Dot wants to live as a foreigner, let her. She only came by today to pick up her check."

Mr. Edison refused to see her and remained upstairs in his office. I was forced to become the intermediary. I had to tell my stepdaughter her father refused to see her. I didn't report his specific comments.

There were tears of sympathy as well as agony between Marion and me. I was pleased that it seemed we might yet be friendly to each other. We hugged and vowed to keep the correspondence flowing between us. She then asked if I would accompany her and see her off on her eight o'clock sail the next morning. I was eager to do that and relayed my intent to my husband.

"No you will *not*, Billie," He snapped. "I will not have it. Dot can go where she wishes. I don't give a hoot." He also had some less kind words for his daughter that I will not repeat here.

Again he was cruel. At that moment I did not feel like a wife or a mother. It was my duty to tactfully relay some of her father's words to Marion.

Her reaction was immediate. She said nothing, but turned, marched past me and breezed up the stairs with me close behind. She had every right to see her father. She refused to be treated in such a callous manner.

We burst into his office. He looked up surprised. I expected fireworks, an all-out fight. I was braced, my heart was beating rapidly.

Marion went around behind his chair. She raised her arms. I expected her to hit him. But then. . . She dropped her arms around her father, placed her face next to his, kissed his cheek and then stepped away.

Mr. Edison's jaw dropped and he swiveled in his chair and looked at his daughter. He could find no words. I was as surprised as he.

"For some strange reason I love you, father," Marion said. "You have given me every reason *not* to love you. I am leaving now and I hope to find friendship and love in another place. I do not plan to return -- ever! Goodbye.

She now turned to me. "I'm sorry for the way I have treated you in the past, Mama, but please understand it was only because of my father's unexplainable rejection."

She reached out to me and we hugged right in front of her father.

I desperately wanted to go with her. I just could not let her leave alone under these strained conditions. My heart was beating double time. I turned to my stubborn husband.

"I am going to see *our* daughter off, Dearie. You can come with us if you wish or you can stay here alone and sulk. I'm taking Angela with us. I will return tomorrow after I see Dot off on the boat."

Marion turned one last time to look at her father who was already back at his paperwork. She looked at me again, tears running down her pockmarked cheeks. "I just don't understand him, Mama."

With that, we quietly left the room. Marion took my arm and we walked together down the stairs, smiling at each other. A carriage was waiting. Angela quickly packed our bags for overnight and the three of us boarded the carriage.

I felt very good. I had defied Dearie's disgraceful rejection of his daughter. Perhaps I should have stood up to him on earlier occasions when he was simply being unreasonable. Not a word was said between us women over the incident. But after a loving hug the next morning at the gangplank, I was convinced my stepdaughter and I finally loved each other as mother and daughter.

The movie tycoon

Encouraged by the success of the kinetoscope prototype at the World's Fair, Mr. Edison gave the go-ahead to Mr. Dickson to move into full production with a wider variety of actors. At the same time he established The Kinetoscope Company and began manufacturing the perfected kinetoscope projection machines in West Orange.

On April 6, the first machines were shipped to central locations in Atlantic City, Chicago and to Holland Brothers, 1155 Broadway in Manhattan where kinetoscope "parlors" had been set up. The parlor in New York had a highly polished floor. Palm trees were set around the room. A plaster bust of Mr. Edison was placed in the window, painted to look bronze. We advertised the event in the major newspapers.

The kintoscopes were lined up along the center of the room, back to back, in two rows of five machines. A brass railing at waist level protected the machines and allowed the viewers to lean forward to get the best view through the peephole. An attractive young woman near the entrance sold twenty-five-cent tickets that allowed the customer to view one row of machines per ticket.

With Mr. Edison and me, Dickson and Insull as observers, the doors opened Saturday at noon, April 14, to a line of customers that extended out of sight aound the corner of the block. The plan was to close at six and retire to Delmonico's for a celebratory dinner -- if all went well.

Happily, our plans did not work out. Our last customer left the room just after one the next morning. The cash box held an extraordinary $120. I made the calculation. Some 480 tickets had been sold!

Tired, and certainly hungry, the four of us patronized an all-night restaurant to celebrate and spend our proceeds on boiled live lobsters from Maine.

In less than a year, two additional franchises were established. One would sell kinetoscopes in Europe and the other would film boxing matches to be shown on kinetoscopes in bars and high-traffic areas everywhere wherever allowed. The machines were sold at a list price of $200 each and the cash flow increased dramatically. Revenues by February 1895 totaled more than $177,000.

Mr. Edison now considered himself a "movie tycoon."

Life at the mines

Mr. Edison was confidant his mining operation would eventually yield fortunes beyond imagination. His compulsion resulted in spending most of the next four years at his mines in New Jersey.

America was still in the midst of financial depression. His reactivation of the mine came at great cost. In addition to the funds his father-in-law had lent him, he had lost most of his General Electric stock and other investments. Yet he called the mines "my Ogden baby."

Until now, Mr. Edison had no place of his own to stay at Ogden. He had roomed and had eaten meals at local farms and boarding houses. But now, feeling flush with success in his other ventures and the *potential* success at the mines, he built himself a very basic two-story "home" in the middle of the mining rubble. It was an American dream house but without the wrap-around porch, flowery landscape and picket fence. The view from every window was barren, black landscape.

Mr. Edison's goal was to streamline his ore milling plant. That began with crushing his ore into refined powder and forming it into briquettes. Why briquettes? The railroads gave him better shipping rates if he used open cars of material impervious to the weather and strong enough to withstand the bulk handling on either end of the journey. This also satisfied the demands of the furnace men at the iron works who wanted a porus, agglomerated product that was easy to handle.

The inventor succeeded at both. My husband was enormously proud that it took only a little over two hours to process an entire railroad car of raw ore into completed briquettes.

The dirty, loud, he-man Ogden mines turned the hills of Edison, New Jersey into black deserts. It was the early days of assembly-line production, a scene quite the antithesis of the less noisy, more techy, sun-filled and fresh-air atmosphere of the workshops in West Orange, where workers sat at tables near open windows and the essence of fresh-cut hay fields drifted in and most of the workers wore smiles and were polite to each other.[66]

Tom had continued to work as a common laborer, ostensibly to learn a trade. It was understood by the family that he would follow his father's lead and never set foot in school again. He was now reassigned to the company store stacking greasy castings. He had no special privileges and he had to report to the superintendent rather than his father. Tom had no love of this job either. In his free time he wandered the barren landscape, in his own world, shooting displaced squirrels and using the hair from their tails to make paintbrushes.

Tom was now eighteen and the worship of his father had digressed into resentment. He complained to me about his sad state and expressed how he respected me.

"Oh, Mama," he wrote. "My job here is degrading and an insult to what creative things I could be doing. I know that Papa is trying to make me a paragon of his "self-made-man" he likes to talk about, but I'm not appreciating it. What is he trying to prove? Why won't he talk with me or just show a little interest in what I'm doing? Can it be that there is room for only one Thomas A. Edison in this world? I feel I am up against an imutable force.

"And look at Marion," he continued. "She does nothing except roam around the world as a free spirit and he still sends her living expenses. What about me? Why is he picking on me? Marion has always been his favored child. That's pretty obvious. When do I get to travel in Europe? William and I have always been left behind when the rest of the family travels. . ."

Tom's complaining placed me in the middle of his conflict with his father. How much of this did I have to endure? It was very stressful.

And now Marion is gone and threatens never to return. And then there is William. Will he graduate from Trinity or will he end up like his brother?

The only consolation I had was my own children, to nourish and to love. I was determined Madeleine and Charles would never wander down the same path that my husband allowed his children to go.

Tom somehow struggled on through the tough winters at the mines and earned a break so he could enjoy summers in the pastoral atmosphere at Chautauqua. There he could mingle with refreshing, polite, spiritual people as well as the Miller family and brother William.

As much as Tom complained, he really did miss his sister. But mostly it was his father, absent of course, whom he was convinced was the only person alive who had the power to give meaning to his life.

Mystery letter from Germany

There was another reason Marion fled to Europe. The story gradually came to us from others with whom Marion was corresponding. She had had a failed relationship with a young man in New Jersey.

She was now in Germany where she resumed another relationship that had developed during her extended vacation in Europe. The man was Oscar Oeser, a German army lieutenant stationed in Chemnitz, some forty miles southwest of Dresden.

Mr. Edison received a letter in the summer of 1894 with a German postmark. It was addressed to him but the handwriting was not Marion's. Since we had not heard from Marion since she left months ago, I was nearly crippled with curiosity. A million horrible thoughts passed through my mind as I examined and re-examined the envelope. I dared not tear it open, and I did briefly consider steaming the flap.

He was just a 'presence'

I remember the time Madeleine, baby Charles and I went up to the mine after it reopened. It was a sunshiny November day. Mr. Edison had been begging me to visit -- preferably without any children. My young ones and I rode with Scarth at the reins. Arriving at the mine, we saw a man who emerged from a hole in the ground. He was dirty and his clothes were rumpled, but he was happy, all smiles and talk and he spent a few minutes with us. Then someone called out urgently to him and he scurried back into the hole. Madeleine was six at the time. She recalled in later years this was the first time she realized she had a father.

I don't blame her. Mr. Edison was never home during the week. If we saw him at all, it was only on Saturdays. He was just a "presence" Madeleine recalled. And as often as he claimed to be home on Saturdays, he was not. He was consumed by other activities. There was, for example, the General Electric dinner on Saturday night at Delmonico's. On other Saturdays he had to make the rounds of one or more of his dozen companies.

At another time, Madeleine remembers, "We took the open carriage and met father at the train station. We were all dressed up that day. I wore a high collar that I hated. Mama wore a beautiful summer dress that I loved. She also wore a fancy hat and just had her hair done. It was a hot day. When the train arrived it was burning soft coal, a black cloud roiling out of the stack and over our heads. Then this man who looked like a filthy beggar got off the train. He frightened me as he moved quickly toward our carriage. He was covered with soot. He climbed right into our carriage and I screamed as he quickly went to Mama, knocked her hat off -- and hugged and kissed her. His sooty clothes got Mama all dirty and wrinkled. And I thought, 'Goodness sakes. Is that man really my Papa?'"

I too remember these stories clearly. I was not yet thirty and friends and neighbors thought it was conspicuous that my husband was never at home.

Mr. Edison wrote me time after time asking me to come up to his mine and stay for a few days or a week. He suggested, "Leave the children at home with Lucy and you can talk to them by telephone. I can work much better when you are here for then I am satisfied and my mind is at rest."

The funny thing is, to entice me, he promised to install running water. But that never happened and I never visited for overnight. He called his new house the "White House," which was also funny. It was a wild stretch of his imagination to compare the President's home to this unpainted shack on a rock pile among his naked black hills in New Jersey.

In another letter he wrote, "I feel lost in not going home to see my darling, dustless Billie. What am I to do without a bath? Some smartweed seeds have commenced to sprout out of the seams of my coat. Think of it, Billie. Your lover turned into a flower garden."

For better or worse

Mr. Edison had often used a pedagogic tone with me since we first met. I was only nineteen. He wore the mantel of a mature, worldly gentleman who felt the necessity of teaching me, the delicate, much younger, innocent woman, about the ways of society and the world.

"If you knew how much I love you darling Billie you would never fear or worry for an instant about such things or ever be jealous. Don't you know that the fixed law of the organic world requires one man for one woman and that all normal well-balanced men never have the least desire to contravene that law, it's only the ill-balanced degenerate and conceited egotist that does such things."[67]

He was suggesting, of course, that the urge to flirt, or worse, with another woman never occurred to him when he was away from me for long periods. I knew well this man's strong desires for me first hand. Did he really want me to think his desires for female companionship were simply tucked neatly away for weeks, sometimes months, when he was away from me? Did he want me to think that a man, so revered by the masses, could not be strongly desired by other women?

I could have recoiled at his often superior attitude and challenged him. But what good could have come of that? From the beginning, I unconditionally accepted my Dearie, for better or worse.

Marion finds a man

The mystery letter was from Lieutenant Oscar Oeser requesting Mr. Edison's permission to wed Marion. He stated he had known her well before she had returned to America. He provided a list of character references, both civilian and military. Lieutenant Oeser said he, as a German officer in the kaiser's forces, also had to request permission from the king of Saxony to marry a foreigner.

Mr. Edison sent off an angry letter to Marion. "Dot. What is the meaning of this foolishness? Of the millions of available American men in this world, why do you find it necessary to marry a German, especially an army officer? These are two negatives against a happy marriage. What kind of life do you expect to find with this man? I am sending your Uncle Simeon [his father Samuel's half brother] to Germany to investigate this man. I am against this marriage and, if the king has any common sense, he too will refuse your request."

Marion responded immediately. "Father. I love you very much. But why can't you give me a little love? I am your daughter. I need your love. I have always needed it. Please, please forgive the way I walked out on you at Glenmont when you refused to see me and say goodbye to me. That hurt me dreadfully. I wanted to hug you and kiss you before I went away, but you wouldn't let me. Please understand that Oscar and I are blissfully happy -- the happiest I have ever been -- except when you and I spent so much time together after mother died. Oscar has accepted my ugly, pock-marked face and he loves me and promises to care for me forever. I can no longer live alone. Please, father, give us your blessing. I will be so proud to have you to walk me down the aisle. It will mean everything to me. Your loving daughter, Marion."

Uncle Simeon's favorable report on Lieutenant Oeser grudgingly passed Mr. Edison's scrutiny. But then, as if penalizing her for choosing this man against his wishes, he refused to attend the wedding. Marion was devastated as was the rest of the family.

Instead, brother Tom volunteered to go, not because he had any great feelings for his sister, but out of brotherly obligation and, perhaps, a perfect excuse to get away from the mines and visit Europe for the first time. He arrived in Germany two days before the wedding and left the day after, delaying his return to America by a month-long European tour.

Tom was the last of her family Marion would see for another seventeen years.

Chapter Twelve

1895-1897

Rechargeable batteries

The first utilitarian gasoline-operated cars began to appear in 1895. For Mr. Edison, who famously developed the first practical use and transmission of electric power twenty years earlier, it was natural for him to begin experiments with inexpensive rechargeable batteries for cars as an alternative to "noisy, smelly" gasoline vehicles.

Initially, Mr. Edison had his doubts about the commercial value of rechargable batteries, until he began experiments with them in isolated electric lighting plants. It was here that generators could be run during the day to charge batteries that powered lights at night.

But it was an entirely new concept to invent a generator that was small and light enough to recharge a battery in an automobile. It wasn't until after the turn of the century that Mr. Edison realized it *could* be done.

Experiments with X-rays

X-rays[68] were discovered in the Netherlands by physicist Wilhelm Roentgen in 1895. These rays were "radiated" from a cathode tube and were able to pass through the flesh and muscle tissue of living animals to produce a shadow image on a photographic plate. Its value in surgery was immediately recognized and the medical profession stampeded toward the process.

Mr. Edison was asked by a professor at Columbia University for help in discovering the most effective fluoroscopic chemicals for lamps and fluoroscopes. He put his laboratory men to work testing crystals in about 8,000 different chemical combinations. Within three weeks he sent the University a fluoroscope with a tungstate-of-calcium screen that enabled a clear shadowgraph of a person's hand that had shotgun pellets embedded in it. A surgeon then performed the first X-ray operation in America with my husband's gadget.

Excitement of this discovery broke out all over America. Mr. Edison went into mass production and supplied X-ray tubes to hospitals and surgeons. At the May 1896 Electrical Exposition in New York, Mr. Edison exhibited a row of fluoroscopes, each with peepholes. Thousands of visitors looked at shadows of the interior of their hands as they held them between the X-ray tube and a screen -- the first such exhibit in the world.

But then, small injuries began to occur in Mr. Edison's lab, injuries that were not readily noticed. Lab assistant Clarence Dally was poisonously affected. His flesh became ulcerated and his hair fell out. He went through several amputations and finally died.

Even Mr. Edison, who was experimenting with the use of X-ray lamps for lighting, suffered a severe eye injury from which he later recovered. He immediately put his experiments aside as dangerous.

Injuries from X-rays, of course, were not limited to the West Orange lab. Many accidents were happening everywhere X-rays were in use. Little was known about radioactivity.

It took as long as fifteen years, and countless injuries and deaths, before protective lead screening came into use and an improved cathode tube was invented.

Mr. Edison's father, Samuel, died in February 1896 at the enviable age of ninety-two. In recent years he had been living with his daughter, Marion Page, at her farm in Norwalk, Ohio.

Mr. Edison and his sister had an argument over where their father's funeral should take place -- in their birth town of Port Huron, Michigan or right there in Norwalk. His sister won out, saying her husband Homer was in too poor health to make the journey to Port Huron. Mr. Edison gave in, for once, to his sister's wishes.

Despite recently becoming deeply involved in X-ray experiments, Mr. Edison pulled himself away from his work in respect to the memory of his beloved father, and his mother Nancy, who had died twenty-five years earlier.

Memories of his father stretched from when "Al" accompanied his father into town on Saturday nights and bought him peppermint sticks to keep him busy while Samuel talked with friends. They might also watch a band concert or they might take the horse and buggy and visit his father's shingle mill. But generally, his memories of Port Huron were negative. It was a backwater, he said, where few of his neighbors understood him.

Samuel was very proud of his inventive son and never ceased to brag about him. He tried to get him to set up his first laboratory in Port Huron, but Mr. Edison called the town a "damn hole" and had the foresight to see that the village of Menlo Park was strategically located on a railroad line only a few miles from New York City and Newark. Samuel relented and Mr. Edison appointed his father general supervisor of the laboratory construction in 1876.

I did not attend the funeral. Mrs. Page wrote me saying it was very good to see her brother after so many years. She graciously blamed his long absence from her doorstep to the distance between Ohio and New Jersey. Their father's body was then transported to Port Huron where Mr. Edison had vowed he would never return. But his reputation preceded him and the town celebrated his return as if they had loved him throughout his youth.

"I became damn tired of listening to reminiscences of a childhood I had no recollection of," he told me. "You know how I detest people fawning over me, or who they think is me. I left town just as soon as they covered father with the good earth."

The lost soul

Tom was hanging on to his job at the Ogden mine by a spider's thread. He was now twenty and a lost soul. Try as he would, he could not penetrate the invisible wall between him and his father. He craved first of all for his father's appreciation of his work at the mine. When that never came, he yearned for nothing but camping in the wilderness, much like Henry David Thoreau's experiences in the wilds of Maine. Tom wanted to study nature in its most primitive form, he wrote, "where not a sound is heard, except perhaps a hooting of an owl on yonder treetop or the roar of a restless panther up in the crevices . . . I plead with you to kindly think of me -- who studies this life in a different view and one who loves you all so dearly -- but love in return is cold.

"He [his father] passed me by . . . and his distractedness never allowed him to wave or say hello. I am invisible. A nonentity."

I tried to answer Tom's letters with encouraging words. I felt for his pain. Tom's letters sent directly to Mr. Edison were futile -- "I wrote to him, but no answers came." I often attempted to mediate between him and his father, but with very poor results.

Summers at Chautauqua in the wild sustained him. He tried to find a way to work at the mines while at the same time satisfy his wandering spirit. His interest in his Ogden job was now waning, but he was afraid of his father. He had always been afraid of Mr. Edison. He called him "sir" and gave him the utmost respect, or was it a feeling of intimidation, when in his father's presence?

"Mother, I want a change -- something that is new to me that is full of adventure. . . Why should I write you about this, for it is a father's claim, but I write to you with a feeling that, being as father is and situated in this world, it would not be advisable to tell this to him, for he has no time for consideration. America's foremost inventor, I often wonder, and think, am I his son. What have I done to be deserving of such a great and honorable Father. And it is his genius I have to blame for these doubtful and restless thoughts of mine. I probably never will be able to please him -- I have no genius, no talent and no accomplishment, I am afraid, it is not in me, but I shall never give up trying. If I could only talk to him the way I want to. I have many ideas of my own which sometime I would like to ask him, or tell him about, but they never leave my mouth."

In a letter to his father about this time, Tom wrote: "I don't believe I would ever be able to talk to you the way I would like to because you are so far my superior in every way that when I am in your presence I am perfectly helpless. I have never pleased you "in anything I ever have done."

And then to me: "If father thought that after I finish college he would give me a position somewhere, I would of course much rather work for him and for his interests. But as this [is] out of the question as he will never have anything for one who is considered by him and probably others in his employ as unintelligent, I have in consequence given up all hope in this direction. . . He told me I was to 'paddle my own canoe' and I am going to do it."

Tom's growing affection for me matched his disaffection for his father. This disaffection extended to Chautauqua where he felt he could no longer stay with his family, even though he lived elsewhere on the campus with friends. He also refused to stay at Glenmont when his father was present.

Tom always believed that his father was the only one who had the power to give his life real meaning. He was not receiving that power, therefore he felt his life was meaningless. "I shall never ask father again for something to do."

Next came Tom's thoughts of suicide.[69]

Ford meets Edison

The Association of Edison Illuminating Companies met in New York City in August 1896. Henry Ford had been working under Alexander Dow at one of Mr. Edison's Detroit electic substations. In his spare time, Ford, the tinkering engineer, was experimenting with building the gasoline "quadricycle." It was built on a buggy foundation with four bicycle wheels, a two-cylinder, four-horsepower, air-cooled engine that Ford made himself from miscellaneous parts found here and there. The vehicle weighed five hundred pounds, had a three-gallon gas tank and no reverse gear. It had two fixed speeds -- ten and twenty miles per hour.

Dow was aware of Ford's tinkering and valued it at the substation. He was also aware of and had seen Ford's creation and was impressed. Dow introduced Ford, age thirty-three, to Mr. Edison, fourteen years his senior, as an employee of his and "a man who has made a gas car." At Mr. Edison's encouragement at this meeting, Ford sketched out the significant details of his car. According to lore, Mr. Edison smacked his fist onto the table and said, "Keep at it!"[70]

From this meeting on, Henry Ford idolized Mr. Edison and it increased year by year, but their paths would not cross again for another decade and a half.

William continued his psychological struggle and poor study habits at Trinity but somehow graduated. He joined our family at Chautauqua for the summer and spent most of his time with his older brother hiking, boating and occasionally seeing Chautauqua girls and attending dances.

The boys at eighteen and twenty also spent time commiserating with each other about their father's lack of interest in them.

"Why is it that father ignores me at the mines when I am doing what he asks of me?" Tom asked his brother, as they lay side-by-side on the Chautauqua beach. "I am so depressed. I feel like crap. In father's eyes I must be a pile of shit that must be deposited with his ore residue on his barren landscape."

"Jesus! Tom. I don't know what to say. I'm shocked. I hate to see you thinking such morose thoughts. Can't you just dump it and have some light-hearted fun here? I also know what it's like to be ignored. School has been a bitch for me. Everyone there envies me because of father's goddamned reputation. They ask me why I'm not like him. They kid me about how lucky I am to have such a famous father. They expect so much of me. Everyone expects so much of me. But I'm trying to ignore it all and you must do that also. We have to think of other things and make our own lives."

Tom turned on his side toward William and propped his head onto his raised arm. "Just how the hell can we do that when our name is 'Edison'?

"At school, everyone expected so much of me. I'm the one who looks like father. They expected me to be another Wizard. When I didn't live up to their expectations, they made fun of me and taunted me saying I was the 'Edison dunce.' I didn't have any of the fellows I could really call my friend and who liked me for what I was.

"Even the girls you and I see here -- are they seeing us because they like us for who we are, or because they want to be seen with the son of an Edison? Damn. It's such a problem."

"Hey brother," William said. "You're depressing me. Let's take the canoe across the lake. We need some exercise."

"You need the exercise, brother," Tom said. "I work at the mines."

"Ok. I'll paddle. You rest."

Tom's opinion of Oscar

Tom revealed to me in a letter more details about his journey to Germany to help with sister Marion's wedding.

"I didn't like Oscar at all, mother. He was conceited and militaristic. He and Marion were greatly upset, of course, that father didn't care enough to walk his once favorite child up the aisle. Oscar asked me what kind of a cruel father we siblings really had. I tried to defend him, but truly, there was no defense.

"Oscar made fun of me because of my job in the mines. He said, 'Join the army. It'll make a man out of you.' That hurt all the more, mother, because it was true. Maybe I should join the army.

"I asked Marion in private what she saw in Oscar but she refused to talk about it. She was obviously enamored by him prancing around in his fancy officer's uniform with badges and medals all over it. With all the pride he displayed, they are going to live in military quarters – a real dump of a place for lowest ranking married officers. It's a major change for Marion who has been living in a grand hotel.

"I'm now on my way to Paris to see France for the first time. William and I were never given the Grand Tour by father. I'm going to grab this chance while I have it. I plan to visit the Left Bank and get a closeup of the lifestyle of the artists and writers and see how it compares with the Village here.

"I love you, Mama. I wish we were traveling together. I know it would be a lark."

The "Edison" curse

Totally ill prepared academically because of his father's misunderstood instructions to the Trinity headmaster, William followed his father's wishes, or was it his desire to follow his friends, and enrolled in a School of Engineering. Yet his father, still oblivious to the mixup at Trinity, used his influence and proudly saw his son enrolled at Yale in the fall of 1897. William did as he was told, albeit with reluctance. Certainly, he believed, his father knew what he was doing.

I was well aware of the fiasco at Trinity and tried to intervene with Mr. Edison, but he would not listen to my reasoning. By the following spring, unable to get passing grades in any of his engineering courses, William dropped out of Yale -- to his father's extreme chagrin and his son's increasing feeling of personal failure.

Because he was an Edison, William's "disenrollment" was noted in the press -- adding a harsher level of public failure for the young man. The reason given to the world was "eye difficulty."

Both boys were now on the loose, rejected by their father, continuously trailed by the press, and plagued with the reality of nowhere to hide. It became obvious to both boys that their name was more of a curse than a blessing.

But now, free of schools, the boys were together again having a few drinks in their father's old haunt, Delmonico's. Tom had endless stories about his two weeks in Paris and his mixing with the artistic elite.

As they examined their jobless predicament, they began to see that the name "Edison" was indeed their rightful birth privilege. Certainly they could benefit from their name to start their own business. Why not? Their father had not offered either of them a decent job in any one of his many businesses. Papa had no right to be the exclusive holder of the Edison name.

The boys expressed these thoughts bravely in a joint letter to their father.

The reaction was swift and brief. "You will *not* run off on your own and contaminate the well-established and respected Edison name. Any attempt to do so will result in legal action."

Challenging their father's threats, the boys resolved to take action. Thanks to their name, they had no trouble raising the capital they believed they needed. The bank assumed their father was behind his sons' business plans. The boys opened companies in the city at 96 Broadway and named them the "The Thomas A. Edison Jr. Improved Incandescent Lamp Company" and the "William L. Edison, Agent for Phonographs, Kinescopes, Roentgen Ray Apparatus, Edison-Lalande Batteries, etc."

This activity was decidedly against their father's wishes. My Dearie ranted and raved around the house for a full day, making it uncomfortable for all of us. Never would he ever allow *anyone* to use the Edison name for any purpose. It was sacred. To my husband, the agnostic, his name was *more* than sacred.

Tom's and William's dreams of entrepreneurship, personal independence and, most importantly, self-worth, were totally obliterated when their father called the bank, cancelled the loans and had both businesses shuttered.

I had to ask myself, isn't it strange that a man, who always did exactly as he wanted, did not allow his children to do anything they wanted? I felt so sorry for the boys.

Chapter Thirteen

1898

Mina is pregnant again

In January, I recognized I was three months pregnant with my third child. Both Madeleine, now ten, and Charles, two years younger, earnestly hoped the new baby would be a girl and that she would have blonde hair. Marion was a blonde, so this hope was not unreasonable.

Our twelfth wedding anniversary was approaching, not that we ever celebrated it, but with it came my hopes that my husband, closing in on age forty-two, might slow down a bit and become an active part of this family. How many more things could he possibly invent?

I had been fearful of overexerting myself in my current state, but I could not ignore my social commitments to the community. Like my husband, I had my job to do, but some days I felt used up and unable to do anything.

I was often very uneasy about my stepchildren. I feared they were giving me gray hairs prematurely. Their lives were so erratic and undisciplined. I knew deep in my heart that the chaos in their lives was not entirely their fault. If their father had only given them a fraction of his time and shown them just the least bit of attention and love, I knew that would have made a great difference. There was not much I could do about their relationship with him. I could castigate and berate my husband. but it would have been totally useless and counter-productive. I tried to love his children -- our children -- but, in reality, I could do little more than sympathize with them and act as a buffer.

But I too was a casualty of his absence. I too got lonely and wished for more of his presence. And when I was down and feeling empty, I realized and firmly believed, that I was here to help him do all that he had to do. He was a great man and a great man must have a great woman behind him. I tried very hard to be that woman.

William joins the Army

Following the business fiascos led by Tom, the Spanish-American War broke out on April 25 and it was William, nineteen, who surprised us all by enlisting in the Army. He signed up as a private in the First New York Regiment of Volunteer Engineers. Not to belittle his intentions, as it turned out this was as close as he ever came to becoming an "engineer." After training, he was sent to Puerto Rico where he was promptly shot in the left foot in the conflict that lasted only three and a half months. He spent six weeks in the hospital and was discharged near the close of the war. It was now publicized that poor William had one additional defeat -- he failed at seeking glory in this war. He never had a chance to fire his weapon.

William returned to New York in late summer and stubbornly set up a business on 59th Street with a partner, G.M. Rogers, a successful businessman who graciously offered his expertise to the young man with the Edison name. Their goal was to sell to bars, restaurants and other public establishments an "automatic picture machine" they named it the Edison Photoscope. The device, that William had actually created himself but neglected to patent, allowed the viewer to see twelve photographs, accompanied by songs from a music box, for a nickel. Never having discussed the plan beforehand with his father, it was William's unrealistic expectation that Mr. Edison would manufacture these machines for them.

"There you go again," his father wrote, expressing his wrath. "You never learn. No! I will not manufacture your so-called Photoscope. It sounds very much like my slot machine. You are an embarrassment to me. It's this Rogers fellow who wants to use my name for his benefit."

William immediately wrote back. "Dearest Papa. It is not Mr. Rogers who wants to use your name. I invited him to join me to help me manage my business. I needed his help, although I'd much prefer your help, Papa. I am using the Edison name because it is *my* name also. I am not competing with you. My machine uses pictures, not movies. Please, Papa. Allow your son to paddle his own canoe."

Mr. Edison shut down his son's business.

Once again it was father against son. William's hope was dashed and resulted in a serious fracture between them.

The Miller boys

In sharp contrast to their cousins, my brothers John, twenty-five, and Theodore, "Thede," twenty-three, had graduated with honors from St. Paul's School. They were also frequent visitors to Glenmont on holidays and whenever they passed through New Jersey. My husband was the prime attraction.

Mr. Edison took a great interest in John and Thede as adolescents and later as they progressed through college. At the same time the two brothers became infatuated with Mr. Edison. For Christmas he gave them a telescope so they would be able to views the stars and planets. He gave them many components from his laboratory so they would be able to conduct their own experiments. This included telegraph keys, wires and a battery. He also gave them a manually-operated generator that, when cranked up to 200 RPMs, sent out a charge that could shock their pet cat. In addition, he gave them a bottle of sulfuric acid so they could make battery fluid but warned them, "Do not to spill this caustic liquid or get it in your eyes for it can be very damaging."

Neither mother nor father commented to me about dangers of some of my husband's gifts. But the boys showed their responsibility by avoiding injury. I can't say the same for their cat.

It had always been assumed that John and Thede would join their brothers at their father's reaper plant in Canton, Ohio. But under Mr. Edison's influence, it appears this may have influenced them to alter their vocational aspirations.

Thede graduated from Yale in May, two years after brother John. The entire Miller family attended the ceremonies in New Haven, Connecticut. Thede was the baby of the Miller family, the favorite. He was handsome, smart, president of the debating society, a wrestler and violinist, as well as an actor. Madeleine, at eleven, was infatuated with her cousin.

Father Miller was preparing Thede to take over his dreams of founding additional Sunday schools as well as new Chautauquas branches throughout America. He also thought that Thede should continue his education by attending law school.

Mina's brothers enter the war with Spain

Father's plans came to a standstill on February 15 when the USS *Maine* was sunk in Havana Harbor.

On April 23, President William McKinley called for 125,000 volunteers. About a million men came forward. My brother John joined the Navy as an engineer on the USS *Marblehead*. Two days later America declared war with Spain.

Just after his graduation, Thede took a more adventurous course and joined Teddy Roosevelt's legendary Rough Riders for the invasion of Cuba.

Father, mother and sister Jane tried to convince the boys this was an "interloper's" war. Thede responded with, "If everyone excused himself for selfish reasons, we would have no army."

Thede sent a letter to mother before he was shipped out. "I think I am doing my duty and trust that you will agree with me. My train leaves right away, so I must close. Love beyond expression from a loving son. Goodbye."

Officially named The First U.S. Volunteer Cavalry, the Rough Riders originally consisted of Indian fighters from the southwest territories, but once Theodore Roosevelt resigned his post as Assistant Secretary of the Navy in May 1898 to lead the group, the ranks quickly filled with a greater variety men. Many of these were from Ivy League schools. They included glee-club singers, athletes, American Indians and Texas Rangers. I was so proud my brother had decided to join before the great rush to glory that followed.

Thede was among the first 12,000 to land at Daiquiri, Cuba on June 22. They were to advance through the jungle and tropical heat to meet the Spanish troops at Santiago. On July 1, the Rough Riders found themselves outside Santiago facing snipers settled in on Kettle Hill. The gunfire kept the men low with what Roosevelt called random fire. Several officers, including Roosevelt, called for the charge on the hill. The troops had no choice but to move forward and take the hill by direct assault. Journalist Richard Harding Davis was among the troops. In a greatly idealistic and imaginative story, he wrote that Roosevelt waved his hat and the troops rushed the hill.[71]

The story I read leaned heavily on romantic images and photos. The reality was far from it. Men were mowed down en masse, including Thede, who believed he was hit in the left shoulder. There was little pain. He didn't think it was serious at the time, but he could not raise himself from the ground. He told his fellow troopers to move on and not to bother with him.

He later learned the bullet had actually passed from the left shoulder, through his upper torso and out his right shoulder. Breathing became difficult. His spinal cord was nearly severed. He was now paralyzed from his shoulders to his feet.

Time passed. He watched as Roosevelt's Volunteers, with reinforcements, reached the top of the hill and repulsed the Spanish. Around him, numberless men were on the ground in various conditions, some trying to move, others motionless.

Thede waited, his breathing more labored.

He was eventually picked up and transported twelve miles over muddy roads to an American Red Cross hospital tent that was overwhelmed with casualties.

He was able to dictate a final letter to mother. "A narrow escape but feel sure I will pull through all right. . . They are doing everything that they can for me. I remain your most loving son and will be with you soon."

As I read his letter, I had to stop now and then to wipe tears away. I feared the worst. I shuddered at the chaotic scene he described. I hoped and prayed that my baby brother would indeed be here with us soon.

That was not to happen. He died on July 7 after slipping into unconsciousness. They buried him right there in a simple grave near the ruins of a burned out building.

A brief telegram with this news arrived in my hands from brother John three days after I gave birth to a boy. I hugged my baby tightly as I wept and decided the boy would be christened "Theodore."

My sister Jennie dies

It was in the midst of the final gasp of the Ogden mining operations in November that my beloved sister Jennie died in Akron. I was visiting my parents in Ohio at the time. She was only forty-three, a mere ten years older than me. It was not a total surprise. Jennie had been very ill with valvular heart disease for a several months and had been married a mere six years. She never had any children.

I wrote Mr. Edison at the mine with my sad news. He responded, calling me "darling wife" and "Billie," with true sympathy, but there was no way that he could accompany me to the funeral. If he left the site for three or four days, he said, he would have to shut it down. Everything, he said, depended on the outcome. He said he had 400 men on the job "and all depends on myself. Had I an intelligent assistant I could have come."

Mr. Edison never even made it home for the Christmas holidays that year. His comment was, "What! Is it Christmas, already?" I sent him a cake, shaped somewhat in the form of his ore mill.

Claiming Thede's body

John Miller was fully engaged on the USS *Marblehead* in Guantanamo harbor and was unable to retrieve his fallen brother's body. A military quarantine had been issued ashore in Cuba after a yellow-fever outbreak.

Stuck on a boat tantalizingly close to shore, John mourned for the brother he had been so close to all his life. He agonized over the reports of the Battle of San Juan Hill that directly followed the Kettle Hill battle. He spilled all his feelings in letters to me and mother. He truly felt the pain and anguish and ugliness that Thede must have witnessed all around him during the battle.

John wrote to father Miller saying he had tried to keep his mind off his brother but it was very difficult to do. "Dear old Thede. How gladly I would have given up my life for him. . . If only I could have gotten here a little sooner and seen him before he died. If Thede had lived, what a glorious homecoming we would have had."

A month after the war ended, Theodore's body was disintered and send home to the Miller family and placed in the family plot in Akron. Father's close friend Bishop John Vincent officiated and delivered a eulogy that our family found very moving.

Mother also thought the ceremony was meaningful and said she believed the event brought the Bishop's family and ours closer together. George was also present. In spite of all my activites at Chautauqua, we had not seen each other since I broke off our engagement years ago. We found ourselves side-by-side. I was curious about how his life had turned out.

I was the first to speak. "Hello, George."

He turned to me. "Hello, Mina. How are you?" He smiled.

"I'm just fine, thank you. How is university life?"

"It's fine."

"Are your married?"

"No."

"I'm sorry to hear that. Why not?"

"You destroyed me."

"Oh. Come on, George."

"I'm serious. What did I ever do to you? You're the one who broke our engagement. You're the one who walked out on me."

"I feel sorry for you, George. I hope you can find happiness somewhere." Without another word I turned and walked away.

The rift between the families was between my father and the Bishop. They stubbornly disagreed over which one of them *first* sparked the idea of creating the Chautauqua Institution. Each had publicly announced it was *his* idea. What difference did it make! They worked at founding it *together*. Instead, they nearly severed the traditional bond between our families.

Tom had no understanding of business. He was also impractical and clumsy with his hands. These handicaps made it nearly impossible for him to deal effectively with experienced businessmen. His name was a magnet and once someone came in touch with him he was easily lost to their advantage. Investors hovered like flies around him, but they seemed to be more interested in using the Edison name than anything Tom could offer them. His earlier ventures with his brother William were failures even before their father halted them. Despite failure after failure, and his father's continuing rebuffs, he still craved to be an inventor of mechanics like him.

Tom had come up with what he called the "Edison Junior Improved" incandescent lamp. In a letter to me he seemed to be confused about whether he had invented something marketable or that his investors were more interested in his marketable name. Regardless of how Tom felt, Mr. Edison, as usual, was *certain* the investors were after the Edison name.

Tom was delighted when the newspapers called the lamp his invention and took his side when his father criticized his son in a New York *Herald* interview. Tom believed his father was jealous and he began to see himself as his father's rival.

The newspapers wrote that Tom learned how to invent by working in his father's laboratory. These reports opened new opportunities for him. He caught the attention of the New York electrical community and this led to his appointment to the Committee on Decorative Effects for the 1898 Electrical Exhibition to be held at Madison Square Garden. This in turn magnified his achievements and created for him a reputation as an inventor.

Soon, Tom seemed to have delusions of grandeur and he hinted to one friend that the federal government was looking to him to work on some crucial experiments. Scheme after scheme followed and for one reason or another they all failed.

I wrote to Tom. "Dearest Tom. What is happening? Why do you keep repeating the past? I cannot believe the newspaper reports. Are the quotes about your statements correct? I wish you would move back to Glenmont and reconsider your future. I want to help you any way that I can."

"Dear Mama. Thank you for your offer, but I cannot live in the same house with Papa. He doesn't try to understand me or give me any of his valuable help and experience. I totally respect him and I would give anything to be an inventor just like him. I wish I could work in his laboratory and learn how to do things the right way. I am now getting some public recognition and I want to make the best of it. I know I have talent. I just have to find it."

Where would all this end? It ended when Mr. Edison became disgusted, once again, with people using his name. He threatened Tom with a lawsuit if he did not stop.

William revealed to Tom that his father said he was through with him also and that he was a total disgrace. Tom, in turn, declared that he would go on "until the law compels me to stop."

Their arguments accomplished only one thing -- a total break between father and sons. In fact Tom was broken in spirit in every way. He began to slip into a frightening psychological tumble.

Chapter Fourteen

1899

Edison returns to his laboratory

Mr. Edison never really gave up on the Ogden mine, but he recognized it would be smart not to invest any more money in it. He had totally dedicated himself to the mine for five years, ignoring his family. He had also lost millions of dollars and was in debt for several hundred thousand more.

One day in 1899 he was on the train with Walter Mallory, his Ogden plant superintendent. They talked about the progress of dismantling the operation. Mallory later wrote that Mr. Edison was in a jovial mood. It surprised him that, after all the years he had devoted to the project and then to have it fail, he could be so lighthearted.

All that was now behind him. He pointed out to Mallory that he was now fifty-three and out of work, but he could always find a $75-dollar-a-month job as a telegrapher.

This gay disposition after a failure was one of Mr. Edison's most positive characteristics. He had reacted the same to many failures. He even boasted about all his laboratory failures. How many failures did it take to come up with one success in the lab? "Take a look at my notebooks," he would say. "Failures are learning experiences that lead to successes. It's only when you quit that you really fail."

I was exuberant. My husband was home again working in his laboratory just down the street from Glenmont. I could visit him. He could be home at night.

The Ogden mines venture was behind him. His motion picture and phonograph businesses were doing very well and were on their own. Mr. Edison had to decide which of the ideas rumbling around in his head he would tackle next. "I have enough ideas to break the Bank of England," he often said.

He had learned that Portland cement[72] was just emerging as a major building material. Roads were now being paved with cement. He foresaw a big expansion of reinforced concrete construction in America. How could he now take advantage of this new industry? He decided he could make use of the big rock crushers that were now dormant at Ogden and grind his own cement. In his pastime he had already designed a long rotary kiln that could be used for making cement.

On April 15 he organized the Edison Portland Cement Company and decided to use the facility to make low-cost concrete dwellings. He set his engineers to work designing molds for various house designs. Each mold would be a section of a house and, when assembled, would be a complete shell of a home ready for the details to be added outside and in.

He bought a tract of limestone rock in eastern Pennsylvania and brought in his "Giant Rolls" crusher from Ogden. Eventually his company was able to grind out 1,000 barrels of cement every twenty-four hours. Mr. Edison calculated that free flowing concrete could cast a six-room house in one piece in about six hours with his specifically-designed machinery. The object was to produce cheap houses for the "working man" in the form of detached dwellings. The result was a pioneering effort into pre-fabricated housing.

In the end his scheme failed to win general acceptance. It cost him about $100,000 before he scrapped the idea. Mr. Edison's cement houses may have worked best fifty years later at the conclusion of World War II when a critical housing shortage developed and cheap, cookie-cutter pre-fab homes became popular.

Lewis Miller dies

Father Miller suffered through an agonizingly long illness in late January brought on by what was variously described as kidneys, abdomen, stomach or, most likely, prostate. In any case the doctors decided on immediate surgery. Mother and I accompanied him by express train from Akron to New York City for the procedure.

But it was the middle of winter and we were caught in a blizzard that stranded our train in the New Jersey meadows. It was a horrible time, beyond words, as my father experienced unrelenting pain. For two days and nights we waited on this immobile train amid the snow drifts, icy cold and very little food until an ambulance finally arrived to carry the three of us into the city.

They catheterized him on Monday, February 13 but the shock, combined with the endless wait on the train, was too much for him. With his loving wife and daughter at his bedside, he held on until early Friday when uremic poisoning took its toll. Father passed away on February 17 at the age of seventy.

His friends and acquaintances remembered my father and his accomplishments affectionately as an outgoing, hospitable man who was generous philanthropically and worked tirelessly at his farm machine factory. He was also devoted to his church in Akron and to the education of young people. In that regard, he was the creator of the now widely adopted Sunday school program. He was also remembered and celebrated as the co-founder of the well-established Chautauqua Institution.

I look at my father similarly and also as a wonderful family man. We eleven children profited richly from his intellectual instruction as well as from the neighbors and celebrities he invited to his dinner table regularly. Father, I believe, prepared me suitably for my husband -- a man of vast talent who needed me to understand him, protect his name and his interests, and to look after his children as best I could. It was not a matter of having an easy married life with a rich man. It was a matter of my defending a life that invents great things and is revered for his contributions throughout the world.

Tom marries a chorus girl

While we in the Miller family mourned the loss of father Lewis and siblings, Thede and Jennie, my twenty-three year old stepson Tom Edison had somehow managed to avoid enlisting in the Spanish-American War. According to my sources, Tom was drinking heavily and had been living with a New York chorus girl named Marie Louise Touhey[73] for about two years. They shared an apartment in the city near Broadway in the West Fifties.

Marie, eighteen, was known in the press as "casino girl," always cheerful, self-confident and full of fun. She was described as having a shapely figure, a pleasant voice and a mass of wavy golden hair surrounding bright blue eyes.

This lovely young woman had bit parts as an actress -- at least until her fateful performance as Parthenia in *La Belle Helene* on the evening of February 16, 1899 when she broke into a spasm of uncontrollable giggles on stage. The curtain dropped and the manager, who had had difficulties with her previously, dismissed her immediately and told her to leave.

She replied sweetly and pleasantly, "You need not tell me when I am to leave. I'll leave when I get good and ready; in fact, I think I'll leave now."

"You can give *her* costumes to Miss Jones," the manager said to the wardrobe woman.

Overhearing this, Marie retorted as sweetly as any actress could, "Pardon me. I am not 'her.' I have a name, and it is Mrs. Thomas A. Edison Jr.!"

With that shocking statement, Marie swept out the door to a gathering of reporters. "Yes," she told them. "Tom and I were married three months ago."

All this was reported in the newspapers. It was scandalous. What the press did not know was they were married against Mr. Edison's wishes, three days *after* this stage incident on February 19. In addition, the new Mrs. Tom Edison Jr. was intoxicated and in the public spotlight, making her rounds in the run-down district of Tenderloin, bragging that she was Mr. Edison's daughter-in-law and his favorite. Marie went on to say the "Old Man" gave her money and she was playing the family for "suckers."

The two were divorced a few months later. As part of the divorce bargain with Marie, Mr. Edison gave her a twenty-five dollar a week allowance on the condition that she not use her married name as a stage name.

Tom's drinking continued. I attributed it to legal difficulties he was having with shaky business dealings he was still having, designed to make use of his Edison name.

Storage batteries

As early as 1896, the few gasoline cars in existence were already belching noxious fumes from their tailpipes. One insightful electrical engineer wrote, "Imagine thousands of such vehicles on the streets, each offering up its columns of smell!" Mr. Edison recalled that statement in one of his professional journals during his commute into New York City in the spring of 1899 as he awaited the Cortlandt Street ferry. Idling engines were indeed noxious.

This was the impetus that set him to work experimenting with safe, compact storage batteries that could replace the smelly gasoline engine. In February 1901, with capital stock of $1 million, he organized the Edison Storage Battery Company.

Fulfilling his dream of a perfect battery took more than ten years of experimentation, trial and error, stockholder rebellion and competitive challenges in France and Britain. It cost him personally $1.5 million plus $2.5 million investment capital by 1910. By 1914 his battery was the sole power for twenty-five percent of the pleasure-vehicle market and more than half of all electric trucks.

But this was about the high point in his competitive battle. Vehicle manufacturers were reluctant to redesign their vehicles to accommodate the battery. It was large and heavy and it needed to be protected from cold weather to save its energy. In an attempt to answer this problem, Mr. Edison designed and began marketing a truck designed around his battery, but it fell short of commercial success.

Electric vehicles might have had a fighting chance -- until his friend Henry Ford revolutionized the entire automobile market with his very popular and economical Model T.

Never to be defeated, Mr. Edison foresaw unlimited new markets for his batteries -- ships and railroad lights, railway signals and switches, submarines, insolated-house lighting, flashlights, miner's lamps, and any number of industrial and household uses.[74]

William marries

William's business differences with his father were compounded when, in November, he too married against his father's wishes. Mr. Edison believed William, at twenty-one, was too young and unsettled to marry. It was also very sudden, quite Edisonian, in my opinion. They had met at a party. It was love at first sight.

It didn't matter to his father that William's wife, Blanche Travers, was the daughter of a successful Maryland farmer and produce wholesaler and the niece of U.S. Senator John Daniels of Virginia. Blanche's family whole-heartedly approved of their daughter's marriage into a famous, well-to-do family. Although the Travers family was dismayed that the young husband was not yet employed, they were pleased at the couple's youthful spirit and optimism for the future. As far as money was concerned, there was little Blanche's farm family could do for the couple. As for Uncle John, he had fought himself up the proverbial ladder to Congressional success and he expected his niece's husband, from a well-connected family, to do the same.

I was opposed to William's unforeseen marriage as well, so much so that I stopped writing to him. This was not smart on my part because terminating communication never solved problems between people. When the press got wind of it they called it an elopement. Looking back, there was much in my life I regretted because I tried to support my often irrational husband. I loved his children and I felt they loved me. I was often torn by the family calamities that took place around me.

Mr. Edison was never tempted to do what other prominent men did for their sons, and what his sons expected him to do for them -- spend a small fortune helping them establish successful businesses of their own, or work their way up the ladder in their father's business so they could eventually run it.

In this regard, William sent me a letter outlining his wrath at his father. He took on the mantel of the forlorn son of a great man -- without a home. He accused me of disinheriting him because, he said, I wanted to get rid of Mr. Edison's first children because they were so much trouble.

William insisted he could "paddle his own canoe." Now that he was of age, he had inherited money from the settlement of his mother Mary's estate. He told his father he wouldn't darken his door again, but hoped that they could eventually find common ground and better understand each other.

Circumstances changed somewhat three months later with the death of Mr. Edison's sister Marion Page. Mr. Edison displayed a degree of loss and weakness toward his sibling with whom he felt close. To him, there were a lot of pleasant, youthful, memories with her. William took advantage of his father's feelings of family attachment and asked for a get-together so he could meet Blanche. He felt certain that once his father met his wife, he would like her. But William was rebuffed. It would be another three years before his father finally accepted the marriage.

During the following years, William ran into the same problem his brother Tom was experiencing with their father. William established another "Edison" company for the distribution of auto parts. Mr Edison was irate, once again, at believing his good name was being corrupted.

Mr. Edison telegraphed William. "You are being used for your name just like Tom, and as you seem to be a hopeless case. I now notify you that hereafter you can go your own way and take care of yourself . . . I warned you not to do it. Your action makes it hopeless for me to do anything again -- I am through -- E."

Then Blanche joined in the conflict, spilling out her own anger of what seemed to be the excommunication of his two sons. "Do you realize," she wrote, "that we [sic] are the children of '*The Greatest Man of the Century*' -- and for them to live on an income of a mere forty dollars per week takes very much more ability than I can display. Surely you would not have us live in a cheap boarding house with plain people."

Mr. Edison became even more resolute after this from Blanche. "I see no reason whatever why I should support my son," Edison replied. "He has done me no honor and has brought the blush of shame to my cheeks many times."

William and Blanche went on to lead a wandering, sometimes homeless, life for nearly ten years, often living in squalid conditions, working menial jobs, accepting public assistance, moving from city to city "paddling their own canoe."

Tom invents a new process

Tom finally entered a promising venture that was based on his own idea. It was a process for hardening steel that he claimed was better than the one that existed because it reduced the weight of the plating while it increased its tensile strength. With the help of his uncle William Holzer, Tom's mother's brother, they formed the "Thomas A. Edison, Jr. and Wm. Holzer Steel and Iron Process Company." Importantly, the process had been tested at the Bethlehem Steel Company and the company said it showed some promise.

Tom had recently broken with his father and now brashly said of himself that he was going to be "his father's competitor."

Unfortunately the whole venture fell apart when Tom's company was sued for services paid for but never completed. On top of this, Tom was also sued for passing bad checks, a practice he had been known for in the past.

His uncle William blamed Tom for forfeiting a promising venture that could have produced generous profits for the both of them. Add to this, Tom's underhanded tricks of writing bad checks and acting arrogant toward his father forced his uncle to ask him to find somewhere else to live.

Another uncle, Charles Stilwell, his mother Mary's older brother, took Tom in.

I found his failures a terrible shame. Tom had indeed invented a promising process that could have won him his long-desired fame and fortune. But it was the weaknesses in his personal habits that did him in. Add to this his embarrassment in the face of his father, combined with his divorce from the pretty "casino girl" and his inability to find a job, all had a further devastating effect on the man.

"Sir," Tom wrote to his father. "Every job I apply for I'm asked why I'm not working for you. I tell them I want to find success on my own, but they come back to me with, 'If you're not good enough to work for your father, I don't want you either.' And that's the way it's been going."

There was no response from his father.

Alcohol continued to haunt him in many ways.

Holidays at Glenmont

Thanksgiving and Christmas events were equally festive and, yes, ornate. I continued the traditions of the Miller family at Glenmont. Present around our table would be our immediate family, assorted Miller siblings and cousins and perhaps some college friends. We were able to seat fifty-two around our table. The fewer empty chairs we had to remove from the table, the better. We were most likely to fill them all on holidays.

For meals, our appetizers were fresh oysters, my favorite, then consommé followed by hard-shelled crabs. Just thinking about this now makes my mouth water. For the main course we had fresh, local turkey, potato croquettes, mushroom patties, cucumber salad, plum pudding, lemon ice along with figs and nuts. At Christmas dinner, we had a miniature chocolate Saint Nicholas at each place setting. Of course the children had their own food preferences and wanted to take a bite out of old Saint Nick before touching anything on their plates.

We tried also to think of our neighbors who lived alone, as well as the local families in need. The children and I delivered three dozen meals with presents around West Orange in the big sleigh. It was the ultimate joy of the season to see the smiles of appreciation and delight. Every few years I was able to get Mr. Edison to dress up as Saint Nick. He fit the role perfectly and I think he enjoyed it -- after we got him through the first visit.

Our Christmas tree was set in the two-story parlor entry at the front of the house. It was first draped with strings of Mr. Edison's multi-colored electric lights. It could be seen at night from the village below through the upper and lower windows. The massive tree was dressed with a wide variety of decorations, from the conventional, to the fanciful, to the children's own creations. Ropes of evergreen, the children's paper chains wrapped around the tree and tiny replicas of some of Mr. Edison's inventions such as his phonograph, his battery and even a model of his electric auto.

Under the tree the children might find a doll, a bow-and-arrow set, wooden building blocks and push toys such as a train or a collection carved farm animals. We also liked board games. Mr. Edison's favorite was Parcheesi.

Set amongst the tree branches, mostly hidden behind the decorations, might be a little box with my name on it. It became one of Mr. Edison's games for me to find that box. In it was most likely a jeweled set of ear rings or a beautiful necklace. He liked to see me decorated when we entertained.

It was also a tradition to invite our help to join us in the evening before Christmas. It was understood that it was our family who gave the presents to them. We did not expect or encourage them to reciprocate. They then joined us around the grand piano where we sang carols.

There might be an early Christmas Eve church service to which I brought the children. Mr. Edison never attended for his own, sometimes vocal, reasons. But he did contribute money to the church when, for example, there was a crisis -- the steeple clock had stopped functioning, the outside of the building was peeling, an ell was needed to house the expanded Sunday school.

Chapter Fifteen

1900-1901

Family vacation in Tampa

With our youngest children well out of diapers, I felt we could now travel as a family. We went south to Tampa in March for a little vacation, taking rooms at the Tampa Bay Hotel. Its architecture was classic Moorish with ornate furnishings -- and the service was truly first-class.

The local press asked if we were going to continue south to Fort Myers. We told them not this year. We were in Tampa simply for pleasure, to relax and get away from winter in the north. Actually, we might have dropped down to Seminole Lodge to see the progress made in upgrading and spiffing up the place after our long absence, but there was still no direct rail connection from Tampa to Fort Myers.

How nice it was to feel the Florida warmth seep into my bones and to amble along the beach with the talcum-powder sand pressing between my toes.

For Madeleine, twelve, and Charles ten, the Gulf Coast beach was an entirely new experience. Shell collecting and sand-castle building occupied a lot of their time, otherwise they were in the hotel pool. Theodore, at nineteen months, would have been oblivious to this environment and remained at home with Lucy.

Mr. Edison chartered a boat and captain and, taking the role of Ahab, was out to catch "the big one." The rest of us accompanied him one day, but the thrill for us soon waned and flopping about on a choppy sea under the hot, mid-day sun took its toll. We begged Papa to take us back to shore which he did, but not without comment.

"Ah, you landlubbers," he laughed. "I was just about to haul in the mightiest piscatorial record ever seen in these waters. Surely he would have dwarfed Moby Dick."

Then, reeling in his line, the great fisherman turned to the captain. "Skipper! Take 'er about and let's get these poor excuses for sea dogs back to port."

He never did catch "the big one" during our visit but he was perfectly happy catching and releasing the lesser creatures.

We returned home quite refreshed.

Madeleine's 13th birthday party

Now that my husband was home from the mines and working just down the street at his new laboratory, he began to take some interest in the activities at Glenmont. Life at home under my guidance turned to maintaining my husband's much deserved status in the world. I had always loved parties and entertaining, but without Mr. Edison around it had been awkward to hold one without him at my side. Now I felt free to pull out all stops -- in a manner close to that in which we were entertained throughout Europe, New York City and, yes, Akron, Ohio.

In the meantime, we did a big bash for Madeleine's thirteenth birthday, I had my secretary, Angela, send out invitations to forty of Madeleine's friends for her party on May 31. All invitees responded and attended. They were each greeted by the birthday girl herself in the grand entrance hall and then sent on to the dining room where I greeted them.

Lucy Bogue, who had given all our children piano lessons, was our guest pianist for the game of musical chairs. With forty participants, thirty-eight chairs had been pulled out from under the table and lined up. The children then marched around the table while the piano played. When the music stopped, all but two would find an available seat. Those two girls then stood at the side of the room and two more chairs were pushed under the table and so it went, eliminating two children each time. The hilarity was wonderful. I did have to manage a few scuffles as two girls fought for the same chair that, unfortunately, was large enough to hold both of them. The only way I could handle the dispute was to have them draw straws.

Lucy was a big help as well when we played several other games: Love The Neighbor, Balloon Volleyball and Duck, Duck, Goose.

We then went out onto the lawn for a potato-sack race, then an egg-in-spoon race and others games until I saw that the children were flagging. What am I saying? Lucy and I were dragging.

We returned to the dining room table where, in our absence, Gracie our cook had placed a large birthday cake. Who sat next to whom was decided by drawing the first or second half a Mother Goose rhyme. Matching halves sat together -- the first half to the left of the second half.

(This may sound like unnecessarily detailed organization, but I have found it helped eliminate some problems. It failed when a child was unable, or unwilling, to follow instructions. Perhaps I should have had another adult or two to help with handling so many children. Frankly, it was a bit much for Lucy and me.)

The birthday cake was decorated with the tiny flags of forty nations. Each of the girls had a flag from one of these nations. We had a flag chart attached to the wall and, as each girl identified the country of her flag, she was given a slice of cake. Need I say this was Mr. Edison's educational game.

Madeleine's party was a success. An adult party would be far less strenuous.

Tom was involved in many other shaky, and likely illegal, schemes while he was living with his Uncle Stilwell. One business was the International Bureau of Science and Invention. It advertised its services as The Inventor's Confidential Friend and Tom was the "expert" with whom his clients conferred and paid outrageous fees in the belief that they were receiving the Wizard's tried and proven advice. Before this progressed beyond the point of no return, his father had it squelched.

Tom then became involved with two businessmen and the Thomas A. Edison, Jr. Chemical Company was formed. Their product was "Wizard Ink Tablets." When dissolved in water, according to instructions, it created a useable ink. But the product advertising falsely claimed, "It is being extensively used by the U.S Government and the principle Banks and Boards of Education throughout the country."[75]

Again, Mr. Edison cut this business short because the product name implied his father's endorsement.

But Tom wouldn't stop. Even after the above incident, Tom's partners paid Tom $5,000 for the use of the Edison name plus $25 a month bonus and the men continued to sell the Wizard Ink Tablets.

Then there was the "Magno-Electric Vitalizer,"[76] a worthless device that Tom had developed claiming to revitalize whoever used it.

Finally, there was the scheme with his Uncle Stilwell. Tom sold him the rights to use the Edison name after his father's death. Uncle Stilwell, in turn, planned to sell those rights to the Columbia Phonograph Company.[77]

All of this led to conflict after conflict with his father and further aggravated his physical and mental health. His excessive drinking degenerated into severe health problems -- anxiety, thundering headaches and vertigo -- that finally forced him to seek help in a sanatorium. It was there he met Beatrice Willard, his very attractive and attentive nurse. A romantic relationship developed during his lengthy recuperation that certainly helped his return to normalcy.

Return to Seminole Lodge after 14 years

Our family finally returned to Seminole Lodge on February 27 for five weeks after a fourteen-year hiatus. We arrived on the steamer *H.B. Plant* with all flags flying in honor of my celebrated inventor. We disembarked at our pier but were quickly met by our caretaker who said the crew had not quite finished upgrading the buildings and grounds. So we all re-boarded for the downtown docks. It was not an easy arrival. In addition to Mr. Edison and myself, I had Madeleine, Charles and baby Thede as well as a maid.

There we met carriages at the town dock that took us to the new Fort Myers hotel, erected three years earlier. But, as they say, "There was no room at the inn." It was full of northern guests who now filled it every winter season. So we piled back into the carriages and moved our considerable group and belongings back to our place and made do with the rooms that were available.

I was so happy to finally put my feet up and rest, but there was a lot of bang, bang, bang. Mr. Edison was getting a headache as well so he finally called a stop to the activity and asked them to continue after we left at the end of the season. So we were able to settle in with only minor alterations unfinished, but all necessary facilities in working order. The landscaping was basic and had cleared us out of the jungle. Mr. Edison's lovely fertile muck was hauled in from the river bottom and spread around the gardens. That allowed us to begin our own gardening and return it to our original plan of years ago.

For both Madeleine, thirteen, and Charles, eleven, these were the years they grew into and became accustomed to the good life -- the privileged life. Glenmont stood alone on the hilltop overlooking the town, like an emerald set amongst diamonds on the face of a crown. The estate was surrounded by eight hundred undeveloped acres. The children's regular playmates were the children of other leaders of American industry. There was Jerome Franks whose father was on the Andrew Carnegie payroll; Henry Colgate the manufacturer of soap and toothpaste; Lloyd Fulton ran the family Newark ironworks; Robert Lincoln, son the assassinated president, was our neighbor during our family summer week or two at Deal Beach on the Jersey Shore.[78]

Family life at Glenmont changed radically for all of us when Mr. Edison began to spend more time with the family. Several newspapers arrived on the doorstep each morning. Selections from the British poets and the Old Testament were studied and considered by Mr. Edison to be good for moral development. They read them together before dining in the evening. I noted that Madeleine secretly read her favorite romantic novels, including *Little Women*, in her room before falling asleep many nights.

Madeleine took great pleasure in having her father near home as she grew into her teens. And I admit I bowed and catered to Mr. Edison's wishes as Madeleine considered him "Master of the House" as did the entire family. She tried to please her Papa in every way. Madeleine listened when he spoke and danced to his music. For her, Papa was certainly second only to God. Everything Papa attempted to do was a lesson of some kind to the children.

Every day before Papa left for his laboratory he visited each of the children's rooms to offer his greetings for the day. On one of these mornings, Madeleine was lounging back in her chair while one of our maids buttoned her high-top shoes. Seeing this, Mr. Edison came downstairs and told me that no child of his should ever be treated to this luxury.[79] Dreaded thoughts of Marion crossed my mind. I nipped it in the bud.

Mr. Edison had a distaste for excessive jewelry. He disapproved of bracelets and forbid red dresses. If he saw me and Madeleine on our way to an event wearing a ring, a pin and a necklace, he chastised me in his gentle way and reminded us of the Oceanic islander who wore half her weight in decorative jewelry.

Charles had an energetic group of friends who enjoyed kicking a rugby ball around Glenmont's private gymnasium located in the basement. They chased each other in war games through the thick woods and brambles. They climbed tall trees to prove their manliness. They used their slingshots to kill barn vermin. On the flat lawn terrace they engaged in bicycle polo using croquet mallets and tennis balls. The mallets sometimes interfered with the wheel spokes and sent the rider flying over the handlebars.

At twelve, Charles was driving the family's electric auto to Carteret prep school downtown.

Outdoor activities for the whole family included spring nature walks around the premises. Mr. Edison used this as another opportunity to lecture as we walked. The surrounding wild woodlands contained a myriad of natural flora. We took cuttings of growth that we had missed from other walks and compared them to our collections of pressed flowers when we returned to the house. They all had common names and we challenged each other to find their correct Latin identities.

At the times we ate breakfast together, it was always meat and potatoes, at least for Mr. Edison. It was also a time for him to educate us by quizzing with questions based on school homework with which he regularly familiarized himself. I maintained vocabulary checklists and used them with the children daily. Before bed time, Mr. Edison oversaw

Madeleine and Charles studying volumes of science reference books in the upstairs library, searching through citations and jotting notes that he might find helpful in his laboratory work.

Mr. Edison had demanded much more of his first daughter when she was school age. I remember Marion complaining about being required to memorize several pages from the *Encyclopaedia Britannica* every day after she left school to travel with her Papa after her mother died.

During evenings at Glenmont after the children had gone to bed, I looked forward to my knitting or other crafts or reading the English poets or looking at the latest issue of *Lady's Pictorial*. Then, after I retired for the night, Mr. Edison remained at his "thought bench," sometimes until nearly sunrise, as he prepared himself for his next day's projects. Regardless of how late he stayed up, he was always up again at 7:30 to begin the new day.

Kidnap of Madeleine threatened

Generally, people who achieved fame and honor in the 19th Century were usually regarded with respect and esteem. Achievement of a venerable goal was proof that it could be done and gave others something to strive for themselves. But as the 20th Century arrived, media-enhanced celebrities who earned a great deal of money came to be regarded with skepticism. The divide between the rich and poor had increased and that brought about increased envy by those whose wealth was far less than they believed they deserved. A few in that category resorted to "easy money," a practice that most often required an unlawful activity. Kidnapping,[80] historically, was one way to acquire wealth quickly.

It is a frightening word for a heinous crime, all the more so because our family fell victim to the threat of kidnapping our thirteen-year-old Madeleine. I still feel the anxiety pounding in my chest whenever I recall the horrible event.

It began with a post-marked, hand-written letter in May 1901 that demanded a “quik delivry of $25,000 cash or your dauter will disapear. this is serious. Do not tell noone. You have 5 days to do it or else.” The letter also gave instructions on how and where to leave the cash.

I was jolted into action and immediately ran to Madeleine who was safely in her room with the substitute governess, Mildred. It was Lucy’s day off. Madeleine had only just walked home from school minutes earlier and I had greeted her normally. Of course now she immediately knew something was terribly wrong.

"What's wrong, mother? What the matter?" she asked with a tremor. She had never seen me in such an agitated state. Mildred stood by, mute.

“Oh! Good,” I said. “You’re okay. Thank God.”

“Of course I’m okay. What’s wrong?

With Madeleine clutched under my arm, I called Mr. Edison at the lab. I had trouble getting the words out, but he understood something was terribly wrong by my quaking voice and said he was on his way immediately.

“What’s wrong, mother?” Madeleine repeated.

“I just had a fright, Madeleine. Not to worry.”

“You frightened *me*, mother.”

That upset both of them. I didn’t know what I was saying. I was so shaken. “I’m sorry. We just received a kidnap note in the mail.”

“What’s a kidnap note, mother?”

“It’s a letter from a bad person, Madeleine. I’ll explain it later. We’re just going to stay in the house right now.”

I felt I had already said too much.

While waiting for his arrival, I gathered Charles, Theodore and Mildred around me as well.

Mr. Edison arrived a few minutes later. My hand shaking, I showed him the letter. He read it, nodded his head and mumbled a few spiteful words.

Mr. Edison had been personally threatened for many reasons over the years and he had always been able to laugh it off, but this was the one threat he took very seriously and immediately swung into action by calling the Pinkerton National Detective Agency.[81]

I don't know the details of what followed, but my job, with Lucy's help the next day, was to keep the children together at home. Waiting. How unendurable it was for me to live through the next several days without knowing when or if anything violent was going be thrust on us at any moment. Round-the-clock shifts of guards were posted at Glenmont, but I had little sleep. Lucy was extremely agitated.

Mr. Edison worked out a plan with the detectives who were very thorough and efficient. Their activity gradually reduced our initial fears, yet our family remained on edge for several months until two villains were finally caught and confessed.

The real tragedy in this event was that of our our substitute governess, Mildred who, for reasons we never understood, felt an extreme degree of responsibility. She was the guardian who was present when I received the threat letter. Initially, both Lucy and Mildred were suspects in abetting the criminals by potentially revealing inside information to the culprits. The frightening and harsh experience of interrogation changed our lovely and sensitive young Mildred. She was never herself again.

In spite of our pleas, Mildred tearfully gave us her resignation, insisting that she felt responsible. We loved her. She had been our alternate governess for many years. Some time later we learned she had committed suicide. To us, it was a tragedy that had no rational answer. Apparently there was no way we could have saved her from what must have been horrific, self-destructive thoughts.

Chapter Sixteen

1902-1903

The Koreshan belief

Fort Myers joyfully welcomed back their famous citizen in early February. They gathered at the town docks as the inventor triumphantly arrived aboard a new steamer named after him -- the *Thomas A. Edison*.

Our family was celebrating another milestone. Mr. Edison had finished his years-long development of his storage batteries and at age fifty-five was ready to take a rest. But his concept of "rest" was turning to another activity and pursuing it with great gusto. That pursuit this season was fishing.

Only a northerner, snow-ice-and-numbing-cold-experienced, can truly appreciate the climate and natural beauty of the tropics. Returning to Seminole Lodge was a panacea for all of us. I immediately set about padding around in our gardens, pulling weeds and taking cuttings of dozens of my flowering beauties to dress up our home inside and on our spacious porches.

Mr. Edison was out on the pier with Madeleine and Charles teaching them the skills of baiting and dropping a hook into the Caloosahatchee. I heard their screams and giggles as he helped them hoist their first wriggling catches onto the pier. I walked out to join in their merriment as my husband verbally unloaded his experience onto them. He was the one who removed the hooks and released the unhappy creatures back into the river so that they might repeat the experience another day.

We learned that Tootie McGregor had sold the Gilliland house, and then that owner traded it to R. Ingram Travers. So we had a new neighbor for the next several years.

Again we were disappointed that we did not have a chance to buy the place. It was awkward living so very close to a stranger, but the Travers family did not spend much time here. We made acquaintances with them and let them know we would be interested in buying their place when the time was right for them, but that happy day didn't arrive for another four years.

In late February we took delivery of a new 25-foot naphtha launch,[82] sent down to us by train from New Jersey to Punta Gorda, accompanied by Freddy Orr, a long-time assistant to Mr. Edison. I was pleasantly surprised to see it was named *Mina*. It was a lovely boat with long delicate lines. It looked very nice at the end of our pier.

Soon Mr. Edison was out in the Gulf on the *Mina* with winter friends thoroughly enjoying his favorite sport. On one excursion near Matlacha,[83] his group caught 180 fish weighing a total of 350 pounds!

For my own entertainment with a lady friend, we attended a lecture by Dr. Cyrus Teed, a physician and alchemist who became a religious leader and, for some, a messiah. He told us how he denounced the idea that the earth revolved around the sun and discovered "cellular cosmogony," his belief that the sky, the earth, the sun and the moon reside within, and at the center of, a hollow sphere. He founded, and lived with his followers, in a Koreshan[84] community of about 250 followers in Estero, a few miles south of Fort Myers. The lecture was interesting although far-fetched in my opinion. Fortunately Mr. Edison was not with us, for I would have expected him to vehemently challenge the good doctor and embarrass me in the process.

One of our few social activities included a dinner invitation from a couple from Williamsport, Pennsylvania who were winter regulars and stayed at the Fort Myers hotel. Mr. Edison liked them because they treated us as ordinary friends making the evening relaxing. We reciprocated a week later and invited them to Seminole Lodge for dinner.

We left for the North in early April.

Schooling

Mr. Edison never acknowledged that he had made a serious mistake by denying Tom and William his personal attention and an early education that would have prepared them for a private schools later. In any case, with my influence, his attitude changed when *our* three children came along and, I have to add, I was now older and more experienced. In contrast to my stepchildren, both Mr. Edison and I were active in influencing, encouraging and loving Madeleine, Charles and Theodore during their schooling. They each *did* demonstrate a talent for science.

Factors that changed my husband may have been his age also, accompanied by a reduced enthusiasm to accomplish as much work as possible with no regard to how long it took.

Madeleine, after graduating from the Oak Place School in Akron in 1906, enrolled in Bryn Mawr. It was here that she showed a great aptitude for science and engineering but, because she was a woman, the social barriers of the time offered no encouragement in either technical education or employment opportunities in that field. I was greatly disappointed when she left college after two years and pursued the life of a socialite.

Charles had a definite talent for an engineering education and attended MIT until he was lured away in his senior year by a company that gave him a business apprenticeship. As time passed, he learned that business management was more appealing to him than working in a laboratory. It was management that prepared him for successful careers in the Edison businesses, politics and government.

Theodore was the only Edison child who excelled in science and engineering, graduated from MIT with a Masters degree and went on to become an inventor on his own like his father.[85]

First tests of electric vehicles

When Mr. Edison came down the mountain from his mine operation, the automobile age had begun. During the ten years he had been gone a bicycle and velocipede[86] craze had taken hold. With the ability to easily pedal a two-wheeler on cushy pneumatic tires at ten miles an hour, passing horse-drawn carriages with ease. The public was experiencing a new freedom. My children had one of the later bicycles with a chain-driven rear wheel. There was one problem. Our home was at the top of a hill. While the children had no trouble going down the hill, returning at least part of the way involved walking. But Charles and Theodore enjoyed being able to ride the two-wheeler to school. Madeleine was a bit hesitant, having to straddle the bar between the wheels. Ladies' bicycles didn't appear until she considered herself too old to ride one.

Now into the new century came the horseless carriages -- motorized phaetons and light coupes with exhilarating speeds of ten, twenty and even thirty miles an hour, powered by steam, gasoline or electricity.

The new technology fascinated Mr. Edison and he bought a gasoline-powered vehicle and it confirmed his belief that they were too noisy and smelly. He then bought several different electric-powered vehicles. The first was the Mark III Columbia, then came the Baker, the Woods and the Studebaker. Charles was the first in the family to drive, at age eleven, and he managed it very well -- a natural. Then I took a hand at it and I have to say I did quite well and enjoyed it. Then Mr. Edison, who had never even driven as much as a horse, gave it a try. He was immediately out of control. He ran a wheel over Charles, the instructor, and put the vehicle in a ditch. He almost fell out head first himself. I'm pleased to say it was only Mr. Edison's pride that was hurt. He never attempted to drive again. Charles was only bruised.

Mr. Edison predicted that the horse as a method of transportation was doomed. He liked the electric car far better than the gasoline powered. The electric was clean, quiet and it didn't have that foul smell. The steam-powered car he felt was too fast, likely to explode and very difficult to operate. He foresaw another market for his rechargable storage batteries.[87] "Who knows more about batteries than me?" he asked me rhetorically.

Thus began my husband's campaign. He felt it was the right time to introduce a battery-powered car that was more practical and efficient than gasoline or steam.[88]

Mr. Edison's work habits

From the time Mr. Edison envisioned a worthwhile project until he completed it, our household was never at rest. His preoccupation removed him from our lives. His work on the improved storage battery was a typical example.

His habit was to rise between 6 and 7:30, eat breakfast and Scarth would take him in the carriage to the laboratory at the foot of the hill. There he expected his co-workers to be at their tables experimenting with their respective projects. In the middle of the day his lunch was sent down to him from Glenmont and he would eat it at his work area. At 6 in the evening Scarth would pick him up and return him to the house for dinner. This was the one time in the day the children and I would have an hour or two with him to discuss our daily interests and concerns -- *if* his mind was not fixed on something else, making him impenetrable.

At 7:30 or 8 in the evening he returned to the laboratory and resumed work. Scarth came by at midnight to take him back to the house but often he would send Scarth home and work another two or more hours. When he tired, or needed deep thinking, he was known to stretch out on top of a work bench and close his eyes for an hour or so. He would then rise and continue working until breakfast. This cycle could continue month after month until he was satisfied he had come up with the results he wanted.

At dinner one evening he told me he recorded to date more than 9,000 experiments in the development of this storage battery but he had not yet solved the problem.

I replied, "Isn't it a shame, Dearie, that with the tremendous amount of work you've done that you haven't been able to get any results?"

"Results, Billie? Why, woman, I have gotten a lot of results! I know several thousand things that won't work."

Weeks later at dinner he wore a broad smile. He said he had now accumulated more than 10,000 experiments on the battery and "I have discovered the missing link in the combination I was looking for."

Mr. Edison had his men begin production on the battery, but during his trials, using the battery in his test cars, he became dissatisfied, stopped production and began a new line of investigation until it worked precisely as he wanted. In the process, he had accumulated more than 150 notebooks detailing with the progress on this particular invention.[89]

Hiring the best scientists, engineers, technicians, managers and supervisors was rarely a problem. There was always a long line of top-notch men who were eager to work for the world-famous, immensely successful man called "The Wizard" who invented things everyone wanted.

Sometimes Mr. Edison himself would do the interviewing of candidates, especially for men who would be working close by him in his laboratory.

Harper's Magazine published an article on Mr. Edison in May 1932, seven months after my husband died. It included an introductory interview he had with M.A. Rosanoff who was a candidate for work in the chemical research section of his laboratory. I think it illustrates his work habits.

"Mr. Edison," Rosanoff asked. "Please tell me what laboratory rules you want me to observe."

This question was a surprise to Mr. Edison who spat tobacco juice in the middle of the floor and yelled, "Hell! There *ain't* no rules around here! We are tryin' to accomplish somep'n. . . Do you believe in luck?"

The trembling Rosanoff replied, "Yes and no. My reasoning mind revolts against the superstition of luck, my savage soul clings to it."

"For my part," the Wizard said, "I do not believe in luck at all. And if there is such a thing as luck, then I must be the most unlucky fellow in the world. I've never once made a lucky strike in all my life. When I get after something I need, I start finding everything in the world that I *don't* need -- one damn thing after another. I find ninety-nine things that I don't need, and then comes number one hundred, and that -- at the very last -- turns out to be just what I had been looking for. It's got to be so that if I find something in a hurry, I git to doubting whether it's the real thing; so I go over it carefully and it generally turns out to be wrong. Wouldn't you call that hard luck? But I'm tellin' you, I don't believe in luck -- good or bad. Most fellows try a few things and then quit. *I* never quit until I git what I'm after. That's the only difference between me, that's supposed to be lucky, and the fellows that think they are unlucky."

Major improvements had been made at Seminole Lodge when our family returned on February 21. The dock had been extended another five hundred more feet into the Caloosahatchee and included a 25- by 12-foot roofed assembly area at the end. My namesake, the *Mina* was now protected in a boathouse alongside the dock.

I was delighted that the interior of the lodge had been painted and wallpapered and the bathroom and kitchen had new and improved plumbing.

Scarth, our chauffeur, demonstrated a hidden skill. He had experience managing small fishing-party boats on the Great Lakes. He was able and quite excited to pilot the *Mina* for us. We no longer had to hire local help with dubious experience.

Recovering from his exhausting work on batteries, Mr. Edison pleasantly surprised me by spending his first week here at his favorite sport of fishing and didn't go near his laboratory. He hauled in a seventy-five pound trout at Four-Mile Island. But when he heard that a hotel guest had caught a 163-pound tarpon, I saw he was envious. He invited me to go with him on his pursuit and we both dropped our lines outside the barrier island. I hooked a big one and played with it quite a while. Mr. Edison became seriously interested in my efforts before my tackle broke and my prize escaped. Tarpon fishing was now the biggest draw for patrons at the Fort Myers Hotel.

With the lodge now brought up to expectations, I felt we could do some entertaining. One of the Edison Portland Cement Company stockholders and his wife spent a few days with us. After the obligatory day of small-game fishing, we took them on the steamer *Suwanee* to Sanibel Island for an afternoon of shell hunting.

We had two more guests and their wives in the middle of March. One was Walter Mallory, former superintendent at the Ogden mines and now vice president at Edison Portland

Cement. The other was Emil Herter, Mallory's assistant and former draftsman at Ogden. The six of us went out in the *Mina* on a moonless night to enjoy the balmy air and gaze at a sky filled with the most glorious collection of stars. Mr. Edison entertained us by, not only naming the constellations, but telling the folklore of each.

Disaster struck in early March when we learned in a telegram from Mr. Mallory that ten men, including the chief engineer of the plant, Edward Darling, had been killed in an explosion at Mr. Edison's Stewartsville, New Jersey grinding plant that Mr. Mallory supervised. A convulsion of telegrams ensued and Mr. Edison had the plant shut down until the cause of the problem -- most likely excessive dust ignited by a spark from the kiln fires -- was corrected.[90]

Gloom hovered over our refuge until we departed on April first.

Settlement with Tom

Tiring of his constant conflict with his father, Tom wrote another letter to his father saying, "I will sign any reasonable agreement with you in which you can dictate your own terms, which will satisfy you forever, an agreement which will deprive me of all future rights to the name of Edison for the purpose of obtaining money and any other matter that is reasonable for the protection of yourself and at the same time myself."[91]

Mr. Edison, driven by self interest, took but a dash of pity on his son and signed an agreement with him in which Tom would not use his own name, much less his father's name, in any business. For this Mr. Edison agreed to give him a weekly allowance of fifty dollars to help him fulfill his current dream of equipping a farm and raising mushrooms in rural Burlington, New Jersey. In addition, Tom received money to buy the farm, restore it and equip it with the necessary farm tools. In effect, Tom was put out to pasture.

This effort began a period of reconciliation between the two.

Patent sharks

Over and over I heard Mr. Edison repeat it. "I'm being plagued by patent sharks! They're going to put me out of business!"

Mr. Edison believed that, because of the unnecessarily complicated and dragged-out legal process to be granted a patent, his concepts were insecure and subject to theft. These patent thieves had no respect for intellectual properties and openly set up factories and produced knock-offs of properties that were legally protected.

At this time, court injunctions filed to cause another party to cease manufacture, were not often permitted. This left Mr. Edison with no other recourse but to sue. But the cost and time of a suit was much greater than the loss to the defendant. Thus, the sharks won.

Mr. Edison's fundamental motion-picture camera was a case in point. The American Mutoscope and Biograph Company infringed on his kinetographic camera. It took six years for his patent to be granted -- and even then there were skirmishes that followed.

Once the air was cleared, Mr. Edison felt he could devote his talents to improvements, such as color photography and an affordable home movie camera.

For the five years leading up to 1908, his movie production was a profitable business. One of his best known, successful and longest lasting movies was *The Great Train Robbery,* directed by Edwin S. Porter and released in 1903. This was an 11-minute movie about a group of bandits who stage a brazen hold-up, only to soon find a posse hot after them. It was the age-old story of the triumph of justice and how good wins out over evil.

This movie and other Edison Motion Picture Company productions were filmed at Orange Mountain Park and Essex County in New Jersey. For this "Western," they used the Erie and Lackawanna Railroad line along the Passaic River as the train line -- not far from New York City.

Chapter Seventeen

1904-1905

The year of the tarpon

Poor Mr. Edison. He began the new year with a bout of pneumonia, gently cursing the damp, frigid weather of New Jersey and restless at having to spend his days in bed or wrapped in a wool blanket next to a cozy fire.

He could be such a baby when he wasn't feeling well, but for me and the children it was good to have him close by us. Theodore, now six, kept him company and played with the old clocks Mr. Edison used to judge the boy's mechanical abilities. He said Theodore showed promise.

By late February, we were ready to travel to Fort Myers. Madeleine, Charles and Theodore were with us along with my sister Mary Emily and, of course, our help.

Our spirits were high as our troupe sailed up the Caloosahatchee to our dock on the steamer St. *Lucie*. This year, everything was ready for us at Seminole Lodge. Mr. Edison's new thirty-six-foot electric launch, *Reliance*, was tied up at the dock and that was his first destination. He went directly to the motor compartment in the stern and checked out the new batteries. An upgraded lighting system had been installed in the house, laboratory and kitchen. The grounds had been well tended and several hundred pineapple trees had been planted.

After dark that first evening, Mr. Edison turned on the new lights that illuminated our fountain and gardens. He also had a powerful light installed at the end of the pier. Our grounds were now available for a stroll night and day.

Charles, fourteen, remembered this visit in detail as "the year of the tarpon." Using mullet for bait, he and his father caught two tarpon their first day out. Mr. Edison's catch weighed forty pounds and he bragged about its size -- the biggest he had ever caught. But shortly, Charles hauled in a 100-pounder that immediately deflated his father's ego. He wanted to throw his "little" catch away but Charles objected and Mr. Edison had both of them stuffed and mounted on the wall.

This was also the year Mr. Edison experimented with the transmission of sound waves under water. Using long and short bursts of steam explosions in rapid succession, in Morse code fashion, he claimed to have reached a distance of four miles through the water. His goal was to be able to communicate up to fifteen miles.

Marion after ten years of marriage

What a pleasant surprise to receive a letter dated August 14 from Dresden. Marion, now thirty-one, said she was happily celebrating her tenth wedding anniversary to her military man, Oscar. Her regret was that they had not yet had children.

Her letter hinted that she missed our family and that her life was often very lonely as Oscar was called away on military missions or he spent too much time hanging out in local bars with his chums.

"I'm concerned about her, Dearie. I wish there was some way we could make her happy. I know that a loving letter from you would brighten her life."

"There you go again, Billie, harping on making our children happy. Dot is how old now? In her thirties? She's cut out her own life, made her own choices. What would happen to her if I were dead? Would she still want letters from Hell?"

"Very funny. I'm not asking you to do anything other than what a good father might do -- write a nice letter and show some interest in her life. Marion has always been crazy about you."

He just didn't understand. All I could do was continue to send my letters of understanding and love, although I knew it was their father they wanted.

The hero of his time

This was the 25th anniversary of Mr. Edison's invention of the carbon-filament lamp. His companies created an impressive display of his 1879 incandescent lamps and labeled it "Edisonia," suddenly raising the inventor's status to a man who had a solid place in history.

To add luster on top of luster, the American Institute of Electrical Engineers treated him to a banquet of 500 guest engineers at the Waldorf-Astoria hotel in New York City. Replicas of his first practical incandescent light were given away as souvenirs. For dessert, ices in the shape of the lamp were served.

I was seated with the wives of the men at the head table. One after-dinner speaker following another attempted to out do the others in praising Mr. Edison on his invaluable accomplishments. I could see that my husband was becoming more and more embarrassed with the excessive homage. He had always said that he was "cursed" with adulation. The city newspaper editors were present and they published lengthy passages of these speeches.

This event marked a number of changes in our lives. First of all, it was only the mid-point of his career. Every year following, the press remembered the anniversary date and celebrated Mr. Edison's life as a national hero. The public could not get enough information on the inventor. It was truly hero worship. He was chosen repeatedly in the popular press as "The greatest," or the "most useful" citizen.

At age fifty-five, he was also my hero and I will take credit for many of the changes in his personal habits. His mode of dress was the most obvious. He now had the desire to look the part of the man he represented. His suits were conservative black; his shirts were white with a collar and string necktie. His waistline had grown but he kept it under control. He had a full head of white hair, although his brows remained jet black. He looked like an old-fashioned gentleman, but beneath that facade he was a non-conformist activist with unfading genius.

Edison's deafness worsens

Hearing had always been Mr. Edison's greatest physical disability. In January he became very sick, once again, after working under great strain. His doctor determined he also had mastoiditis and must to undergo a dangerous, radical surgery. He survived the operation but from this point on my husband was another step closer to being totally deaf.

His accompanying sickness continued and I knew that time in southwest Florida would be the best medicine. That was not to happen. He returned instead to his laboratory where he watched the testing of battery cells. The news from his lab was most discouraging. Even after ten years of labor, they had not yet had a breakthrough.

"This is very disheartening, Billie. It is a puzzle about where to turn next. There is too much that is magical about a battery."

Indeed. Mr. Edison's proven success at using his empirical methods of research now seemed to be failing him in battery chemistry.

Automobiling was fast becoming the thing to do among the middle class in their leisure time. For our family also, boarding the motor car and traveling[92] up the coast and into New England was the height of enjoyment in the good weather.

At Mr. Edison's insistence we needed to get away for more than just day trips this summer. This was a two-week jaunt, beginning in mid-August, in a couplet of 1905 White[93] steam-powered cars. Charles nicknamed them Disaster and Discord and were capably driven by him and my brother John. Our party of eight also included Madeleine, my sister Grace, niece Maggie Miller and, of course, Mr. Edison and myself. Baby Theodore, only seven, remained at home "to take care of Miss Lucy."

Our cars were handsome and Mr. Edison didn't purchase them simply at random.

"I bought these vehicles beause of their style, comfort and performance. Mr. White got rid of that old 'buggy' look. The '05 is one of the first of have it's engine up front under a hood. If you had been reading the newspapers like you should, Charles, you'd know the White, named Whistlin' Billy, just set a speed record of about seventy-five miles an hour at the Morris Park Track. But don't you get any ideas to beat that record this week, Charles. These machines are better than Stanley's steamers and more dependable. Besides, if it's good enough for President Taft, it's good enough for us."

That was true. With four of us to each car, we were very comfortable with our suitcases and picnic baskets and, camping equipment. We were all in high spirits when we headed north from Glenmont on a circumnavigation through Vermont, New Hampshire and Maine.

We made a bee line up through central Massachusetts and spent our first night in Keene, New Hampshire, among the smallest mountains in the state. It was a long first-day drive and we eagerly settled into our rooms in the hotel before our evening meal. The boys weren't a bit tired. They wiped the dust off the cars, checked out the mechanics under the hood and answered questions from the curious on-lookers.

The next day we continued north along the east side of the Connecticut River, through Bellows Falls, in and out of Vermont, to scenic Dartmouth College, in Hanover. The college invited us in for lunch and we were given a tour of the campus. Charles commented that he'd like to spend his college years right here. He liked their engineering laboratories, as of course, did his father.

From Hanover we took a "shortcut" over to Plymouth on a very rough and hilly road. I thought we would get lost and have to turn back. But our drivers carried on bravely with Mr. Edison's confidence using his ten-year-old Rand McNally atlas.

We took a break in the tiny town of Campton Village, New Hampshire and had lunch on the banks of the gentle Mad River. Apparently it was only "mad" in the spring thaw.

The roads worsened the further north we traveled. Mr. Edison read the map wrong and our road ended in the town of Lincoln that featured a very foul-smelling pulp mill. There wasn't enough daylight for us to get out of town to find the main road and we were told there were no inns nearby.

That didn't deter Mr. Edison. We had brought our tents and he loved camping. We found a suitable area just out of town and away from most of the smell.

"Adventure!" Mr. Edison trumpeted. "Everyone should take up camping." The boys set up camp under our leader's direction. We spent the evening around the campfire and under a beautiful canopy of stars. Charles entertained us with a comical script he had written about a day in the life of our family.

Mr. Edison was up at dawn -- 4:30 that morning. He had the coffee perking and bacon, sausage and eggs cooking as he rousted the rest of us out of bed. The aroma of his cooking won the competition against the pulp mill's emissions.

The atlas was vague and didn't show the local roads. We conferred with the owner of the Lincoln general store on the best way to continue east and then north -- well aware that getting directions from the local population could be hazardous to our health. But it turned out fine. We just had to slow the boys down as we navigated the back roads, struggling east through the mountains to Wonalancet and then on up to Conway. It was slow going -- but adventurous.

Once on the Conway road we were able to pick up speed until we received a long-overdue tire puncture. The boys quickly made the repairs and made our way to Bartlett where we spent the night in the small, but comfortable Bartlett Inn.

Well rested, we left early after a good breakfast at a local diner and sped north up and up through the magnificent Crawford Notch. The boys raced the train that was high above us until we reached the height of land. We won the race and celebrated our feat at the railroad station. Everywhere we went our twin cars generated comments. We even had comments from a couple of train passengers who looked down and saw us speeding toward the same destination.

In haste, or was it fun, the boys raced each other along the straight-aways until, I think it was Disaster, lost power and broke down. It took some six hours of the greasy work for the boys to find the problem and then repair it. Mr. Edison was very proud of their results.

We stopped for the night in Bretton Woods, in the western shadow of Mount Washington, at its namesake hotel, a massive structure that dominated the landscape. From our room we could see the black smoke of the cog railway[94] engine, high above us, crawling up the mountain.

Full of anticipation at ascending the highest mountain in northeastern America ourselves, we boarded the train soon after breakfast. The summit was free of clouds and the sky blue. It couldn't have been a better day. Better than advertised, the ride was both frightening, a little sooty and very steep in places. We women feared the brakes would let loose and we would slide down the tracks to our certain death. The boys hung out the windows and wondered aloud what it would be like to slide down the mountain on a board straddling the tracks.

At the summit, Mr. Edison talked with the sooty-faced engineers about the mechanics of the cog-driven engine and watched closely, in his white suit, as the men oiled the dirty machine, refilled its boiler and labored in the driving compartment. Then my husband noticed a couple of gasoline cars in the parking lot. He had to visit them and talk with their drivers about their experience driving up the carriage road. He wondered aloud to me how his battery-in-progress might fare as it powered up to the summit. Would it survive the eight-mile ordeal?

We took our mountaintop suite in the three-story, ninety-one room Summit House that had withstood the fearful blast of winter winds for about twenty years. But today there was very little wind and it was quite hot in the sun. The boys were all over the summit. They toured the original sixty-four-foot-long stone building, the first structure on the mountain in 1852.

The boys disappeared for hours and I was very concerned. I learned they had descended a trail through a pristine garden of arctic-like flora to the head of a huge ravine.

My enjoyment was dining at a surprisingly elegant table and a Delmonico-quality meal. Mr. Edison's enjoyment was sitting on the deck and talking with a man who owned an engineering business. He happened to be very familiar Edison batteries and had used them successfully.

The Mount Washington experience was the high point (no pun intended) of our tour. The boys talked us into spending a second night so they could follow another trail from the summit down to a pond called "Lake of the Clouds." From there they continued hiking to an adjacent summit called Mount Adams.

The girls met other young ladies their age. They played cards and board games. The view didn't interest them and time seemed to drag. I was happy to sit beside my husband and meet other couples who happened by. It was nice. There were no reporters and the people we met didn't fawn over the inventor. They generally brought up stories of their interest in New England and the White Mounains in particular.

It was glad to be off the mountain. We back-tracked again and headed directly east from Conway to the Maine coast. We spent our last few days in Ogunquit, Wells and Kennebunkport enjoying the salt air and walking ankle-deep in the water at the edge of the beaches. The children played in the waves, built sand castles and buried each other.

We stopped in Boston and visited the Paul Revere house. This led to my history-buff husband's suggestion that we follow Paul Revere's route out to Lexington, just a few miles west. There we viewed his statue. On then to Concord where we toured the homes of Nathaniel Hawthorne, Louisa May Alcott and Ralph Waldo Emerson. Filled with the lore of the area we aimed Disaster and Discord for home through Connecticut.

Apparently Mr. Edison had not yet had his fill of adventure. He instructed the boys to drive straight through New York City -- and we did. But we lost ourselves in Harlem in the middle of the night until we found a friendly street-car driver who gave us directions to the Holland House were we stayed for what was left of the night.

It was good to get back to Glenmont. My diary was packed with these wonderful memories.

Charles the playwright

Charles at age fifteen showed a remarkable talent for writing, not the least of which were his plays. His ability showed itself in 1905 when he wrote a comical drama of manners that depicted the Edison family at dinner. The characters were me, Mr. Edison, Madeleine, Charles, Lucy the governess and my younger brother John. The setting was just after the Spanish-American War and after John had graduated from Cornell and had come to live with us while he worked for Mr. Edison.

The drama[95] provided rare insight to the intimate times of our family. It also was a foretaste of what Charles was to pursue in Greenwich Village during his carefree years preceding his entry into serious business life.

Chapter Eighteen

1906-1907

The railroad arrives in Fort Myers

Our family arrived in Fort Myers, as usual, by boat. Our group included Madeleine and several of her schoolmates and Charles, Theodore and my sister Grace.

During our absence since 1904, the Atlantic Coastline Railway had finally been extended to Fort Myers. The importance of this event cannot be over estimated. It brought the promise of a transfusion of life, growth and sophistication to the area. It connected the sleepy little town to the rest of the world. This wonderful convenience became our regular means of arrival and departure as well as for others who might never have visited the Everglades otherwise.

A second major change was our purchase of the former Gilliland home from Ingram O. Travers, along with an adjacent, triangular parcel that squared off our property.

Downtown Fort Myers was growing and filling the hotel with tarpon hunters who competed for the largest tarpon caught during the season. And a second hotel, The Bradford, had been built. It joined the Fort Myers Hotel that ungraded its status with the touristy name of the Royal Palm Hotel.

Fort Myers was changing rapidly. With it came the first automobile brought to town.

Our big travel entertainment this season was a tour on the *Suwanee* up the Caloosahatchee, through the Disston canals, Lake Flint, Lake Bonnet, Lake Hicpochee to Lake Okeechobee. On the lake itself our tour passed Fish Eating Creek, the mouth of the Kissimmee River and Taylor Creek on the north shore. Okeechobee is a very large lake. In fact, it is the largest body of fresh water in Florida and second only in size to Lake Michigan as the largest lake completely within the contiguous United States. Land actually dropped out of sight during our passage. To carry this a bit further, our captain said Okeechobee is about the size of Rhode Island. But suprisingly, its average depth is a mere nine feet.

The captain was quite friendly and informative. He told us that it was he, in 1883, who hauled in the first dredge that began the massive operation of draining the Everglades by connecting Lake Okeechobee with the Caloosahatchee River.

Early Florida farmers wanted to drain a large part of the 4,000 square *miles* of Everglades to create more farmland. Most people thought the draining project would be "as simple as pulling a plug." Ditches were dug and water flowed, but it was a slow, expensive and highly controversial process.[96] Mr. Edison thought the project was conceived by "damned fools" bent of destroying Florida's natural beauty, plants and wildlife.

Later this same year, Mr. Edison hired the same boat and captain and we crossed the bay to visit the lighthouse on Sanibel Island, taking all our family and guests. Looking at the iron structure of the lighthouse took only minutes. Most of the party much preferred walking the beach and searching for beautiful shells for which the island is most noted.

The San Francisco earthquake

We had just arrived home from Florida when we read the horrible news of the San Francisco earthquake that hit the city on April 18, 1906.[97] Its epicenter was the downtown and the rupture extended a great distance outward. The violent shaking lasted about one minute and was felt hundreds of miles away. The death toll from the quake and resulting fires was at least one thousand. Eventually, it was judged to be one of the most significant earthquakes of all time.

Fortunately Mr. Edison had no significant manufacturing operations in San Francisco.

The phonographic craze

During the early years of the 20th Century Mr. Edison's favorite invention was selling faster than he could produce them. He sent a letter to his several thousand retailers in May of 1906 apologizing for the delays in delivery of the phonograph and promising he would soon catch up.

This was the result of the "phonograph craze" that was spreading across the country. His cylindrical records, made of hard wax, had sold more than two million. He insisted his records produced acoustics superior to the Victor Talking Machine disk records.

Also, the content of his records was directed toward the popular "cracker-barrel" public, offering Negro melodies, love songs, waltz tunes and brass-band marches. And then his "canned opera" was coming into vogue. His competitors, Victor and Columbia, were selling their disks at two dollars. Mr. Edison's cylindrical records were only thirty-five cents.

Finally in 1912, he decided to make a disc record of his own but he ran into difficulties almost immediately. He called out what he referred to as his "insomnia squads" and they spent about a month working as much as 112 hours a week. It worked. His final product was made of hard plastic that eliminated much of the hissing sound that competitive records experienced. My husband was elated and he vowed to make his machine the world's "greatest musical instrument."

His sales volume soared past seven million records per year by 1914 as his content included ragtime and his choice of star vocalists.

Tom, and the nurse who cared for him in the sanatorium, fell in love. As their relationship developed, Tom's drinking and anxiety over his father's demands mitigated. Now, with a modest allowance and real estate, Tom finally had the wherewithal to ask his nurse, Beatrice Willard, to live and work with him on his mushroom farm along the banks of the Delaware River. For the next few months they lived in happy anonymity under the name of Mr. & Mrs. Thomas Willard.

Two months into living together, Tom learned that his first wife, Marie Touhey, the spunky New York "Casino Girl," died from a drug overdose. The incident greatly shook Tom. He calculated that she was only twenty-four. He reported the news to us and Mr. Edison was gracious enough to pay for Miss Touhey's funeral and write an obituary in the New York *Herald Tribune*.

Tom still carried more than an iota of feelings for the ever-cheerful, fun-fun girl and insisted on attending her funeral. Beatrice accompanied him. They were the sole attendees.

This brief fling in Tom's young life was news to his fiancée. But quite coincidently, it was Miss Touhey herself who indirectly brought Tom and Beatrice together. Her wild and immature behavior certainly contributed to the drinking problems that landed Tom in the Sanitarium where nurse Beatrice helped bring about his recovery and their love for each other.

Tom and Beatrice were married on July 7, 1906. It seemed that their life would be one of idyllic harmony.

This was one marriage that met Mr. Edison's and my approval.

Madeleine enrolled at Bryn Mawr College in September 1906. I couldn't believe my first child was going out into the big world. She was an impatient student and found her academic life tedious.

"Why I have to use the metric system instead of inches and quarts is pure nonsense," she wrote. "The instructors all gathered around me in an attempt to make me understand it all. And in the laboratory I'm a danger to both myself and my friends. I gnash my teeth and end up crying in frustration.

"Trigonometry is no better. Do you remember when I needed a tutor just to survive the multiplication tables? And psychology? My brain is too puny to understand this stuff."

I very much wanted my daughter to earn a four-year degree. Her brain wasn't puny, it was her lack of ambition. I know she could have excelled in all her courses. She could memorize and understand pages and pages of Mr. Edison's encyclopedia information. But subconsciously, she asked herself, where am I going with this college degree? Will I get a job in a science laboratory? Will I become president of a college? Will I earn a decent income to support myself, to be independent? She must not have believed she could have achieved any of the above. But the only women that her father hired filled menial positions at the least amount of pay. Yes, she could be a teacher in the lower grades. She could work in a factory tending a machine. Just possibly she could become a nurse.

I believed Madeleine had been pampered, and perhaps even favored, at the Oak Place Secondary School in Akron which was administered by my sister Grace. There was no pampering at Bryn Mawr. In spite of her early complaints, I hoped she would settle down and become a student.

She received fine grades in English and history but what she most enjoyed was her social life that she undertook with gusto. Drama classes and Glee Club were her favorites she shared with two other new freshmen friends -- Peggy James, the daughter of the renowned psychologist William James, whose *Principles of* Psychology was used as Madeleine's undergraduate text, and Mary Worthington, the niece of the Bryn Mawr president, Martha Carey Thomas.

Madeleine lost her pal Peggy to depression, an unfortunate malady of her father's as well, and she dropped out during the second semester. This had a profound effect on Madeleine and she followed suit and returned to Glenmont after completing only two years. This was very disappointing for me.

A damaging freeze

Ewald Stulpner, who we hired after our long absence, now preceded us to Florida each year to prepare for our arrival. He reported that an unusual freeze had taken place at our property and it had damaged a portion of our bamboo garden. The temperature in early January 1907 had only dropped one-and-a-half degrees below freezing, but that was all it took. Thankfully, he said, our fruit trees survived.

Our family didn't arrive in Fort Myers until February 27. We were able to take the train the entire distance for the first time. The only child with us was little Theodore, nine. Both Madeleine and Charles were in college. My guest this year was my oldest brother Ira, his wife Cora and their daughter Elizabeth.

As usual, now that he was in his sixties and slowing down a bit, Mr. Edison spent most of his time fishing on the *Reliance*. With the excitement downtown of the annual tarpon contest, he was still hoping to catch a big one like Charles caught the year before.

We began stepping into local activities a little bit at a time. We visited the Fort Myers Woman's Club and the inventor dutifully signed his name in their guest book and then left. I stayed on and told the story about my father co-founding the Chautauqua Institution. I was already a member of the Women's Club and I reaffirmed my interest in their activities by giving them a check for $120 to go toward creating a permanent town library.

Since my long-term plans included visiting Fort Myers most winters, I had stationery printed with "Seminole Lodge" in the letterhead. I planned to use it here for all my social activities. I considered our winter estate to be mine while Mr. Edison's activities revolved around his play at fishing, boating and working on his dock.

I now used the former Gilliland cottage as a guest house with a living room and dining room on the first floor with a separate structure housing the kitchen that would be used for both houses. Now, with the kitchen removed from our cottage, we made this our master bedroom. It had closets, a private bathroom and a drop-from-the-wall ironing board.

Meanwhile, Mr. Edison was extending his dock even further into the river with a pavilion at the end next to his boat house. This continued to be the longest dock on the Caloosahatchee.

The Royal Palm project

Among our most noticeable and lasting beautification projects in Fort Myers was the Royal Palm project. The town was growing rapidly in population, tourists, hotels and stores. Yes! There was now a store featuring women's fashions. The arrival of the railroad created an immediate growth explosion. I saw this growth happening. But growth in itself does not always bring beauty. The town fathers were busy adopting and revising bylaws and guidelines as fast as they could, but I felt they needed something for the pure beauty if it. Mr. Edison and I loved palm trees from our first arrival. We particularly liked the Cuban Royal Palm for his height, girth and majesty.

These trees were not native to Florida, but they were very plentiful in Cuba.

We thought it would be a valuable beautification project to line both sides of Riverside Avenue, which was later named McGregor Boulevard, with these palms extending from downtown outward for about a mile. We would provide for the construction of protective boxes around each tree, fertilization and care for one year, and necessary replacements for two years, provided the town agreed to care for them ever after.

We told the Fort Myers *Press* about our plan[98] and they published it on April 4. We wanted to avoid the town fathers and get the plan in front of the public immediately, avoiding potential political obfuscation and delay. The *Press* article said it would make Riverside Avenue the most beautiful avenue in the state.

The proposal moved very rapidly. The Town Council met the day the article appeared. They formed a committee. The committee met with us to learn more and to sign an official agreement. The Council accepted the proposal along with a letter of thanks.

Contractors came forward with tree proposals and prices. Mr. Edison finally accepted a proposal. The Everglades had some growth of Royal Palms, but they were not as plentiful or healthy enough to fill the order. Besides they were not as regal as the Cuban variety. It was determined 564 trees would be needed when they were spaced twenty feet apart on both sides of the boulevard.

The deal was settled. Trees were ordered from Cuba. All parties were pleased.

Assuming our tree proposal would eventually be completed, Mr. Edison had a six-inch well drilled on the east side of Riverside Avenue to be used exclusively during the planting and initial caring for the Royal Palms.

Our family left for home at the end of April after only two months in residence. All further business was done through Stulpner and by telegram to Mr. Edison.

Edison the laboratory scientist

Once again Mr. Edison's health was failing after twenty exhausting years of labor on batteries, the Ogden mines, cement projects and his phonograph. In recent years he had acute trouble with his ears. He had X-ray damage to one of his eyes and his stomach. In addition, he had to deal with the stresses of international celebrity which, although it was good for business, it caused pressure to live up to the expectations of others. The press constantly badgered him and our family.

Further, his long-time secretary from the Menlo Park days, John Randolph, gave in to his daily stress of managing Mr. Edison's financial and business operations and committed suicide by gunshot. When hearing of Randolph's demise, he rushed to the widow's home and saved her from commiting the same.

Finally, he was feeling a great sense of inventive accomplishment, but he now lacked the energy and drive that carried him through his first four decades.

On his sixtieth birthday, February 11, stout and round faced, he publicly announced that he was giving up the commercial aspects of his businesses to work exclusively as a scientist in his laboratory. He told me his plan was to study chemical and electrical characteristics that he had encountered over the years but had no time to study in detail. He would now work at his leisure doing anything that met his fancy. His spirit had never faded.

William invents a new spark plug

In 1903 William wanted to open an automobile garage. Mr. Edison was pleased to see that William had a plan and gave him money to get the business started. But then William, probably recognizing he had little business acumen, took in a partner who convinced him to name the business Edison Automobile Company. This enraged Mr. Edison, as it always had, and he squelched the deal.

For the next few years William worked for other automobile companies, gaining experience. He also developed a new type of spark plug in his own laboratory. William showed promise and Mr. Edison was finally impressed. Maybe one of his sons would become an inventor after all. Frank Dyer, Mr. Edison's business manager helped William set up his business. Very soon, however, he was in financial trouble. Dyer found William to be headstrong, full of vanity and conceit. He also spent money freely.

But the main fault that ended this business was William advertising his spark plug as having "the full approval of my father, Thomas A. Edison." His father strongly objected and demanded that he refrain from using this wording. And this led to William complaining that "he not only takes no interest in anything that I may do but, if I am not sadly mistaken, he simply despises me."

Even I had to admit that William never learned from experience.

Mr. Edison pointed out to me that William never thought of approaching the automobile industry about his new spark plug.

My answer was, "Why didn't you suggest that to him in the beginning so he wouldn't feel he had to rely on strangers?"

His response was, "There you go again. He's a grown man. Men have to look out for themselves."

William did look out for himself by taking advantage of his father's friendship with Henry Ford. He wrote and asked

Mr. Ford for help with his new sparkplug and his other automobile improvement ideas. Mr. Ford took interest and gave William some suggestions but William never followed up. It never occurred to him to visit Mr. Ford personally as well as other Detroit automobile manufacturers. Opportunities were forever escaping William's grasp.

Charles enters Hotchkiss

Charles entered the highly selective Hotchkiss preparatory school in Lakeville, Connecticut for his junior and senior years. He was not particularly prepared academically but he applied himself with gusto, struggling with every subject, including German and geometry, both of which he had failed in the past. He passed most of his other courses but without distinction. He simply yearned for vacation when he could goof off and listen to phonograph records in his room.

My, my. When I read his letters I felt a sinking sensation in my heart. Was Charles going to be the same as the rest of our children? Where was the ambition and drive of his father? It's no secret that children of very successful people have difficulty achieving. Maybe Mr. Edison somehow sapped his children's energy and drive. Their father never had anyone drive him or encourage him. He thrived on his successes that he created. But then again Mr. Edison had no one to tell him he couldn't do something. As he strove to get ahead the name Edison meant nothing. He had no one to live up to.

Charles and Madeleine had been given every opportunity on a gold platter. I prayed that both would take hold of themselves and grab the gold ring that was just beyond their current reach.

Perhaps the "gold platter" was the very problem. But what could I do about it? Is there some way to change and reroute my children? Oh! It was so very difficult.

And what about my beautiful, nine-year-old, blonde-haired Theodore? Will he be different? Will he take a different path? Is he different from the others?

Theodore goes to summer camp

Theodore was only nine when he went away from home for the first time to the ritzy Camp Pasquaney on Newfound Lake in Hebron, New Hampshire. Founded eleven years earlier, it offered activities over during a seven-week session in sports, singing, nature hikes, skits and shop projects. It limited the number of campers to one hundred.

I was a bit worried about him of course, but he didn't appear to suffer from homesickness and his letters home showed concern only for his dog Snowy and if he could buy a camp banner that cost a pricy $1.25. He also talked about his diving off the raft and how brave he was to do the "polar-bear swim" at sunrise while the "lazies" were sleeping.

Theodore was never sent away to boarding school like his five his siblings. He was eight years younger than Charles and, thinking that Theodore might be my last child, as Mr. Edison approached his mid-sixties, I wanted Theodore in my life as long as possible with the help of Lucy who hadn't retired yet. Theodore remained at Glenmont and attended Montclair Academy in West Orange. His grades were always good, although his report card might also have a note about his "inattention" and "being silly." If that was worst they could report, I was quite happy.

Chapter Nineteen

1908-1909

The Royal Palms arrive

In mid-January Stulpner informed us that the Royal Palms had arrived in Fort Myers from Cuba. Towles, our contractor, had imported eleven hundred three- to six-foot trees that he planted and watered and cared for. But most of the palms died after five or six months, possibly from frost or disease.

He then ordered thirteen hundred additional trees from Cuba and planted them. A year later, after a drive down McGregor Boulevard, we noted that most of the Royal Palms were doing very well.

"Grammach" dies

We received word from Alice Holzer that her mother, Margaret Stilwell, died at her home in Hamilton, Ontario. Affectionately called "Grammach" by Tom and William, she cared for the boys briefly after their mother Mary died. I still recoil when I remember my visits with Mrs. Stilwell before and just after Mr. Edison and I were married. She was always bitter toward Mr. Edison for the way -- she felt -- he treated Mary. Margaret's son Charles Stilwell worked for Mr. Edison in the Hamilton office setting up a lamp manufacturing factory. Our relationship with Margaret ended when she moved to Canada to live with Charles.

In mid-February, Mr. Edison was admitted to Manhattan Eye, Ear and Throat Hospital where he remained until early March. He underwent two operations for an acute abscess in his deaf left ear. Four days after discharge he and our family left for Fort Myers.

I was very concerned for my husband's health, both physical and mental. The stress for all of us was unspeakable. I arranged for private railway car from the Pennsylvania Railroad Company. With us were Theodore, almost ten, Madeleine and her friend Margaret Gregory, and a young Dr. Page, who had been one of the attending physicians during the ear surgery. He planned to remain with us for ten days.

Many of the comforts of home were with us in the railway car, including Mr. Edison's Poland Springs Water, ginger ale, chicken, sirloin steaks, lamb chops, bacon and fresh vegetables. Mr. Edison wanted no canned vegetables, only crackers and cheese, tea, coffee and green olives.

The train left with us from Newark and arrived in Lakeland, Florida thirty-six hours later. Our car was switched onto the Atlantic Coast Line that took us into Fort Myers, arriving a little after noon.

During the ride I wrote to Charles, at Hochkiss, and told him how much I wished he was with us. I also complained about the Florida heat, and my dislike of Stulpner the caretaker, and how I very much liked the private railway car.

Young Dr. Page seemed to have developed a romantic liking for Madeleine's friend Margaret. Although he looked after Mr. Edison attentively, he was like Margaret's shadow otherwise.

Our arrival at Seminole Lodge brought some excitement. The new caretaker, Doyle, nearly burned the house down by over-stacking the grate in the kitchen stove. It took a bucket of water to douse the flames and make a huge mess. It amazes me how large a floor area a little water can cover.

Mr. Edison was now feeling much better. He chartered the *Suwanee* once again and invited thirty guests from the new Royal Palm Hotel as guests. We fished and had a luncheon on board that included fish chowder. Finally we ended up playing the card game Whist.

I wanted to be more involved in the social circles in Fort Myers. We were invited to the Fort Myers Yacht and Country Club for a reception and dance, but Mr. Edison didn't want to go. So I didn't go. I probably should have gone and brought Margaret, Madeleine's friend, and Mr. Edison's Dr. Dalton, who replaced Dr. Page. But I didn't. On the other hand, if I had gone I probably would have met a lot of people and then I would have been obligated to go to all their functions and they would have been hurt if I didn't go at all. I want to mingle, but I hesitate for some reason. Maybe I'm afraid of being the star of the show, since I am the one-and-only Mrs. Edison. I go round and round on this.

Madeleine as debutant

With Madeleine now at home and declaring she had never intended to seek a four-year degree from Bryn Mawr, I felt compelled to launch her formally into New Jersey and New York society. What better place to throw this party than at Glenmont. I hired the well-known and respected Victor Herbert and his orchestra.[99] Victor, by the way, acted also as "musical advisor" to Mr. Edison at his Phonograph Works.

I went all out and invited more than three hundred guests for the June event. Mr. Edison put up a fuss.

"I despise the ordeal of shaking hands with so many people I don't know, and don't *want* to know," he complained. "Besides, my presence will take attention away from Madeleine and void the whole purpose of this do."

"Do as you want, Dearie. Probably most of them agreed to come in the hope of meeting you and not caring a whit about meeting Madeleine. I would hope that you can make a brief appearance at the very end. Your daughter will appreciate that."

The inventor mumbled something and scurried away happily to his laboratory.

All guests passed through an arbor of pink roses and palms at the Glenmont entrance and then along the receiving line of Charles, Theodore, Madeleine and me. Tom and William were invited but had other important things to do. I ignored queries for Mr. Edison's presence and directed attention to Madeleine, the guest of honor.

The press was invited and the flash of camera lights added a certain degree of spectacle and gave Madeleine the added attention I wanted her to have. Of course one of the main purposes was to have her meet the parents of potential suitors. We were anxious to have her marry someone we could approve of, but we weren't forcing the issue. If we didn't show her off, probably no young, eligible man of our choosing would ever notice her.

Naturally, Madeleine had been nervous before and during the time the first guests passed through the line, but she quickly recovered and exuded her genuine, gracious personality. I was very proud of her.

The luncheon was informal and set out on our dining room table. The guests were encouraged to take their plates to chairs located throughout the first floor and under a tent on the grounds overlooking the town. Drinks, and finally desserts, were distributed by the caterer's staff.

Mr. Edison eventually appeared, as suggested, mid-way through the meal. He must have been hungry. He was dressed in his best and looked his most distinguished. He and I sat together on lawn chairs and chatted with those who came by. His hearing was best when outside rather that in an echoing room. Guests who thought they could talk business with Mr. Edison were cut off with, "Excuse me. Now is not the time."

Madeleine insisted on circulating on her own without me at her elbow. She was pleased to meet and converse with a number of attractive, and sometimes interesting, young men. After all, wasn't that one of main reasons for the event?

Later the same week, Madeleine held her own sit-down luncheon that included all her out-of-town girl cousins and some friends. Papa was the guest of honor and took his place with the young ladies at the head of the table and entertained them with humorous stories about his youth and travel adventures. He was interrupted several times with giggles and laughter and hand clapping. When he finished, he announced that he had difficulty with his hearing so he would just sit among them and read a book. The girls indulged on fruit salad, steamed salmon, decorated muffins and ended with a four-tiered cake smothered with chocolate sauce while Edison himself worked on a single pork chop, applesauce and peas, totally engrossed in his reading.

Monhegan Island retreat

For a dramatic change following Madeleine's brief college career, I took her and Theodore to Monhegan Island, Maine in August to visit their aunt Grace Miller who often spent her summers there in one of the thirty wind-scoured cottages or at the only inn.

We sported the ten-mile, rather lumpy, mail-boat ride from Port Clyde and took rooms in the Old Monhegan House Inn, located in the heart of the small village near the church and post office. There was no transportation around the small island. One had to hoof it, weather the salty wind in our faces and enjoy the unique views.

The island had a long history involving pirates and Indians that Theodore took a great interest in reading about. My sister

Grace was an accomplished artist. She circulated with the famous painters, such as N.C. and Andrew Wyeth, who often spent time on the island. She had suggested Madeleine bring with her a set of paints and brushes and join her in capturing the beauty of the retreat.

While they used their brushes, Theodore and I walked the rugged heights of the north coast, sat on the ledges and watched lobstermen hauling their traps and sailboats on the horizon bending to the uninterrupted winds of the open waters. We searched the cove and rocky crags where pirates might have hidden their treasures. Terns, gulls and other chattering seabirds circled and dipped and glided around us. Island sounds of the wind, the splashing waves and the bell-buoy clang just off the cliff were the constant. How beautiful, I thought. Yet how lonely and apart from the busy world.

Our week-long visit made a permanent impression on the children. They brought home their souvenirs of shells and, for Theodore, an empty lobster shell saved from a delicious dinner.

Madeleine the party girl

How curiously like me Madeleine was becoming. We both enjoyed socializing and entertaining people. In early 1909, now twenty-one, she circulated with an itinerant crowd, in her estimate of, "forty or so" friends who spent a lot of their time partying, dancing, attending gala balls, motoring to football games near and far and coming home well after I had reluctantly gone to bed without greeting her. In her words, she was having "a grand" time. As her mother, I had mixed feelings about her cavorting, but it didn't appear to be harming her. She continued to be my same, happy, laugh-filled daughter. Among her friends was one young man, John Sloane, whom she referred to as "my boyfriend." He lived nearby in South Orange which was primarily a Catholic town.

Toward the end of the summer, her college friend, Peggy James, invited Madeleine to spend some time with her at the family home in Chocorua, New Hampshire. Madeleine immediately accepted and wrote home that she was "having a fine time and not to worry about me and my gentlemen friends."

Should I now worry?

Peggy had two attractive, uncommitted older brothers and Madeleine tried to find common ground with each of them. Billy had quit Harvard medical school after two years and now strived to become a painter. With him, she said, she would "go into aesthetic and soulful rapture about colors and cloud effects. . . but he seems not to take to that kind of thing."

Harry, former editor of the Harvard *Crimson*, had spent time working in Washington at the Department of the Interior and then graduated from Harvard Law School. Madeleine thought she could get along with Harry "if I had the nerve. But certain marks in his 'physiognomical' character rather trouble me. He has eyes that have the iris set up too high so that too much white shows."

One afternoon she and Harry had a picnic on a hillside. It was an idyllic setting. When they left, as she was scrambling down the hill, she caught her skirt on brambles and it ripped open yards of material. It was awkward and embarrassing, she reported, as she had to hold her skirts with both hands as they returned to the motor car.[100]

Although Madeleine's correspondence and friendship with Peggy continued, nothing of her relationships with the James boys ever developed.

Fading motion-picture business

As Mr. Edison's phonograph sales and popularity soared, it was the beginning of the end for his motion pictures. It began with the firing of the talented Edwin S. Porter and his assistant

William J. Gilroy, the men who produced *The Great Train Robbery*, *The Life of a Policeman* and *The Life of an American Fireman* and many others, all successful. Edison Studios had created about twelve hundred films. Porter, who had been with Mr. Edison for eleven years, had resisted the new popularity of nickelodeons, a jutebox that Mr. Edison favored.

In 1908 Mr. Edison formed the "Motion Pictures Patents Company," nicknamed the "Edison Trust," in what I thought was a shameful attempt to shut out smaller movie producers -- a rare act of Edison greed. His company was later shut down after being found guilty of antitrust violation in 1915. In 1918 he sold his all film interests.

Mr. Edison tried to cover up his disappointment by telling me he had never been interested in becoming a movie director or in producing films. I said, "Humbug! You had a great deal of fun mixing with the actors and watching the eventual movie."

He lowered his head as I told him the truth. "Yes. I guess I did."

I knew also his inventive interest lay in solving technical problems of color, for example, or building an affordable home movie camera.

He never said so, but I know he regretted firing Porter who went on to greater acclaim that the inventor could have shared.

Edison and Ford meet a second time

As I understand it, Henry Ford, owner of Ford Motor Company, and four other car companies in 1909 were involved contesting a patent infringement suit filed by George B. Selden, owner of Selden Motor Vehicle Company and the Electric Vehicle Company. It was a critical fight for Ford and others to break up the Selden monopoly.[101]

At some point during this eight-year battle Ford walked into Mr. Edison's lab unannounced and asked him for advice, knowing that Mr. Edison had great experience in defending his inventions from monopolies. My husband gave Ford advice that led to a stunning defeat for Selden. It destroyed Selden's cash flow. He gave up building cars and focused instead on building trucks. Ford now admired his friend all the more.

Ford was a single-invention man, whereas Mr. Edison was protean yet he often envied Ford's business efficiency and commercial success. Mr. Edison always addressed Ford as "Henry," yet Ford never failed at calling his friend "Mr. Edison." They were different men in most ways yet they came to admire each other for *some* of their differences.

Mr. Edison was a quick thinker and raconteur; Ford was a boring talker. Mr. Edison considered Ford somewhat of a simpleton; but later he became afraid of Ford, for "I found him most right where I found him most wrong." Mr. Edison never claimed to love the masses; Ford did, early on. Ford earned fame in 1914 for paying a minimum wage of five dollars a day, while my husband was still paying half as much.

Somehow, their friendship lasted a lifetime.

William's house in the country

As difficult as it was, William and Blanche stood their ground and never begged from either family. I had begun corresponding with the couple and sympathized with their problems of getting their life together. As the years passed, I kept their father informed of their woeful status. So it was a surprise and a relief both to me and the now thirty-something-year-old couple, when in 1909 Mr. Edison accepted the fact that his son, although childless, was married. I believe he might even have been amazed that their marriage endured through the decade of hardship.

The relief came as a substantial, regular income, that allowed them to buy a farm in the country as Mr. Edison had done for Tom. The couple set up a poultry farm in New Jersey where they bred and sold turkeys, ducks, quail, pheasants and even homing pigeons. The income also allowed William to live the life of a country gentleman, visit me at Glenmont on holidays and circulate among the men's clubs in New York City. It became a comfortable life with the woman William loved.

The houses are connected

The family arrived in mid-February with Madeleine, Theodore, some friends, and, of course, the maids. The Fort Myers mayor greeted us at the train and thanked us for beautifying the town with the rows of Royal Palms along McGregor Avenue. Mr. Edison in turn thanked the mayor for the biggest improvement in town -- kicking whiskey out and voting the town dry on the previous town ballot.[102]

Mr. Edison was in a funk. He had just lost an appeal that prevented his phonograph company from selling his machines in New York. In addition there was a heavy cash penalty. In retribution, he took it out on the innocent fish in the Caloosahatchee.

His mind cleared a bit when he received an invite from the sport fishermen of Rockport, Texas inviting him to their waters across the Gulf for a week of good tarpon fishing. Mr. Edison replied with an invite of his own saying, there are so many tarpon and fish near my place in Fort Myers that it raises the river level eleven inches every season.

An elegant evening party was thrown at the Royal Palm Hotel by Mrs. Hermance who regularly wintered here. The event was to honor my husband, beginning with a tea with dinner following. There were sixteen guests. Following dinner we gathered in the music room and parlor for conversation, music and dancing. Believe it or not, I was able to drag my Dearie onto the dance floor for a few rounds.

Recovering from the economic problems of two years ago, I ordered changes previously requested at Seminole Lodge to continue. The most exciting was the arborway, a pergola, between the two houses. The trelliswork on both sides were to be covered with ivy and colorful climbing floras.

Honored with a gold medal

We traveled to Stockholm, Sweden not long after we returned from Florida. It was our first trip to a Scandavian country. The vistas were beautiful; the city was clean and architecturally unique. We attended a formal reception and dance sponsored by the Swedish Royal Academy of Sciences, founded in 1739.

Mr. Edison was honored with a gold medal for his inventions of the phonograph and the incandescent light.

Mr. Edison's autobiography

At age sixty-three, Mr. Edison decided it was about time to record the details of his life for posterity. During much of 1908 and 1909 he filled several notebooks with personal reminiscences that were later published in two large volumes, co-written and edited by Frank Lewis Dyer, the inventor's long-time assistant, and Thomas Commerford Martin, former president of the American Institute of Electrical Engineers.[103]

The Introduction in the book begins: "Prior to this, no complete, authentic, and authorized record of the work of Mr. Edison, during an active life, has been given to the world. . . These volumes aim to be a biography rather than a history of electricity. . . A great deal of this narrative is given in Mr. Edison's own language, from oral or written statements made in his reply to questions addressed to him with the object of securing accuracy. . ."

My name is mentioned. "Acknowledgments must also be made of the courtesy and assistance of Mrs. Edison, and especially of the loan of many interesting and rare photographs from her private collection."

But, somehow, Mr. Edison, in his personal life story, forgot his family. His autobiography contains *not a single word* about his two wives and six children!

Tom and William settle for less

In a 1909 letter to Mr. Edison's biographer, Frank Dyer (a letter that did not appear in his book), William complained that his father always criticized him, Tom and Marion.

"For ten years I have not received what might be called a fatherly letter," William wrote, "but on the other hand each and every one contained the statement similar to, 'You can paddle your own canoe' 'I'm through with you' 'if you don't make this go your name is Mud' and other very encouraging (pardon the sarcasm) statements."[104]

Try as they might, there was nothing the children could do to please Papa. He failed to prepare them for our marriage; he never offered fatherly advice; he was too ready to find fault; and expressions of love for them never happened.

Mary's boys never came close to achieving their dreams of becoming like their father who, for some unknown reason, they continued to idolize. They craved the opportunity to please him.

In the end, his boys were forced to settle for what their father finally gave each of them -- a farm in the country, apart from Glenmont, the laboratory and my three children.

Charles enrolls in MIT

In the fall of 1909 Charles enrolled in MIT. He rented rooms at No. 6 Louisburg[105] Square, an exclusive residential area of Boston's Beacon Hill. At Mr. Edison's suggestion, Charles studied general science without focusing on any particular specialty. His father's goal was to prepare him to take on a management role in Thomas A. Edison, Inc. But Charles felt "constrained" by the academic structure and chose instead a variety of electives. His grades were mediocre and for this he apologized time and again, but Charles never offered an excuse.

He joined the Delta Psi fraternity and went on slumming parties, but he also joined an informal reading and study group. It met twice a month over crackers and coffee or beer at the apartment of a young English professor and playwright who greatly encouraged Charles' writing in which he had enjoyed dabbling as a teen.

Chapter Twenty

1910-1911

Fort Myers celebrates 25 years

The town of Fort Myers celebrated its twenty-fifth anniversary on March 9 and Mr. Edison was the guest of honor and sat with other local luminaries. As usual, Mr. Edison declined to make a speech, but simply waved his straw hat to the crowd who returned several "Hip, hip, hoorays."

There was a parade along McGregor Boulevard and through town led by cowboys, a team of oxen pulling a wagon with a chicken coop and a blown up photograph of the old, dirt-street, downtown -- all staged to represent how the town had modernized over the past quarter century. This was followed by colorfully flowered floats of town organizations, a new town fire truck and then a line of shiny automobiles with their horns honking.

I was thrilled to visit the new Royal Palm Theater where we were given a tour and then watched live entertainment and silent movies. The hand-out advertised forthcoming plays and musicals. It wasn't Broadway, but it was a good start -- all very nicely presented. Fort Myers was building its social life and from this point on I believed I could include our local theatre as part of our entertainment of visitors.

Many improvements had taken place at Seminole Lodge as well. I held a reception on the east porch for my younger sisters, Mary Emily and Grace, Madeleine, and some of the Fort Myers social dignitaries. Set up on the new pergola, musicians provided a background of contemporary and classical selections.

One of these guests asked if we had considered installing a swimming pool. We had not, but now that Mr. Edison had the suggestion in his head, he began with some drawings. Before the season was over, a ferro-cement pool was under construction. It would be filled from the well that was drilled previously for irrigating the Royal Palms. As if to justify the expense, my husband said a pool would also be a good nearby water supply in case of fire.

Cement houses at Glenmont

Never giving up on an idea he still felt was plausible, during the summer of 1910, Mr. Edison built two experimental two-story cement buildings on the grounds of Glenmont. They became the gardener's cottage and a garage. This was the last gasp of his idea to produce inexpensive housing for the working man. Years earlier he had dropped the idea as too far afield and distracting from his other businesses. Unfortunately, he wasn't able to stir up enough interest to continue.

My thinking probably represented that of everyone else. I was recoiled at the idea of cement houses. But once these buildings were painted and decorated, I was unable to tell the difference between our cement buildings and our conventional buildings. For no other reason, these unique structures added interest to the property tours we gave our friends and guests.

Edison batteries conquer Mt. Washington

The headline in The New York *Times*[106] read:

Automobiles Complete Long Endurance Run;
Trip of 1000 Miles Including Mount Washington Climb
Proves That Edison Battery Is No Longer a Myth.

The two "electromobiles," a Bailey and a Detroit, set out from the Touring Club of America, Broadway and 76th Street, New York City with two men each and their necessary travel gear. The machines were equipped with Edison batteries. Mr. Edison was determined to prove that electric autos were better than gasoline ones.

The trip took four days solely because the batteries had to be recharged at the few and far between electric stations along the route. Their first resting stop was Waterbury, Connecticut and from there the cars took different routes. The Bailey's next stop was Pittsfield, Massachusetts, while the Detroit went by way of Hartford, Springfield and Boston. The Bailey reached Manchester, Vermont on the fourth night and drove over Peru Mountain with its steep and rugged road. The Detroit crossed Massachusetts, through Lynn and Topsfield on Rt. 1 to Portsmouth and on to Portland and Poland Springs, Maine.

The Bailey passed Claremont and Newport, New Hampshire and Lake Sunapee with a night stop to charge up at Plymouth. The Detroit continued on to Bretton Woods. They both met at the Mount Washington Hotel. The next day they drove around the foothills of Mount Washington to Jackson and recharged. This was to be the end of the planned trip. The drivers considered the effort a huge success and they were ready to return to New York.

But, in the glow of having proven the value of the Edison batteries, Mr. Edison, ever the seeker of publicity, sent a telegram and urged the drivers to continue on and drive up the carriage road to the summit of Mount Washington.

They did, but the weather was against them on that steep 14-percent, and often 20-percent grade. They achieved seven of the eight miles before they were forced to stop due dangerous conditions. The drivers spent a sleepless night in the cold but were rewarded with a finish the next morning. A crowd of well wishers greeted them at the summit. The batteries survived the climb and the freezing weather.

There was nothing else to do now but drive home. The Detroit route was from Bretton Woods, past The Old Man in the Mountain, Franconia Notch, Manchester, Waterbury and New York City. The Bailey went by way of Poland Springs, Portland, Portsmouth, Amesbury (the Bailey's birthplace), Boston, Worcester, Springfield and New York.

The New York *Times* closing words were: "This trip alone, not to mention many others, goes to prove that the long-talked-of Edison battery is no longer a myth, but an accomplished fact, not to be scoffed at, but to be regarded with awe and serious interest."

Other newspapers picked up the story and Mr, Edison received the attention he wanted.

What does God mean to you?

Mr. Edison was always getting headlines as a result of some statement, often controversial, that he made to a reporter. Newspapers always sought the ideas expressed by "the most popular man in America." He was newsworthy and certainly his name sold papers.

God was the subject in late summer when a reporter from *Harper's Weekly*[107] asked, "What does God mean to you?" The question sounded simple enough but, for many, it was the answer that was not simple. Frankly, I was the one who tried to attend church regularly and I took our children with me before they grew up and left our nest. My husband and I rarely talked about God or religion. I was aware of his views. Thus, any discussion we had was usually limited to mundane matters of repairs or other needs at the church. On these subjects he was usually open-minded.

My outspoken husband's sincere, but perhaps not fully considered, answer to the reporter during this interview was, "A personal God means absolutely nothing to me." He went on to say that God was an "abstraction." Superstition was his enemy. Most people were "incurably religious." And, "billions of prayers" are not enough to halt a natural catastrophy.

The response from the magazine's pious lay readers and the religious press were angry attacks on Mr. Edison. The postman delivered bags of mail instead of the normal batch with an elastic around it. We had to ask the help to give us a hand opening and sorting the wheat from the chaff, so to speak.

Response from the clergy by mail and from their pulpits spoke out against my husband's "Unitarian and materialistic" views. He was placed in the company of Tyndall, Huxley, Darwin and this suited my Dearie just fine. They were among his favorite authors when he was growing up. Mr. Edison did not flinch. He stood up to the noise and maintained his beliefs for which he saw no need to modify or defend.

I neither agreed nor disagreed but kept giving my services and money to the Methodist Church in East Orange. I continued to invite clerics and other guests to Glenmont for dinner as I always had. But, when six Methodist bishops showed up at one occasion, my husband embarrassed me by walking out of the room saying, "I'm not listening to any more of this nonsense."

Eventually we came to an understanding. I would continue to invite church people to dinner, but we would not discuss religion in his presence. He agreed to this and life went on.

Much later, my husband qualified his beliefs about God and admitted the *possibility* of a supreme being.

We left this all behind and took our family on a European tour.

Madeleine is nervous

Madeleine visited her Aunt Grace and my mother at Oak Place, the Miller estate. The report to me from Akron was that Madeleine appeared very nervous and unsettled. It appears my daughter spoke in confidentiality to her elders. My daughter had been spending time in the company of John Sloane and his family. She should have been nervous because Mr. Edison had forbidden her from seeing her "boyfriend."

When I mentioned this to Mr. Edison, he immediately checked out the Sloane family. They were respectable and the boy's father owned an aircraft plant and was doing a booming business with the government. But the family was Catholic.

My husband's hackles went up and his popish prejudices were revealed.

"We have to put an end to this," he said. "I will not allow my daughter cavorting with a Catholic. It is dangerous. She'll soon be worshiping the Pope and kissing his ring."

"Now, now," I said trying to smooth his feathers. "He is only a friend among her other friends. She could very likely have a lot of Catholic friends."

"Humbug and hogwash, Billie. One thing leads to another and they could become serious and that leads to only one thing -- marriage and a house full of another generation of Catholics. I will not have it! I want you to speak to her and tell her in no uncertain terms that she will not see this boy."

"If you feel so strongly about this, I think you had better speak with Madeleine."

"Billie! The children are your responsibility. You will speak to her. You threw that debutante party for her and she met a hoard of Protestant boys. Is this some kind of sordid rebellion?"

If the written word could reflect Dearie's forceful words, they would fill a page in bold, sans serif type. He was as stubborn as a mule.

I spoke with Madeleine a few days later.

"How is your friend John Sloane?" I asked innocently.

"Fine."

"Tell me about him. I'm interested in your friends."

"He's just a friend. He's one of our crowd."

"Is he a boyfriend?"

"What are you getting at, Mama?"

"I want to know about him, that's all. You didn't invite him to your coming-out party."

"No. I didn't. But I wish I had."

"Why didn't you?"

She looked and rolled her eyes. "Because you and Papa wouldn't have approved."

"Is that because he is Catholic?"

"So you know! Did Gramma Miller tell you? What a snit! I can't tell my secrets to anyone!"

"This is very important to us, Madeleine. We don't want you marrying a Catholic."

"Mama! He is a *friend*. He's *not* my suitor."

"I hope not, darling. This would make your father very unhappy."

"Well don't you worry about it."

"I do. I was married at your age. That was what your big party was for. We had hoped that the party would result in some of those young men asking for you for your hand."

"Some to them are in my crowd. You never know."

"We just want you to be happy. You have a better chance of being happy with your own kind."

"Kind? *Kind*? Is a Catholic a different species of human?"

"You know what I mean. He is a different religion with different beliefs."

"You mean like a Buddists and Jews?"

"Madeleine! Marriage is tough enough when you have the *same* beliefs. You don't have to go out and complicate things by finding someone who thinks differently."

"Yes, Mama. Thank you for the lecture. I hear you."

That ended our conversation but I don't know that anything was resolved.

We decided to vacation in Europe in the summer of 1911. The trip was an effort to pull the family together before they scattered on their own. We traveled in two groups -- about a month apart. I was in the vanguard with Madeleine, twenty-three, who sulked and didn't want to go and Theodore, ten years younger, who was quite the opposite -- excited at making his first ocean voyage. We three, along with governess Lucy and chauffeur Scarth, took an escorted tour of Holland, Belgium and England. At Mr. Edison's suggestion, we used fictitious names, and avoided the largest cities to escape the press.

Charles, now twenty-one, and Mr. Edison sailed on the *Mauretania*. The two were developing an adult relationship. Since Charles now had three years of MIT, as well as a bit of business experience, they found each other to be interesting companions.

During their voyage, Charles later told me, he saw from his deck chair his father at the rail with a couple other men. They were holding folded paper airplanes over their heads and discussing how the different designs reacted aerodynamically. Minutes later, the men were peering over the rail watching the water roil against the bow as the steamer cut through the waves, now talking about skin friction of water against metal and how it could be designed for more efficiency.

Mr. Edison introduced his new friends to Charles. They were Henry James, the novelist, and Peter Cooper Hewitt, the scientist and inventor. The author had been staying with his brother William's daughter, Peggy and family in Chocorua, New Hampshire, since the famous psychologist died of a sudden heart attack in August 1910 at the age of sixty-eight.

We docked in Liverpool and Charles drove them (his first experience driving in the left lane) by way of Coventry to London. Charles described his drive between the hedgerows as being swept along a trough of green. They picked up Sir George Croydon Marks who gave them a tour of Parliament. The MPs were in an historic debate at the time and they witnessed the vote that abolished the House of Lords veto power over the House of Commons.

The two men ferried across the Channel to Boulogne where they met up with us. We were all in good spirits as Scarth drove us in a Daimler along the Normandy coast, stopping at a unique chateaux each day to take in the sights.

We passed through beautiful Saint-Malo that was once a walled city on the coast guarding the mouth of the Rance River, inhabited for centuries by fearsome pirates. Another pleasant stop was Mont Saint-Michel, the unique island commune in Normandy. Then we rode back through the Loire valley with its many castles and gourmet meals.

Finally, we went on to Paris where Mr. Edison had arranged to meet up with Marion and her husband Oscar rather than side-trip to Germany.

Seventeen years had passed since we had seen Marion, now thirty-nine. She wrote from her summer retreat on the river Rhine that she was thrilled at the prospect suggested by her father, saying her happiness scale has soared fifty degrees. She said that, in anticipation of the visit and as a courtesy to the family, Oscar had begun taking spoken-English lessons. She said, parenthetically, she and her husband had never spoken English together. Marion's only complaint was that she had to travel at all. She said she had sleepless nights thinking of the prospect.

As Mr. Edison had feared, it was in Paris that the press discovered us. The sleuth was E.A. Valentine from New York *World*. He intercepted Madeleine and begged her for a meeting with her father that she firmly rejected.

The actual meeting between the Oesers and the Edisons was friendly and cordial. Marion hugged her father far longer than he preferred, and she and I hugged as well, but far less than I wanted. Marion had not seen Madeleine and Charles since they were quite young and, of course, she had never seen Theodore. The four young adults conversed easily. Oscar made his best effort in English but it was very limited. Marion filled in as translator. We had dinner together and spent a single night in the city. We parted ways the next morning. Marion displayed some tears and that was it. No one knew when we next would meet.

Our family drove on to Switzerland, spending more time than elsewhere in Geneva and Lucerne. In spite of Mr. Edison's trick of packing the car and loading the family before announcing his departure, Mr. Valentine proved his expertise at his job and pursued us.

While motoring the challenging roads of the Austrian Tyrol, Mr. Valentine suddenly came down with a heart condition, possibly related to altitude sickness or an overdose of strychnine. In that ailing condition, he begged Charles for a few words from the Great Man so he could file his story with the paper. Mr. Edison, appreciating a man who carried on under difficult conditions, relented and the two spent some time on the deck of an Austrian inn at Klagenfurt.

The interview, and a rest at the inn, seemed to cure the reporter who Mr. Edison and the family had now taken a liking to. In fact, he was invited to continue with them on their tour.

The happy group, now involved with refreshing stories from Mr. Valentine's experiences, went on to Vienna and then Budapest. Here Mr. Edison had an emotional reunion with a former employee and friend who had worked closely with him at Menlo Park. They went for a walk to enjoy the city, but were soon closely followed by the local press. But their reunion was a success, regardless.

Back at the inn, the manager gave them a private room where the family was given a personal serenade by a local troupe. Meanwhile the manager secretly set up the main room and, as we prepared to leave, an elaborate reception was given the inventor. As I watched my husband walk around the room meeting and greeting people, I thought it was doubtful that *any* businessman, with an obsession only for money, ever enjoyed *life* more than Mr. Edison.

We sailed for home at the end of September.

Mina's brother Robert dies

My brother Robert Miller, Sr. died in Chautauqua on July 26, 1911. He was four years older than me and the husband of Louise Igoe. Early in his career he had worked with my father at his Altman plant in Canton, Ohio. In 1899, the year our father died, Robert was appointed postmaster general at Ponce, Puerto Rico by President William McKinley, who was also a personal friend of our family. Robert was only fifty years old.

I didn't see Robert much because of his job in Puerto Rico. Fortunately I did see him at Chautauqua before he passed away. He had some kind of lung infection that made his breathing progressively difficult. His was a very difficult death of suffocation, but his condition was made somewhat easier by the drugs that were admistered to him.

Three of my ten siblings had now passed away.

Chapter Twenty-One

1912

Edison -Ford business relationship

Henry Ford was a household name by 1912. He had fought off George Seldon's lawsuit and the Model T was a common sight throughout America. Ford was still refused membership in the Association of Licensed Automobile Manufacturers (ALMA), but he felt he didn't need its endorsement. He felt he was doing just fine without ALMA's endorsement.

He bought an abandoned sixty-acre racetrack in a suburb of Detroit and built a huge steel and glass factory for his Model T. It was here he created his unique, and famous, moving assembly-line production from which an automobile emerged every two-and-a-half hours. Each worker along the line was assigned only a single task in the assembly. From where each man stood, the part he needed was sent to him on a conveyor belt.

Mr. Edison and I were invited to tour Mr. Ford's new plant. It was like nothing either of us had ever seen. My husband scratched his head in marvel at the system after only the first few minutes of the tour.

"By golly, Henry" he said. "When I think how I could have used this system in any number of my factories. This is brilliant."

Ford now wanted to share his success with the man he so admired.

"Mr. Edison," Ford began in the only address he ever used for his friend. "I need a battery for the Model T. In fact, I need a generator and a starting motor as well. I'd like you to design and produce these for me."

Thus began another phase of their relationship.

"I've been thinking about this for a while," Ford said. "I will guarantee you a minimum of $4 million a year in orders and I will advance you $100,000 now in anticipation of eventual delivery."[108]

Mr. Edison paused and I could see the gears in his head spinning. "That sounds like a very generous offer, Henry. Let's put it on paper."

For the next few years Mr. Edison set to work on the project, with Ford advancing him another million dollars for research and development, but the inventor could not come up with a practical, integrated method that would work.

Yet, Ford continued to admire Mr. Edison in every way and their friendship blossomed unabated.

Madeleine and friends in Fort Myers

Our journey to Fort Myers this year included three of Madeleine's friends, one of whom was Peggy James. Madeleine, now twenty-three, believed that Seminole Lodge and climate would help Peggy recover from her depression that had been heightened by her father's death less than two years earlier.

It worked. Peggy, who had never been to Florida, was totally captivated by the tropical beauty and surprised by the luxury of our estate. The four girls lived in the adjacent "guest cottage." They entertained themselves independently except for meals when they joined Papa, Theodore and me. Madeleine told me that Peggy wrote home to her mother that her mental state had rapidly returned to normalcy and she gushed over her lodge's wide porches and the French windows that overlooked our uncountable number of bold flowers that "almost defy reason."

The swimming pool installation had been completed since our last visit. I wrote to Charles, who was now back at MIT, that the girls enjoyed the pool immensely. I had been reluctant to visit Fort Myers this year, but now I raved in my letter to Charles about the sunshine and the birds and how I really loved it here.

Three-time Democratic presidential candidate, William Jennings Bryant, toured Fort Myers and stopped by our estate for a brief visit. His visit happened during my initial beautification project of the town and was well underway with the planting of more than two thousand Cuban Royal Palms. I shook hands with Mr. Bryant, but Mr. Edison was not to be disturbed in his laboratory.

Mr. Edison treated us all to a day out onto the Caloosahatchie on the steamer *Suwanee* with Captain Menge. We fished over the sides and had a little bit of luck. Peggy saw her first wild alligators. As the boat approached, these creatures wriggled off their sunny spots on the sandbanks and dipped menacingly into the river. Peggy was startled, but Madeleine assured her that alligators only did this because they felt safer in the water and were not a threat to us. Peggy was not convinced.

More of a threat, I felt, was our handsome boat captain Menge himself. His flirtations with the girls on our four-day trip to Captiva Island and then on to Lake Okeechobee I thought were excessive. Maybe I was jealous. The girls didn't complain. In fact, Madeleine and her friends scribbled a little poem about him.[109]

We made frequent trips on our own electric launch, *Reliance*. One evening a week or so later, sans Menge, we took Madeleine's friends out at night on the *Reliance* and skimmed silently through the water. The girls marveled at the calls of owls, herons and whippoorwills as each performed its own serenade just for us. Unfortunately, Mr. Edison was never able to hear these beautiful sounds of nature.

When it came time to leave for the north, near the end of April, we all dreaded it and wished the bliss could continue. I wrote Charles that "Seminole Lodge is the place . . . It is better to enjoy Papa's free time with him [here] rather than to be home where his is busy."

The shocking news of the sinking of the Titanic on April 15 had just reached us before we boarded the train. We all found it frightening and extremely depressing as we read the horrible details.

Edison at age sixty-five

He wanted no special party for the event, but he couldn't keep us from singing "Happy Birthday" to him. He was now sixty-five.

"I don't know where all the years have gone," he remarked. "My life has just hummed along day after day, eighteen hours every day, and suddenly I wake up and I'm old. I don't want to look in the mirror any more. This man in the mirror has too much to do before he gets old."

His fan mail this year was especially heavy on what these admirers considered an important mile-marker.

"Humbug!" the inventor said. "It doesn't change anything."

In answer to the most most frequent question asked of him, "What is the secret of your success?" he had an answer.

"Work. I work twice as many hours as other men. Since I've done that for forty-five years, that makes me ninety. Add twenty years for my youth and we're up to one hundred and ten. Add eighteen more hours a day for the next twenty years and I'll be one hundred and fifty. I don't eat much. I don't sleep much. And I don't shut off my blood circulation by wearing tight clothing."

Mary Emily Miller marries

My younger sister Mary Emily Miller, finally married, at forty-five, in June to businessman William Nichols, also from Akron.

Mary graduated from Wellesley College in 1888 and did a lot of traveling in Europe with our sisters, Jennie and Grace. She lived most of her years at Oak Hill with father and mother.

In 1909 she had what was thought was a mental breakdown and spent time in the Battle Creek Sanatorium in Michigan until we invited her to stay with us at Glenmont during much of 1910. She bemoaned her life as a maiden lady and said she envied everything about my life.

Then she met Mr. Nichols, a widower, who cheered her up. It was a good match. Their wedding was very simple and we did not attend.

Improved inventions announced

In the fall, Mr. Edison announced the production and sale of two improved generations of his products.

The first was Diamond Discs, Thomas A. Edison, Inc.'s first entry into the disc market after generating the cylindrical record for so many years. Although Victor, Columbia and others had been in the disc market for years, Mr. Edison's new discs were unique in the phonograph industry. They were a quarter-inch thick and would *not* play on Victrolas or with steel needles. They would play only on Edison phonographs with his diamond stylus. Victor products could be played on an Edison machine but it required an adaptor that could be bought from Edison, Inc. separately. These discs were used until 1929 when Mr. Edison shut down his phonograph production entirely.

The other product was the "Home-Projecting Kinetoscope," a home cinema projection system, that was announced in an advertisement in the magazine *Edison Works Monthly,* published October 1912. I found the advertising copy of that time far different than we would see today in advertisments. Here is a taste of it.

"With the advent of the Edison Home Kinetoscope, there has come a new and powerful force for education and entertainment. For there is within that little machine all the magic of Aladdin's Lamp. Wither lie your inclinations? Would you investigate the mysteries of the world's great industries, learning the processes by which various commodities are prepared for your use? Or would you explore the beauties of distant lands? Loll at ease in the depths of your spacious arm-chair and summon before you the pomp and splendor of India, the picturesque charm of Japan, Italy with its wealth of mythology and its history more wonderful than fiction. Or perhaps you have not yet marveled at the scenic grandeur of our own land. Whereever [sic] fancy leads, you may pursue to the far ends of the earth. Would you laugh? Comedies sparkling with irrestible fun and rich with rare humor, stand ready to tickle your senses. If you would sound the depths of the drama, beautiful tales of love and adventure, stirring scents of heroism and devotion, with now and then a touch of pathos, attend your slightest wish. Or if you love history you may witness some of the greatest events which the world has ever seen.

"The Machine Itself -- The Edison Kinetoscope is neither a toy nor a delicate and complicated mechanism but that combines simplicity, safety and effectiveness. It is simple because Mr. Edison realized, when designing the instrument, that it would be operated by people who are not scientifically or mechanically trained, safe, because the source of light is carefully protected, and effective, because it compares favor-ably in design, material, workmanship and finish with the professional types of Edison Projecting Kinetoscopes that are used in theatres and other public places."

This ad was accompanied by photos of the carrying case and the projector, the reel-to-reel filmstrip and the hand crank on one of the reels for the user to manually wind the film through the projector as it is cast onto a screen.[110]

Mina's mother dies

Mother taught me well. She passed away in October at the age of eighty-two. I delightedly saw myself in her in all respects. I strived to be the unselfish, other-directed person she was.

As an example, my Dearie was first in importance in my life. I tried always to take his side of an argument, although that often hurt in regard to his children. For them I could only try to help them understand their father's often cold, yes, brutal stubborn streak. I often had to donate my soul to his children to help them survive a rough period with their father.

I traveled to Akron and attended the church funeral service for my mother with my seven surviving siblings and their families. Father, who had passed away twelve years earlier, was in our thoughts as well. We children all agreed we had a very special upbringing and were sent off into the world with the best credentials.

At the collation that followed I noticed a good looking man who looked a little familiar. I went over to him.

"Excuse me," I said.

He turned to me. It was Edward Hughes, an old suitor of mine. "Mina!" he said happily. "I'm so sorry about the loss of your mother. She was a wonderful woman."

"Edward. Thank you. How very nice of you to attend. How are you doing? You look just great."

"Thank you. I don't see Mr. Edison with you."

"No. He found something more interesting he had to attend to. How about you? Are you married?"

"I sure am, but Susan hasn't been feeling well. So I'm batcheloring it."

"Do I know Susan?"

"I don't think so. She never lived in Akron. She's from Boston."

"Oh. How nice. Do you have any children?"

"Yes. Two sons, both of whom are in law school and I hope will join me at my company after they graduate."

"I haven't seen you at Chautauqua."

"No. I never returned after college. We live in Franklin, Pennsylvania and I have my business there. How about you? Do you still visit Chautauqua?"

"I'm there with the children every summer for a couple months. My family's still very active there as you can imagine."

"Your father? Is he. . ."

"Oh. I'm sorry. You didn't hear. He passed away in ninety-nine. He was seventy."

"He was a very good man. I wish I had known him better."

"Well, we were still young. You came to our family dinners now and then."

"I did. Excuse me, but I had a real crush on you. It hurt when you became engaged to George Vincent."

"You can blame my mother for that, Edward."

"I should have fought harder for you. But then Mr. Edison came along and I didn't even have a fighting chance."

"You never know," I said coyly.

"Do you have children?"

"I do. I have three stepchildren and three of my own. They range in age from forty-nine down to fourteen. Two girls and four boys."

"That's a houseful."

"Actually its only the youngest who's at home now."

"Very nice."

"Do you and your wife ever get out to the New Jersey area?"

"Yes. I come through on my way to the city occasionally."

"Mr. Edison and I would love to have you two visit some time. Here's my card."

"How could I resist? Thank you. I'll give you a call when things shape up in that direction."

"Very good. Well. It's been very nice to see you, Edward. But I should be circulating."

We shook hands and parted our ways. I was impressed by him. He had grown into quite a distinguished gentleman.

Chapter Twenty-Two

1913-1914

Charles drops out of MIT

After surviving the first two exhausting years at MIT, Charles spent the summer of 1911 camping in the mountains of Arkansas. He was probably already thinking of quitting the studies in which he was not especially interested. He had some deep thinking to do on his future.

Charles did return to MIT in the fall, but he was still indecisive on an educational major coupled with his lack of interest in any form of engineering. He dropped out midway through his senior year in 1913 -- much to Mr. Edison's delight and my disappointment. Would I ever have a child with a four-year college diploma?

His father's delight turned to disappointment when Charles' lure was not his father's business, but the Boston Edison Company. They offered him fifteen dollars a week as a floater, an apprentice, moving from department to department, learning all phases of the company. He spent a year at the company soaking up valuable skills, but when summer returned his wanderlust took over and he requested a leave of absence to tour the country. The "Edison" name worked in his favor and the company granted him the time off.

Charles told us his plans. He and his MIT friend, Bob, were going to tour the West before settling down.

Charles drove his motor car to Denver where he picked up Bob and began their adventure. They were soon lost on the

13,204-foot Argentine Pass that crossed the Continental Divide -- the highest named vehicle-accessible pass in Colorado. An adventure it was indeed. The the snow had not yet completely melted in May. At times they had to push the vehicle over the drifts. They eventually made it to Colorado Springs and there they experienced their first rodeo. It was there he sold his motor car and opted for the train that took them to California by way of the Grand Canyon.

Bob was now running low on funds. He decided to sell his prize Western-style sterling silver belt buckle to the train conductor who had shown an interest in it. The boys ended up in San Francisco where they bumped into two friends from Menlo Park, the sons of men who had worked for Charles' father. The four joined forces and shared an apartment on Bush Street, just off Market, happily wasting their time in pubs and lolling on the California beaches eyeing the girls.

It was mid-August when Charles returned. He was poised to rejoin Boston Edison. To my surprise, and certainly to Charles, his father offered him an apprenticeship at Thomas A. Edison, Inc. with a starting salary of ten dollars more per hour than Boston Edison was paying him.

Charles accepted.

This was a significant step on Mr. Edison's part. It was the first time he had offered an apprenticeship to any of his children. But why Charles? He had never shown any particular interest or skills in science or engineering. His preference at MIT was management and he had never shown any desire to work for his father. But what Charles did have was the lingering rapport he developed with his father during our last trip to Europe.

Charles began his apprenticeship in November 1913. His future was cut out for him. Unlike his father, however, Charles had competing interests that occupied his mind.

Talking pictures Introduced

Improved synchronized talking pictures were first introduced by Mr. Edison at Keith's Colonial Theatre in New York on February 17, 1913 and were shown to enraptured audiences for several months.

As Mr. Edison explained it to me, accurate synchronization of the picture with the sound had been the problem from the days of the Black Maria when the effort was strictly manual trial-and-error, matching the motion picture with the sound on a separate phonograph. Mr. Edison said, how nice it would be if someone could "do for the eye what the phonograph does for the ear." Moving pictures, by 1913, had already gained great popularity. Adding sound, beginning with Mr. Edison, was the frosting on the cake. It was a big hit and all the more people patronized movie theaters.

But it wasn't until the 1930s that truly synchronized sound was finally taken off separate recording devices and recorded directly onto the camera film itself by inventor Lee deForest.[111]

Charles' other interests

Charles Edison also had a hearing loss. Although it was nowhere as pronounced as his father's severe problem, it plagued him all his life.[112] In spite of this infirmary, he loved piano improvisation. He enjoyed writing as well as reading. He had always been attracted to the Bohemian life of the Greenwich Village cafes, saloons and chess parlors. When the clock struck five at Thomas A. Edison, Inc., he bee-lined it to the Village to join the crowd of artists, musicians and writers. His poetic side reveled in the Village atmosphere that exuded the offbeat that he loved. He dressed the part as well, conforming to the Bohemian style with his wide-brimmed felt hat, a kerchief around his neck and a baggy mismatch of shirts and trousers. He smoked a pipe and was a familiar sight as he wandered the streets and visited his many talented friends.

He still wrote his own play scripts and, after he and others become frustrated with the difficulty of breaking into Broadway, decided to open his own theater. His goal was to give himself and others an opportunity to publicly present their artistic works on stage. It was a philanthropic gesture[113] to help serious, struggling, usually unemployed, theatrical artists.

With the help of his friend Guido Bruno,[114] a multi-lingual impresario who was known for his notorious poetry, the two briefly partnered in opening the one-hundred-seat Thimble Theatre at 10 Fifth Avenue. It was an immediate success and attracted painters, composers, actors, poets and writers, and playwrights of every description: Marcel Duchamp, Albert Gleizes, Wallace Stevens, Edna St. Vincent Millay, William Carlos Williams. Charles' creation became the exuberating milieu during the 1920s for everyone exploring the arts in New York City.[115]

It looked like Charles had found the right combination of a steady income and the artist's life while thriving at both.

Following weeknight performances, Charles caught the "Owl Train" home in the wee hours of the night, yet he never failed to report to his office at nine.

Welcoming Edison, Ford and Burroughs

In late February 1914 we arrived by train in Fort Myers to a splendid hullabalo. Fortunately we were given warning at an unscheduled stop just before Fort Myers when the mayor and a band of local officials boarded the train and accompanied us into town.

Traveling with our family as guests were the Henry Fords and their son Edsel and John Burroughs the noted naturalist. A huge, festive crowd greeted us with a band playing, automobile horns blaring, flags and banners waving.[116]

Ford, now fifty-one was at the peak of his fame with his Model T and his acclamation at having recently given his auto-plant employees a three-shift, eight-hour work day and an unheard of daily wage of five dollars.

Burroughs, at age seventy-seven, was at his most famous as well, through his unique and popular writing of his perceptions of the natural world, much like Henry David Thoreau.

We exited the train and were guided to the front of a line of about thirty automobles, mostly Model Ts. Mr. Edison, Madeleine, Charles, Theodore, Lucy Bogue and I were seated in the lead car with the Mayor at the wheel. The Fords and Mr. Burroughs were in the automobile behind us. With the marching band in the lead, we were paraded all the way to Seminole Lodge. There we thanked everyone and escaped to relative seclusion as the band drummed it up and slowly faded away.

The joys of a carnival

Other than fishing, perhaps a circus, a carnival or a Wild-West show was Mr. Edison's most enthusiastic dramatic diversion. He liked and appreciated showmanship and he demonstrated his own knack for it throughout his life -- from peddling his newspapers and snacks aboard the train as a youngster, to bragging about his numerous achievements to the press. He was expert at attracting public attention.

The annual Fort Myers Carnival was in town during the gathering for the Edison annual camping trip. Mr. Edison invited Ford and Burroughs to accompany him to the carnival. The highlight this season was automobile racing at the Motordrome. Mr. Ford was delighted to see modified Model Ts among the contestants. Gleefully, my husband and Mr. Ford cheered as the competitors raced at speeds greater than sixty miles an hour, kicking up clouds of dust on the oval dirt track.

"That's one mile every minute!" Ford exclaimed. "I had no idea my T could go that fast."

The trio wandered through the Midway stopping to shoot rifles at moving ducks and throw balls at milk jugs, laughing and making jokes, refusing the worthless prizes they won.

They ended up at Roy Jennier's Society Circus and watched the daring Ed Millette do his famous head-balancing act on a trapeze.

Mr. Burroughs, the quiet bird watcher, was agog and wide-eyed at all of this brash and noisy activity amid throngs of undulating carefree people. But he was a good sport and kept up with his rowdy friends.

Camping in the Everglades

All that excitement behind us, the most memorable event of this season's visit was our camping trip sixty miles into the Everglades in five Model T Touring cars and, I think, two Cadillacs. Plenty of room for all of us, our troup also included a cook and three guides, with tents and all the camping needs of an army.

Ever since his arrival, Mr. Burroughs found considerable pleasure discovering one species after another, commenting, "I never thought I was coming into such a tropical country as this. Fort Myers reminds me of Honolulu and Jamaica. It is one of the most beautiful spots I have ever seen."

The idea of camping, as Mr. Edison explained it, was to "go down to the Everglades and revert back to Nature. . . We will get away from fictitious civilization." The men were actually following Mr. Burrough's goal to "worship God's truth in Nature."[117]

"Indeed," Mr. Burroughs has written, "when I go to the woods or fields, or ascend to the hilltop, I do not seem to be gazing upon beauty at all, but to be breathing it like the air. . . I am not a spectator of, but a participator in it."

As I recall, with the help of Charles' and Madeleine's reminiscences, the road soon ended and we were plunging through pine woods and bouncing off palmetto roots. Then there were sandy areas where we'd have to get out of the cars and push, then wet areas we splashed through. I truly thought we were too deep into a jungle that would consume us and we would never return to civilization. We finally arrived at a place called Rock Lake where someone determined we should camp.

The guides set up the tents. The cook cooked. The rest of us sat in our folding chairs and observed nature until dusk fell and the mosquitos discovered us. We retired to our respective tents behind insect netting.

In the middle of the night we were hit by a violent tropical storm. The gale howled. The ridge pole broke in one tent and it collapsed. The occupants dashed to other tents. Heavy rain thundered on the canvas tents and tarps and we were soon standing in water. The tents leaked and sagged. We were all huddled in the wildest confusion, as Madeleine described it. We wrapped bedding around us and that too became soaked. Our naturalist remained mummy-like, curled in his blankets, in a corner on his cot, apparently "worshipping God's truth."

Finally the storm, for which it was quite evident we were ill prepared, passed and we shivered and complained until daylight finally broke. A makeshift clothesline was stretched between trees and the warmth of the sun appeared. The groundwater dissipated. Somehow the cooks were able to start a fire and soon the aroma of bacon waffed among us. Spirits gradually improved and sarcasm reigned with comments on how comfortable the beds were and how well we had slept. Mrs. Ford said she felt selfish being totally under water when the rest of us had only been half under. After such a boring night, she said, she demanded that she be shown a big snake. Each of us tried to improve on the other's stories and this resulted in howls of delight as the sun warmed us and our world dried out.

We spent one more night in the outback and then returned to civilization.

We had planned a several-day cruise to Lake Okeechobee, but after their three-week visit our naturalist and our industrialist guests decided to return to their northern homes.

Planned also was a visit to the local grammar school. Mr. Ford and Mr. Burroughs delayed their departures and fulfilled their commitment and visited the school children. Each gave short talks about their respective interests. It seemed to hold the children's attention and gave them a mind-picture of the world beyond Fort Myers.

Correspondence between my husband and Mr. Ford included a thank-you for the time they had in Florida, and the comment that he now had 1,000 cars a day rolling off his assembly line. The statistics were simply mind-boggling to me.

In his letter, Mr. Ford also stooped to advise my husband on the injurious effects of smoking, particularly cigarettes. Mr. Edison, the cigar smoker, replied in good humor, that he employed no person who smoked cigarettes.

World War I begins

On June 28, 1914, Archduke Franz Ferdinand of Austria and his wife Sophia were assassinated in Sarajevo by Gavrilo Princip. It was part of a movement that became known as Young Bosnia. The event led directly to war. The news was shocking and I kept informed of the consequences of it daily.

It was an extremely bloody war that engulfed Europe until 1919 with huge human losses and very little ground won or lost -- certainly nothing was gained. It was fought mainly by soldiers in trenches with an estimated ten million deaths and twenty million wounded. Man's extreme inhumanity to man had raised the hope that this would finally be "the war to end war." In reality, it set the stage for World War II.

Mr. Edison immediately became involved in the war effort.

For the fourth time we had a child who chose to marry someone who did not meet Mr. Edison's approval.

To our dismay, Madeleine and John Sloane had spent the year prior to their marriage in a four-story walk-up apartment in Greenwich Village located across the street from the Bohemian-famed Brevoort Hotel on Eighth Street.

Because of Mr. Edison's obstinate disapproval of popish religion, I suffered Madeleine's absence from my daily life. My husband rejected the Catholic Sloane family. I fought hard, independently of Mr. Edison, to get the family to agree to have the wedding at Glenmont and, I succeeded. But now the relations between our families were poised to collapse because of one person.

I faced Mr. Edison directly. "You know that it's because of your obstinate and blind prejudice that Madeleine felt she had to live away from us, out of our lives, for the past year. I am determined to have her wedding at Glenmont and I won't put up with your foolish behavior over this. I couldn't bear the same disaster with my children that you had with yours.

"You might be glad that they will not be married in the Catholic Church. They have agreed to marry in our home with a priest. The Sloane family had the grace to compromise on something that is important to them. Their ideals are no less important than yours. You should be very happy and grateful.

"Your refusal to attend our daughter's future in-law's polite engagement dinner invitation was most embarassing. Where is your dignity? Where is the high ground that you stand on? What did you expect to gain from that ignorant behavior? Madeleine was in tears for a full week. Mr. Sloane is a highly respected gentleman from a good family. He is an inventor just like you. Madeleine's fiancé is well educated and intelligent, polite and gentlemanly. What does that make you?"

Mr. Edison held up his hands in surrender.

"Billie, Billie, Billie," his said tiredly. "You have flayed me down to my bare bones. My flesh may never recover from the lashing you have dealt me. Forgive me, my love of my life. I have sinned and I need your forgiveness."

I melted before him. "Ah! You are absolutely impossible sometimes. I don't know how I have survived these many years. Of course I forgive you, because I know you will make amends. At the very least I want you to show up and shake hands with the groom and his father. I want you to smile and say something nice to the groom's mother and simply be the man I have always thought you were."

"Do I have to kiss the priest's ring?"

"Don't be sarcastic. Be very happy and loving toward our daughter. I don't want *her* running off to Europe."

Mr. Edison recoiled as if attacked by a charging bull. "Oohh, that stung, Billie. It really hurt."

"You know very well that it could happen, Dearie. You know it very well."

Somehow I pulled it all together. He grudgingly acquiesced.

So, on June 17, 1914, at 4 PM, my beloved Madeleine married her longtime "boyfriend" John Eyre Sloane. The service was held at Glenmont and performed by the Rt. Rev. Mgr. Brann of New York.

Rare ferns and hanging baskets of orchids and roses adorned our home. One end of the drawing room where the ceremony was performed had an elegant old tapestry displayed as a background. A bank of acacia and flowering mimosa plants was against one wall. Next to this was a tall silver candelabra.

As the guests were arriving, the Nathan Franko orchestra played Grieg's "The Wedding Day," Bohm's "Calm as the Night," and other selections by Liszt, Ganne, Mozart and Godard.

I wore a gown of salmon pink chiffon with a sash of tangerine color trimmed with ostrich feather tips that were tinted to match my gown. My hat was brown.

Charles Sloane, the groom's brother, was the best man. Ushers included my sons Charles and Theodore, my brother John, and five friends of the family. Unfortunately, Marion, Tom and William, although invited, were unable to attend.

Mr. Edison entered the room with Madeleine on his arm. He was smiling, despite being tucked into his tuxedo and stiff white shirt. The bride wore a robe of cream colored chiffon velvet, with a bodice of old rose point and duchess lace that I had worn at my wedding. Family lace also formed part of the train that fell in graceful folds and was surrounded with a narrow wreath of orange blossoms. She carried a shower bouquet of lilies of the valley and white orchids.[118]

The couple knelt on a cushion that was used by Dearie and me at our wedding.

My sisters, Margaret and Rachel Miller were the maids of honor. They wore gowns of mauve taffeta, the skirts draped with turquoise blue tule, and leghorn hats. They carried bouquets of yellow roses from my gardens. There were six bridesmaids, friends of Madeleine. Once again I regretted not having my friends as bridesmaids in my wedding.

The event was truly splendid and Mr. Edison remained through much of the reception that was held on the lawn. A buffet followed, served at individual tables.

Following their honeymoon, they moved to Plainfield, New Jersey where Madeleine's father-in-law owned a successful bi-plane factory, producing planes that were purchased by the U.S. government for use in the European war.

The Edisons visit the Fords

We were in Dearborn visiting Henry and Clara Ford in August 1914 soon after war broke out in Europe. Americans early in the war were disinterested in the conflict, yet sympathetic for those involved. Mr. Edison offered his thoughts to the newspapers when asked.

"It makes me sick at heart, and mankind as a whole, to see this war. Those military gangs in Europe piled up armaments for years until something had to break."

As with most other Americans, he remained neutral during the first year of the war and said he would have no part of it.

Ford, as one of the world's largest industrialists, traveled around the country saying his heart was also set to keeping out of the war. But he was adamant about bringing the warring parties to the peace table.

By early September, Mr. Edison announced the opening of a new plant in Silver Lake, New Jersey for the manufacture of phenol[119] and other chemicals that were in short supply in this country.

The advantages of Mina's children

My children had definite advantages over Mr. Edison's first three offspring. By the time Madeleine came along, Mr. Edison's name was a household word. She, Charles and Theodore and, yes I, grew into his fame with all the privileges that came along with it. Mr. Edison was more assured of himself and, as we all grew older, my husband became more relaxed in his success as the dean of American inventors. He began to see that it was to his advantage for Charles and Theodore to get an MIT education and therefore help him in his businesses. And, of course, with age, Mr. Edison softened, was less dognatic, was more fatherly and found more time to enjoy his family.

But regardless of his feelings about my children, he still harbored bad feelings about Marion, Tom and William and he put them out of the way, generally out of his life.

Despite how persistently I tried, and how his boys tried with my help, to become a part of our family, Mr. Edison's will prevailed. And then, with his children grown, it was too late to make corrections in individual traits already well established.

Charles the executive

Mr. Edison was fifty-seven and his son twenty-four when Charles began to take his job seriously at Thomas A. Edison, Inc. He was obliged to cut back on his activities in the Village as his father gave him more and more responsibilities. He enjoyed most of the work but cared nothing for bookkeeping and accountanting and thrust that on others. But Charles could delegate. That was a weakness of his father.

Immersed in the business, Charles quickly became aware of the vast size of his father's enterprises. He knew of no other man, no other inventor, who had ever been involved in so many details of a giant corporation, creating, manufacturing, selling and raising payroll money than Mr. Edison. Within ten years Charles was his father's lieutenant and chief managerial man. But his father continued to demand the final word in the whole business until the day he died. That was fine with Charles, except for the inevitable conflicts when new-school met old-school in a discussion on which way was the "right" way to solve a problem.

Charles had his first crisis in this regard early in his apprenticeship when a sudden disaster struck. The Edison works in West Orange had been rolling along piling profits upon profits when on December 9, 1914, about six in the evening after his father had gone home, a fire broke out in the center of the factory quadrangle where chemicals and flammable motion-picture film were stored. The fire was out of control from the beginning. The factory fire team was quick to bring in the hoses but the water pressure in the village of

West Orange was insufficient. Fire apparatus from neighboring towns were also ineffective because of the water shortage. The chemicals set off a full conflagration. The firemen were overwhelmed and one man died.

Charles was working late and was present to help direct but he was overcome by what was described as the "horror of the scene and his immediate despair." Although the adjacent buildings were of concrete, "fireproof" construction, they were insured for less than their value. Workers removed and relocated as many valuable supplies and equipment as they could, but the loss was more than one million dollars.

Mr. Edison was called from dinner and he met up with Charles as they watched the activity. "Where's mother?" Charles later recalled his father asking him. "Get her over here, and her friends too. They'll never see a fire like this again."

The disaster was frightening even from my Glenmont advantage a half mile away. I shook violently as I watched the flames shoot high into the sky. Fortunately, the library and the main laboratory buildings were out of the way and survived. When Mr. Edison returned to the house and I greeted him with my condolences, he said, "Oh shucks, it's all right. We've just gotten rid of a lot of old rubbish." Once again my Dearie could shrug off his incalculable emotional and physical losses.

Charles and his father began reconstruction immediately and employed fifteen hundred men. By New Years day 1915, less than a month later, new buildings were up and most of the regular workers were back at their places in two shifts producing the first new phonograph *disk* records that brought in nearly ten million dollars that year.

Charles had found his calling.

The diva and Mr. Edison

Anna Case was the first American, native-born, Metropolitan Opera diva that had no formal vocal training. She was the daughter of a blacksmith in New Jersey. She was leading the chorus and playing the organ at church in her hometown for twelve dollars a month before she was fifteen without ever having a music lesson. Later, she took some lessons from a local teacher who had to give her student up because her potential was too great. Anna was sent on to a teacher in New York. At twenty, the very beautiful Miss Case made her Metropolitan Opera debut and moved up quicky taking starring rolls within six months.

Mr. Edison snatched onto her talent and made many recordings, establishing her as a concert singer. She became his soprano during his Diamond Disc years. He told me that Miss Case sang with none of the "vibrato" that had always bothered his injured ears.

When Miss Case was overheard absently singing along with her Edison records in a music store, the owner was told by his customers that they could not differentiate between her live voice and that of the Edison records. His success with Miss Case prompted him to send her on national tours. He also used her for tone tests in front of 200,000 people over the next year. The audience, wearing blindfolds, was asked to listen to both Miss Case and then the record. They too were unable to tell the difference. Edison held one of these tone tests in Carnegie Hall on March 20, 1920.[120]

Chapter Twenty-Three

1915-1916

"Lusitania" is torpedoed

The sinking of the British ocean liner *Lusitania* in Irish waters by German U-boats on May 7, 1915, was the last straw in American neutality. Once again I was shocked when I picked up the newspaper and saw the headlines. Of the 1,959 passengers, only 761 survived. The dead included 128 Americans. The country was enraged and we hastened to enter the war.

Initially, Henry Ford preached pacifism against what he called his business opponent's desires, "purely manufactured evil -- an orgy for money." Ford put together a delegation of influencial people that planned to travel to Christiania,[121] Norway on a mission of personal diplomacy, saying he had proof that the "International Jew" had initiated the war for their own financial gain.

Ford was attacked with a torrent of ridicule. Clara begged Ford not to go. The boat left for Norway with, as some described, a boatload of college students, eccentrics, peace-nuts and journalists. Before the boat even reached Norway, Ford realized he was in an impossible situation. He swallowed his pride and returned to Clara. But still, he said, he did not regret the attempt.

Mr. Edison had preached the importance of submarines two months before the sinking of the *Lusitania*. He envisioned a vast fleet of American underwater warriors that would protect the eastern coastline and be "peace insurance." Mr. Edison stopped short of calling for war but preached "preparedness" through the press.

The Secretary of the Navy, Josephus Daniels, had recently signed a valuable battleship and submarine battery contract with Mr. Edison for an estimated $15 million. Daniels had recently publicly advocated that the country concentrate on becoming ready and yet he also advocated eventual disarmament. As a result, Daniels and Edison spoke the same language and sought the same goal with a long-range plan to rule the seas with a viable war craft.

Edison serves his country

In mid-summer 1915, Josephus Daniels, after consulting with President Woodrow Wilson, formally asked my husband to take charge of the new "Department of Invention." Its function was to consider technological ideas and suggestions from civilians and the military. Mr. Edison would chair it. Others on this board included the young Franklin D. Roosevelt who was then assistant secretary of the Navy under Daniels.

The first 100,000 ideas and suggestions that came in to the board overwhelmed it. The ideas were well meaning but essentially useless. Not wanting to spend his time behind a desk shuffling paper, Mr. Edison immediately gave up his chairmanship and took the honorary title of president. The board also revised its mission to that of supervision of research projects with the specialized Navy departments. This resulted in the establishment of the first Naval Research Laboratory. For the next year or so this only occupied part of Mr. Edison's time. But that promised to change dramatically as the war in Europe hovered over them.

In October 1915, we were joined by Charles, my sister Grace and Cora and Henry Ford to attend the Panama-Pacific International Exposition in San Francisco that celebrated the opening of the Panama Canal some months earlier.

On the way west we stopped in Indianapolis to visit the poet James Whitcomb Riley and evangelist Billy Sunday in Omaha. Unfortunately I did not record Mr. Edison's discussions with these men. All I can say with confidance is they were lively and respectful.

One of the featured events in San Francisco was "Edison Day" that was built around the huge Edison exhibits of his inventions over the years. Mr. Ford was just as much a hero and the two of them rode together in an open car through the streets of the city.

For my husband, there were more exciting things to do. Harvey Firestone and his wife Idabelle and Henry and Clara Ford joined us for a visit with Luther Burbank. Burbank was a pioneer horticulturalist and botanist who developed more than 800 varieties of plants that included vegetables, grains, fruits, flowers and grasses. At dinner, Mr. Edison grilled him on his interests in goldenrod for the making of rubber and then on fibers in other plants for use as filaments in electric lamps.

We were disappointed. Mr. Burbank's interest was confined to developing improved *food* sources. In any case, we invited him to visit our Forida winter estate to see our gardens.

Another interest for all of us was a tour the city that had been so ravenged by the earthquake and fires nine years earlier. We toured displays that showed before and after photos. The recovery was quite remarkable. But Mr. Edison's question was not unique when asked of the redevelopment. "Aren't you afraid you're going to have another quake?"

The answer was his own. "Of course. Everyone is afraid of another quake, tornado, flood or a repeat of any disaster. But what do you do? You can't leave the area and go elsewhere. A similar event might occur there. So this is what you do. It's the very same as inventing. You start all over again -- with confidence."

We took several sidetrips, one of which was to the Lick Observatory, operated by the University of California. We toured the huge Dome at the top of Mount Hamilton near San Jose. We were invited to stay until after dark and peer through the huge telescope at the heavens. Never at a loss for words, Mr. Edison had to ask, "Have you been able to see God?"

The answer was, "Not yet, but we are feeling very close to Him during our observations."

Deadly explosion embarrasses Edison

The bad news first. Less than one year after Mr. Edison signed a $15 million contract with the Navy for ship and submarine batteries, the 1916 new year began with an explosion aboard the U.S. Navy's E-2 submarine in Brooklyn Navy Yard. Five men were killed and ten others wounded. The cause was attributed to a hydrogen gas leak from Edison batteries being installed while the submarine was in drydock.

The good news. An inquiry into the disaster confirmed that leaks in Mr. Edison's batteries were infinitesimal and that the E-2 explosion was purely accidental. The same batteries were being used in many American and foreign ships during the world war and had been proven quite satisfactory.

The New York *Times* gave its report on January 17, confirming their safe use. "The Edison cells have been in use on submarines for a long time, although this is not generally known. Mr. Edison is not in the munitions business, and he has not sold any since the war but before that, three submarines of a certain European power were fitted with these batteries. They have not met with any accident."

Leading up to American participation in the European war, Preparedness Parades, with the stars and stripes proudly displayed, had been taking place all over the country. Mr. Edison was determined to participate in the New York City Preparedness Parade on May 13. I begged him not to go. At age seventy, it would be an exhausting experience for him. It was controversial and bomb threats were common. But, as a member of the Naval Consulting Board, all of whom were marching, he felt an obligation. I then leaped into the spirit of the event and joined him in the march. I'm so glad I did. And my Dearie did just fine. If anything, I was the one who tired.

Beginning at City Hall Park and continuing up Broadway and Fifth Avenue, more than 125,000 civilians marched among dozens of drum corps and brass bands. At the head of the parade was a huge 95- by 50-foot American flag. All of us marchers carried a flag of one size or another and most spectators held flags as well.

The overall effect of all the parades indicated that America was ready to enter the war and defeat the enemy that also threatened the United States.

A similar parade in San Francisco two months later was violently interrupted by a suitcase explosion. Ten bystanders were killed and more than forty were wounded. Two radical labor leaders, Thomas Mooney and Warren K. Billings were convicted in the rush to judgment. Two weeks before their scheduled execution, President Woodrow Wilson asked California Governor William Stephend to look further into the case because of suspected corruption of the prosecution and false testimony. Both men were pardoned and the real killers were never found.

So my fear of marching in the New York parade was not entirely unfounded.

My sister Grace marries

In mid-February my sister Grace Miller, at age forty-six, married businessman Halbert Kellogg Hitchcock. The wedding took place at Glenmont.

I was so happy for her. She was very close to my family and we had traveled extensively together. I was greatly relieved that she had finally found a good man who could make her happy and promised to take the best care of her.

Our *first grandson is born*

Our first grandchild, Thomas Edison Sloane, was born to Madeleine on March 4, 1916. His name, following family tradition, was named "Thomas Edison." It signaled for me a chance to reconcile with Madeleine after two years of what can only be described as our "banishment" from their life because of our silly differences over religion. We had tentatively mended our disagreements out of the mutual need to bring our family together again for the wedding, although apologies never passed Mr. Edison's lips.

As it turned out, Papa was thrilled with his first grandson, named "Teddy." At age sixty-nine, the "old man" acquired a new enjoyment of holding a newborn, yet a touch of resentment continued between our families.

I visited Madeleine and held Teddy for a couple hours and chatted. He was handsome, of course. I hated to leave Teddy for Florida so quickly.

Getting away from the war

It was just Mr. Edison and me when we arrived in Fort Myers in late March for a four-week vacation. The dread of war in Europe seemed to have had very little effect on the locals. My husband's duties with the Naval Consulting Board had not yet taken much of his time. Getting away from that part of my life was nice, but I already missed grandson Teddy.

Mr. Edison's only gripe the first week was the apparent absence of tarpon. He complained that the commercial fishermen were either catching them all or scaring them away from their natural feeding grounds. He found the best fishing otherwise from his pier.

In a complete change from his normal disinterest in children, my husband invited the entire School for Boys on Captiva Island for a short visit to his "jungle" habitat and then he even entertained them with his fishing stories, gave them a tour of the laboratory and houses and personally served them iced lemonade and cookies. His new interest in children was heartening.

Near the end of April we reluctantly returned to Glenmont.

Ford moves next door

Mr. Ford and my husband had become very close friends over the years through travel and camping adventures. Although they disagreed on some rather major social and political issues, they had enough in common to bind their friendship.

In May, Henry Ford was notified that a five-year-old house, located on the opposite side from our guest house, called The Mangoes, was for sale, a fact unknown to us. The property extended out to the shore where it had 177 feet of frontage on the Caloosahatchie River. Mr. Ford was interested. The sale price was $25,000. Photographs were sent. More photos were sent and Ford made an offer of $20,000 and refused to barter. His offer was accepted.

Purchasing a home next to his best friend made sense to him. I can't answer for Mr. Edison, especially after the horrible Gilliland incident.

As Mr. Edison gained confidence in Charles and gradually turned things over to him, the Edison companies became better organized and showed a healthy, yet uneven, balance sheet. Shutting down the expensive movie business helped the cash flow.

There were problems, of course. Prices of raw materials in the face of war were inconsistent. Rising inflation versus wages brought tensions to the middle management. Strikes needed management. Profits were on a rollercoaster.

Charles was a very good businessman, but his father was an inventor. It was not always a good mix, especially when the patriarch wants things done his way. So, they had lively discussions that more often than not leaned toward the inventor.

Charles had trouble sleeping during these times. He dreamed of his days in Greenwich Village when he didn't have a care, writing plays and managing a playhouse. He considered quitting the family business. His father was making too many mistakes. He just didn't understand the current business problems. Mr. Edison was micromanaging the most trivial things. Charles spoke to me about these problems and having to bow to his father's judgment.

"The real problem is, I can't fire Papa," Charles began. "But he has become a pest. He wants me to run the business and then he interferes with how I want to run it. We get into the most ferocious arguments. It's very frustrating. I'm tempted to quit and let him do what he wants. Often, I simply stop arguing and do what I want regardless and he let's it pass. I think he just wants to feel he is needed. I know *I'm* needed."

These issued continued well into the 1920s but Charles stuck with it.

In late August Mr. Edison initiated the second of what would become annual automobile camping trips with three of his buddies. This one toured through Vermont and New York State. He provided six-passenger gasoline touring cars for the party and trucks followed with the tents and camping equipment, food, camp servants and drivers.

I noted that he didn't use electric cars. "I'd much prefer electric," he said. "But they're too much trouble when you have to stop at some inconvenient place short of your goal and get the batteries recharged. Some day I'll have a battery that'll last a thousand miles."

Mr. Edison and Harvey Firestone, left Glenmont on August 28, covering eighty-two miles over rough country roads and spent their first night in the Catskill mountains just southwest of Albany. Henry Ford had planned to meet the group along the way, but pressing business interfered.

The next day they stopped in Roxbury, New York and picked up John Burroughs at his home. The three-some traveled on through Lake George, the Adirondack mountains, across the north tip of Lake Champlain before heading home south through Vermont and then a night in the Massachusetts Berkshire Hills.

Mr. Edison told me that he always sat in front with the driver. Presumably that meant Firestone had to sit alone for the first leg. They bounced along the pot-holed dirt roads, some times at forty miles an hour. Burroughs, age eighty, said all the bouncing began to bother him after a while. He commented that Mr. Edison was well padded and could take the bumps.

"You can be kind to your automobile or you can be kind to your body," my husband said. "To hell with the automobile. Step on the gas pedal."

Back home safely, Burroughs wrote my husband. "That was a fine trip and I enjoyed it. I had been sick during the summer and the jolting in the auto made me think I couldn't stand three days of it. But then, the further we went, the more miles I wanted to go."

In the mountains Burroughs offered a description of Mr. Edison with his geology hammer poking around the rocks like a hungry monkey taking samples. My man was always curious.

The naturalist was again in a new situation. He was not accustomed, like his younger friends, to traveling with servants. He said the trip was like the luxuries at the Waldorf-Astoria on wheels.

Ford vowed to be with the group the next time.

Chapter Twenty-Four

1917-1918

Germany declares all-out war

Germany declared all-out submarine aggression in the shipping lanes during the early weeks of 1917. They were the confident masters of the oceans with their sneaky, silent, invisible submarines preying as far afield as our own Atlantic coast.

Our country had been passively ignorant as Germany built its huge war machine and President Woodrow Wilson wasted two and a half years delaying our arms buildup by attempting to keep the United States neutral.

Finally, on April 6, 1917 the United States joined its allies, Britain, France and Russia and entered the war. Americans traveling overseas had no idea that war was imminent in Europe. Thousands were caught by surprise and afraid to sail home across the Atlantic.

Marion saw the war buildup early on, right from her own apartment window in Chemnitz. The passage of military vehicles and foot-stomping soldiers became increasingly frequent. She lived and watched in fear as her German-army-officer husband spent more and more time away from her on military maneuvers.

Two months before the U.S. entered the war, Mr. Edison had been spending most of his time working on secret experiments using the open expanses at Eagle Rock Mountain here in West Orange.

But now that war had been declared, Mr. Edison left Glenmont and moved to the national's capital for his full-time naval work. He was surprised to find himself under full-time security by the Secret Service. He initially worked sixteen-hour days from his Washington hotel room.

With his father gone, Charles regained his nightly sleep habits. He was in full control of Edison, Inc. He could do as he pleased without the micromanager second-guessing him.

Theodore, nineteen, was able to accompany his father on many of his missions -- he was a man his father could rely on, who understood him and had his inventive mind.

During this time I also spent some time with my husband at sea when his work area was near Key West. I was worried about him. While experimenting with phenolic acid in his lab, a mixture exploded and injured his eyes temporarily. He felt ill and I wanted to be with him on board the ship. It was obvious the crew considered me a nuisance, but I put up with the discomforts of life on board ships and looked after my man.

During his initial work for the Navy in the Naval Research Lab, Mr. Edison had many run-ins with navy brass as he required them to to perform tasks outside their comfort zone. This led him to complain to Secretary Daniels about the typical Annapolis graduates who headed military bureaus. He saw them as hesitant to do anything beyond which they were trained, such as be creative and experiment with new ideas. He was convinced at this time that no military research would be possible if the admirals who ran the Naval Research Laboratory were allowed to continue. As a result, Secretary Daniels gave Mr. Edison free rein to contrive anything that would interrupt or halt the German U-boats from the havoc they were wreaking.

During his year and a half with the Navy, Mr. Edison contributed forty-eight projects that helped do just that, including a periscope with a rotating, spray-free viewfinder; submarine sonar rangefinders; a new nighttime travel route plan for merchant ships to avoid the German peril; refined shore-to-sea torpedoes capable of penetrating thick iron hulls; rapid-fire Venetian-blind signals capable of transmitting forty words per minute; a hydrogen-detecting alarm to warn of undersea explosions; smudge decoys that ape the smoke from a steamer to lead the Germans astray; a device for the quick turning of ships; another device for locating submarine guns and torpedos; an anti-torpedo net; hidden lights; collision mats.[122]

Of particular importance was a sonic device that used a submerged phonograph diaphragm to record the noise of submarine engines or the noise of a torpedo being discharged. On recognizing this noise, the ship would immediately turn ninety degrees from its original heading to avoid the projectile.

No matter how busy my husband was, he sent daily dispatches to me via naval communications. "We are now firing smoke shells from a three-inch gun and they work well"; "A Naval man is making my mine detector and a war-boat will take it to Guantanamo Bay, our big Naval station in Cuba"; "From your lover as ever steady, reliable and unchangeable."

Obviously, Mr. Edison's Naval Research Lab was not the only one working feverishly to combat U-boats. The General Electric Laboratory had a team of experts, headed by Dr. Willis R. Whitney. They devised a "listening device" to be used in conjunction with the De Forest radio telephones. These were used on submarine chasers with considerable success. When Mr. Edison heard their successful trials with this, he was elated.

His service for the Navy had been frustrating for him, but in the end, official navy reports show that he had created dozens of practical and life-saving inventions that were adopted by the service.

Correspondence from Marion during the war build-up was distressing to say the least. Her life in Germany was changing rapidly. She now found herself out of the city and stuck in an isolated army garrison as Oscar trained for battle.

She was alone more and more. When not on army maneuvers, Oscar often spent nights drinking with his buddies. He might even bring them home in the early morning, banging on the door to let them in. She would escape to the bedroom and had no option but to listen to their loud bragging of conquests of bar maids and whores. It was disgusting, filthy talk. In an effort to throw them out, she was hissed at and booed and Oscar joined the others in total disrespect.

It was one of those nights that she overheard Oscar bragging about a woman with whom he said he was spending time when Marion thought he was on training maneuvers.

"Depression suddenly swept over me," Marion recalled later, stunned at the thought the man who had loved her so passionately was doing the same with another woman. "I faced him when he sobered up and he told me it was none of my business. Can you imagine? We then had a terrible fight and he disappeared for several days. For the first time I saw our twenty-three years of marriage unraveling."

Soon after this, Oscar was mobilized. War was now a reality. He was frightened. Marion was frightened. They parted on speaking terms but she knew their marriage was doomed. She was very much alone. She saw through her window hundreds of ragged, half-starved Frenchmen as they were marched by under German guard. Artillery fire was getting louder and shaking her windows. Articles in the newspapers were more venomous. Marching soldiers, heavy guns and stomping boots were always on the streets.

In her own formerly upscale neighborhood, she wrote home, people were going into garbage cans looking for food. Children were wandering alone. Bread lines were ever longer.

Germany was not prepared for a long war. The country depended on imported foods and raw materials. Rationing took effect. The domestic potato crop was poor the first year. People ate animal feed and turnips. Death from malnutrition, exhaustion and disease was rampant.

Among the sad letters she wrote to me, "If we have a loving father in Heaven why does he let millions of his innocent children suffer so and the guilty ones go unpunished? I wish I could run away from it all."

Marion's childhood fears of the night returned. For days she lay prone with suicidal thoughts, her nerves producing sharp tingles in her arms. Her legs became weak. She experimented by washing away her reality with liquor, but that only made her violently sick and with pounding headaches.

She could not decided what to do next. Her world had fallen apart.

Tom's problems with alcohol

"The farm is falling apart. The furnace has failed and the roof is leaking. We can see through cracks in the walls," Beatrice wrote during the summer of 1917. "Poor Tom is of little help for he is back at the bottle feeling morose and gloomy. He promises over and over that he wants to renew his life and pull things back together. But it never happens and his contrition continues.

"Tom says he is taunted by ghosts that constantly hound him to fulfill his most urgent desire of becoming like his father. His head is full of Edison ideas that are struggling to get out. Tom has his father's genes. He *is* his father but he is plagued with the failures of his past that did nothing but cause embarrassment to his Papa.

"He and I have prayed that his father would help him by understanding how very much they are alike and then give him a little guidance toward achieving his ideas. But Mr. Edison is so stubbornly protective of the holy Edison name, Tom knows an understanding between him and his father will never happen."

I thoroughly understood Tom's problem. I was well aware of Mr. Edison's stubbornness. Protecting the untarnished holy grail of the Edison name was never to be questioned -- even if it came at the expense of his children.

Tom's devoted wife continued to care for her husband as he suffered his terrible headaches and dizziness. "Because of this and his frustrations, he lashes out at me for the most minor things. It's just horrible."

The couple, in a rare move, joined our family for Thanksgiving at Glenmont where alcohol was rarely served. Beatrice told me confidentially that she received her strength to put up with her problems from her religion. "Tom is far from well," she said, "but the weight of my Cross is Love, and with my faith strengthening at every heartache, I patiently look for Victory."

Tom spent the holiday quietly, shyly, watching his father, searching for a break in his ever-present control of the activities to have a father-son talk -- a talk about anything -- just a few meaningful words together. It never happened.

Being a confirmed teetotaler, Mr. Edison was unsympathetic to his son's alcoholism. He callously remarked to Beatrice that he had already invested "huge sums" for a cure at a sanatorium and it appeared to him that, since she had cured him once, she ought to be able to do so again.

Before they left for home that Thanksgiving day, Mr. Edison, in an effort toward an apology, gave Beatrice a sum of money to have their 100-year-old farmhouse repaired. He also expressed his hope that she could do the same for Tom.

The war was now in full motion. Marion decided she had to escape. Girding her strength, she carried two suitcases with nothing but the "essentials" and took train and bus the two hundred miles toward the Swiss border. She was frightened. Her transportation was frequently stopped and her papers and bags searched.

There was a long line of people on foot waiting at the border to enter Switzerland. She suddenly saw herself as a refugee, void of personal power and influence, at the mercy of the clerks and non-coms who harrassed her. She observed that some passed through the gates while others were apparently refused entry and had to return.

What was the difference? Marion was racked with fear. She had only her German passport for identification. Would they let a German citizen pass through into a neutral country? What if they turned her away? What would she do? There was nowhere she could go.

Marion gritted her teeth with a determination she hadn't felt in years and joined the end of the line. The person in front of her was a woman about her age who appeared to be alone. She spoke to her in German. The woman shook her head. "I'm afraid to talk to strangers," she replied in German and turned away.

The line moved very slowly, but finally the woman in front of her was allowed to pass through after answering a few questions that Marion was unable overhear.

Marion's turn came. She handed a Swiss-uniformed woman her passport and she examined it. She asked Marion a question in German. Marion answered in English.

"You're an American," the inspector now said in English, recognizing her accent.

"I am."

"Where is your American passport?"

"It expired."

"Why do you want to enter Switzerland?"

Wthout a thought she said, "I'm trying to escape my German army-officer husband."

The woman smiled. "Welcome to Switzerland," she said in English and handed back the passport.

Marion also broke into a broad smile. "Thank you *very* much madam."

She crossed into Basel, Switzerland. She was safe. She was elated. She took a room in the Hotel Schweizerhof and immediately sent us a telegram.

Cautious not to reveal information that might be used against her, should her words be censored, she wrote:

"My darling family. I am living in Basel now, alone. During my trip I have been very much afraid and alone. I would like to return home but, with the dangers in the Atlantic, it would not be wise. I love you all. May peace come quickly. Love, Marion." The message included her return address at the hotel.

I was elated at her terse message and pleased she was safe. I had so many questions for which I ached for answers, but I knew as an outsider, it was impossible to understand the conditions of war she had experienced and what she had gone through just to arrive in the neutral country. I would learn no more until the war ended.

She remained in Switzerland until the Armistice was signed, continuing to receive financial support from Papa by way of bank transactions. But packages could not be shipped during the war. Dependable communication with me was no longer possible.

Marion was alone once again but her life was much more tolerable.

After a six-year courtship to his college heartthrob, Charles announced his marriage with only *three days* notice, but the couple had an explanation.

Charles had not been to Fort Myers since he began work with his father five years earlier. He told me he was fatigued. Carolyn had never been to Florida but she had been very busy as coordinator of the 2,200-bed Harvard Medical Unit that had been sent overseas to care for the sick and wounded on the front. It was her job to enlist doctors and find supplies and send them overseas. Having been at it since America joined the war, she too was worn out. They allowed themselves a week to regain their strength.[123]

On the second day of the couple's arrival, Charles surprised Carolyn by asking, "Do you want a large wedding?"

She looked at him quizzically. "Are you proposing to me?"

"I am."

"I don't need a large wedding, Charles."

"Good. Then let's get married here and now."

"Great idea!" Carolyn said enthusiastically. "We couldn't pick a more beautiful spot."

They sent telegram invites to their widely separated relatives up and down the East Coast announcing the impromptu date of March 27 -- without explanation! Mr. Edison was on a naval vessel in the Florida Keys doing his work for the Naval Consulting Board. Theodore was on uninhabited Man Key with a number of sailors and other workers living in tents and coordinating efforts with Mr. Edison on the ship. I was on shore in Key West with other wives in comfortable quarters.

I told Mr. Edison that I was going to the wedding. I was geographically the closest relative. He said he and Theodore were too wrapped up with his Navy obligations. Responding to

Charles, he telegramed, "The sooner the better." I took a boat to Fort Myers. This was a second wedding we could endorse.

John and Madeleine could not make it. They were in Washington with the children. Her response expressed the fear that the newspapers would imagine the worst for Charles in a hasty wedding. With William and Blanche, they had called it an elopement.

Carolyn's mother[124] lived in Vermont and said she would celebrate with the newly weds later.

The couple had their wish. This was quite the opposite of a big wedding. It was intimate. It took place on the lawn at mid-afternoon at our retreat. The little altar held two candles burning in front of three decorative trees -- a Japanese umbrella, a cinnamon and a camphor. The ceremony was graciously conducted by the Rev. F. S. Shore of the Fort Myers St. Luke's Episcopal Church. In the absence of Mrs. Hawkins, I walked the bride down the red-carpeted garden aisle. Witnesses were governess Lucy Bogue and butler Henry Horsey.

The honeymoon was a Model T drive to the beach where the couple planned to catch a fish or two, cook them over an open fire, and dine together with a bottle of wine. But this plan failed. The evening mosquitos joined them and invited all their friends and relatives to the party. The humans were forced to desert the pesky creatures.

On April Fool's Day the newly married couple left for West Orange by way of Key West on the steamer *City of Philadelphia*. They left me at Key West to wait for my busy husband. Carolyn returned to Boston where she completed her work with the Harvard Medical Unit.

The couple soon rented a small apartment on Park Avenue in West Orange. They had no garage so they left their Model T parked on the street. The apartment soon became inadequate and they moved to a "proper" cottage in Llewellyn Park near Glenmont.

Finally, his job with the Navy was over and the "Old Man" returned to work at Edison, Inc. in November. Differences between father and son reemerged.

Theodore works on his own invention

While Charles was honeymooning at Seminole Lodge, Theodore, twenty, was helping his father by working on a war apparatus of his own on Man Key. His project was finding "a way of getting large quantities of explosives carried short distances with a very light apparatus." From early March to late May 1918, he and several sailors and a cook lived in six tents and worked in an abandoned 14-by-32-foot shack. They had lights supplied by a generator. The crew, living out in the open on an exposed key, experienced scorpions, an octopus, a tarantula and high-wind storms.

He wrote me telling of sand fleas that appeared every evening about dusk and "bite like hell." He was relatively close to me geographically at Fort Myers and said he would try to visit, but it was doubtful. Sunday was a half workday when they relaxed by playing poker and craps. They also bet with each other on the shots they made with their weapons. But seriously, he said, they were making progress on what he described as a big engine with wheels -- "our biggest wheel went 500 feet when shot at 1,000 revolutions per minute."[125] Whatever all that meant.

More interesting to me was Theodore's descriptions of bird life in the Keys. He told of an Oven Bird that ventured into his tent. His tent mate caught a fly and the little bird ate it from his hand. He said he attracted birds by leaving a dead fish out in the hot sun. The fish attracted flies and the flies in turn attracted birds.

In other news he said his father had visited him on the island and Theodore demonstrated his gun to him. His father said it was interesting and then outlined some tests he could do to develop it further.

William is drafted

The comfortable life of the man-about-town was suddenly interrupted in July of 1918 by a draft notice from the Army. William was not disappointed. Here was another opportunity in which he might yet achieve glory and hero recognition in the European war. After all, the poultry business had become boring. William, at forty, was placed in the tank division and served in Great Britain and France.

Fame and glory escaped him, however. He was miserable as he served his country as a sergeant in the salvage and repair section of the army as "a mere foreman over a bunch of mechanics." He appealed to his father to use his influence to either upgrade his rank or secure for him an early discharge. Not surprisingly to any of our family, Mr. Edison ignored his son's plea.

William was finally discharged when the war ended in 1919. He returned to his wife and poultry farm.

Edison's second grandson is born

Madeleine's second son, John Edison Sloane, was born on April 21, 1918. Mr. Edison and I were at home for the delivery and Papa was just as thrilled with the second grandchild as he was with the first. Relations between our families were far better.

The young Sloane family was having financial problems. Madeleine had been trying to live the life to which she was accustomed. She revealed to me that there was never enough money to satisfy her "needs."

"We never go out to eat and there is never any money for travel," she said. "I can't remember the last time we went dancing. John says airplane sales are way down since the initial contract with the army. And now there are a lot more people in the airplane manufacture business. Competition is tough. His parents are struggling also."

Mr. Edison could sympathize with his daughter. He didn't lend the couple any money for the airplane business, about which he was skeptical, or for their household budget, but he did pay off the mortgage on their house.

Madeleine was appreciative and said she was trying to live a life of fiscal responsibility.

Another gypsy tour

Henry Ford, now fifty-five, had missed out on the previous tour because of business demands, but he would not miss this one. Mr. Edison and Harvey Firestone made arrangements for a tour in the summer of 1918. The destination was the Great Smoky Mountains and it would be far more elborate than the New England-New York tour of 1916.

Now, dear reader, you might ask why these millionaires, the heads of leading industries, in the mid- to golden-years of their lives, choose to cook potatoes over a fire, sleep in a tent or under a tree, and swat flies and other insects? It was incomprehensible to the press and the general public.

But Mr. Edison explained in a note, saying, "While mankind has been slowly drifting into an artificial life of merciless commercialism, there are still a few who have not been caught up in the meshes of this frenzy and who are still human, and enjoy the wonderful panoramas of the mountains, the valleys and the plain, with their wonderful content of living things, and among these persons I am proud to know my two friends, John Burroughs and Henry Ford."[126]

The pair set off in their caps and dusters for the Catskills. where they stopped for John Burroughs at his home in

Roxbury again. Then the three sped on to Pittsburgh and picked up Ford and Firestone.

The caravan rolled through the little villages in West Virginia and North Carolina, stopping only for gasoline or for a look at something that attracted them. It was at these stops that locals gathered to gawk at them and examine their road machines. Some had never seen an electric light yet they recognized the man who invented it.

Ford was taken aback when one group didn't recognize *his* name and had never seen a Model T. But that pleased my husband and he said "Good." He knew they would have a good time in that area -- without being hounded by the locals.

They found a meadow and their tents were erected. While Ford swung an ax and cut wood for the fire, Mr. Edison sat in the car reading or simply meditating in their pastoral setting.

There was really no need for them to do any labor for they had brought along their help. Close behind them on the road was the kitchen truck and several supply trucks that provided the comforts Mr. Ford found necessary, Mr. Firestone enjoyed, Mr. Edison accepted and Mr. Burroughs found ridiculous and rather embarrassing for a naturalist accustomed to roughing it.

In the morning men washed up in a brook. Mr. Edison had removed his coat to wash but left his shirt and string tie on. He had slept in his clothes and traveled the next day in his always-rumpled suit.

Their lead car broke down in a far corner of West Virginia. It was Ford who removed his coat and crawled under the vehicle and made the repair with a piece of metal he found at a nearby blacksmith shop.

Around the campfire at night, these captains of industry talked about the raging war, Ford's political interests and their problems with employees and strikes. John Burroughs felt left out. He led a life of thrift and relative poverty, while the others talked about their contempt for earning vast amounts of money that they insisted meant so little to them, that industrial products, commodities and inventions represented true wealth. They believed bankers were parasites and Jews were "goldbugs," out to take every advantage of them.[127]

Yet here these men were, pretending to flee crass materialism by living in tents. Mr. Burroughs was the oddball of the group to me. Was he that desperate for friends to play with? Mr. Ford even advertized their camping tours in advance. Movie cameras and newsmen followed their tours. Ad men and publicity agents created publicity stunts for them. A truck near the end of one caravan carried a huge sign that read, "Buy Firestone Tires." The motor caravans increased in size over the years and by 1919 reached a length of fifty vehicles. Politicians jumped into the act. President Warren Harding at one time sat in the flickering light of their campfire.

I heard most of these stories second hand and I didn't want to believe them. It all seemed so contradictory to our refined and quiet life at Glenmont.

The war ends

As the Allies pushed toward the German border on October 17, the alliance between the Central Powers began to collapse. Germany itself began to fall apart from within. By November 9 the Kaiser and all the royal familes had abdicated and slipped across the border into the Netherlands and elsewhere. Meanwhile, hunger and popular dissatisfaction precipitated revolution throughout the country. The Weimar Republic was announced and peace feelers were extended to the allied British, French and American armies.

The armistice was signed at five in the morning of November 11 between the Allies and Germany at Compiègne, France in a railroad car parked in a French forest near the front lines. The terms of the agreement called for fighting to end along the entire Western Front at precisely eleven that morning. Cessation of hostilities did indeed end that morning on the eleventh hour of the eleventh day of the eleventh month of 1918. More than four years of bloody fighting came to an end with neither side gaining significant ground.

The world, and our family, breathed a great sigh of relief. But many believed the war was so horrific, took so many lives, left so many wounded, and destroyed so many families, this *had* to be "the war to end war."[128]

Or was this human naiveté?

Marion visits Oscar in the hospital

With the war finally ended, Marion, still in Switzerland, learned from her German friends that Oscar had a nervous breakdown and was in a Nuremberg hospital.

"I had to visit him," she wrote. "I had to see how he had changed. I prepared myself for the difficult return to the war-devastated country. Arranging for reliable transportation was difficult. Hoards of refugees, returning and leaving, often blocked the road and my driver had to u-turn and find another route. I kept questioning why I was making this journey. What was I going to gain?

"I found the hospital and I located Oscar, although he did not look like the man I had known so well. But he recognized me. He was on a bed in a ward among fifty other wounded soldiers. There was no privacy. I was shocked to see that his hair had turned totally white. He showed me his mangled left leg that had been splintered by a large caliber shell. He was told it would eventually mend but he would have a significant limp. He spoke about the horrors he had witnessed and how his fatherland had been 'unfairly' brutalized and destroyed. He said he hated the Americans and the British who had brought his country to its knees. The malvolence I saw in his eyes frightened me. He asked why I had deserted him. 'Why didn't you wait for me?'

"By way of an answer, I asked about his lover and he turned his head away. I pressed on, asking what she had that I didn't. He ignored me. I shouted and screamed at him, not aware of what I was doing, until I was shaken by a Red Cross nurse who brought me to my senses. At age forty-seven, I now knew my marriage was over."

Chapter Twenty-Five

1919

Depression after the Great War

Charles had managed the Edison empire with quiet efficiency and it thrived during the war years while his father was away on his naval assignment. When the Great War ended two major events took place. The economy went from inflationary boom times to stagnation and the second worst depression in the history of the country.

Secondly, Charles rode the war years with much success but with his father's return, yet in the terrible economy, came his demand to take over the management once again. The Old Man, seventy-two, ordered major cuts in personnel and even eliminated the personnel department that Charles had toiled over recently and reorganized. The two of them faced each other in a raging dispute over personnel policy. Mr. Edison reminded him, "Hell. We don't need them. I'm doin' the hirin' and firin' around here now." Yet Charles personally counted fifteen unnecessary people in the laboratory "who weren't doing a damn thing." But because of his father's sentimental reflections about his precious laboratory they remained on the payroll. This disagreement soon passed. Charles was another of his sons who all but worshiped his father yet found it very difficult to deal with him. Charles hung on.[129]

It seemed like every year Mr. Edison fired and hired another manager of our Florida estate. A married couple was now doing the duty, but Mr. Tinstman was doing other work as well and his wife had taken his place. However, it appeared my husband was pleased with her work.

To my surprise we now had a cow on the property that my husband, in his wisdom, wanted for his diet of fresh milk. In fact, he was drinking a dozen glasses of it a day. But the cow needed to have a tubercular test and there was no veterinarian in town. Fortunately, Mrs. Tinstman had a personal physician who agreed to do the test. All was well now for the milk drinker.

Before we left for Florida, Mr. Edison, now seventy-two, said, "I feel just fine. You can stop worrying." He reminded me, "The three generations of males from whom I'm descended have lived between 104 and 99 years, my father Samuel being the latter. Even if this age decline ratio continues, I can expect to live until my late eighties."

I thought, who can argue with a man who thinks in that convoluted way?"

Madeleine and her two little boys visited with us along with Theodore, my younger sister Mary Emily and her husband, William, and a nurse.

It was a relaxing month, our first visit since the we entered the war and Mr. Edison's important part in it. He needed this rest. The family made good use of the new pool. We did some fishing on the pier.

The inventor was spending much less time in his laboratory so he arranged to have some of his chemicals, raw materials and the two huge dynamos shipped back to the West Orange lab. Miscellaneous equipment and tools were sold locally.

Every good garden should have its own bees. I had my own hives at Glenmont. Our caretaker had bees brought in for our new hives but apparently they weren't happy with their new home. They moved elsewhere. Mrs. Tinstman was going to try again in our absence.

Mr. Edison tidied up our Seminole Lodge property title, half of which was in my name and half in his, by placing it all in my name. It was a nice gesture and I thanked him for it. In spite of what he said about living to an old age, in reality he had in mind the potential of an earlier death. I was greatful to him for relieving me of what might have been a burden after his death.

We left for home on April 10.

Burroughs' notebook

John Burroughs, the naturalist, always carried a small notebook and pencil with him for jotting his thoughts on the birds and other wildlife he observed as well as the ideas of others he thought interesting that were expounded in his presence. I never saw that notebook, but I know that Mr. Edison saw it and found it interesting enough to tell me about its contents.

Burroughs, a "child of the woods" as Henry James once remarked, had only met Henry Ford in 1913. Their meeting came about after Burroughs had written in one of his many magazine articles that the automobile was a noisy and "befouling" machine. In answer to this comment, Ford, who was an admiring reader of the naturalist's writings, shipped a Model T directly to the writer's doorstep at his farm on the Hudson River. The authority on bird calls and woodland serenity was soon seen at the wheel of the Tin Lizzy speeding around the countryside with his granddaughters in obvious, joyful enthusiasm.

Soon after expressing his thanks to Ford, he was invited to visit the industrialist at Fair Lane to celebrate the unveiling of a bird fountain that had been constructed from stones

Burroughs had donated from his farm. The men, with so many opposites between them, became friends.

In the summer of 1919, Ford, Firestone, Burroughs and my husband went on their sixth annual camping ritual. This time it was New England. Although this should have been simply a camping trip for four men, the entourage and its followers had grown to excessive proportions.

It was on this trip that, according to Mr. Burrough's book, he felt offended as Mr. Ford ranted on and on about the Jews, that they caused thefts and robberies around the country; that they caused inefficiency in the Navy; that the Jews caused the war. Mr. Ford specifically named Jay Gould, widely considered a "Robber Baron," as a perfect example of the Jewish avarice he abhored.

Burroughs, who had known Mr. Gould since childhood, pointed out to his recent friend that Gould was a "tried-and-true Presbyterian." The satisfaction resulting for the others lasted only a moment. Ford continued his vicious anti-semitism. Burroughs wrote that he could not make himself continue recording Mr. Ford's diatribe. It pained him too much.

I know Mr. Edison had a touch of anti-Semitism himself on occasion, but it was more conventional. He pointed out the Jewish businessmen in Germany were far "more keen and alert" than the lowbrow German industrial leadership. Mr. Edison otherwise looked kindly on the Jews, calling them "remarkable and mysterious" in their isolation from the rest of mankind. "I wish they would all quit making money. The trouble with the Jew is that he has been persecuted for centuries by ignorant, malignant bigots."[130]

All of this made me wonder just why my husband had a relationship with Mr. Ford. And Mr. Burroughs. How did he fit in? What was the commonality? Mr. Edison trusted Mr. Ford. In fact he was the only man he had come to trust since a similar confidence had been demolished by the Gilliland debacle.

The New England trip, according to Mr. Edison, was quite satisfactory. He said nothing negative about it.

Theodore excels at MIT

Mr. Edison had always been impressed by Theodore's technical aptitude. He loved to experiment. It was no challenge for him to perform his father's alarm-clock exercise, by taking it apart and reassembling it in just a few minutes. At age fourteen, he was mildly wounded when he experimented with explosives in an effort to invent a bomb that could float on water and explode if a hostile vessel touched it resulting in terrible damage.

After graduating from Montclair Academy, Theodore helped his father with some military experiments in the Florida Keys during the war and before he entered MIT in September 1919.

Theodore received excellent grades at MIT in both the sciences and engineering, specializing in theoretical physics. He took to his classes with alacrity and even studied through the summer following his freshman year.

"I have no time to write," he told me, although at my insistence he did *telegraph* me daily. "My day is filled with classes, study, food and sleep -- classes and studies mostly."

In his junior year Theodore felt he could begin to participate in extracurricular activities. In addition to his life-long winter interest in ice skating, he played six sets of tennis on the one afternoon he had no classes. He swam at the Cambridge YMCA and he was elected treasurer of the Aeronautical Engineering Society.

I was anxious about all his busyness.

Tom & Beatrice move to West Orange

After "the war to end war" finally closed, Tom and his loyal wife Beatrice gave up farm life and moved to West Orange, not far from Glenmont. Beatrice happily reported that Tom had not touched alcohol since our Thanksgiving two years earlier.

Mr. Edison was greatly pleased at Beatrice's success in curing her husband, but she attributed Tom's cure to the mild reconciliation between him and his father that resulted in a challenging job at Mr. Edison's Research Engineering Division. Tom said he would have no problem at all working for his brother Charles despite being a decade and a half his senior.

I admit that I had exerted some influence on Mr. Edison by expressing Beatrice's belief that Tom was indeed an unproven carbon copy of his namesake. But Tom's reaction to the proffered job did not result in unrestrained glee. He saw it as a challenge -- a put-up-or-shut-up deal, under the direction of his sympathetic stepbrother Charles. Tom's job was to examine incoming patents and determine which ones were worthy of developing. Charles told me Tom felt a "gigantic strain" in his job, but he persevered, only occasionally giving in to one perceived illness or another.

Beatrice was happy with Tom's steadfastness at the job, but she knew he had still not received the expressions of satisfaction and praise from his father that he continued to crave.

Mina's older brother marries

My older brother, Edward Miller, now sixty-one, finally found the love of his life. She was his twenty-two-year-old housekeeper, Elizabeth Ann Lewis. He had resisted marriage until he met this young woman.

He worked as vice president in father's company, Altman Miller & Co. and became president after father died in 1899. Most recently he started a real estate business. He had lived all his life in the Akron family home with my other unmarried siblings.

I didn't attend the wedding and they didn't plan anything special. I didn't know the girl, but frankly, I thought the age difference was rather unusual. But, who was I to be critical? That's what some people thought about my marriage to Dearie.

Chapter Twenty-Six

1920-1921

My calendar of events

Mr. Edison and I had our thirty-fourth wedding anniversary on February 26, the day before we left for Florida. I reminded him and he gave me a hug and a kiss. If he had done any more, such as buy me flowers, I would have collapsed in a dead faint.

For well over half of our marriage I had to manage my life by myself. I was lonely and felt deserted during many of those first few years. But then I caught hold of myself and decided on my own path. That path involved helping others. I had the money. I had the time.

I started with the church in West Orange. Following my father's lead, I gave money to add an ell to the sanctuary for Sunday School classrooms, a small kitchen and a Fellowship Hall for the mingling of the congregation and for coffee and cookies following the church service. This was also a good time to give the entire building a new coat of paint as well. The whole project was very well received.

But perhaps more important than that, once a week we served hot meals in the church Fellowship Hall and opened our doors to everyone -- the less fortunate as well as our regular members. And we mixed and developed new friendships. I was shocked to learn how many families in our area had so little -- so little income and so little food. It inspired me to initiate the first "food pantry" in West Orange and it was welcomed by hundreds of people. It took a lot of time, energy and generosity of many others to keep the pantry well stocked. It was used most heavily during the winter, of course, when vegetable gardens were frozen over. During the spring and summer, the church provided vegetable and flower seeds to those who wanted gardens. These activities gave our congregation, and other churches that joined in with us, real meaning to their lives as well.

In Fort Myers I did very much the same. The town, during the years when we first arrived, had only a single "federated" church that accepted all denominations and beliefs. Working with the clergy, I gave money to add a new and larger sanctuary building and converted the former church into classrooms and, you guessed it, a Fellowship Hall. With the membership's guidance, we also bought new hymnals and prayer books to accompany the new pews.

Each of these projects took many meetings, months and letters going back and forth. What a difference it made. The congregations in both towns increased substantially.

My life was also consumed during the summers at Chautauqua. My brother Ira and I both served on the board of directors of the institution. I spent a lot of my time behind our family cottage on the grounds of Miller Park beside the lake. I installed flagstone walks that weaved through the park and its many flower and shrub gardens. My horticultural talents blossomed and I planted petunias, foxglove, columbine, hydrangea, violets, bluebells and forsythia to name a few. I placed wrought iron benches throughout so visitors could sit and enjoy the scene with the lake as a backdrop. It all tied in nicely with the Chautauqua Bird & Tree Club that I helped organize in 1913.

I was the founder of the Fort Myers Round Table of community leaders whose task was community improvement. I brought chapters of the American Red Cross and the Salvation

Army into both the Oranges and Fort Myers and worked with them.

Mr. Edison never drank alcohol, but I admit I had a glass of wine now and then with the ladies. I was a member of the Anti-Saloon League of America and the Orange Orphan Society. I visited the orphanages at least once a month and worked with a group that actively sought families for these children. Our group also inspected the orphanages for cleanliness and that the children were being fed and treated well. It was a major responsibility and we took it very seriously.

For seven years I belonged to the West Orange Improvement League, keeping the city clean and its its politicians on their toes.

None of these activities interfered with taking care of my husband and children. I gladly gave up evening and weekend meetings when family activities were planned. I always believed in family first. I never liked the term "housewife." I was a wife to my husband and mother to my children. If someone wanted to call me something, they could call me "home executive."

At home itself I had a myriad of duties. I had a full staff and a huge house to oversee. I had parties and social engagements to plan and to lead. Although our butler, Henry Horsey, managed the details of house and staff perfectly well, he still looked to me for my preferences.

My cook always wanted guidance. Mr. Edison was not the problem. He usually ate the same meat and potatoes day in and day out. I wanted variety for both me and for my children. I wanted fresh vegetables and fruit. Head Gardener, Tom, planted, maintained and weeded all our gardens and, in the fall and winter, the gardens moved into the greenhouses. I could still have fresh vegetables and fresh-cut flowers most of the year.

And then there was my husband. He was such a creature of habit. He had an endless list of likes and dislikes and he was demanding in some respects. He always slept in a nightshirt. He said pajamas were binding. He wanted me to lay out his underwear and clothes for the next day because he didn't want the chambermaid to see his private clothes. He was always up by seven. He wanted me standing by the door, ready to open it, with his coat on my arm, when he left for work. I always sent him off with a kiss on the cheek and he'd say a few affectionate words.

He also wanted me to be the first person he saw when he arrived home, the time of which was impossible to anticipate. If he came home late, he would call my name from the entrance and, if no answer, he would chase me down.

Morse Code continued to be a major part of our lives. At dinner with the grandchildren or guests, if he couldn't follow the conversation, he would look at me and I would fill him in with taps.

The New York *Times* was his must-reading in the evening. The paper was always placed in his armchair by the fireplace in his study. That chair was his and his alone. Not even the grandchildren could sit in it. His favorite cigars were the mildest of the Cuban. He smoked four each day. At the time, they sold at two smokes for a quarter. I was responsible for maintaining the supply of cigars, both at Glenmont and in Florida.

I ordered all his suits for him from his favorite tailor in the city that he had used for fifty years. The tailor knew that the suits had to "breathe." I never did learn what that meant.

My husband did find time now and then to show his love for me. Talk and thoughts had to be cleared away. For him to be absorbed in thought was his regular nature, but at these times, I had to be absorbed in his thoughts as well. This sometimes took a great deal of effort on my part. When we were alone and in bed, I was Dearie's "dearest Billie." There I could draw on what I will call "the spirit." I was quiet with his soul.

Early on in our marriage I needed this loving. Those were the days when I felt the most insecurity and self-doubt.

Repairs needed at Seminole Lodge

Our family arrived at Fort Myers in late February. This year our guests for the first time were my sister Mary Nichols and her husband William, along with my niece Rachel Miller, nineteen.

This season we were made aware that our cottages were in need of a lot of repairs. For some reason Mr. Edison thought his paradise had always cost too much and now he complained about having to repair them. Of course the buildings were now thirty-four years old and set in climate where the use of wood from the Maine forests may not have been suitable to begin with. The buildup of paint over the years had to be removed before a fresh coat could be applied. Instead of scraping off the excess paint, the workers used blowtorches and in the process the kitchen wall caught fire where the wood was rotten. But it was extinguished and no real harm was done.

Every year we had our property manager send boxes of fresh Florida citrus to friends, neighbors and management. This year the volume of shipments reached fifty-seven cartons, but we knew the northerners all appreciated fruit out of season.

Downsizing the business

The post-war economy was still on a downturn. During the war years the Edison companies experienced a boom in phonograph sales, but by the end of 1920 a serious drop in sales necessitated a reduction in production as well as employees. Charles and his father had some serious disagreements on how to go about cutbacks because the cuts in management involved many of Mr. Edison's long-time, loyal men. The end result was Mr. Edison's "economy campaign." There was too much management and too much overhead. He reduced the number of managers, engineers and workers by two-thirds![131]

At the same time, however, Charles increased efficiency and production by buying new equipment and introducing new methods of operation.

Charles was greatly annoyed because many of the other improvements in the business that he had introduced were eliminated. It had become a matter of survival for the business. For a time, former workers in West Orange dispised the Edisons for the reduction in employees. It was a very difficult time for everyone. In the end, Charles admitted his father was correct. He did what needed to be done for Edison, Inc. to continue, while other businesses throughout the country did not survive.

Marion divorces Oscar

I was not surprised when Marion wrote in 1921 that, after twenty-seven years of her childless marriage, she had divorced her cheating husband Oscar Oeser. I immediately thought, oh, good, Marion is coming home. But that didn't happen. She said she had a lot of wounds to heal. She would never return to Germany. She had found a perfectly comfortable home in Switzerland.

Marion filed for divorce soon after visiting her husband in the German hospital, but with that country's bureaucracy destroyed and in chaos, the action went nowhere. Finally, her father's unexpected help arrived. He found a way to speed up the process. His daughter was finally free from the marriage he had been against from the beginning. A contrite daughter wrote her father.

"Thank you, Papa. Thank you for your help in ridding me of my unfaithful husband whom I loved for so many years. I am still comfortably settled in Switzerland and I have a lot of pain to resolve. I am creating a plan of what to do for the rest of my life."

Mr. Edison was mum. He had done what he felt he had to do. It was now up to me. I wrote Marion.

"We are so pleased that you are safe and comfortable. Your father sends his love. We both wish you will return to America and settle near us. I don't want to sound pushy. I understand that you have a lot to resolve but I feel that with our help and love it could be much easier for you to make your decisions here."

Marion's response came in the return mail. "Thank you for your consideration of my future. I am sure America will eventually be in my plans."

The wives join in the camping trip

Except for the brief trip into the Everglades, this was the first year the wives were "invited" to join the men on their camping trip. But this invite did not take place without some discussion. The women's argument was, why should the men have all the fun? We want some camping fun also. Mr. Edison complained about how complicated it would become with seating in the cars. Who will sit with whom. Is a separate car necessary? Who will drive? Then there are separate sanitary facilities and how about the sleeping accommodations? Do we need an extra tent? He went on and on. "It's not that we don't want you, it's just that it complicates everything. And he brought up the disasters that happened on our Everglades trip, which of course had nothing to do with the women. This was the "open road" trip. Very different.

I refused to listen to his complaints. "The wives are going with you. You men will love it!"

We gathered at the Firestone home in Columbiana, Ohio where Harvey and Idabelle and their son Harvey junior graciously hosted us. With us also were Henry and Clara Ford and their son Edsel. President Warren Harding joined us as well, giving excuses for the absence of his wife, Florence, who became "ill" at the last minute. Missing was the camping regular, John Burroughs. He had died the year before. With the naturalist in mind, the tenuity of life was felt among the group, spurring an increased determination to enjoy the moment.

Mr. Firestone had wanted this trip to be simple and gypsy-like, but it quickly degenerated as it had the year before, into a festive parade, attracting the press and anyone with an auto who wanted to become a part of the convoy. The men were constantly photographed and interviewed and encouraged to act like overgrown children. On a hot day, Mr. Ford, for example, was likely to call a halt to his driver, leap out of his car, strip off his shirt on the run, and jump into an icy stream, with the usual attention of a gaggle of photographers.

Mr. Edison now had me with him in the front seat of the lead car along with the driver. Dearie chose the routes, preferring to visit or pass through villages rather than cities. If we were approaching a group of children at the side of the road, he sometimes stopped and handed out candy.

At the end of the day, he located an open field and the work crew set up all the tents in a circle around our campfire. It looked like a Civil War bivouac. We brought our own fire wood so we wouldn't have to scavange. The kitchen truck was set up for our meals. Pardon me for even mentioning this but, set up at a discrete distance were the "necessaries tents" for men and women. The workers set up their own nesting area, a larger compound on the periphery, available to the press as well.

The highlight of each day, apart from the actual drive, was simply sitting around the evening campfire. Although we initially sat as couples, the women soon moved together with their own talk, yet we were also tuned into the men's conversations. Not surprisingly, the men generally talked about their business interests whereas we women focused on clothing and decorating our homes.

As the evening went on, the men's conversations might degenerate into jokes and fun-making of each other's idiosyncracies. One in particular that I overheard was Mr. Edison commenting that President Harding was a "real man" because he chose to chew tobacco rather than smoke cigars. A disgusting habit as far as we women were concerned. But his comment brought on great howls of laughter.

Although I enjoyed the women most of the time, I was happy also when the trip ground to an end and we each returned to our own ways. Frankly, I did not enjoy camping en masse.

Chapter Twenty-Seven

1922-1923

Ella Piper's Beauty Parlor

We celebrated my husband's seventy-fifth birthday late this year, although the cards and telegrams from others around the world piled in on time. We were in Fort Myers with the Fords. The celebratory event, at Mr. Edison's request, was to be fishing. An advance team prepared Seminole Lodge and Gracie had dinner ready soon after we arrived on the afternoon train.

The Fords arrived in their private railroad car, with their cook and butler, very late in the evening. The local newspaper reported they were asleep on arrival and remained in their car until morning when Mr. Ford left the railroad car and Clara, and walked to the Mangoes.

The Fords visited us soon after breakfast and the men left for town in the Model T that Mr. Ford had given my husband in 1916. The industrialist was at the wheel. They were like two teenagers when they were together. They visited the local Ford dealership where he introduced Mr. Edison.

In the meantime, we women toured downtown Fort Myers. A great variety of shops had sprung up in recent years so Clara and I had a fine time together. One particular place I enjoyed during previous visits was Ella Jones Piper's Beauty Parlor on Hendry Street. Ella and I had become good friends because I had my hair and nails cared for here and Mr. Edison stopped for his haircut when his regular barber was not available to come to our house. Ella was a classy lady and had no problem generating conversation. This was probably the best place to get caught up with the local news since our last visit. I introduced Clara Ford who was as captivated by Ella as I.[132]

Fishing occupied the men much of the two weeks of the Ford's visit, either on the pier or out in the boat. They had hoped to snag a tarpon, but that didn't happen.

Soon after we left for home, Charles and Carolyn arrived for a vacation. They took the boat out in quest of tarpon, going directly to Yellow Fever Creek on the north side to the Caloosahatchie near Fort Myers. Charles reported to me that they fished for what seemed like hours until he noticed a very large fish under their boat. As the story goes, Charles threw a harpoon in Ahab fashion and pierced the monster but it didn't give up. It began charging the boat repeatedly until it was exhausted. It turned out to be a sawfish, sixteen feet long and some six hundred pounds. He sent me a copy of the newspaper article describing his catch. As some newspapers are apt to do, he said, the story was greatly exaggerated, but then again, Charles' stories most often reflected his modesty. He was so unlike his father in that respect.

A visit to the GE Schenectady plant

It was a reunion of sorts, coupled with great curiosity as Mr. Edison made his first visit to his General Electric Schenectady plant in twenty-five years. The huge plant had grown to 18,000 workers, a far cry from the little Edison Machine Works of long ago. President Gerald Swope gathered the employees into the parking lot for an overwhelming greeting for their namesake and founder. A small ceremony followed at which a bronze plaque dedicated to him was placed on the door of the laboratory that he had founded.

A tour followed during which he observed hundreds of technicians and scientists at work fulfilling a goal that Mr. Edison had only been able to dream.

He watched a demonstration of a man-made lightning bolt of 120,000 volts that zapped a bar of tungsten steel. The bar disappeared into a cloud of vapor.

Particularly interesting to my husband was the recent development of using tungsten as a lamp filament. Tungsten was the material the inventor tried to use years ago. It was one of the experiments recorded in his notebooks that he rejected.

Among other developments that had Mr. Edison shaking his head in wonder was the 100,000-candle-power lamp and the photoelectric mechanisms that reproduced sound on tape for motion pictures and phonographs.[133]

In spite of all this wonder, Mr. Edison left Schenectady with a negative feeling. He could not understand how huge corporations, whose employees worked together in groups and held many conference meetings could possibly accomplish as much as dedicated scientists working alone. The "weight of organization" seemed to him to slow down the process or even halt it. It led him to ask, "Where is the lone entrepreneur?" At the same time, he saw that there would always be a place for individual genius that could find a niche for invention and beat the huge corporation at its own game.

William rebuffed once again

Still striving to become his own man in the technology area he so admired in his father, as well as to find relief from chicken farming, William jumped once again into mechanics. He invested in a small radio shop in New Jersey. So much time had passed since his last foray into a business, and with his father so much older, he was sure that adding the Edison name to his shop would be ignored.

Not so. Mr. Edison came down on him with a vengeance and threats.

William wrote his father. "I thought I received several jolts during the war over in France worth taking notice of but they were nothing compared to this. Papa, just what is your reason for trying to throw a wrench in the cog wheel of my honestly built and honestly arrived at radio set?"

My heart went out to William once again. He never understood his father and, as a result, he would never learn.

Edison's third grandson is born

Madeleine's third child was born on March 2, 1923. The family had trouble coming up with a suitable name. They wanted a name that had not yet been used in the considerable alphabet of Edison and Sloane given names. There were too many Charles, Frank, Harry, Henry, Homer, John, Samuel, Simon, Thomas, Theodore and William names in the family.

They finally decided on "Peter" and his middle name would continue the tradition -- Peter Edison Sloane.

The young Sloane family was still settled in South Orange and they were still having financial problems. As strong and as independent as Madeleine was, she had trouble asking her father for help. She commiserated with me, writing and rewriting drafts of a letter to send to Papa and, finally, she sent it. It resulted in the payoff of the new mortgage on a larger house to hold their growing family.

Although she was well aware of the tribulations that her stepsiblings, Marion, Tom and William, were experiencing with Papa's wrath, she was envious of her sibling's unlimited free time and for their aggravatingly "childless and egotistical" lives. Maintenance of the three young boys kept her very busy along with her keeping the home up to her orderly standards.

Papa and I were regular visitors to the Sloane household. We often made time to be with our grandchildren so Madeleine could escape with a friend for a free afternoon. Mr. Edison was soon testing his grandchildren's abilities with his alarm-clock-technology test. He seemed pleased.

A paved road reaches Fort Myers

I saw my first Burrowing Owl this season. I recorded it in my lifetime observations. How strange that a bird should live in a hole in the ground, especially a hole that another mammal had dug. These smallest of North American owls are brown spotted, have long legs and distinctive eyebrows above their bright yellow eyes. Their under feathers are white. It makes me wonder how they keep so clean. And what happens to them in their hole during a heavy rain?

The town was finally raising funds to pave the road into Fort Myers from the north. We contributed $500 toward the $17,000 in total contributions. The improvement was another step toward beautification. The dust stirred up from increased traffic had become very bothersome.

We and the Fords went to the Arcade Theater and watched Charlie Chaplin movies. A downcast Mr. Edison was disappointed that none of his movies were shown.

The Fords had their new Lincoln this season. We all made good use of it traveling down to Estero and Bonita Springs. That part of the county is beautiful but still quite undeveloped. The news at Ella's Beauty Parlor was the proposal to cut out a large section of South Lee County and create two new counties to be named Collier and Hendry.

Edison, Ford and money

Mr. Edison and Ford, both wealthy men, had always professed that they had no desire for great wealth. My husband earned earned income of more than $1 million annually and Ford earned many times more than that. Mr. Edison, in a speech that was read for him at the convention of motion picture producers said, "You must never think of profits, but only of public service."[134]

I will restrain myself and not comment on this statement from these two American capitalists.

What represented true wealth to Mr. Edison was not cash, but commodities and industrial products, although he rarely seemed short on cash. By 1922 the value of the American light and power industry alone had grown to more than $15 billion!

Mr. Ford stood fully behind his friend's beliefs regarding money. Ford said in 1930, "Our prosperity leads the world, due to the fact we have an Edison. His inventions created millions of new jobs and he has done more toward abolishing poverty than all the reformers and statesmen."

I agreed. They both did their part Ford in creating good jobs.

Theodore graduates from MIT

To my everlasting joy, my baby Theodore, my last child, graduated from a four-year college program in June 1923. I traveled to Cambridge to witness the event that I had so hoped Madeleine could have accomplished and that Charles had come so very close to reaching.

Commencement 1923 was a year of firsts at MIT, we were told. This was the first graduation at which both faculty and graduates wore academic gowns and caps. It was the first at which graduates received a diploma personally and in alphabetical order. And this was the first MIT commencement in which a "loud-speaking apparatus" was used.

Somehow I was favored with a seat near the platform. I waited patiently as the graduate's names were called. I heard the name "Theodore Miller Edison" called and I watched as he crossed the platform proud and erect. I saw him receive his diploma from MIT's eighth president, Samuel Wesley Stratton. At that very moment, the sight flashed back through my mind of the time, twenty years ago, when I watched my brother, "Thede," graduate from Yale in 1898.

At the conclusion, we found each other in the crowd. It was a wonderful moment as I hugged Theodore. He handed me his diploma. It said he had graduated "with distinction."

Chapter Twenty-Eight

1924 - 1925

Theodore meets Anna

Mr. Edison was anxious to have Theodore join him at the company. But Theodore was as strong willed as his father and declined the offer. In the fall of 1923 he returned to MIT for a post-graduate year studying mathematical physics, a field Mr. Edison had always made fun of. Theodore received his Masters Degree in the spring of 1924.

In January, the very middle of his intense year in graduate school where he had enrolled in sixty-five credit hours of courses a week, he found time to go to a dinner party at the home of a school friend. There he met Anna Maria Osterhout, the daughter of a distinguished professor of botany at Harvard. She was as tall, athletic and blond as he was. They shared interests in swimming, skating and tennis. Anna exuded the élan that captured Theodore's heart. Three years his junior, she was enrolled in the Harvard pre-med program. She was healthy, fit and headstrong -- a girl who drove her own car! As if anything could be wanting for Theodore, she was cultured, a good cook and she loved the theater and music. If there was any fault, it was an occasional stinging flash of temper.

Within a week, they were dating. He invited her to see Oscar Wilde's *The Ideal Husband*, and the next day they attended a violin recital by Jascha Heifetz.

Theodore reported all these details in letters to me and I worried that I might soon be left out of his world. But then he reassured me with a falsehood I could live with saying, "You're far and away my best girl!"

By spring, however, their relationship grew into romance and Theodore drove her in his flivver from Cambridge to the Ipswich countryside for picnics and fresh-from-the-ocean clams and lobster.

Anna accepted Theodore's proposal in July.

Oscar marries his mistress

I received a painful letter from Marion in the summer of 1924 saying that her former husband had just announced his marriage to his long-time mistress, Clara Berger.

Marion wrote, "The newspaper announcement with their pictures brought this woman into reality. Until this, she had only been a vague, hateful creature who was stealing my man. Now to actually see them. . . It hurt terribly. It stabbed me in the heart. I knew I shouldn't have been surprised, but it hurt anyway. My Oscar, my lover of more than twenty years was now taking formal vows with the woman who replaced me. For the first time I could clearly see my former husband with this younger, beautiful woman wrapped tightly in his arms and he was looking at me, and I at him, and he was grinning smugly. Depression overtook me and I felt very sorry for myself for days."

The decline of the phonograph

It was not easy for Mr. Edison to watch the slow, steady decline of his favorite invention, the phonograph. He believed new methods of selling it were needed as well as new technology, such as a longer-playing record. How wonderful it would be, he dreamed, if a two-hour record could be created. Then we could listen to a series as long as "The Decline and Fall of the Roman Empire."

In fact, the decline of the phonograph was most likely due to the growing popularity of the radio -- an innovation in which his sons William and Charles had seen as a promising business but which Mr. Edison shot down and vehemently resisted as a passing fad. He told the press that the radio would be a destructive influence by ruining the public's "aesthetic aptitude." How could the radio ever compete with the acoustic clarity he had developed so well in the phonograph?

Both Charles and Theodore had eventually convinced their father to begin manufacturing radio receivers. But with the long delay of obtaining licenses from patent owners, mainly General Electric, Westinghouse, RCA and Bell Telephone, this brought him up to 1928, the eve of the Great Depression when the move to a major new technology was unthinkable.

Theodore accused his father of opposing new ideas until it was too late. William heard about their interest in radio and was smug at implying I told you so. Radio receivers and electronic phonographs were two examples of delayed reaction to innovation. Theodore, who was considered the most talented of all his children by friends and relations, regarded his father with mixed feelings of respect and puzzlement.

Unfortunately Mr. Edison could only be in a funk. His mind still raced, but his body couldn't keep up with it. The future seemed to be moving toward the radio and the electronic phonograph business, but at age seventy-eight he just didn't have the energy to tackle anything new. He couldn't keep up with his children's ambitions.

Rubber redux

Harvey Firestone took the train south with us this season, disembarking at St. Augustine. We continued on through Lakeland where we were greeted by a class of school children and well-wishers.

As part of our mutual desire to become very active in the town of Fort Myers, we allowed Morton Milford, editor of the Fort Myers *Press*, to meet us at Lakeland and interview us on the train as we headed south. Of more interest to Mr. Edison this time than talking about himself was the editor's report on the availablility of tarpon in the area, the just-opened *wooden* auto bridge across the Caloosahatchie, the status of the Tamiami Trail from Tampa that had come as far as Punta

Gorda, and the development of the newly established town of Everglades City.

We invited the entire senior class at Fort Myers High School to visit our estate and have their photos taken with the great inventor. I gave a tour of our gardens and tried to give it a lively flavor, but the questions kept returning to my husband's activities.

Our friend Harvey Firestone, the tire baron, showed up at our place in March with experts on rubber trees from Singapore and Liberia. Mr. Edison told them about his efforts with goldenrod, about which they showed only polite interest. The experts were studying the possibility of raising rubber trees in the southwest Florida climate.

An experiment with the guayule rubber plant, that is native in the Southwest and Mexico, was undertaken by Ford on seven thousand acres he had purchased in LaBelle, Florida. Guayule was a waist-high, woody shrub that regenerates and needs very little water. Firestone doubted that Ford's experiment could yield the volume and quality of resin that was needed for the U.S. consumption of rubber.

Ford's experiment failed for several reasons. The LaBelle guayule plantings died after a hurricane came through and drowned them. Another problem was, after harvesting, it took the plant four years to regenerate. Firestone's prediction was accurate. The acreage necessary for the volume of resin needed would have to encompass the entire state of Florida. Grayule was certainly no substitute for the rubber tree. Obviously, Mr. Ford did not do his homework.

Advocating public parks

I had the good fortune to speak before the Board of Governors of the Fort Myers Chamber of Commerce. I explained how important it was to have parks and open areas in every community. I suggested that open areas of land should be set aside now, as soon as possible, for recreation of all kinds, otherwise a rapidly growing town could become a dense, unattractive cluster of buildings cutting out the sun.

People of all ages must have open, grassy areas where they can sit, walk, relax and play in the fresh air. The areas must be large enough so that the daily noise of traffic and business is but a background murmur. Open areas should be skattered around the town, easily available to residents from one end of town to the other. I emphasized that every delay in securing this open land would mean fewer options in the midst of rapid growth and the rising cost of the land itself.

I had a sympathetic audience. I was pleased. The president of the Chamber challenged the board to take action and expressed his appreciation for the Royal Palms that had been planted along McGregor Boulevard. He said that open areas throughout town would do just as much as the palms to beautify the town and make it attractive and welcoming.

I was asked to join the subcommittee on open areas and I accepted their invitation.

Theodore tours the Pacific Northwest

In the early summer of 1924, Mr. Edison again asked Theodore to come to work for him. Again Theodore rejected the offer. He told his father he was finally free and he was going to do what his siblings and parents had done and visit the West Coast.

He did, and he particularly enjoyed the wild and rugged mountains and the churning sea along the coasts of northern California, Washington, Oregon and British Columbia. He explored the Columbia River in a raft with a guide, and toured the Olympic Peninsula and its parks, Mount St. Helens and Mount Rainer. Like Charles, he loved the freedom of the open road and camping wherever he found fresh water, level ground and a pleasant vista.

I arranged to meet Theodore in Washington and we spent several days doing some, let's say, "civilized" camping. I just wasn't fully able to release my "baby" yet.

During Mr. Edison's last years we were most likely found in Florida than elsewhere. The gardens at Seminole Lodge now had thousands of tropical plants along with our botanical laboratory and a staff of botanists.

The cost of rubber continued to rise throughout the war and it was one of the most important commodities of the industrial world primarily because of the automobile needs of four pneumatic tires, tubes and a spare.

Henry Ford was on a different mission this season. He wanted to purchase Mr. Edison's Fort Myers laboratory and contents and move it to his Greenfield Village[135] museum in Dearborn, Michigan. But, Mr. Edison had already sold a good number of his tools and equipment to the local blacksmith, William Ross. Ford beelined it to Mr. Ross' business and promptly bought back all the tools and equipment that included, engines, drill presses, lathes, an anvil, hand planes and a myriad of other hand tools.

After Ford scurried off to locate more Edison memorabelia, Mr. Edison and I set of on an adventure with the owner of the local Lincoln dealership. He chauffeured us along the newly paved Tamiami Trail to Naples[136] where the pavement temporarily ended. The town was even less developed than Fort Myers was twenty years ago. There was a lot of swamp and a lot of alligators. The sole industry was citrus. As we toured the area we could hear the lively whistle of the Orange Blossom Express as it puffed north from the Naples Depot loaded with oranges and grapefruit..

The next morning we continued south through Marco and out onto a point of land to the village of Caxambas. It was here that Baron Collier[137] picked us up in his beautiful yacht *Volemia* and took us through the Ten Thousand Islands to Everglades City, a new development by a rich New York advertising tycoon. The ride was glorious. Mrs. Collier, a naturalist herself, identified all the birds and wildlife we saw on route.

On the way home, Theodore noticed a wounded heron that had a broken bill. We stopped and he performed miraculous surgery on the bird and let it fly away, happily, I hoped.

In December 1925, Fort Myers was completing plans for an airport just south of the city on the Tamiami Trail. It would be a stop on the air route from Tampa to Miami. We were told the flight would take an hour and a half and cost $32.50. The cost of a bus over over the same route to Miami was $20.

Fort Myers was modernizing rapidly.

The most difficult husband in America

I was shocked beyond belief when I picked up my copy of the July 1925 issue *Collier's Weekly*[138] and read the headline declaring Mr. Edison to be the most difficult husband in America. About a month earlier I had been interviewed by *Collier* editors Conan and Weir and had spilled my heart out. I told them that I had dedicated my life to this great man and thought it worth my effort a thousand times over. Certainly he had few real friends. No, he didn't really have any hobbies. And yes, his work was his first love.

Yes, he was stubborn, particularly with his first three children with whom he absolutely failed, in spite of my efforts to intervene on their behalf. He never had a relationship with any of them, except for the scant year of two with Marion after his wife, Mary, died. The one consistent thing he did do for his children was minimally support them financially when he refused to let them use their "Edison" name in their unpredictable business ventures. Mr. Edison felt that any use of his name by others would corrupt it and his empire would crumble in a pile of rubble.

His children by our marriage I saw as considerably different, thanks to my maternal instincts, my greater age and maturity and their father's less stressful work years. He found time to be with them on occasion and play educational games with them. He was teasingly affectionate at times, but then distantly present and unapproachable.

All of the above may be true but I didn't want to dwell on the negative aspects of my husband. His great strength was his genius. His genius made him who he was. He had little control over how he was created by God. He was a driven man who was compelled to create. He was loved and respected by the world for the things he did to change and improve our lives. I strongly believed that my place in his world was to love and defend the man who accomplished all his marvels.

I was comforted by remembering the New York *Times* headline: The Most Popular Man in America."

Marion returns to America

We received a very heartening letter during Christmas of 1924. "I have decided to come home," Marion wrote. "Your encouragement and expressions of love for me have been very welcoming. I am curious to see my brothers and sister and meet their spouses."

She wrote to her father. "It is a great trial that I cannot speak with you. I cannot help but remember when I *could* talk with you. I often remember you reading *Evangeline* to me as I sat in your lap."

On February 25, 1925, after more than thirty years in Europe, Marion returned, first of all to Canada, to visit her mother Mary's sister, Alice Stilwell Holzer, in Hamilton, Ontario. They hadn't seen each other for thirty or so years. Mrs. Holzer had taken the responsibility of caring for Marion and her two younger brothers immediately after their mother died. They had a tearful reunion which turned out to be their last. Mrs. Holzer would die less than a year after Mr. Edison passed away in 1931.

Marion arrived at Glenmont a month later. She and I quickly found common ground as adults during the few days before her party. Our seven-year age gap was now insignificant -- we were both in the fifth decade of our lives! I arranged a lavish family welcoming party for Marion. Theodore's wedding was scheduled for two days later. We did not want to dilute either event by celebrating it on the same day. I made Mr. Edison promise he would be at both events.

Four of our children came with their spouses: Tom and Beatrice, William and Blanche, Charles and Carolyn, as well as Madeleine and John Sloane and they were accompanied by my three grandchildren, Thomas, John and two-year-old Peter, all with "Edison" as their middle names. Theodore came with his fiancée, Anna.

If age difference were to matter at all at this time, it would have been between Marion, 52, with no children, and Madeleine, 37, with three children. Marion focused instead on her three Sloane nephews. It was obvious she loved children and they responded to her well.

The 78-year-old patriarch of this considerable family arrived a bit late but he was in good spirits. He surveyed the clan and then made a point to personally speak with each of them.

For Marion, the reunion was momentous. Most of her memories of her father went back to her pre-teens. There was but one time when she saw him in between and that was when the family met with her in Europe fifteen years earlier.

The man had aged. He had slowed down. He was portly, although still handsome and certainly dignified. She couldn't help but hug him, and when she pulled away, she was teary. Here was the man she knew best when he was a young man, when they traveled together to shows and dined with him in Delmonico's and bought his cigars for him. Now he was an old man.

But age had caught up with the whole family. I was older. All her siblings were older. Everything had changed in her absence.

All of us had expected Papa to make a speech, but that didn't happen. It was Marion, the elderest child who decided to speak to everyone.

"I am overwhelmed by what has happened here in my long absence," she began. "I am struck by what I have missed. It has been wonderful to begin to get to know you all again. I truly regret having deserted you. I look back at my life in

Europe and I ask myself what do I have? What did I bring back with me? What do I have to contribute to this wonderful family? What do I have to give to this family?

"The one person who has gone far out of her way to keep in touch with me over the years and I'm sure with each of you also, has been Mama."

A rousing cheer erupted -- for me!

"She supplied the love and, if I may say it, Papa supplied the money that kept us from drowning in our own mistakes. All of us have made mistakes, but somehow we have overcome them. Surviving the 'Edison' name alone has been our greatest hurdle, I think. We have a great Papa who didn't ask for fame and fortune, he simply did what he was compelled to do, what he was driven to do, what no other man in this world has ever accomplished. The world loves him. We love him. And we have all pined to be closer to him. But it wasn't his fault he was at arm's length. He was driven by demons that are foreign to most other men.

"Papa and Mama. We love you and thank you for all you were able to do for us in this difficult life. Amen."

Again there was applause, even Papa, although I don't know how much he heard.

Marion's speech generated a bit of embarrassment here and there. We were all aware of our successes and our failures. But this was life, and we were gathered here today to share our belonging to this family -- the Edison family -- for better or worse.

Marion spent a week with Mr. Edison and me. I was happy to see the two of them spend time alone together. Near the end of her visit we three drove north and investigated properties in Connecticut. He bought her a beautiful farm in the countryside of Norwalk. It was there Marion made her home, surrounded by nature and living on a decent monthly pension from her Papa -- his way of showing his love to his oldest child.

Two days after Marion's welcome, April 25, we regrouped. The simple wedding was held at Glenmont. Both Anna and Theodore demanded simplicity and limited it to a few friends and family.

Immediately after the ceremony they left for Maine in Anna's motor car with Anna at the wheel. Arriving late in the night, they spent their first night of marriage camping on a deserted beach near Kennebunkport. The next day they took the ferry over to Monhegan Island where they spent a week in a cabin enjoying the solitude.

In the days following, they moved back to an apartment in West Orange. Anna continued her pre-med studies at Harvard and Theodore was appointed director of research and engineering at his father's business.

Chapter Twenty-Nine

1926 - 1928

Spring training

We escaped to Fort Myers for our fortieth wedding anniversary while Mr. Edison was still in a funk over the economic depression. Charles had written me about his failure of confidence in his father in running the businesses in such bad times. He felt he could no longer fall back on his father's wise counsel because the management of the business was becoming more complicated and beyond his comprehension. Charles said the business was now on his shoulders alone and that provoked his father's anxiety.

Arriving at the train station in Fort Myers, our family was met by the usual large and friendly gathering of well-wishers, an event that cheered my husband at least temporarily.

With us also were two of Madeleine's three sons, Ted nine and Jack seven. Meeting us also was a local Boy Scout, Bob Halgrim, who, at Madeleine's suggestion, I had hired to provide the boys with a creative and enjoyable variety of activities during their visit, such as fishing, canoeing, sailing, swimming, life-saving techniques in the pool and exploring nature in the Fort Myers area. This high-school senior was given the unusual responsibility of disciplining the boys as he saw fit. It was not an easy task -- until he gained their respect. Madeleine arrived a couple weeks later with her youngest, Peter, who was only two. As it turned out, Bob was so effective with her boys Madeleine hired him for the summer and he returned with them to New Jersey.

The "Edison Pioneers," a group of early Edison employees, now friends, had been meeting annually for a number of years on Mr. Edison's February 11 birthday. But the "old man" was not able to attend this year's gathering at the Hotel Astor in New York. In his absence, *all* of his children except William attended the event as guests of honor. I was immensely heartened by my children's rush to please their father and his closest work buddies.

The Fort Myers *Press* took advantage of Mr. Edison's seventy-seventh birthday and was permitted to interview him on a number of subjects. At this time Henry Ford was on a crusade to rid the country of jazz music and the foxtrot and replace it with "old-fashioned" dances. Mr. Edison commented that the idea was foolish and it would never succeed. And on dancing in general, an activity for which he had no enthusiasm, he commented, "If a chimpanzee had a sense of ryhthm, he would dance himself to death."

The Philadelphia Athletics were at Terry Park for spring training and Mr. Edison decided he wanted to go to a ball game and meet their manager Connie Mack.[139] They met and Mr. Edison, dressed in his standard black suit and straw hat, was handed a bat. After two strikes he "swang" and slammed the ball into the outfield. At this performance Mack offered Mr. Edison a contract to play regularly. Mack then gave him a tour of the fairgrounds where, coincidently, the first annual County Fair was taking place.

In the meantime, I was at a luncheon downtown at the Royal Palm Hotel. I was summoned to the phone where I was told my oldest grandchild Ted had been run over by our chauffeur. Madeleine had not yet arrived from the north so I felt responsbile. I rushed back to the lodge and was greatly relieved to see that Ted had only a scratch on his head and a couple bruises elsewhere.

Charles is named president

Six months after Mr. Edison knocked Kid Gleason's baseball into the outfield, he stepped down from Edison, Inc. He appointed Charles president of his empire in August 1926. Mr. Edison remained company chairman but, in reality, it was an honorary position.

The effect was twofold. Mr. Edison would still have full control of the use of his name and his public image, playing to the press with his country-boy, homespun, philosophical comments on every subject the reader-conscious press posed.

Secondly was his presence in the laboratory where he elected to continue working. Lab assistants were accustomed to having the Old Man working side-by-side with them. That was the way it had always been.

Ford removes the Fort Myers lab

Disassembling the original laboratory building and shipping it to Ford's Greenfield Village in Dearborn, Michigan had already been accomplished this year when the Fort Myers Chamber of Commerce belatedly expressed an interest in moving and preserving the historical lab to a location within the town. They said it had been of historical interest in the town for forty-one years and it should remain in town.

I agreed with the Chamber. Fort Myers and this lab was where my husband did much of his work. Why shouldn't it be left here and become part of the town's legacy? But it was far too late.

Mr. Edison confirmed to the Chamber that this plan had been part of a long-time agreement with Mr. Ford along with the original Menlo Park laboratory. But the town persisted, writing to Ford himself telling him of the town's wishes. But Ford replied that the building parts and contents had already arrived and plans for its erection and preservation were already complete, noting that Fort Myers did not have any such detailed plans.

It was apparent the inventor no longer looked at Fort Myers as his workplace. At age seventy-eight, his "jungle" was now reserved for relaxation at fishing and boating.

He didn't anticipate another calling that was about to take place.

Celebrations

Although he had missed the three previous gatherings of the Edison Pioneers, he did attend the celebration for his octogenarian year on February 11, 1927 by delaying his annual voyage south. They met at the Robert Treat Hotel in Newark. His good friends Ford and Firestone were also present.

Our family left for Fort Myers eight days later and were greeted at the train station by Mr. Edison's long-time assistant, Fred Ott in his Ford flivver.[140]

We celebrated our forty-first wedding anniversary two days early on February 24 by attending the Arcade Theater to see Harold Lloyd star in "The Freshman."

At my arrangement that week, we accompanied about 150 orphan children from Arcadia. We met the train along with the Fort Myers band and groups from neighborhood churches and civic associations. We all went over to Terry Park and watched the vaudville performance of the Johnny Jones Show.

Mr. Edison then brought all the orphans over to Seminole Lodge for a tour, home-made ice cream and a swim in our pool. He also joked and played with a group of Johnny Jones Show adult little people.

In March, we hosted members of the Philadelphia Athletics at Seminole Lodge. I called it the largest party Mr. Edison ever hosted. He served his cigars along with fruit punch and, of course, the banter of his "at bat" grew spontaneously into some kind of a World Series star performance, with a good deal of laughter.

The quest for rubber continues

From 1924 on, the cost of rubber continually increased for several reasons. Demand was the most obvious reason; a British-Dutch cartel that controlled world rubber production threatened to curb the supply; the British Rubber Restriction Act, that became effective in 1922, cut rubber production and doubled the cost; the vast rubber plantations of southeast Asia came under the control of the Japanese before World War II; and, in 1925 when balloon tires were introduced, air tubes in the tires used additional rubber.

The United States in the mid-1920s was using as much as seventy percent of the entire world's rubber supply.

Henry Ford pleaded with Mr. Edison to get cracking and do something about either creating a domestic supply of rubber or finding a substitute. Mr. Edison, at age eighty said, "I will -- someday."

So much for relaxation at fishing and boating.

My husband surprised me once again. He went back to work by organizing the Edison Botanic Research Corporation in 1927. Its challenge was to do just as Ford had requested. All talk, dreams and thoughts in the Edison family turned to rubber. He collected an extensive library on the subject covering four centuries, from when the Spanish first brought balls of natural rubber to the Old World. He made detailed studies of early attempts to synthesize rubber. He sent scientists out to many countries, as well as Florida itself, charged with collecting samples of latex-bearing plants.

He now planned to do all his rubber research in Fort Myers. Ford had taken away his old lab. He needed a new lab. He drew up new lab specifications.

But, partly because taking on this new challenge and overworking an old body, my husband became sick, suffering from uremia, yet he continued working toward a solution unabated. He commented to Madeleine in 1928, "It takes ten years to study one family of plants, and here I am racing with the angel of death all the time."[141]

Tamiami Trail completed

One month before our family arrived in Fort Myers, Mr. Edison sent an entire railroad car of supplies, equipment and tradesmen to replace the original laboratory that he had given to Ford. It was built anew and surrounded by barbed wire to give the impression that high-security work was under way within. Fred Ott supervised the operation. With him was the head of the West Orange botanical laboratory and seven more chemists and aids.

All was ready when he arrived. Greeted by fifteen hundred townspeople at the train station, he told them he was here to work on his rubber experiments and nothing else.

He was excited. He thought of this as a new beginning -- as it was more than a half century ago in his Menlo Park laboratory.

But Mr. Edison was not feeling well. I answered for him when the press asked. I told them he was troubled by old-fashioned dyspepsia and I had placed him on a milk diet.

We had with us this trip Mr. Edison's cousin, Edith Potter, and my sister-in-law Florence Miller with her two children, Nancy, five, and Stuart, two. For help we had two servants, our regular maid, Laura, and our cook, Gracie, who was thrilled with the new kitchen appliances that had been installed since her last visit.

The first thing Mr. Edison did was inspect his new laboratory. Then he organized his staff so they could begin working on plant specimens. He had a full contingent of staff, trained, experienced, ready and eager to set to work.

The recreational director for the city thought it would be nice to sponsor a town-wide birthday party for Mr. Edison that would be held in the municipal auditoruium. I convinced the inventor that he should attend although he referred to the idea as "poppycock."

Charles Lindbergh had been invited for the February 11 birthday event. The now world-famous flier had completed his trans-Atlantic flight the previous May 21 and was still collecting alcolades by hopping around the world. His present schedule was through South America and the Caribbean countries, arriving in Havana on February 8 -- just a two-hour flight away from us.

I agreed to send the cable invitation to San Juan and a response came on February 3. Mr. Lindbergh apologized and said the earliest he could arrive would be two days after the party. But he sent his "admiration and best wishes" to my husband.

His flight path on the thirteenth would have sent his plane over Fort Myers on his way to St. Louis by way of Cedar Key. But, none of us saw or heard a plane fly over.

Harvey Firestone was at the party. He asked Mr. Edison about his loss of flesh. His milk diet had caused him to lose about forty pounds. Mr. Edison answered his skinny friend, "You're no fatty yourself!"

We celebrated our forty-second anniversary with the Fords and Florence Miller. We went to the County Fair and toured the events with the police chief. During our tour we ran into Conrad Menge, brother of Captain Fred Menge. Conrad joined the tour and suggested they stop at the "flea circus." We did. A man appeared with a flea and hitched it up to a wagon the size of a fingernail and the flea pulled it! Mr. Ford got the biggest kick out of that flea![142]

On April 5 we made our first trip across the completed Tamiami Trail to meet Harvey Firestone in Miami. Their discussion was rubber. Before the end of the month I made that same trip again with Mrs. Clarence Chadwick to attend a state beautification meeting. Both of us spoke on the beautification of the Tamiami Trail in particular. While we were in Miami, my husband was in Everglades City to congratulate the recently named Seminole chief, Josie Billy. We all made very good use of that new road.

We held our first open house to the public at Seminole Lodge in celebrattion of the Tamiami Trail opening. We each went about our own business and let the public do what they might. But interviews with either of us was prohibited.

It was a very exciting season, the longest yet. We left for home on June 12. As we boarded the train in the midst of a hundred or so well-wishers, Mr. Edison joshed with the crowd saying, "I don't want to leave, but she makes me," and then pointed to me.

Appreciation to a high school senior

Alvin Lampp was a Fort Myers high school senior when he worked one summer for the inventor-turned-botanist. His job at the new Fort Myers lab was to test specific plants for rubber content following specific instructions from Mr. Edison. There were some twenty plants in each of 500 plots from which he took clippings for testing. Each of the 10,000 plants was numbered and identified. It was drudge work, but young Lampp was tireless and Mr. Edison remembered him. When he graduated, I cornered him and presented him with an autographed set of Mr. Edison's biography.[143]

The Lewis Miller Centenary took place at Chautauqua on July 24. I could not believe my father had been born a century earlier. Mr. Edison and I and the entire Miller family attended. I was still a little uneasy about our relationships with the Vincents. Firstly for breaking my engagement with George Vincent forty-three years ago and, secondly, the silly, but important to the men, of whether it was the bishop or my father who *first* came up with the idea for Chautauqua. I never understood why they couldn't take joint credit.

But Bishop Vincent had given a moving tribute to my brother Thede who died so young in the Spanish-American war, and the same with his eulogy to my father at his funeral in 1899.

Leading up to what I considered this momentous event, I became worried over who of Chautauqua importance would be attending and speaking. I approached Arthur Bestor, president of the institution, and suggested inviting specific colleagues of my father's whom I would like, but Bestor failed in getting them to accept. It sent me into a deep depression.

Then I got hold of myself and I invited my friends -- the Fords, the Firestones, the Ochs and Sperrys, and Anna Studebaker Carlisle from Akron, all of whom knew my father and agreed to attend and some of whom spoke.

The event was a grand success. The speeches did my father honorable. The symphony orchestra, conducted by Albert Strossel, played a wide range of artists, including Berlioz, Wagner, Debussy, Gluck, Brahms and Handel.

Father's children and the grandchildren were given a grand reception at the Bird and Tree Club. This was where I, their "Auntie Ga," had spent many hours with each of them while wandering Chautauqua's rustic areas searching out the beautiful gifts nature had to offer.

Chautauqua had come a long way in its twenty-five years since the men founded it. By 1928, more than twenty spin-off Chautauquas dotted the country, and each of these had dozens of smaller tent assemblies that spread my father's vision. I was very proud to have been brought up in this heritage.[144]

Ford's Greenfield Village

In October Mr. Edison and I traveled to Dearborn, Michigan to visit Henry Ford's new museum of the history of American invention and industry, named Greenfield Village. There we saw his historic laboratories imported from Menlo Park and Fort Myers. It was a permanent monument to Mr. Edison's life work. Mr. Ford, the very man who once publicly debunked much of written history as nonsense was now validating the past with physical evidence.

Ford had bought a vast spread of rural land and peppered it with 19th Century farms, churches, taverns and farmhouses. It was a huge museum of the industrial revolution from giant locomotives to antique looms and farm equipment from the Puritans through the 1800s.

But hovering over all of this was the man the industrialist most revered, Thomas Edison. Ford was driven to preserve my husband's legacy *in total*. In addition to the laboratory structures, he had gathered up every invention, tool, machine, vehicle, hammer, chemical, generator, electric lamp, work-bench, library that Mr. Edison had ever touched. He toured the countryside looking for any relics that the inventor had sold, cast aside or given away that he could find. The search was exhaustive. Ford spent about $3 million in this undertaking for the Edison displays alone and $10 million in 1929 dollars overall on Greenfield Village.

We walked the grounds and much of it seemed weirdly familiar. Mr. Edison was taken aback. To see all his life, including an exact replica of Menlo Park before him at one time was overwhelming.

The Lights Golden Jubilee was scheduled to open on October 21, 1929. Ford raced to complete his Greenfield Village site to coincide with the Jubilee.

Congressional medal

The governments of Chile, Russia, Japan and others had honored Mr. Edison for all his contributions to mankind over the years, but the United States had done nothing. True, he had been given personal credit by the President Roosevelt for having served in the Naval Research Laboratory, and he had been offered a Distinguished Service Medal which he had refused. But there had never been an overall award from his own country for his considerable inventive genius.

At the suggestion of one of Mr. Edison's industrial friends to Andrew Mellon, then secretary of the treasury, Mr. Mellon went to Congress and suggested they correct this unpardonable oversight. Congress took action and, by resolution on May 21, 1928, Edison was awarded the Congressional Medal of Honor. Andrew Mellon himself visited the "Wizard" at his West Orange laboratory and made the presentation. About the same time, President Coolidge paid honor to the "wizard of electricity" during a radio address that marked the forty-ninth anniversary of the first practical incandescent lamp.

These events left Mr. Edison appropriately recognized by his government. His modest comment was, "I was glad to have served my country."

Chapter Thirty

1929-1930

Celebrity 82nd birthday party

During the fall of the previous year, without Mr. Edison's knowledge, I had a small private office for my husband constructed on the site of the original laboratory that had been shipped to Michigan. It was directly behind the house and just perfect for his ramblings at night.

It was located in a lovely spot next to the garden surrounded with scarlet bougainvillea. A trellis in the midst was covered with blooms and ivy. A number of small beds of shrubs and perennials completed the setting and made the area quite inviting.

The little office was organized inside with his desk, chair and library of botanic and chemical subjects. It had a front porch with two rocking chairs. Greatly surprised when he first first saw my effort, he found it useful to meeting with the press that could gather in a sem-circle front of the porch. His new botanic research lab, now fully fitted out on the opposite side of McGregor Boulevard, was just the right distance for his visits during the day.

We arrived in mid-January to the regular crowd of greeters. My husband seemed to be in good health which I attributed to the removal of his teeth in early fall. And he had now regained his weight, thanks to giving up his milk diet.

President-elect Herbert Hoover was on the the east coast at Belle Isle in Miami. Word was out that Mr. Hoover planned to visit Mr. Edison on his 82nd birthday. My husband was asked if he was going to Miami to visit with Mr. Hoover. His reply was, "Hell, no. He can come visit me."

The press expected Mr. Hoover to come to Fort Myers by way of the newly paved Tamiami Trail. To everyone's surprise, however, Mr. Hoover arrived on his yacht *Saunterer*, sailed up the Calhoosahatchie, anchored in deep water and took a tender that tied up at Mr. Edison's pier. My husband greeted Mr. Hoover with "Hello, fisherman." Mr. Hoover remained in the area for a few days, fishing from the *Saunterer*, catching two sailfish much to his delight.

The President-elect then joined Henry Ford and Harvey Firestone who arrived for the birthday celebration. With all these celebrities present, Seminole Lodge was packed with press arrivals from far and wide.

But then the press was ejected from the area and six autos arrived to carry the birthday celebrities through downtown Fort Myers. Town officials rode in the first car. The second car carried Edison, Hoover, Firestone and Ford with the Secret Service close on their tail. Then came Mrs. Hoover, myself and the Hoover's son.

The tour passed through Edison Park, drove by the recently completed Edison Park School, lined with students, and continued south on Cleveland Avenue and zig-zagged through other streets of town including Evans Avenue where Negro students lined the street. The parade finally went through the business district to Broadway and Main Street to MacGregor Boulevard and back to Seminole Lodge.

That evening, through the wonders of radio, Mr. Edison gave a 100-word address to the nation after being introduced by our son Charles who was still in West Orange. The radio address was simultaneously heard also from speakers at the Fort Myers municipal auditorium to a group of about two hundred and fifty.

Among the letters of congratulations was one from widow Lillian Gilliland expressing her thoughts. Pleasant memories of her years of kindness and generosity to me flooded back. I immediately replied with my gratitude for her good friendship.

The next day I had the three celebrity's wives join me at a meeting of the Women's Community Club downtown.

Some days later Mr. Edison went fishing with his friend Captain E.L Evans. My husband snagged a very large tarpon that made several high jumps out of the water, but then dove under the boat and tangled the line in the propeller.

I have to say that I had some success fishing that day also. While out in the Gulf I hooked and, with a good deal of help, landed a 100-pound stingray.

The night before we left for home, the Roundtable which usually met at Seminole Lodge, met this night at the Arcade Theater for a farewell party. I was pleased that my brother, John Miller, went out of his way to be present.

Light's Golden Jubilee

The Light's Golden Jubilee, the fiftieth anniversary of the invention of my husband's light bulb, opened at Henry Ford's Greenfield Village in Dearborn on Monday, October 21, 1929.

General Electric Company, which had absorbed the Edison original electric-light businesses years earlier, recognized the promotional value of tying their company with the name Edison. They had planned to have their celebration at GE head-quarters in Schenectady and have Mr. Edison light a lamp to set off the company's exposition.

The trouble was, my husband was never consulted. When an old friend relayed this information, his former boss, Mr. Edison, saw no reason why he should give free advertising to General Electric and commercialize his name. Edison was furious and vowed to show GE a thing or two and would have nothing to do with the company. GE appealed to both my husband and Mr. Ford to accept the GE celebration and Schenectady site, but both men were adamant. It would be held in Dearborn.

I had always been skeptical of Ford's Greenfield project. It seemed to be one of his gigantic publicity stunts. Both Madeleine and I believed Ford was also taking advantage of the elderly Mr. Edison by Ford's instinct for self promotion and aggrandizement. I thought back to my husband's "camping" trips and saw Ford and Firestone as shrewd men taking advantage of my husband's name for press coverage. I have to admit I enjoyed the Ford family's comfortable, indeed, luxurious style of living, but it was not my way. His endless display of their possessions were forever around us. I found this unbecoming. Money can't buy everything. It was my wish that Mr. Ford would show his spiritual side.

I couldn't influence my husband either. He didn't care what I said in this regard. Ford was his friend and he didn't mind being "used" by him.

We had been staying at the Ford mansion, Fair Lane, the weekend before the Jubilee began. Monday the twenty-first began cold, wet and dreary. Mr. Edison arrived by wood-burning train to the replica Smith Street station. With us were President and Mrs. Hoover and the Fords. Then some 500 "dignitaries," under the watch of the press, toured the Greenfield Village buildings through muddy streets in covered, horse-drawn carriages.

In the evening we had a formal candle-light dinner in the still-unfinished Independence Hall replica. All three of my children were present with their spouses, but Marion, Tom and William were no-shows. Among the guests were John D. Rockefeller, Charles Schwab, Marie Curie, Adolph Ochs, George Eastman, Walter Chrysler, Will Rogers and Julius Rosenwald. The event was broadcast internationally by radio with a special connection to Albert Einstein who cautiously praised Mr. Edison -- cautiously, because my husband was not in his league as a scientist.

The ultimate deification of my husband came after dinner when he, Ford and President Hoover visited the candle-lit Menlo Park laboratory and climbed the stairs to the second floor. There, at a table, sat Francis Jehl, who was just a lad when he worked for the Wizard but who was now on Ford's payroll. He sat among all the bottles and fixtures of the original lab.

The very select group watched Jehl create a dramatic and lengthy preamble, while an announcer in the background broadcast to the world in a hushed, suspenseful whisper the details of the event. An impatient Mr. Edison broke the near silence in his startlingly loud voice, "Light 'er up, Francis. Light 'er up."

Jehl finally reenacted the lighting with a model of the original Edison lamp and great applause erupted from the crowd in the Independence Hall where I was listening and, it was assumed, the world listened as well.

As millions of listeners thrilled at this great moment, it seemed to me that *everything* was right with the world.

But was it? The Old Man found the excitement very tiring. The little group returned to Independence Hall where President Hoover was to make the principle address. I met Mr. Edison just outside the door of the hall where he told me "I won't go in!" He was weak. With help, we moved him to a chair where he broke down and wept -- totally exhausted. He was brought some warm milk and he recovered a bit, able now to enter the hall and take his seat at the place of honor.

Messages from around the world were read and President Hoover made his speech, but my Dearie heard none of this as he sat slumped in his chair, absent of color, as pale as death. I was truly frightened that my husband was dying on the spot and wanted him out of the place.

I motioned to the President's physician and he and others helped my ailing man to a room adjacent to the hall where he reclined on a couch, eyes closed, breathing faintly. The doctor gave him some medication and he was carried on a stretcher to Mr. Ford's residence where we remained for several days as he recovered and the Stock Market crumbled.

When he did recover, he sat up and said, "I'm tired of all this glory. I want to get back to work."

The 1929 stock market crash

The intoxication of the Roaring Twenties came to an abrupt end. It seemed that *nothing* was right with the world. The Dow Jones Industrial Average had peaked at 381.17 on September 3 and on October 24, "Black Thursday," the market lost eleven percent of its value. Panic followed throughout the industrial world. For days, more and more investors deserted the market sending it to a loss of thirteen more percent. From there it fell and fell further.

At the same time, Mr. Edison's managers were still in the process of shutting down all Edison domestic phonograph operations. Among the last disc records released was Frankie Marvin's new hit, "She's Old and Bend (But She Just Keeps Hoofin' Along)."

In Fort Myers, five freight cars packed with goldenrod arrived for processing. My husband believed he could now make rubber that was acceptable to industry. His search for rubber had now ended. He was able to create one hundred pounds of rubber from one acre of goldenrod. After more than ten years of experimentation, Mr. Edison commented, "Job had no idea of what real patience was."

My husband seemed to spring back to life once we were back in the peace and quiet of Glenmont. But after a few days Mr. Edison became restless and suggested we hold Christmas in Fort Myers this year.

We were on the train once again and arrived at Seminole Lodge on December 5. As it turned out, we spent more than six months there, our longest visit and Mr. Edison's last.

Unlike Christmas Day at home, the day here was quiet with only a few guests for dinner. We had a tabletop tree with tinsel and a few colored balls. While the rest of us had the traditional menu, Mr. Edison was back on his milk diet exclusively. We received presents from people we knew and from people we did not know -- gifts from clothiers, shoemakers, candle makers, tobacco barons and book publishers.

Back home in Glenmont, Charles reported his siblings celebrated Christmas with the usual huge tree and, of course, Edison colored lights. I called home and had a nice chat with everyone. This brought on mixed feelings about being so far away from my family on this particular day.

Harvey Firestone visited us after the holiday and said he was still using imported rubber but he was certain that within the next decade thousands of acres of Florida land would be devoted to raising one of Mr. Edison's plants and that would make domestic rubber economically feasible.

It was soon after the new year that I decided to give my own interview to *American Magazine*, a popular family publication in which I had confidence of a fair story. I asked my husband to sit with me and the journalist. I gave her a rather intimate picture of how I understood Mr. Edison thought and worked. I explained how he had always been stoic about his lack of hearing and it bothered him that he was unable to enjoy his favorite song, *I'll Take You Home Again, Kathleen*.

Then Mr. Edison interrupted and said how "talkies" really spoiled the movies. He said acting had disappeared from the screen and how he would like to see Mary Pickford or Clara Bow once again in silent pictures. He said moviemakers now concentrate on the voice rather than the acting.

I thought the interview went well and the published story met our approval.

Later in January some Navy pilots at the Naval Air Station in Pensacola flew into Fort Myers airport and joined us for dinner. The next day they provided us with air stunts directly over Seminole Lodge. One of these was called a "knee hang." The entire show certainly tested our ability to crank our stiff necks skyward for such a long time.

Mr. Edison's eighty-third birthday brought Ford and Firestone once again to our door. The day started with a press interview. Twenty-five reporters and photographers gathered. I have a very nice photo of the three men sitting on the steps together outside the Botanic Laboratory.

We then went to the dedication of a memorial plaque in Evans Park honoring both of us. It included our images! Speeches were made and I could truly feel the town's affection for both of us in the midst of the reported two thousand residents around us.

Mr. Firestone offered to take me up in his big tri-engine, all metal airplane. Mr. Edison was not interested. It was my very first flight and after suppressing my initial fear I enjoyed myself. He then offered flights to the general public at two dollars each. Fifty people took advantage of his offer.

Charles reported that he was taking his vacation in Arizona rather than Florida this year. He acknowledged that he would have enjoyed fishing, the beach and getting a tan, but he felt he wouldn't get any exercise. He was apologetic. He needed a break from Edison, Inc. where he had been phasing out the phonograph and radio businesses and the distressing job of letting employees go at such a terrible economic time.

Charles wrote, "The old expense guillotine is running red with gore and by the time you get back . . . I will effect a balancing of receipts. . ."

We left for home on June 11, 1930.

I watch over Mr. Edison

During his last two years, Mr. Edison spend less and less time in his laboratory. It seemed to me that his lab was the only interest that kept him alive. Milk was his only food that his perennially troublesome stomach accepted. He lingered in bed later and later into the mornings and sat in his rocker at home. His contact with his workers continued as they came to the house with reports on his goldenrod rubber experiments. I watched over him like an eagle with its eaglets. We took daily rides together over the country roads of New Jersey.

He tried to work or read in his office upstairs and I sat by him doing my domestic, religious and social work. We both had telephones and a board of buttons to call various servants for each of our needs.

Colonel Charles Lindbergh called and said he was in town. My husband insisted we visit Newark Airport to see the pilot. There, the inventor conferred with the pilot on certain problems on landing and takeoff. One particular problem was fog. Edison saw that some means must be developed in order for pilots to see through fog and low-lying clouds.

His body may have failed him, but my Dearie's mind was as active as ever. How very frustrating it was, he said, to be unable to continue as an active doer.

In spite of his infirmities, just after the first of the year he filed his 1,093rd patent application. It was his last. It was for a component in an electroplating process.

Chapter Thirty-One

1931

Edison's fourth grandson is born

Madeleine was still in the hospital after giving birth to her fourth son on January 8, when she received a congratulatory telegram from her father with umpteen suggestions for names. He listed Percy, Victor, Claude and Clarence, "or something unusual," but the name Madeleine and John had chosen, Michael, was not among them. Madeleine was willing to compromise. She settled on Michael Nicholas Samuel Edison after her grandfather Samuel. Mr. Edison found that to be just fine.

Mr. Edison's last trip to Florida

The baby now safely in the world, we left for Florida on January 20. I suspected this would be Mr. Edison's last trip, although I had thought the same in other years. Things were different this year. My Dearie did not immediately visit his adored new rubber laboratory. In fact he didn't visit the lab or appear in public until his 84th birthday which had bubbled up into something of a another national holiday.

The birthday event this year was the dedication of the new concrete bridge over the Caloosahatchie that replaced the 1924 wooden version that was totally inadequate.

He slept late on his birthday, but he rose in time to venture out into the world. We took an open limousine to his only scheduled appointment, the dedication of the bridge that had been named after him. Surrounded by the governor, the mayor and other officials and the press, he cut the ribbon with a giant pair of shears followed by a cheer from everyone. He didn't speak, but he did smile and wave his favorite straw hat.

Back at Seminole Lodge and his little office building, he answered questions from the press. One question concerned unemployment during the deep depression the country was experiencing. He answered, "The question is several sizes too large for me." What do you think of sound movies? "I never heard one."[145] Einstein's theory? "I don't understand it."

That night he met in his office with Harvey Firestone. A brief newsreel was taped in which Mr. Edison gave answers to a number of questions, ending with, "How does it feel to be eighty-four years old?"

"Well, he answered, "it feels very fine to be eighty-four years of age, if you don't have anything the matter with you. But I have a little trouble now and then, but that's because I'm getting old. But I've got a lot of ginger yet!"

He certainly did have ginger. During these last months he seemed to recover a bit and he returned to the laboratory to check on the status of the goldenrod experiments that were continuing with a full complement of chemists. He was also planning to build a botanical research facility on property in Georgia owned by Henry Ford. Mr. Edison believed, once again, he was on the verge of a breakthrough for producing a viable substitute for natural rubber.

Journalism students from the one of the local high schools approached me for an interview with my husband. I invited them to Seminole Lodge and gave them a tour, ending with a visit to the laboratory. There they faced the man they had been eager to meet. Mr. Edison had trouble hearing the young people's questions. I had to code him to understand.

One question from a serious female student asked, when would girls receive pay for technical work like the boys. Mr.

Edison answered, "That is hard to answer. But if education can be converted to finding a way to eliminate the drudgery of housework, you've gone a long way."

He answered a few of their serious questions, but then switched to telling them witty stories about his life and inventions which the young people found very amusing.

Mr. Edison had another chance to see Connie Mack and his Athletics playing at Terry Park. When we arrived, the game was in the third inning against the Boston Braves. Mr. Edison walked out onto the field, the players paused and the spectators rose to their feet and cheered. The Athletics won the game 3-2.

This happened also to be "Connie Mack Day" and it had brought the mayor of Fort Myers to the field. He gave a speech with a tribute to the team and a gift of a Panama hat to Mack.

In early June, Charles and Carolyn visited Seminole Lodge for a short vacation and to accompany us back to West Orange. We welcomed them at the train station. Charles enjoyed southwest Florida as much as his father and spent most of his visit on the Gulf with a guide fishing. Mr. Edison and I were out on a second boat the day Charles successfully hauled in three tarpon. Instead of being envious of his son this time, Mr. Edison simply urged his son on when the line tightened and Charles played it into the boat. Each of these was released, of course, saved for sport another day. The men already had their tarpon trophies.

We left for home in mid-June with my husband much healthier than when he arrived. Mr. Edison instructed his laboratory personnel to ship everything related to his rubber experiments back up North. Our family stood on the platform at the rear of the train and waved farewell to our many friends and neighbors.

Mr. Edison was soon back at his roll-top desk.

Mr. Edison holds his fourth grandson

Michael Edison Sloane was six months old by the time we returned from Florida and Madeleine and John brought their baby to us. For the first time Mr. Edison and I held our fourth grandson. It was a wonderful moment for each of us, my octogenarian seated, infant in his arms, beaming down on him. The baby reached out for a pencil hanging by a cord next to him, grabbed it and pulled the pencil toward him. "Bright boy," his ailing grandfather commented with a smile. This was the only time he would see the child.

This was Madeleine's fourth child, all boys, the oldest of whom was now sixteen. She would be our only child to bear us grandchildren.

Theodore starts his own business

Frail as he was, Mr. Edison still had a firm hand on his companies in his ninetieth decade. Theodore, in his fifth year as an Edison company man, was becoming more restless now with each day that passed. He told me he felt like a missing cog in the presence of his father and Charles. This I could understand. He was bored. He felt that any decision he made could be overridden by the other two. More and more often he left his office to work on inventions of his own that had nothing to with Edison companies. After all, he had joined his father's company originally out of loyalty to his older brother at a time when he thought the Old Man was backing off.

"I don't think I should be working here," Theodore told Charles. "My mind is more and more frequently elsewhere thinking of some rather radical ideas of my own which I am eager to try out."

With me as his secret mentor, Theodore plunged ahead on his own and rented a small office in East Orange close by his apartment. In early March he filed corporation papers under his name for a company called *Calibron Products, Inc.*, chartered to do general research and experimentation and at the same time offer engineering consulting services. The first product produced by Calibron was special graph paper for making perspective drawings.

Theodore had not yet told his father about his new venture, in spite of my telling him "the sooner the better."

Less than a week passed when the local newspaper discovered recent the public corporation filings. The headline across the top of the *Orange Currier* front page shouted, "Break in Ranks of Edison Clan."

Theodore responded to the paper, "This is not the first time that a member of the Edison family has helped to organize an outside venture. My interest in the new company does not affect my connection with Edison Industries." At the same time, he notified Charles that he was resigning as a director and as a member of the executive board, but he would continue at the laboratory only until a successor was found. He further wrote to Charles, "You will probably find that you have greater freedom of decisions if I am not around."

Charles was not surprised, and agreed that the change was probably for the best. The rest of the family was not surprised at the transition.

Theodore's delay in telling his father was undoubtedly his fear of being the recipient of his wrath as had happened with both Tom and William, and he pleaded with me to help convince Papa that, should Calibron fail, the "stigma" would reflect only on Theodore and not the Edison companies.

His wife Ann joined in on the effort, reminding me that "children with as forceful and distinct personalities and abilities, as your three, must fulfill their ambitions each in their own way."

We were in Florida while all this occurred, reported to me by my children as the situation developed,

Frankly, I was as fearful of Mr. Edison's wrath as my children were, so it was late May before I approached my Dearie. I told him the facts and then began to present all the arguments the family had accumulated.

"Billie, Billie, Billie," he began, perhaps lost in thought about his preparation of remarks he was about to wire to the National Electric Light Association in Atlantic City. In short, the aging patriarch simply waved his hand in dismissal. "Don't worry about such things," he said. "My children have done well."

Then, as I sat beside him, he turned to his microphone and spoke his words to the association: "My message to you is to be courageous. I have lived a long time. I have seen history repeat itself again and again. I have seen many depressions in business. Always, America has come out stronger and more prosperous. Be as brave as your fathers before you. Have faith. Go forward."

I reported this to Theodore. He was greatly relieved. He began full force inventing on his own.[146]

Mr. Edison's final experiment

As my husband's health began to seriously fail during his last two or three years, he finally took a greater interest in his health. His diet became his final experiment. For much of his life he had been troubled by diabetes and stomach problems and he had always read medical literature trying to understand his inner workings. His personal doctor, Hubert Howe, confirmed that Mr. Edison had "a profound knowledge of medicine." His interest in chemistry led him to an understanding of physiological chemistry and pharmacology. Following the teachings of Luigi Cornaro, author of *The Temperate Life*,[147] he had been experimenting with diet all his life and took the recommended treatments for his stomach problems. He said to Dr. Howe, "If I were to follow your advice and take all the drugs you suggest or all that the physician in you advise me to subscribe, I would become worse. The fact is my liver is out of order and my kidneys are not in just the condition they should be. I will remedy that very speedily. My cure will be a change in diet."

He discovered that milk relieved his gastric pain. He cut back on other foods and increased milk consumption. Finally, he gave up other foods altogether. For three years he consumed nothing but milk -- more than a pint of milk every three hours. In May, five months before he died, he was drinking seven to fourteen glasses of milk a day! Dr. Howe confirmed that milk was giving him the nutrients and fluids he needed. But, he lost strength and weight. The doctor then modified his diet to include some food. His diabetes was controlled by insulin.

Mr. Edison's physical activity involved moving from bed to chair to bed. I watched him deteriorate daily and he valiently consumed whatever it was at the moment he felt would extend his life.

Three weeks before his death, his doctor was distressed by the lack of improvement in his condition. First his eyesight failed rapidly; then his hearing became so bad that the unique timbre in my voice was the only sound he could recognize. I was beside him nearly full time and held his hand that now ceased communicating. I was well aware that my Dearie was dying. Then drowsiness gradually came on and he slipped into a coma.

We began to make detailed preparations for his funeral. All of us were fully aware, and in trepidation of, the public tributes that would be offered. Our family arrived from far and near. In the early morning of October 18, a major era passed away.

I was long braced for my Dearie's passing, but to have it actually happen still filled me with grief. I was alone with him at that moment and I sobbed uncontrollably. I held his cold hand, the intimate, living instrument through which we had communicated most clearly. My rock, my pillar of strength, my love of nearly a half century was gone from my life. How would this change my life that had been so tightly bound to his?

It was no secret to the outside world that Mr. Edison had been dying. Reporters had gathered in town on twenty-four hour alert. Cards, letters, telegrams, poems and other forms of sympathy arrived by the hundreds.

For two days, Mr. Edison's body lay in an open casket in the library at his laboratory. Thousands of mourners passed by him with at least one member of the family sitting alongside.

Even before his death, the newspaper tributes and stories of his unique life filled their pages. The National Broadcasting Service aired the memorial services and played his favorite songs.

President Hoover sent his wife; Harvey Firestone and Henry Ford and their wives stayed in upstairs rooms at Glenmont. An hour-long memorial service downstairs was broadcast up to their room.

Finally, at President Hoover's request, Americans were asked to shut off their lights at 10 PM to observe one minute of silence in respect to the "Inventor of the Age."

A private funeral

Three days later, Mr. Edison's body was returned to Glenmont for a family ceremony. I went down early and sat in quiet meditation with my husband. Charles had come even earlier and had rearranged the seating, placing me again in the first row with Theodore, Madeleine and him to my right. Tom, William and Marion he placed in the second row. But then I changed the seating order as the children filed in. Madeleine sat to my right with Theodore, Charles and Tom in the front row. In the second row I placed Marion, William, Blanche, Carolyn and Beatrice.

The service was led by Dr. Stephen J. Herben, pastor of our church where I had been an active member for many years. Dr. Lewis Perry, headmaster of Phillips Exeter Academy, read the Twenty-Third Psalm. Other readings and music followed.

We then went on to the interment as darkness began to fall. Dr. Herben read a brief poem. The coffin was gently lowered and each of us stepped forward and dropped a white rose into Mr. Edison's grave.

Thy will be done

Charles and Theodore were the two favored sons. They received 80 percent of Mr. Edison's estate -- some $12 million between them. They were also named co-executors for the balance of the estate with the power to distribute the balance among the remaining children. In addition, after returning from Florida on July 30, three months before he died, Mr. Edison composed a codicil. It stipulated that the other four children, Marion, Tom, William and Madeleine each receive $50,000 a year for life from shares of the Edison Portland Cement Company.

I received nothing, nor did I expect anything. I had already been adequately provided throughout my life with corporate shares and real estate that I was grateful to have Charles look after for me. I also had money from my father's estate.

William was the first to challenge his father's last wish. He was furious that his stepbrothers Charles and Theodore were the favored sons and received millions of dollars while he and his three other siblings received a mere pittance.[148] He threatened to sue and fight the structure of the estate as it was outlined in the will. He said it was prejudicial to him, Tom, Marion and Madeleine. Resentful as his three siblings were, they refused to fully back William. Theodore couldn't abide with the turmoil and resigned as co-executor dumping the problems into Charles' lap.

Inevitably, the content of the will was made public as were the internal family squabbles. Tom took the lead and went public, saying, "I loved my father as the dearest and most god-like parent a man could have, as a genius, with the world sharing my pride."

In the months that followed, Charles was able to halt William's threat to file suit. Charles told the New York *Times* that the deal between the siblings was an "agreement" and not a "settlement," implying we were still a tight family.

I was so proud of Charles and the way he accepted the responsibility thrust at him. He deftly tackled and resolved the problem under the threatening glare of his siblings.

When Charles showed William his carefully drawn proposal, William accepted it and said he was satisfied with his eventual share of the estate. How this was accomplished I was never told.

Chapter Thirty-Two
1932 - On

Life after death

As I write this now, in 1945, I am eighty wonderful years of age, just three years younger than my Dearie when he passed away fourteen years ago.

Contrary to some beliefs, we did find life after death. My routine of many years gradually melted into a life of my own that included my family more inclusively. It troubles me to say that we were all glad the "wrath of Papa" was gone, but certainly an undercurrent of various degrees of fear among us had evaporated. All seven of us discovered we now had the opportunity to develop new lives.

But first, we had to survive the seeming endless tidal wave of respectful, yet annoying, tributes that inescapably swirled around us. Newspapers, newreels and radio all gushed their praise of The Genius of Light, the Great Inspirer, the Conqueror of the Unknown, The Revolutionizer, the Foremost Among Creators, the man who was the personification of the power of human intelligence.

Adapting to the new life didn't happen overnight. Each of us had to re-learn how to think and act and our success at doing that varied greatly. Papa's ghost hovered over each of us in various forms. Years of habit, years of thinking a certain way, years of reacting to Papa's stimuli had to change before a new life could emerge.

Holding some of us back was the "Edison" name itself. Its very mention to anyone anywhere elicited a response. It was the one lingering burden that would never change. None of us ever had a private life. None of us would *ever* have a private life.

I made a point of engaging myself in each of my adult children's lives.

Tom ends his life

The least able of his siblings to cope was Mr. Edison's namesake, Tom. Nearly four years after his father's death, August 25, 1935, Tom's body was discovered in a seedy hotel room in Springfield, Massachusetts. He had registered under an alias. In recent years he had been coping with the effects of high blood pressure and heart disease. An autopsy revealed the death was the result of heart disease. No mention was made of the empty pill bottle beside him on the bed.

Tom had always suffered some degree of depression. He had a weakness for alcohol. He insisted he loved his father but it was obvious he never understood how to please him. Life with father was always negative. His father never showed any love, as we understand it, for Tom. The only gift he shared was a modest income, as if to say, "Take this and stay out of my hair."

His father eventually provided a farm in the country for Beatrice and him, but it was a dead end for Tom. It was boring. Conniving business sharks continued to plagued him, eager to take advantage of his magic name.

Beatrice, the nurse who had once cured him in the sanatorium, saw her husband once again decline mentally and physically, but she could do nothing. Together we tried to cheer Tom and get him involved in something more interesting to occupy his time. But we failed. Tom's life was the epitome of tragedy. He was fifty-nine.

His loyal wife Beatrice received Tom's share of the codicil agreement for the rest of her life.

William the country gentleman

William's life was not much different than Tom's. His life-long tendancy was to imitate his big brother. His business attempts were also squelched by his father, and he and his wife Blanche were also eventually farmed out by Mr. Edison. His big difference from Tom was using his income from Papa to live the life of a "country gentleman." He was able to take advantage of his name and use it as a social wedge. He never experienced his brother's depression or fondness for alcohol. Cancer plagued William in his final years and he also died at age fifty-nine, two years after his brother.

Countess Marion Oeser

Marion Oeser, seventy-two, appears to have survived far better than Mr. Edison's first two boys. She lives the inventive life of a wealthy, widowed countess from Germany on her spacious farm in Norwalk, Connecticut. She retained her married name as a buffer against the press and uses the title "Countess" for social status. She maintains an apartment in the New York as well for shopping and theaters and enjoys seasonal contrast of the residences.

Since her father's death, Marion has been freed from her life-long desire to have her Papa's full attention. This has allowed us to become friendly peers. The seven years difference in our ages is now meaningless as we both have reached retirement age. We have been guests at each others houses several times and have shopped in New York together. Marion has spent time at Seminole Lodge with me as well as at Chautauqua.

We are both able to look back at our early lives with greater understanding. We can now laugh at the hurdles we have both had to leap over the years.

Mother Madeleine

Madeleine and I have the best possible mother-daughter relationship. At fifty-seven she is still very social and is active in many local organizations. I'm pleased to see she is following right in my footsteps. It gives us a lot to do together.

As I write this, my grandchildren range in age from 14 to 29. Three of them have completed college and are on their own. Young Michael is wildly independent, quite an outdoorsman, having matured quickly competing in sports with his three older brothers.

"I worry about Michael. He is such a daredevil attempting to do everything his brothers do. John, of course, tells me not to worry." [149]

Madeleine acquired the political bug about the same time as Charles. She unsuccessfully ran for Congress in 1938.

She continues on looking after her husband and children in a very happy marriage. [150]

Charles the politician

Charles, at age forty-four, took a leave of absence from Thomas A. Edison, Inc. four years after his father died. He found himself on the short list being considered as a Democratic candidate for the U.S. Senate. He opted instead to serve as secretary of the Navy under Franklin D. Roosevelt from 1937 to 1940. The political bug had caught him. He ran for governor of New Jersey in 1941, was elected, and served all through World War II. Finally, this year, he returned to the family company.[151]

Theodore the inventor

Much to my disappointment, Theodore had walked away from his father's trust in him to act as co-executor of his will.

The pandemonium initiated by William and the outcry by his siblings was more than Theodore could take. He said in a flash of anger he didn't care about the money. In any case Charles, the steadiest of them all, accepted the responsibility.

One year after his father died, Theodore's first patent was approved. It was for a device that eliminated machinery vibrations. He was content at his small company, Calibron, where he could spend most of his time inventing.

He and Anna built their home in a thickly wooded section of Llewellyn Park, not far from Glenmont. Like his father, he could walk down the hill to his business. Anna continued at Rutgers University and graduated with a degree in pharmacy. This led her to a position at the Merk Institute for Therapeutic Research, close by me in Rahway.[152]

The good life

As for myself in the years following my Dearie's death, I had a lot of his habits to get over. His rigid routine was my routine. When that suddenly disappeared I had to find a substitute for my time. But it all turned out to my favor. I no longer had to be at the front door morning and evening. I no longer had to accommodate him in many ways. I had a new freedom -- a freedom I greatly disliked during the entire first half of our marriage when he traveled so much and spent so much time at his disastrous mining operation in Ogden.

But, although I miss him, I quickly learned to love my freedom. My times at Glenmont, at Chautauqua and at Seminole Lodge were open-ended. I had ample time at each to continue with my civic, environmental and church work and to be with any one of my children on occasion.

Then something happened during one of my visits to Chautauqua in 1934, about three years after Mr. Edison died. I became reacquainted with Edward Hughes, one of my close childhood Chautauqua friends. His wife had died and he was at loose ends.

I won't say that we fell in love. We didn't. But we enjoyed each other's company and mutually agreed that it was nice to have a compatible, enjoyable companion. One year after meeting we decided it would be convenient to marry and do some traveling together. At our common ages of seventy, we did. We married on October 1935 in a simple wedding with our friends. I took his name, believing it would give me the privacy I often yearned for.

We travelled well together, moving between my three homes and in New York City, Boston and Monhegan Island. In 1937 we spent three months in Europe, mostly in French Provance and northern Italy.

But then, a bit more than four years after we married, Mr. Hughes died, and once again I was alone but I continued my activities, at a reduced pace and life went on.

This book is probably my last great effort. I've told it the way I believe it happened. May God bless you all.

Mina Miller Edison

Afterword

On February 11, 1947, Mina officiated at Edison's 100th birthday after which she unlocked his rolltop desk that had been sealed by Charles ever since his father's death. The event brought back numberless memories of her fifty-three years with the inventor as she and her son looked through his papers and items.

Mina died at Chautauqua on August 24, 1947, her summer home since her father co-founded it seventy-one years earlier. Her life was celebrated by a gathering of 7,000 friends and acquaintances in the outdoor amphitheater. She had touched each of these people in some significant way. Their earnest voices sang "Abide with Me" as a tribute to her life of sharing with others.

Major Characters

Burroughs, John - Naturalist, poet, writer. 1836-1921.
Edison, Anna, neé Osterhout - Theodore's wife, 1901-1993.
Edison, Beatrice, neé Heyzer - Tom, Jr.'s second wife, 1882-1950.
Edison, Blanche, neé Travers - William's wife - 1879-1950.
Edison, Carolyn, neé Hawkins - Charles' wife - 1883-1963.
Edison, Charles - Mina's second child, 1890-1969.
Edison, Charles Pitt - William Pitt's son, 1860-1879.
Edison, Harriett - Edison's older sister, 1833-1863.
Edison, Madeleine - Mina's first child, 1888-1979. See also Sloane
Edison, Marie, nee Toohey - Tom, Jr.'s first wife, 1880-1906.
Edison, Marion ("Dot") - Edison's first child, 1873-1965, married Oscar Oeser, 1865-?.
Edison, Mary - Edison's first wife, neé Stilwell. 1855-1884.
Edison, Mina ("Billie"), neé Miller - Edison's second wife, 1865-1947.
Edison, Nancy - neé Elliott, Edison's mother, 1811-1871.
Edison, Samuel - Edison's father, 1804-1896.
Edison, Theodore - Mina's second son, 1898-1992.
Edison, Thomas Alva - Papa, Dearie, The Wizard, Old Man, Mina's husband, 1847-1931.
Edison, Thomas Alva, Jr. - Edison's son, 1876-1935.
Edison, William Pitt - Edison's brother, 1831 - 1891.
Edison, William Leslie - Edison's second son, 1878-1937.
Firestone, Harvey - Tire industrialist. 1868-1938.
Ford, Henry - Auto industrialist. 1863-1947.

Gilliland, Ezra - Edison's best friend in the telegraph years and close business associate until the phonograph incident. 1846 - 1903.

Gilliland, Lillian - Edison & Mina's matchmaker.

Hughes, Edward - Childhood friend of Mina and her second husband, 1862-1940.

Miller, Jane Eliza, "Jennie," Mina's oldest sister, 1855-1898.

Miller, Lewis - Mina's father, 1829-1899.

Miller, John, Mina's brother, 1873-1940.

Miller, Mary Emily - Mina's sister, 1867?-1946.

Miller, Mary Valinda - Mina's mother, 1830-1912.

Miller, Mina - Lewis & Mary's daughter, Thomas Edison's wife, 1865-1947.

Miller, Robert Anderson, Sr. - Mina's brother, 1861-1911

Miller, Theodore ("Thede") - Mina's youngest brother 1875-1898.

Oeser, Oscar, 1865-?, married Marion Edison in 1895.

Sloane, John Edison - Edison's second grandchild, 1918-1990.

Sloane, John Eyre - "Jack," Madeleine Edison's husband, 1886-1970.

Sloane, Madeleine, nee Edison - 1888-1979.

Sloane, Michael Edison - Edison's fourth grandchild, 1931-1948.

Sloane, Peter Edison - Edison's third grandchild, 1923- ?

Sloane, Thomas Edison ("Teddy") - Edison's first grand-child, 1916-1990.

Sloane, Thomas O'Connor, Madeleine Edison's father-in-law, 1851-1940

Stilwell, Margaret Crane, Mary Edison's mother, 1831-1908.

Vincent, George - One-time fiancé of Mina Miller. 1864-1941,

Vincent, Rev. John Heyl - Co-founder of Chautauqua, 1832-1920.

Selected Bibliography

Baldwin, Neil. *Edison: Inventing the Century*. New York: Hyperion, 1995.

Burlingame, Roger. *Henry Ford: A Great Life in Brief*. New York, 1955.

Chautauqua Institution. (www.ciweb.org/).

Dyer, F. L., T. C. Martin and W. H. Meadowcroft. *Edison: His Life and Inventions*, 2-volume set. New York, 1910.

Dyer, Frank Lewis and Thomas Commerford Martin, *Edison, His Life and Inventions*. The Project Gutenberg EBook #820, 2006, 2013.

Israel, Paul, Director and General Editor, *The Thomas A. Edison Papers Project*. (http://edison.rutgers.edu.)

Israel, Paul. *Edison: A Life of Invention*. New York: John Wiley and Sons, 1998.

Josephson, Matthew. *Edison: A Biography*. New York: Francis Parkman Prize Edition, History Book Club, 2003.

National Park Service. (www.nps.gov/edis/historyculture).

New York *Times* Article Archive. 1851 to Present.

Smoot, Tom. *The Edisons of Fort Myers: discoveries of the heart*. Pineapple Press, Sarasota, Florida, 2004, 2011.

Venable, John D. *Mina Miller Edison: Daughter, Wife and Mother of Inventors*. Charles Edison Fund, 1981.

End Notes

---

[1] Mina is pronounced my-na, not mee-na.

[2] Dyer, F. L., T. C. Martin and W. H. Meadowcroft, *Edison: His Life and Inventions*, 2- volume set. (New York, 1910).

[3] The New York Times, July 23, 1922. Edison received the most votes when readers were polled: "Who are the twelve greatest living American men?"

[4] Scarlet fever was a very serious childhood disease, but today is easily treatable. It is caused by the streptococcal bacteria (strep throat) that produces a toxin which leads to a fever and a red rash that can spread over the body.

[5] Baldwin, page x.

[6] See www.delmonicosrestaurantgroup.com/restaurant/about-history.html. "America's First Restaurant."

[7] Edison had a low tolerance for child rearing. His two younger sons, Thomas Junior (Dash) and William now lived in Menlo Park with Edison's mother-in-law, Margaret Stilwell.

[8] The self-educated Edison had a very low regard for formal education and this had a substantial negative effect on his first three children as will be seen in later chapters.

[9] Both Edison and Mary had never learned the social graces of the time. Edison chewed on cigars and spat on the floor of his laboratories. He cared not a whit what *he* looked like. But he wanted Mary and Marion to be well dressed.

[10] Dyer. Patent No. 422,577, "Apparatus for Speaking Telephones," dated October 21, 1884 was the first listed. There followed six other co-patents through November 24, 1886 involving telephone circuits, railway signaling and railway telegraphy.

[11] The World's Industrial and Cotton Centennial Exposition took place in New Orleans from December 1, 1884 to May 31, 1885. It was one of the many popular expositions at which Edison displayed his inventions.

[12] But it was Joseph Swan, a British physicist and chemist who first demonstrated the light bulb in England in December 1878, but did not get it patented until two years later. His house in England was the first in the world to be lighted. Meanwhile Edison was experimenting independently in America with his version of a light bulb using bamboo for the filament. It was the 1881 International Electrical Exhibition in Paris that Edison's incandescent lighting system established dominance over his rivals. The two men joined in a cooperative deal and formed the Edison & Swan United Electric Light Company, popularly known as "Ediswan," was established in 1883, selling lamps with a cellulose filament that Swan invented. Although Edison continued experimenting with the bamboo filament, when he created Edison General Electric in 1892, that company adopted the cellulose filament that was much brighter and longer lasting. Edison's introduction of lighting to the world is still celebrated on his birthday, February 11, with a "Parade of Lights" in Fort Myers and other cities.

[13] See swanboats.com. The Boston Swan Boats first appeared in 1877 when Robert Paget was given a license to operate a new kind of boat in the Public Garden lagoon. The foot-propelled boat became popular instantly.

[14] See www.lighthousefriends.com/light.asp?ID=367.

[15] Lillian Gilliland was a matchmaker. During Edison's visit to their home she gave the often-unkempt man lessons on how to be a gentleman and how to mix with ladies of refinement. At first he rebelled, but then, as the lovely ladies passed before him, he could see the value of heeding her advice.

[16] Nathaniel Hawthorne (1804 to 1864), American novelist and short story writer. Edison was referring to Hawthorne's "Passages from the English Note-Books." Mina too was well read. Their common love of books provided much to talk about. During this summer activity, Mrs. Gilliland had asked

her guests to write a diary about their thoughts and activities during their visit. This inspired Edison's diary that covered a period of two weeks. Mrs. Gilliland's motive was to generate grist for drawing room discussions in the evening.
Read the diary at: ariwatch.com/VS/TheDiary-OfThomas Edison.htm

[17] Marion, nicknamed Dot, as in Morse code dot and dash, was Edison and Mary's first born. She was eleven when Mina first met her at the Gilliland's beach rental in Massachusetts. Dot missed her mother and became attached to her father. In later years she recalled that she had considered Mina to be too old to be a playmate and too young to be her mother. They were only seven years apart in age.

[18] The Chautauqua Institution was cofounded in 1874 by Mina's father, Lewis Miller, and Bishop John Vincent of the Akron Methodist church. It still operates today as a non-profit adult education center and resort and is located on the banks of Lake Chautauqua in Chautauqua, New York.

The "Chautauqua idea" quickly resulted in many copycats all over the United States. In its own words today, it "is a not-for-profit, 750-acre community on Chautauqua Lake in southwestern New York State, where approximately 7,500 persons are in residence on any day during a nine-week season, and a total of over 100,000 attend scheduled public events." (www.ciweb.org/our-mission)

[19] Edison's 1885 Diary, page 34.

[20] The Thomas Edison Papers, Rutgers University. The marriage took place January 25, 1887.

[21] Samuel Insull (1959 - 1938) worked for Edison in various business endeavors, such as building electrical power stations across the US. With other Edison "Pioneers," he founded Edison General Electric.

[22] Mina Miller was born in Akron, Ohio on July 6, 1865, the seventh of eleven children.

[23] George Vincent was the son of Bishop John Vincent, cofounder of Chautauqua with Mina's father. George and

Mina had been friends since childhood and it was always assumed they were destined to be married.

[24] Edward Everett Hughes was also a promising suitor, but his marriage to Mina would not take place until 50 years later (1935).

[25] Elizabeth Cady Stanton July 19, 1848 speech. www.libertynet.org/edcivic/stanton.html

[26] Exactly when electricity was first introduced to Chautauqua is not known. What is known is the house at 43 North Lake Drive was already wired for electricity by 1890, but the owner was not able to use it by something other than a battery until 1893 when the Castle Power House was built. It was a competitor of Edison, Charles Francis Brush, that founded the Brush Electric Company, and actually installed the system. See "The Chautauquan Daily," August 27, 2011.

[27] Edison's first job was as an itinerant telegrapher with Ezra Gilliland. The use of Morse code between Edison and Mina was essential because of his poor hearing. Code enabled them to carry out their courtship in privacy. See many sources, including "Edison: A life of Inventions," 1998, by Paul Israel, page 247.

[28] In 1885, at the age 38, Edison had already invented the phonograph and the first practical electric light system, along with related switches, fuses and generators. He built electric railways, held more than 100 patents covering electric lighting, electric railway systems, batteries and generators.

[29] To understand the relative purchasing power of money in Mr. Edison's time compared with today, let me suggest these two Internet calculators. If not a precise calculation, at least it is fun to try.
http://www.dollartimes.com/calculators/inflation.htm
http://www.measuringworth.com/uscompare/relativevalue.php

[30] From the diary of Thomas Edison, 1885.
http://edison.rutgers.edu/NamesSearch/SingleDoc.php3?DocId=MA001

[31] Ibid.

[32] Ibid.

[33] Edison was a pioneer in prefabricated houses, preceded, it is believed, only by Lewis Miller who assembled his pre-fabricated house at Chautauqua. Later, Edison went on to build and sell concrete houses that were built using pre-cast molds. See The Boy's Book of New Inventions, by Harry Edward Maule. Chapter IX is titled "The Romance of Concrete." Edison also founded the Portland Cement Company in Maine.

[34] As a young, unmarried woman, Mina never traveled alone. During her courtship there was always her mother or an older sibling to accompany her any distance. The ten-hour train ride between Akron and New York for either Mina or Edison was brutal. Mina stayed with her sister Jennie when meeting with Edison in the city.

[35] www.nps.gov/edis/historyculture/mary-stilwell-edison.htm.

[36] Edison created the first string of Christmas tree lights in 1880 and strung them in a fir tree just outside his Menlo Park laboratory during that holiday season. It was one of Edison's promotional schemes because the passengers in every train that passed by saw the wondrous display. However, it would be another forty years before Christmas tree lights would become tradition.
www.loc.gov/rr/scitech/mysteries/christmaslights.htm.

[37] The New York Times, July 7, 2006. "A Grand Wedding Gift Reopens for Viewing."

[38] Kinetoscope was the first motion-picture viewer in Edison's movie production company. Kineto-, as a prefix, relates to motion.

[39] Lieutenant Frank Toppan is a mystery man, mentioned only once in Baldwin (page 170) and in the New York *Times* article of the wedding [spelled Tappan], but no mention by any other Edison biographers. One other use of the name is in the New York *Times* dated April 29, 1900 in which an Ensign Frank Toppan was elected treasurer of the first annual meeting of the Naval and Military Order of the Spanish-American War. The meeting was held at Delmonico's, a restaurant Thomas Edison frequented.

[40] The New York *Times*, February 25, 1886. "Mr. Edison's Wedding. The Electrician Married To A Millionaire's Daughter."
[41] Eventually it would extend all the way to Key West. Flagler's foresight in the 1880s led to the eventual development of Florida's east coast.
[42] Eli Thompson was a Fort Myers native and superintendent of construction of the two houses and the laboratory. Edison and Gilliland had met Thompson a year earlier and had hired him to supervise a number of projects at the site.
[43] Mina's technical drawings, Rutgers, The Edison Papers, [N314] Notebook Series -- Fort Myers Notebooks: N-86-03-18 (1886).
[44] Edison's business office was now at 65 Fifth Avenue in New York City, not far from Marion's boarding school. He had his own problems -- catching up on the work he had missed while away and experiencing his first labor strike. The workers at his facility in Brooklyn had labored many extra hours trying to keep up with orders. They walked out. The workers had been very much aware of how Edison's businesses were thriving and they did not believe they were getting fair wages. They were willing to work a nine-hour day, but they wanted to be paid for ten hours. They wanted double pay for overtime. They also learned they were getting paid twenty-five percent less than the workers at some other companies.

Edison was afraid the strike would spread though his other factories and this could result in the lights going out. He was also afraid of unionization. He decided it was time to consolidate and relocate out of the city. He shut down his city operations moved his factories to Schenectady, New York taking with him two hundred men who were willing to move.
[45] Among a series of letters between sisters that reflect Mina's emotional adjustment during the spring, summer and fall of 1886.
[46] Israel, page 260. A detailed description of Edison's new laboratory in West Orange.

[47] Laboratory Notebooks, 1886; The Edison Laboratory Archives.
[48] www.edison.rutgers.edu/generator.htm. The dynamo's bipolar magnets were two tall pillars the men called legs. The all-male staff of the laboratory named it Mary Anne.
[49] The first version of the phonograph used *tinfoil* on which sound was recorded, but many people thought voice recording was trickery. In one example, Bishop Vincent, co-founder of Chautauqua, expressed such doubt and asked Edison if he "could speak a few words." The bishop then rattled off a number of Biblical names. Mr. Edison played the recording back to him. The astonished Vincent said, "There isn't a man in the United States who could recite those names with the same rapidity." (From *Edison: His Life and Inventions*, Chapter X)
[50] For a detailed description of the events of this alliance, see Baldwin, page 187; Josephson, page 328; Israel, page 289.
[51] The New York Times, October 19, 1931, "If he [Edison] had a needle to find in a haystack he would not stop to reason where it was most likely to be, but would proceed at once, with the feverish diligence of a bee, to examine straw after straw until he found the object of his search."
[52] Coincidently, Thomas Edison was elected President of the American Institute of Electrical Engineers four years before Tesla's speech.
[53] Baldwin, page 200; Josephson, page 343. Both write fascinating accounts of the AC-DC wars. See also Israel, beginning on page 325. Israel covers the subject in great detail but, strangely, never mentions Nikola Tesla.
[54] The edible ice cream "cone" made its first formal introduction at the 1904 World's Fair in St. Louis.
[55] The Eiffel Tower was erected in 1889 as an entrance arch to the Paris Universal Exposition, alias 1889 World's Fair. It was named after Gustave Eiffel, the head engineer.
[56] www.tour-eiffel.fr

[57] The Siemens company was the first to introduce the electric railway and the electric elevator in 1879 and 1880 at the Berlin Industrial Exhibition.
[58] Smallpox is caused by the Variola major virus. Some experts say that over the centuries it has killed more people than all other infectious diseases combined. The last case was reported in 1977.
(www.nim.nih.gov/medlineplus/smallpox.html)
[59] Israel, page 339. Mr. Israel describes the Ogden mining venture in great detail.
[60] Josephson, page 378. Mr. Josephson's account of the Ogden mines takes a different approach and is a good addition to Mr. Israel's story.
[61] Baldwin, page 225.
[62] After years of experimentation, Edison discovered the light bulb filament that lasted well into the 20th Century.
[63] As we will see, this was one of the properties Henry Ford found as invaluable Edison history and moved it to his Greenfield Village museum in Michigan.
[64] Baldwin, page 255.
[65] The national bestselling novel, "The Devil in the White City" by Erik Larson, published in 2003, vividly relates events, including Thomas Edison's activities, at the 1893 World's Fair.
[66] Baldwin, page 245.
[67] Ibid, page 250.
[68] Wilhelm Röntgen named them "X-rays." The "X" stands for "unknown."
[69] Baldwin, page 260.
[70] Ibid, page 303.
[71] Ibid, page 266.
[72] It is named "Portland" because its color resembles the stone quarried on the Isle of Portland off the British coast.
[73] Israel spells Tom Jr.'s wife's name Touhey; Baldwin spells it Toohey.
[74] Battery power is, of course, direct current. With his batteries, Mr. Edison had no competition from his foe alternating

current which cannot operate portable or stand-alone devices. And eventually rechargeable batteries became standard equipment for all automobiles.

[75] http://edisontinfoil.com/taejr/wizard.htm
See this web site for a reproduction of the advertisement.

[76] http://edisontinfoil.com/taejr/magno.htm
See this web site for several advertisements and illustrations of how to use the Vitalizer.

[77] Israel, page 391.

[78] Baldwin, Page 285.

[79] The Edisons had six inside maids at this time, along with a nurse, cook, cook's helper, waitress and laundress.

[80] The word "Kidnap" dates back to 1648, according to the *American Heritage Dictionary*. "Nap," a variant of "nab" combined with "kid" forms the slangy word. It was first used when kidnappers secured labor for use in the Colonies. Unfortunately, it is used today when people of note in particular are captured and held for vast sums of ransom.

[81] Pinkerton Agency was the first and the most famous detective organization. James McParland was the living embodiment of the agency who solved many famous crimes. See "A Law Unto Himself," by Ben Macintyre in the New York Times, December 20, 2013.

[82] Naphtha-fueled external combustion engines replaced steam boilers on small boats because they were safer. Steam boilers were larger and heavier and could explode if improperly managed.

[83] Matlacha is pronounced MAT-la-shay. The community is located on Pine Island, Florida.

[84] Cyrus Teed adopted the name "Koresh," the original Persian of his name Cyrus. His beliefs were called Koreshanity.

[85] Israel, page 394-397.

[86] The velocipede is any of the early bicycles with pedals attached to the huge front wheel, with the rider high off the ground.

[87] A survey taken in 1899 indicated that of 100 motorized vehicles, 90 were battery powered.
Carriage builders, such as Studebaker and Columbia were building carriages and installing light motors with batteries.
[88] Josephson, page 404.
[89] Dyer, Frank Lewis, and Martin, Thomas Commerford, "Edison, His Life and Inventions," 1910.
[90] Smoot, page 66.
[91] Israel, page 391.
[92] Other Edison family automobile travel included, 1903: through New England and Canada; 1906: New York State and Canada; 1908: the Pacific Coast; 1911: Europe.
[93] www.whitesteamcar.com/White_Steam_Car_Registry/History.htm
[94] www.thecog.com/cog_history.php. On July 3, 1869, the "Old Peppersass" became the first cog-driven train to climb 6,288 feet to the top of Mount Washington. Its construction followed that of the "carriage road" that was completed in the late 1850s.
[95] Baldwin, page 307. Includes the full three-page drama.
[96] By 1920 fewer than 900,000 acres had been reclaimed and Florida's reclamation project was considered a financial failure, but the damage had been done. The Everglades today receives less than one-third of his historic flow south, and in that flow are fertilizer contaminants and other runoff. In addition, the wildlife-rich wetlands are only half the size they were when draining was initiated in the 1920s. The federal government and Florida signed a 30-year federal plan in 2002 to repair at least part of the Everglades natural water flow and wildlife. See: http://perc.org/articles/who-drained-everglades.
[97] See: http://earthquake.usgs.gov/regional/nca/1906/18april/index.php
[98] Smoot, page 81. Here are the complete details of the Royal Palm Project. The palms still grace MacGregor boulevard after more than 100 years.

[99] Victor Herbert (1859-1924) led the Pittsburg Symphony from 1898 to 1904 and composed and published several successful operettas including *Babes in Toyland* in 1903.
[100] Baldwin, page 313.
[101] Josephson, page 456.
[102] Smoot, page 95.
[103] Dyer and Martin: "Edison: His Life and Inventions," 1910. More recent biographers have disparaged the Dyer book as fanciful and inventive. Edison was a wonderful storyteller about his youth and on through his inventions. *Authorized* biographies and autobiographies are, by their very nature, subject to editing out of information not wanted by the person written about. Therefore it is not an unbiased account. But for the unvarnished facts of one's life, experts suggest later biographies, such as those cited in these End Notes and the ultimate authority, Rutgers University. (www.edison.rutgers.edu/)
[104] Israel, page 394.
[105] Pronounced "looissberg," not "louieberg."
[106] The New York *Times*, October 16, 1910.
[107] M. A. Rosanoff, "Edison in His Laboratory," *Harper's Magazine*, September, 1932. (http://harpers.org/archive/1932/09/edison-in-his-laboratory/)
[108] Baldwin, page 322.
[109] Smoot, page 110.
[110] http://blog.thehenryford.org/2013/12/home-projector-wars/
[111] http://www.leedeforest.org/Home.html
[112] One of the big mysteries surrounding Edison's life is why he never attempted to invent a device that would improve his hearing. His reported answer was: "How much have you heard in the last twenty-four hours that you couldn't do without?" and "A man who has to shout can never tell a lie."
[113] *Bruno's Weekly*, August 14, 1915.
[114] Guido Bruno (1884-1942) was a small-press publisher and editor in Greenwich Village, sometimes called "the Barnum of Bohemia." He lived in a Washington Square garret where, for

an admission fee, one could see just how a "true Bohemian" lived. You could also purchase his magazines there.

[115] Baldwin, page 350.

[116] Smoot, page 112. An excellent account of this visit.

[117] Josephson, page 458.

[118] The New York *Times*, June 18, 1914.

[119] "Phenol" was used in WWI to make explosives, "trinitrophenol." At the outbreak of WWI, phenol was in short supply and most of it had been imported from the United Kingdom. But it is used for other things as well, such as aspirin and Edison's Diamond Disc phonograph records. When war broke out the British stopped exporting phenol. As a result, Edison opened this plant to fill the gap.

[120] Baldwin, page 339, wrote, this "was Edison's purpose, after all, to meld the pretense of music appreciation with blatant commercialism."

[121] Christiania's name was changed to Oslo in 1925.

[122] Baldwin, page 346; Israel page 453.

[123] Smoot, pages 139-141; Baldwin, page 353.

[124] Mrs. Ada Hawkins was the widow of Dr. Horatio Gated Hawkins who was a morphine addict who drowned himself in Vermont's Connecticut River. She was the mother of three daughters, one of whom was Carolyn. Ada and Carolyn dedicated their time during the war to relief work.

[125] Smoot, page 142. See a detailed description of Theodore's experiments.

[126] From the Henry Ford Library. This is a note by Edison that was placed within a bird fountain on Henry Ford's estate at Fair Lane in Dearborn, Michigan.

[127] Josephson, page 463.

[128] Montague, Charles Edward (1867-1928). From *Disenchantment*, Brentano's (1922), page 228.

[129] Josephson, page 354.

[130] Baldwin, page 333.

[131] Israel, page 454; Smoot, page 151.

[132] Smoot, page 157.

[133] Josephson, page 466. An excellent account of Edison's visit to Schenectady.
[134] New York *Times,* February 16, 1923.
[135] See www.thehenryford.org/village/index.aspx
[136] See www.naplesdowntown.com/history.htm
[137] Baron Collier was the owner of most of the land that became Collier County.
[138] Edison.rutgers.edu/Martha Conan and H. Weir, "The Most Difficult Husband in America," Collier's Weekly, July 18, 1925, pages 11, 42-43.
[139] Smoot, page 189. See a full, entertaining account of this meeting as reported in the Fort Myers *Tropical News*. See also Baldwin, page 369.
[140] A flivver is defined as slang for *any* small car that gives a rough ride. Also, a Ford flivver was a single-seat aircraft that Henry Ford described as his "Model T of the Air."
[141] Baldwin, page 384.
[142] Smoot, page 206. Mr. Smoot goes into interesting detail about Mr. Edison's party.
[143] Dyer and Martin: "Edison: His Life and Inventions," 1910.
[144] Baldwin, page 390.
[145] Mr. Edison wittily meant this literally.
[146] Theodore accumulated 80 patented inventions by the time he died in 1991.
[147] *The Temperate Life* was first published in Italy in 1558 and translated and printed in many American and British editions.
[148] A "pittance" indeed! $50,000 in 1931 dollars was equivalent to more than $700,000 in 2014 buying power. See the following calculator.
http://www.dollartimes.com/calculators/inflation.htm
[149] Michael Sloane, the youngest of Madeleine's children, died at age eighteen in a mountain-climbing accident in the Austrian Alps in September 1949.
[150] Madeleine sat on the board of directors of Western Union during the 1950s. Mina always thought her daughter had a talent for business and this was how she finally expressed it.

Madeleine gave birth to her only daughter on February 14, 1979. It was an exciting event at first, but much to the family's grief, the baby died shortly thereafter.

[151] Back at Thomas A. Edison, Inc. in 1945, Charles took the company public. Ten years later, the company was sold to the McGraw-Edison Company and Charles became titular chairman.

Charles and his wife Carolyn became active in restoration of historic buildings in the Long Island area. They preserved his father's West Orange laboratory and his mother's Glenmont home by donating them to the National Parks Service, to become the Edison National Historic Site.

Charles and his wife continued their involvement in many civic projects, following the tradition of his mother. He died of a heart attack on June 30, 1969 at age seventy-nine.

[152] Theodore inherited more than a million dollars from Mina's estate. Reaffirming his lack of interest in great personal wealth, he established a mutual association that divided profits of Thomas Edison, Inc. among the blue-collar workers.

Like his mother, Theodore was sensitive to the environment. He founded a preservation society in Florida to protect an area of cypress trees near Fort Myers that also included families of ibises and egrets.

Theodore's interest extended to Monhegan Island where he spent some of his childhood. Here he founded Monhegan Associates whose goal, under his own guidance, was to preserve for posterity the ecological features and rugged headlands that faced the Atlantic. In addition, the Associates' goal was to protect the simple and friendly spirit of the island.

Theodore was among the first to speak out against the Vietnam War. He bought a full-page ad in the New York *Times* in 1966 speaking out against the killing and maiming of our opponents at great cost in lives and money.

Theodore was the last of the Edisons. He and Ann lived into their nineties. He died in November of 1992 and Ann died of a heart attack just two months later in January. They had been happily married for seventy years.

The End